PRAISE FOR *THE ETCHER*

"Bryan Garner, one of the nation's leading experts in legal language and writing, takes us on a voyage of discovery about a virtually unknown Viennese etcher, Oskar Stoessel, who escaped Nazi Germany, came to the United States, and produced some masterly etchings of President Roosevelt, Supreme Court justices, and other notables. Garner's wonderful storytelling skills and numerous reproductions of the art have saved Stoessel from obscurity and provided us with a great read."

> —ARTHUR R. MILLER
> University Professor & Dean of Tisch Sports Institute
> New York University

"The intersection of law and art is not heavily traveled. But in this engaging book, Bryan Garner painstakingly recovers the life of Oskar Stoessel, a Viennese émigré to our country and Europe's finest etcher, and along the way he deftly limns the details of Stoessel's friendship with Chief Justice Harlan Fiske Stone, who assiduously promoted the artist's career, not least by sitting for him and prevailing on his fellow justices to do the same. This tale of friendship, personal indebtedness, and gratitude will appeal to lawyers and art lovers alike, which is no mean feat."

> —HON. MORRIS S. ARNOLD
> U.S. Court of Appeals for the Eighth Circuit

"Bryan Garner has produced a fascinating, charming, and highly entertaining portrait of one of the twentieth century's most remarkable artists. A Viennese refugee from Nazi persecution just before World War II, Oskar Stoessel managed, in a few short years, to record stunningly elegant etchings of Supreme Court justices from Hughes to Jackson to Douglas, as well as a host of other luminaries from Franklin Roosevelt to Cordell Hull. This is a spellbinding and eye-opening contribution to law, history, and art. I will cherish this remarkable book and share it with dear friends as holiday gifts."

—THEODORE B. OLSON
Former Solicitor General of the United States
Partner, Gibson, Dunn & Crutcher

"*The Etcher* is an intriguing story (told by one of America's most intriguing minds) of an artist who, unbeknown to almost all of us, touched the lives of some of the 20th century's most important political and legal figures. It is a worthwhile story of art, law, success, failure, and more than a touch of antisemitism. The world is a smarter place for its telling."

—GARY S. LAWSON
Philip S. Beck Professor of Law
Boston University

"This book works on so many levels. On one, it's the story of a now-obscure artist and his relationship with the chief justice, which leads to his commissions to etch the other justices. But there are so many others. The story is about an art form that fell out of favor, about a powerful man (tinged perhaps with antisemitism) who undertakes to help a Jewish immigrant, the relationships between the justices, and brothers who excelled in the United States while their loved ones fell to the Holocaust. It's about the arc of life. And it's about perseverance, loyalty, and love."

—RICHARD D. FREER
Robert Howell Hall Professor of Law
Emory University

"A fascinating look at how some of the most revealing visual portrayals of Supreme Court justices came about—and at the personal networks linking the justices and their friends during World War II. The reproduction of Oskar Stoessel's etchings is worth the price of the book."

—MARK V. TUSHNET
William Nelson Cromwell Professor of Law
Harvard Law School

"This is an intriguing story of how a World War II refugee from Nazi Austria quickly became the etcher for Supreme Court portraits, as well as for President Franklin Delano Roosevelt. The reproductions of his work throughout the book make one nostalgic for an art form now seldom seen."

—MARY KAY KANE
Dean Emerita, University of California Hastings

"This is a richly textured resurrection of the life of a great artist, reminiscent of Clarence Brown's revival of Osip Mandelstam. Like Brown's work, it reflects the conviction that even the most powerful and malicious of dictators cannot ultimately efface art. It also serves to remind us of the immense contribution to American culture made by gifted and desperate persons fleeing oppression. Garner's pen is a perfect match for Stoessel's etchings and, like them, vividly brings their subjects to life."

—PHILIP BOBBITT
Herbert Wechsler Professor of Jurisprudence
Columbia Law School

"How appropriate that Bryan Garner—as careful a master of the written word as one can imagine—would come to be fascinated by the life of a master of etching, as careful an art form as one could imagine. And that Garner's insights into that life are ultimately drawn from the artist's own words—and those of his correspondents. And finally, that the life of the artist—like Garner's—was one characterized pivotally by a set of engaging, enthusiastic, and enduring relationships."

—ROBERT B. AHDIEH
Dean, Texas A&M University School of Law

"Fleeing fascism, Stoessel had faith that his craft could win him favor in America, even in the corridors of power. And this gem of a book shows how at a disputatious time in Court history, imperious judicial figures could share a generous affection for Stoessel and an aesthetic appreciation of his work. Implicitly confirming that etching could reveal the true personality of the subject, the justices show their poignant human (and gently vain) side, hoping that the etchings would enhance their legacies."

—ROBERT WEISBERG
Special Assistant to the Provost
Stanford University

"*The Etcher* is a compelling story written with clarity and sympathy by one of our finest writers. The book is beautifully illustrated with works from the subject, an immigrant etcher who arrived in this country at the beginning of the Second World War. His friendship with justices of the Supreme Court, including the Chief, Harlan Fiske Stone, is told in exquisite detail to reveal long-forgotten facts unearthed through painstaking research. The story is all the more remarkable because it resonates so perfectly with today's tumultuous political climate."

—CHARLES L. "CHIP" BABCOCK
Partner, Jackson & Walker LLP

"*The Etcher* offers an intimate and fascinating glimpse not only into an artist's life, but also into the personalities and temperaments of Supreme Court justices. Bryan Garner writes clearly and effectively. His insights reflect his intimate familiarity with life at the Court (he was a close friend of Justice Antonin Scalia). Garner proves himself to have been indefatigable in tracking down Stoessel's work and the relevant correspondence. Profusely illustrated, the book brings Stoessel's art to life. Especially impressive is how Garner succeeds in catching the flavor and spirit of the times. I know the Court and its justices well (I clerked for Justice Hugo Black), and as I read this book, I could almost imagine myself at the elbows of the justices here depicted, warts and all."

—A.E. DICK HOWARD
White Burkett Miller Professor of Law
and Public Affairs
University of Virginia

"This short book packs a lot of detail into an accounting of a little-known corner of Supreme Court, World War II, and art history. It's an easy and informative read, and well worth it."

—KENNETH S. KLEIN
Louis & Hermione Brown Professor in Preventive Law
California Western School of Law

"*The Etcher* is a serious accomplishment from a versatile polymath. Bryan Garner has crafted an illuminating biography of an artist who, within years of fleeing Europe during World War II, became one of America's most popular portraitists. Backed by original archival research, Garner's book plumbs Stoessel's success, his challenges as a refugee, and his unusual relationships with some of the era's most influential power brokers. *The Etcher* packs in a string of stunning revelations and collects many wonderful examples of Stoessel's art, enabling the book to serve as both a keen biography *and* a serious retrospective."

—NOAH MESSING
Legal-Writing Instructor, Yale Law School

"We all know Bryan Garner as the magisterial arbiter of legal style. But this gem shows his deft hand at storytelling, a fascinating parable of the European immigrant who finds his moment in the sun producing stunning etchings of Roosevelt and his Court but then fades from view. If you're like me, you'll come to the end wondering how you've never heard of Oskar Stoessel. A must-read for all interested in the inner history of the Court."

—RONALD J. MANN
Albert E. Cinelli Enterprise Professor of Law
Columbia University

"This book is about 'friendship, personal indebtedness, and gratitude,' in the words of Bryan Garner, himself a master of words. It is an easy but instructive read about an Austrian refugee, Oskar Stoessel, whose elegant, insightful etchings, many of Supreme Court justices whom he doggedly pursued, and courtly letters, especially with Harlan Fiske Stone, interlace the book. Garner's admiration for Stoessel's hand, head, and heart enriches a testament to the best of photography's rivals."

—JAMES R. NAFZIGER
Thomas B. Stoel Professor of Law
Willamette University

"One of the greatest American artists you've never heard of—Oskar Stoessel—emigrated from Nazi Austria at age 60 and quickly became Washington's favorite portraitist. Bryan Garner takes us inside Stoessel's relationships with Supreme Court justices and others, telling his story alongside reprints of Stoessel's elaborately designed etchings from the author's personal collection. The quick read and exquisite illustrations take us back to mid-20th-century Carnegie Hall, racial divisions, and immigrant struggles. Fascinating account, beautiful pictures."

—DEREK A. NEWMAN
Newman Law
Seattle & Los Angeles

"Garner rescues from obscurity a leading Austrian etcher, Oskar Stoessel, who came to America as a refugee before World War II and soon made etchings of major American leaders, including President Roosevelt and all the justices of the Supreme Court. Set against a background of rivalries on the Court and storms of war, this short but deeply researched and richly illustrated book tells a tale of friendship, the highest levels of government, and artistry."

>—THOMAS D. ROWE JR.
>Elvin R. Latty Professor Emeritus of Law
>Duke University

"*The Etcher* deals with the fascinating friendship of Oskar Stoessel, Austro-American etcher and painter, with U.S. Supreme Court Justice Harlan Fiske Stone. Not only does this book make good reading, it also contains many photographs of Stoessel's art, which adds to its value. In short, this is a very well-written and interesting book worth reading."

>—HON. THOMAS BUERGENTHAL
>International Court of Justice (retired)
>Lobingier Professor Emeritus
>George Washington Law School

"In one short, crisply written book, Bryan Garner has recovered the legacy of émigré artist Oskar Stoessel, provided a remarkable gallery of Supreme Court portraits from the 1940s, and documented the extraordinary kindness of Chief Justice Harlan Fiske Stone. *The Etcher* offers a welcome glimpse of calm amid the storm of war and the heated controversies among the justices."

>—JOHN V. ORTH
>William Rand Kenan Jr. Professor of Law
>University of North Carolina

"The artist Oskar Stoessel managed to achieve something that eludes most lawyers—unanimity on the U.S. Supreme Court. In *The Etcher*, Bryan Garner tells us how Stoessel, a Jewish refugee from Austria, was able to create the portraits of all nine sitting justices in the midst of World War II. The book is beautifully written and illustrated, with an important story about the nature of artistry, and an equally important subtext about the contribution of refugees to American progress."

—STEVEN LUBET
Edna B. & Edneyfed Williams
Memorial Professor
Northwestern University

"Bryan Garner goes beyond his skilled work as a lexicographer to bring us the history of an Austrian portraitist who immigrated to the United States in 1939. This émigré's skill and his person soon won the admiration of some of the District of Columbia's most important men, including FDR and the entire bench of the U.S. Supreme Court, all of whose portraits he completed. Admirably illustrated, this fascinating book will hold the interest of virtually any reader, and for Supreme Court buffs, it will be impossible to put down."

—R.H.H. HELMHOLZ
Ruth Wyatt Rosenson
Distinguished Service Professor of Law
University of Chicago

"Professor Bryan Garner, the world's leading legal lexicographer, has written a gem of a book. Turning his attention away from legal texts, he has now focused on the engraved image, as produced by a little-known artist and etcher, Oskar Stoessel. This fascinating story, as told by Garner, shows Stoessel to have been a remarkable man and artist with both artistic and social gifts. An Austrian refugee who escaped the Nazis, Stoessel established himself as the artist of choice for the Washington elite of the Roosevelt period, capturing the images not only of President Roosevelt but also of the members of the United States Supreme Court. Professor Garner has brought Oskar Stoessel, his art, and his period to life. For anyone who cares about the law, World War II, or art, this book is a must-read."

> —MICHAEL H. HOEFLICH
> John H. & John M. Kane Distinguished
> Professor of Law
> University of Kansas School of Law

"In *The Etcher*, Bryan Garner continues to give us a look at the humanity of justices on the highest court in the land, how they think and communicate and see the world. This story is a must-read for those whose life is in the courts and anyone interested in an inspiring immigrant story of success."

> —TERENCE CONNOR
> Hunton & Williams, Miami

"This book is a treasure trove, with gems of biography, history, and art packed into a classically written narrative. Just over 250 pages, including reproductions, the biography of Oskar Stoessel, a world-class portrait etcher, is a joy to read. It can be and truly should be read in one sitting; and in truth, once started, it is impossible to put down."

> —NEIL H. COGAN
> Professor of Law
> Whittier Law School

"Bryan Garner crafts the fascinating story of Oskar Stoessel, an Austrian Jewish etcher and refugee from Hitler's Europe, and his relationships with FDR, members of the Supreme Court, and other governmental officials. Garner's narrative raises intriguing questions about the antisemitism of the time. Did Stoessel's subject know that he was Jewish? Would it have mattered? Notions of art, society, and friendship are intertwined in this engaging account."

—STEVEN M. BARKAN
Voss-Bascom Professor of Law Emeritus
University of Wisconsin

"This is a remarkable story, painstakingly researched and beautifully written by one of the foremost legal writers of our generation. The story of the unlikely relationship between Justice Stone and a Jewish refugee is truly compelling. And the happy result of that relationship—striking etchings of all the justices of the U.S. Supreme Court—is exquisitely represented throughout the book. Bryan Garner turns out to be not just great at legal writing, but great at *writing*."

—DANIEL J. CAPRA
Reed Professor of Law
Fordham Law School

"A remarkable story, generally unknown, about art at the Supreme Court. Well worth reading!"

—EUGENE VOLOKH
Gary T. Schwartz Distinguished Professor of Law
University of California at Los Angeles

THE ETCHER

THE LIFE AND ART OF OSKAR STOESSEL

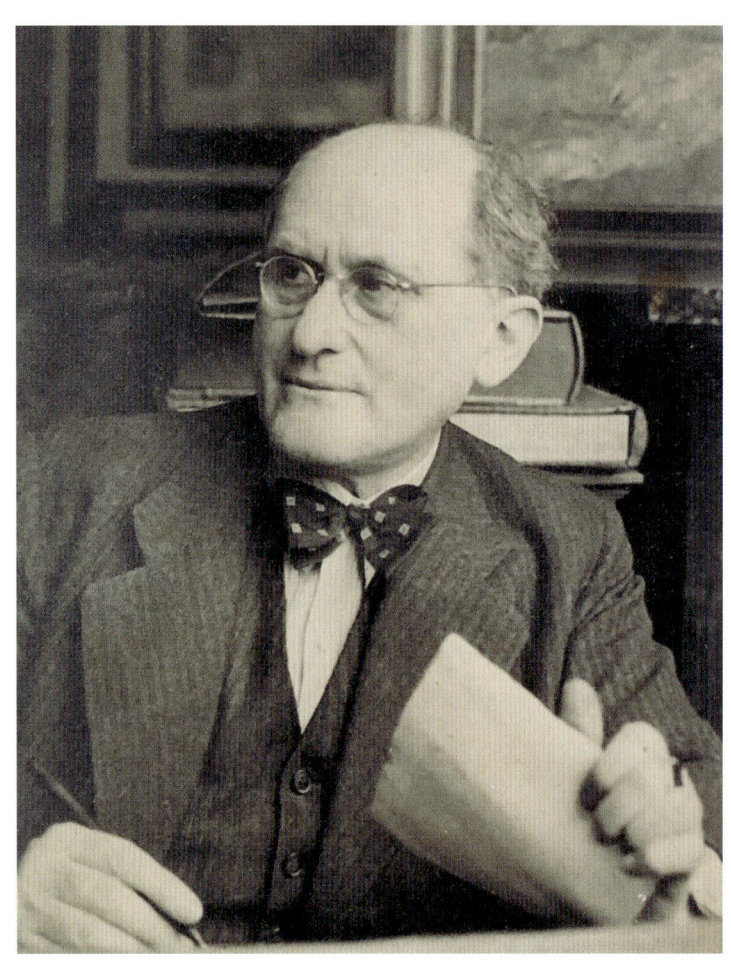

THE ETCHER

THE LIFE AND ART OF
OSKAR STOESSEL

BRYAN A. GARNER

GODINE · BOSTON

Published in 2025 by
GODINE
Boston, Massachusetts
www.godine.com

LIBRARY OF CONGRESS CATALOGING-IN-PUBLICATION DATA

Names: Garner, Bryan A., author.
Title: The etcher : the life and art of Oskar Stoessel / Bryan A. Garner.
Description: Boston : Godine, [2025] | Includes bibliographical references
    and index.
Identifiers: LCCN 2024059346 | ISBN 9781567928402 (hardcover)
Subjects: LCSH: Stoessel, Oskar, 1879-1964. | Etchers--Austria--Biography.
Classification: LCC NE2048.5.S76 G37 2025 | DDC 767/.2092
    [B]--dc23/eng/20250127
LC record available at https://lccn.loc.gov/2024059346

Permission to reproduce Oskar Stoessel's correspondence and art was sought from and
given by his only known relative—his great-nephew David H. Heichler. Permission to
reproduce the holdings of Neue Galerie Graz/Universalmuseum Joanneum was kindly
given by its executive director, Dr. Peter Peer, who also granted permission to quote
from his correspondence. The justices' papers at the Library of Congress have been dedicated to public uses such as the use reflected here. The artwork in the archives of the
U.S. Supreme Court has been reproduced with the kind permission of the Archivist's
Office at the Court. The most prolific private collector of Stoessel's art, Dr. Roman Theo
Carbon of Erlangen, Germany, has generously sent images from his collection as well.
Permission to reproduce items held at the National Gallery of Art in Washington, D.C.,
including David Finley's correspondence, was kindly given by the Gallery.

FIRST PRINTING, 2025
Printed in Canada

Know ye what etching is? It is to ramble
On copper; in a summer twilight's hour
To let sweet Fancy fiddle tunefully.
It is the whispering from Nature's heart,
Heard when we wander on the moor, or gaze
On the sea, on fleecy clouds of heaven, or at
The rushy lake when playful ducks are splashing;
It is the down of doves, the eagle's claw;
'Tis Homer in a nutshell, ten commandments
Writ on a penny's surface; 'tis a wish,
A sigh, comprised in finely chiseled odes,
A little image in its bird's-flight caught.
It is to paint on the soft gold-hued copper
With sting of wasp and velvet of the wings
Of butterfly, by sparkling sunbeams glowed.
Even so the etcher's needle, on its point,
Doth catch what in the artist-poet's mind
Reality and fancy did create.

—Carel Vosmaer (1826–1888)
(translated by Jeanne Clant van der Mijll-Piepers)

TO THE MEMORY OF MY FRIEND
JUSTICE ANTONIN SCALIA,
WHO ASKED ME, "WHO WAS OSKAR STOESSEL?"

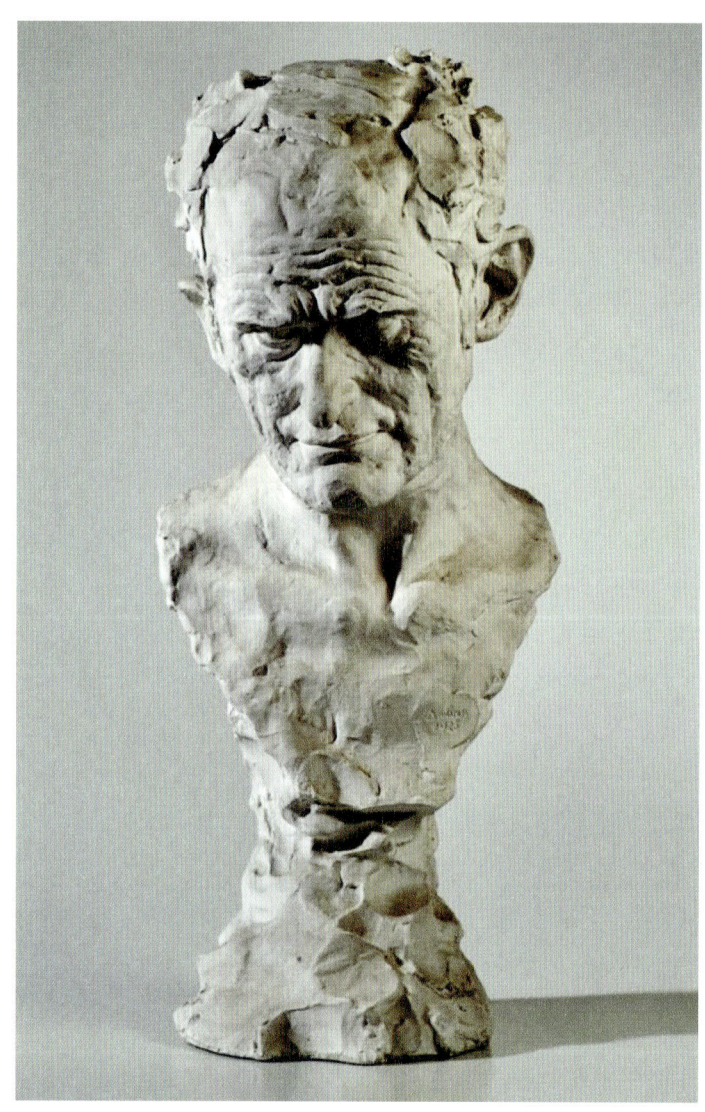

Bust of Oskar Stoessel
by Gustinus Ambrosi (1893–1975),
completed in 1925, when Oskar was 45

CONTENTS

PROLOGUE

THE strands of the extraordinary story that follows have mostly lain buried in files at the Library of Congress and a few other archives. The art world knows little today of Oskar Stoessel despite his significant creative accomplishments. Only a few details are known about his first 60 years or his last 13. But the files of the U.S. Supreme Court justices from 1941 to 1951 contain a great deal of revealing correspondence to and from the artist, whose life is otherwise bookended by a surprising obscurity.

What *is* known, though, is that Oskar was a portraitist of serious genius and a profoundly humane man with a great capacity for friendship. His story resonates, and his art endures.

Though tormented by personal worries about the safety of his family back in war-torn Austria, Oskar might well have found the years 1940 and 1941 to be professionally rewarding. Barely 11 months after arriving as a refugee in New York in March 1939, he obtained an hourlong sitting in the White House with President Franklin Delano Roosevelt to etch what First Lady Eleanor Roosevelt would later declare to be her favorite portrait of her husband. Soon after, Associate Justice Harlan Fiske Stone of the United States Supreme Court (soon to become chief justice) befriended Oskar and helped arrange sittings with each of the other justices—an unprecedented feat. Hailed as the finest portrait etcher in Europe, perhaps in the world, Oskar soon attracted the attention of the National Gallery of Art. On short notice, his work received an exhibition at the prestigious Corcoran Gallery in Washington, D.C., and soon he was selling his work through the Harlow Gallery in New York. He made friends wherever he went, and his etchings were widely praised.

Six months after arriving in America, Oskar was followed to New York by his younger brother, Ludwig, an actor who had enjoyed success in Austrian, German, and British films. Ludwig would soon be frequently cast as a character actor in Hollywood movies, including the 1942 classic *Casablanca*.

Oskar and his brother had fled violent antisemitism in Austria. But both encountered antisemitism even after arriving in America: despite the efforts of Justice Stone, who continued helping even after becoming chief justice, Oskar couldn't find the steady job he yearned for. It was hard then, as it can still be, for a transplanted 60-year-old to find employment.

Meanwhile, the brutal convulsions back in Austria meant that his own family was in grave danger. Austria's far-right party, the National Socialists, had been destabilizing Austria since the early 1930s. Once the Nazis succeeded in gaining supreme power in Austria, their pogroms, expulsions, and eventually systematic genocide would reduce the Jewish population there from 10% to half of 1%.

The menacing encroachments occurred gradually at first, but what began as thuggish vitriol evolved into systematized murders. The whole time, Oskar simply wanted to be left alone to create his art in peace.

CHAPTER 1

The Nature of Etching

ESPITE Oskar Stoessel's being a masterly painter, his passion was etching—an art form that began losing its popularity and cachet after the rise of photography in the late 19th century.

Traditional etching is a printmaking technique that uses a corrosive liquid to etch lines into a metal plate, usually copper. Often working from a pencil sketch, the artist evenly applies a waxy, acid-resistant ground to the plate, scratching a linear design through the ground with an etching needle. The plate is then subjected to acid, either in a bath or by hand, that corrodes or "bites" a design into the metal exposed through the ground. Etching requires considerable knowledge of and experience with the acid's strength and the length of exposure. When the ground has been removed, the plate is ready for inking and printing on a specialized roller press. A thick, viscous printing ink is then applied to the plate so that it fills the grooves. The excess surface ink is wiped away with the palm of the hand or a rag. Some artists leave or add a thin layer of ink on the surface for tonal effects. To make it sufficiently malleable, printing paper is prepared by soaking and then blotting the excess moisture. The artist places the plate face-up on the movable bed of the press, carefully applies the paper to the plate, and then covers it with felt blankets to evenly distribute the pressure of the etching press's rollers. The artist then runs the plate through the press, producing an impression on the paper that is a mirror image of the design on the plate. Artists must consider in their planning that the impressions will be the reverse of the design.

Sometimes the printmaker will use a drypoint needle with a sharp point to scratch directly on the soft copper without using a ground or acid. The needle displaces the metal of the line to either side of the groove, leaving a fragile burr that yields a rich, velvety line. In comparison to traditional etching, in which

Samples of Stoessel's early portraiture in Austria; one is a tinted etching.

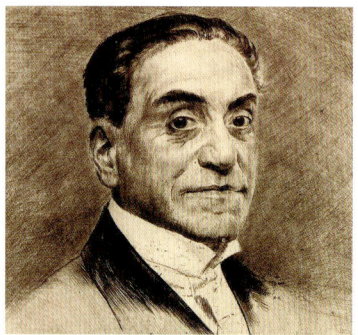

Alexander Girardi (ca. 1910)

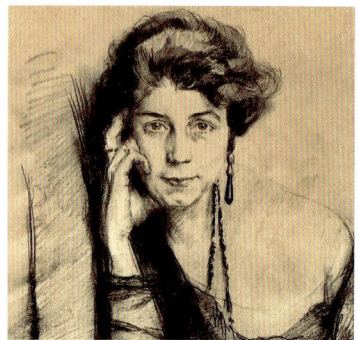

Unknown subject (1920s)

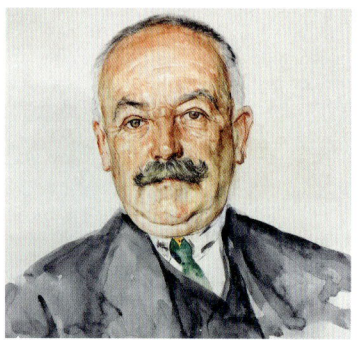

Unknown subject (Graz, 1923)

the lines can be rapid and sketchy, drypoint technique is slower and less forgiving.

But Oskar was not just an etcher. He was more specialized than that—or, more accurately, he gradually became so. He was primarily a *portrait etcher*, an occupation that carries unique challenges. One is that a portrait must not only reflect the sitter's features accurately but also please the subject who has commissioned it. This combination requires considerable diplomacy from the portraitist, who as an artist must be willing to flatter vanity within the constraints of plausibility. Further, a successful portrait captures the mind as well as the face. A fair degree of psychological astuteness is involved. And a successful portraitist must be not just artistically talented and well trained but also socially adept enough to win sitters, to engage them while sitting, and to satisfy them with the experience and ultimately the result. These challenges are even greater when the sitters are, as they tend to be, grandees. As William Blake wrote in reference to Joshua Reynolds, "Only portrait painting [is] applauded and rewarded by the rich and great."[1]

Why *etching*, though, as opposed to painting or photography? The art has an ineffable classicism: it instantly antiques the image represented, as if it belongs to the ages.

1.   William Blake, "Marginal Notes to the Discourses of Sir Joshua Reynolds, 1798" (ca. 1808), in Edwin John Ellis, *The Real Blake: A Portrait Biography* (Chatto & Windus, 1907), 371 (quoting a handwritten marginal note).

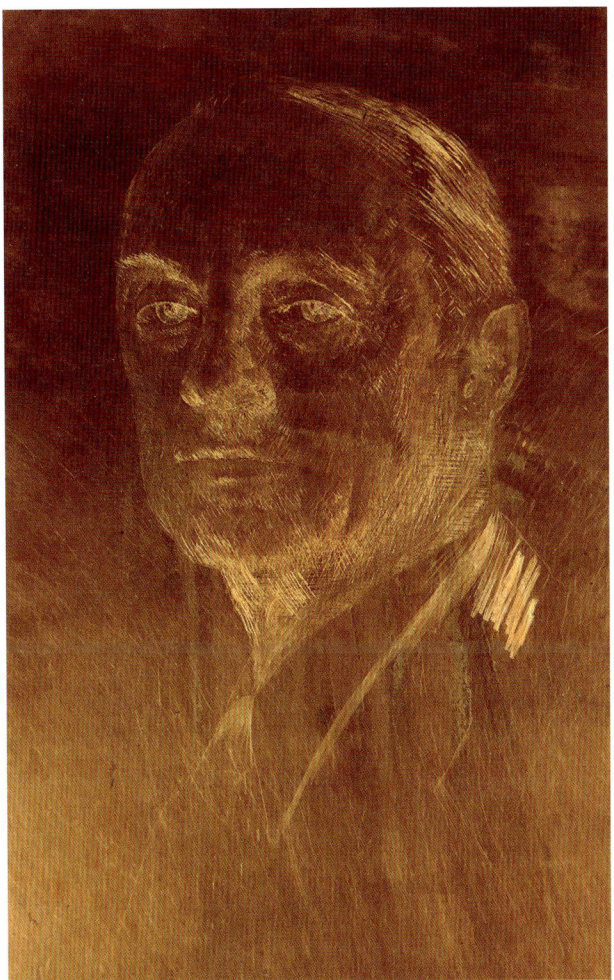

As can be seen here, the copperplate itself involves subtlety in wispish lines. Everything (naturally) is reversed and mirror-imaged, as in hot-lead printing. Often Oskar would portray a floating visage, with minimal surroundings. This type of work requires great sensitivity and a heightened sense of nuance. It also demands a hint of cari-cature——an emphasis on qualities that suggest character. Many of Oskar's etchings are far more revealing about the subject than a mere photograph might be.

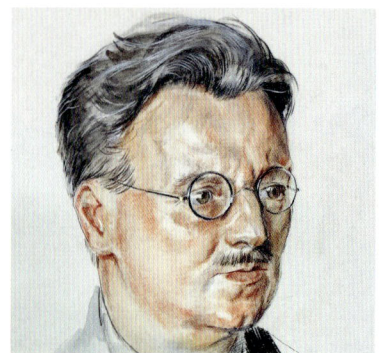

Heinrich Wastian (Graz 1923)

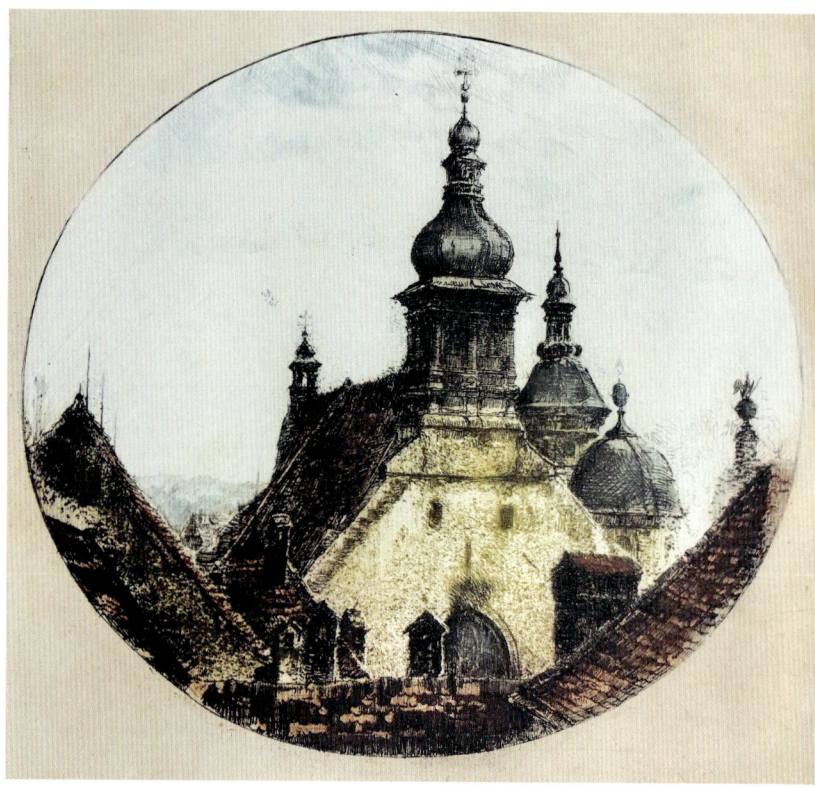

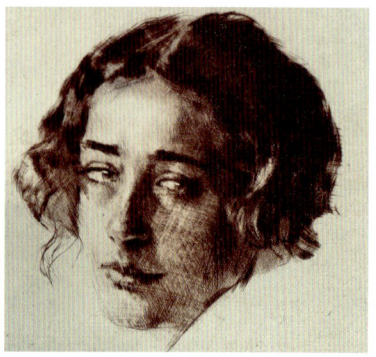

Unknown subject (Graz 1914)

Spires of Graz (ca. 1921)

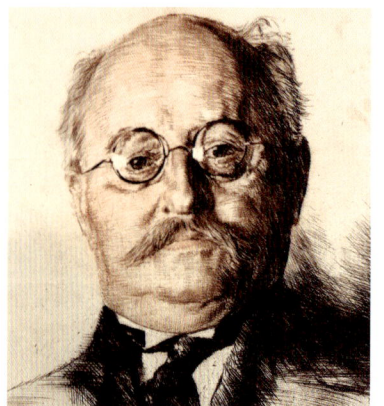

Fritz Winterberg (ca. 1920s)

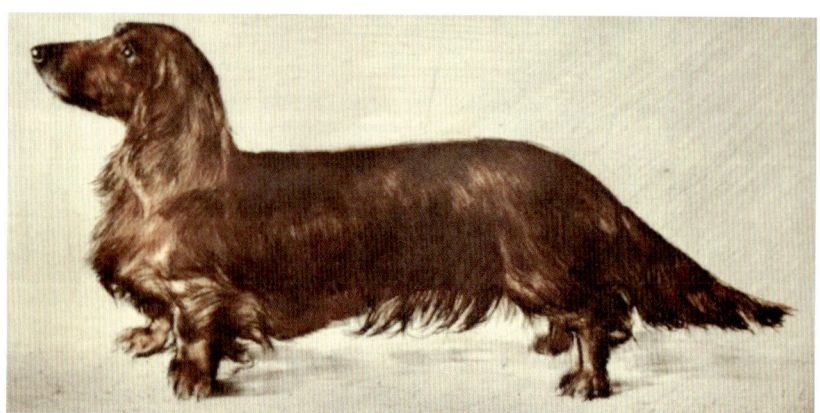

"Long-Haired Red Dachshund" (1925)

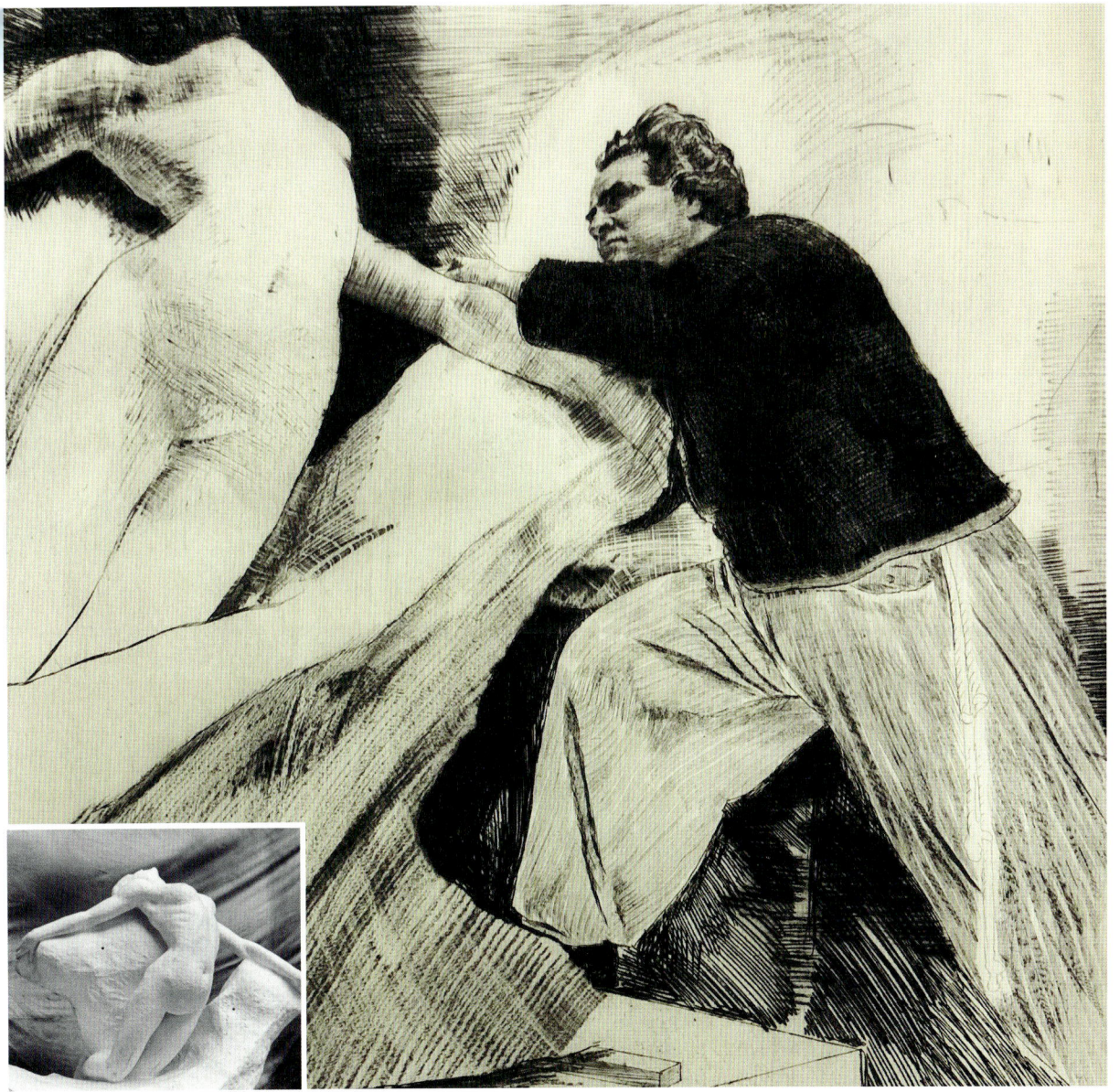

Oskar's etching of his friend, the sculptor Gustinus Ambrosi (1893–1975), as he was finishing a piece entitled "Die Blüte" ["The Blossom"]
(1932). (Ambrosi's bust of Oskar appears on the frontispiece to this book.) Ambrosi was both a sculptor and a poet. Among his more than
2,000 sculptures in bronze and stone are busts of Nietzsche, Mussolini, Goethe, and Richard Strauss. In failing health in 1975, he com-
mitted suicide. His former studio in Vienna has been turned into the Gustinus Ambrosi Museum.
INSET: *The finished sculpture.*

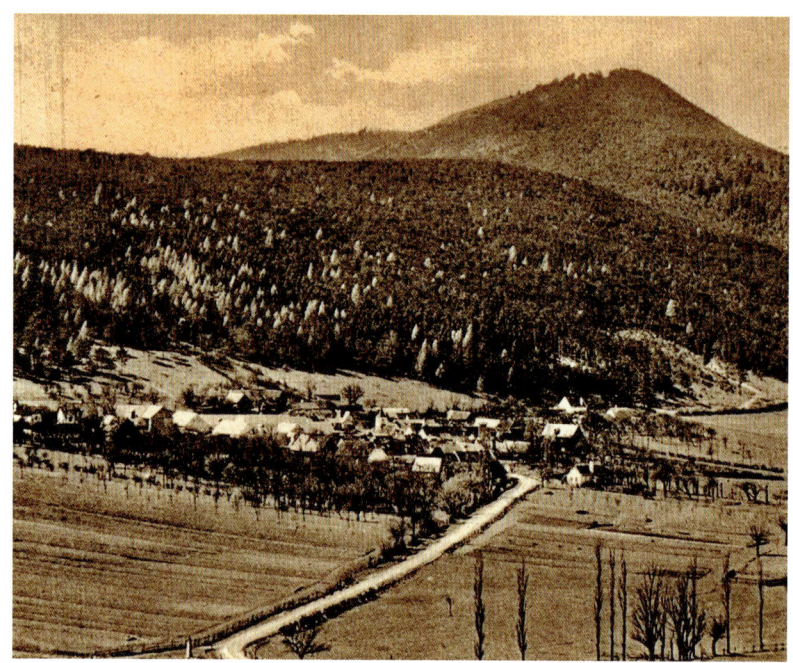

The village of Neunkirchen (ca. 1900)

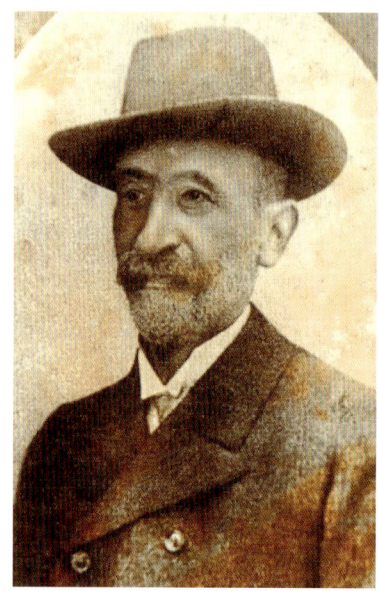

Oskar's uncle Max Stössel (1844—1909)

CHAPTER 2

The Blossoming Artist

OSKAR STOESSEL was born January 11, 1879, in Neunkirchen ("New Church"), Austria—south of Vienna. He was the eldest child in a Jewish family that had moved there decades earlier. Many Jews lived in the region. His parents, Leopold and Berta Stössel, were merchants who also maintained a small farm. They had four children: Oskar, Ludwig, Wilhelm,[1] and Isabella. After Ludwig was born in 1883, the family moved to Lockenhaus, a town closer to Graz. Leopold had family members there, such as his brother Max. It was in Lockenhaus that Oskar's two youngest siblings were born.

In 1892, the family moved to Graz, where Oskar attended secondary school and a technical college, graduating in 1907 with a civil-engineering degree. But as early as 1900, he had begun taking art lessons. Soon he was studying with the acclaimed painter Constantin Damianos. Then he began studying with Leo Diet, the Czech artist who since 1895 had taught at the Kunstgewerbeschule (Arts and Crafts School) in Graz. Although Diet is primarily known as a painter, he also taught other graphic arts such as etching.

In November–December 1907, Oskar participated in an art exhibition sponsored by the Styrian Artists' Cooperative in Graz. An art magazine asserted that Oskar's work in particular must be "given honor."[2] He was exhibiting alongside his teachers Damianos and Diet.

It might well be that Oskar took his engineering degree to satisfy his parents that he would have a practical vocation. His heart seems not to have been in that

---

1. Little is known about Wilhelm (1890–1929), apart from the family knowledge that he existed. David Heichler, Isabella's grandson, has a photograph of Berta with Wilhelm—known to Isabella's daughter, Elsa, as "Uncle Willie."

2. *Die Kunst* (Munich), 15 (1907): 271.

line of study—after all, he didn't attain the degree until he was 28. And from the time he was 21, he was devoting attention to art. His knowledge of engineering, though, surely enhanced his painting—especially in architectural renditions.

Once Oskar graduated in engineering, he was off to Vienna to seek admission into the Imperial Academy of Fine Arts. To qualify to sit for the grueling two-day exam in October 1908, he had to submit some samples of his art. He turned in those pieces, together with his paperwork, at the handsome Renaissance-style building at Schillerplatz. One of his fellow applicants was Adolf Hitler, who was now submitting his preliminary work for the second time; he had passed the first step in 1907 but failed the examination. This time, Hitler was screened out at the first threshold because of his unsatisfactory work. But Oskar was allowed to take the exam.

Having crossed the first hurdle, Oskar now had to submit to a strictly timed series of tests in which he had to choose from among designated subjects to draw. Many were religious in nature. On the first day, the subjects included Cain's killing Abel, Adam and Eve's finding Abel's body, the return of the Prodigal Son, death, mourning, farewell, and the expulsion from Paradise. On the second day, the applicants were expected to select from among these subjects: the Magi, the blinding of Samson, the Good Samaritan, pilgrims, prayer, peace, evening rest, an episode from the Flood, night, the fishermen, and the storyteller.

Soon the Academy posted the results, with "satisfactory" or "unsatisfactory" beside each applicant's name. Oskar was accepted. Now he had the break he'd been hoping for: to study with the newly named professor of art, the celebrated etcher Ferdinand Schmutzer. For the past eight years, Oskar had been preparing for this opportunity.

When his studies began in October 1908, the school records noted—as was usual at the time—that he was Jewish. His enrollment card was marked "jüdisch (mosaisch, israelitisch)." He studied assiduously at the Academy for five years. There was an interruption, though, in 1911, when he was briefly suspended for failing to pay his tuition and fees. His and his family's finances were continually strained.

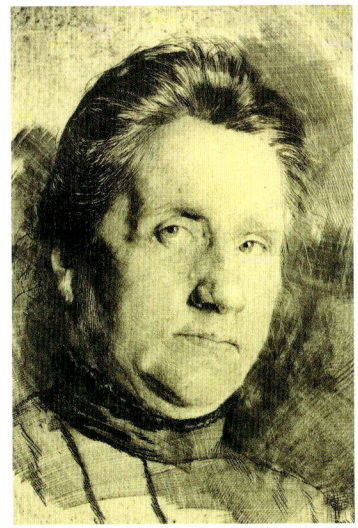

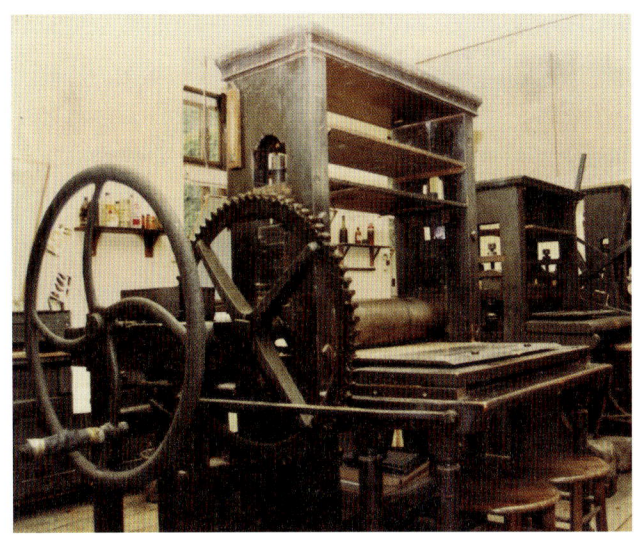

Oskar's earliest etching of his mother, Berta Stössel (ca. 1912)

The type of printing press used by Oskar—especially for large plates. He may have used this very press: in the early 2000s, it was in the same Viennese shop as a collection of his copperplates.

Of all Oskar's teachers, Ferdinand Schmutzer (1870–1928) undoubtedly exerted the most profound influence both artistically and logistically—that is, in the practicalities of earning a living as a printmaker and portraitist. Although Oskar didn't know it at the time, his progress from painting to etching followed the same path as Schmutzer's.

For the rest of Oskar's life, his paintings would show the influence of Damianos and Diet: it was an impressionistic style, typically (in oils) using the impasto technique of thickly applied paint retaining palette-knife strokes as well as brushstrokes. His watercolors were likewise impressionistic. Although some of his landscape etchings showed hints of impressionism, on the whole these pieces as well as his etched portraits were highly exact and naturalistic. Like Schmutzer, Oskar imbued his etchings with a classic realism. They were sometimes almost photographic, with a slight twist. This dichotomy between Oskar's impressionistic paintings and his realistic etchings would always remain part of his work. He never forsook painting, even though he was devoted to etching.

To understand Oskar's work as an etcher, we must know something about his most significant teacher. More than any other student of Schmutzer's, Oskar began by closely mimicking his teacher's techniques and then modifying and refining them. We can learn a great deal about Oskar's artistic development by examining Schmutzer's.

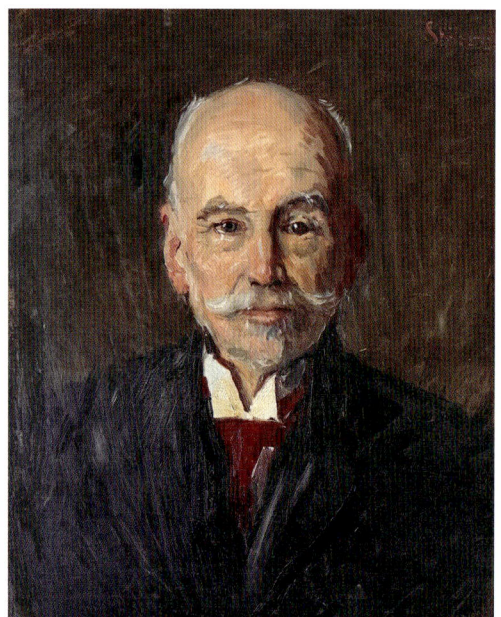 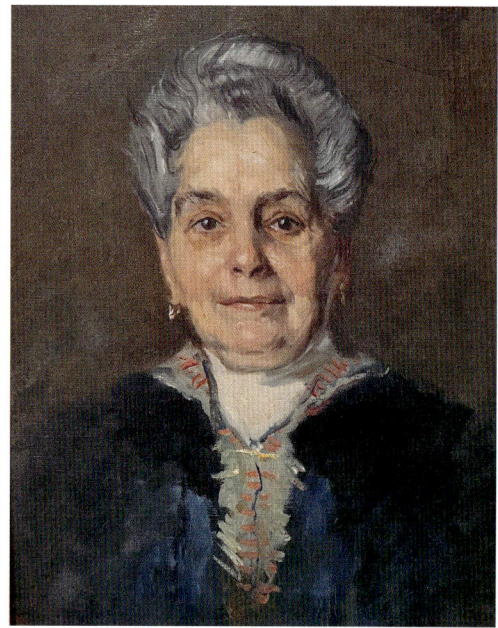

About 1915, Oskar painted portraits for the parents of his friend, the artist Max Robathin (1882–1970), who lived and worked in Graz. At left is Richard Robathin (1848–1938), a factory owner and iron dealer. His wife, Johanna Janschitz (1856–1949), is noted on the back of the frame as being the daughter of a district judge in what is now Slovenia. The couple married in 1875.

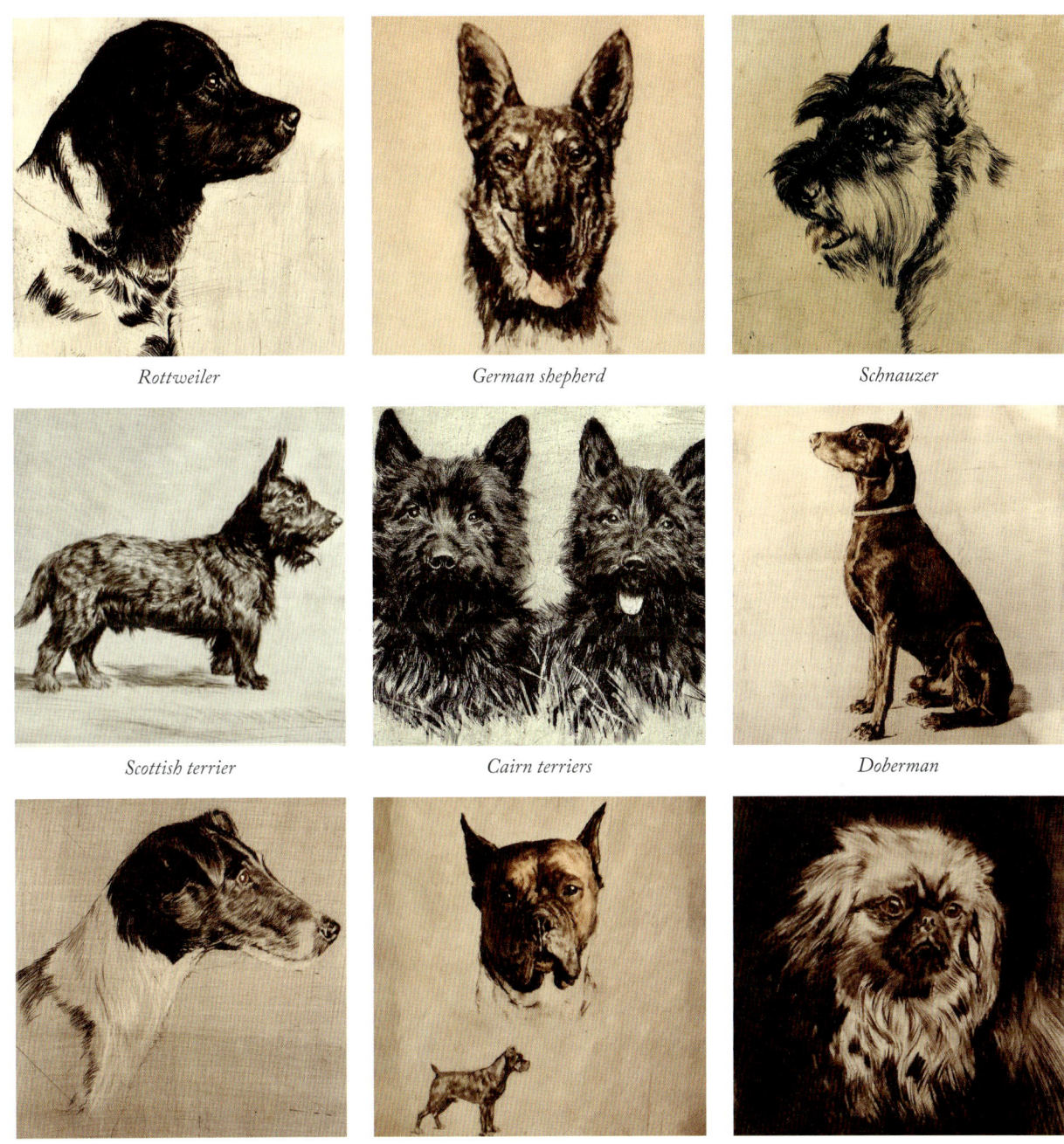

Rottweiler

German shepherd

Schnauzer

Scottish terrier

Cairn terriers

Doberman

Fox terrier

Boxer

Pekingese

In the mid-1920s, Oskar etched a series of dog portraits for the Styrian Society for the Promotion of Purebred Dogs (see page 61).

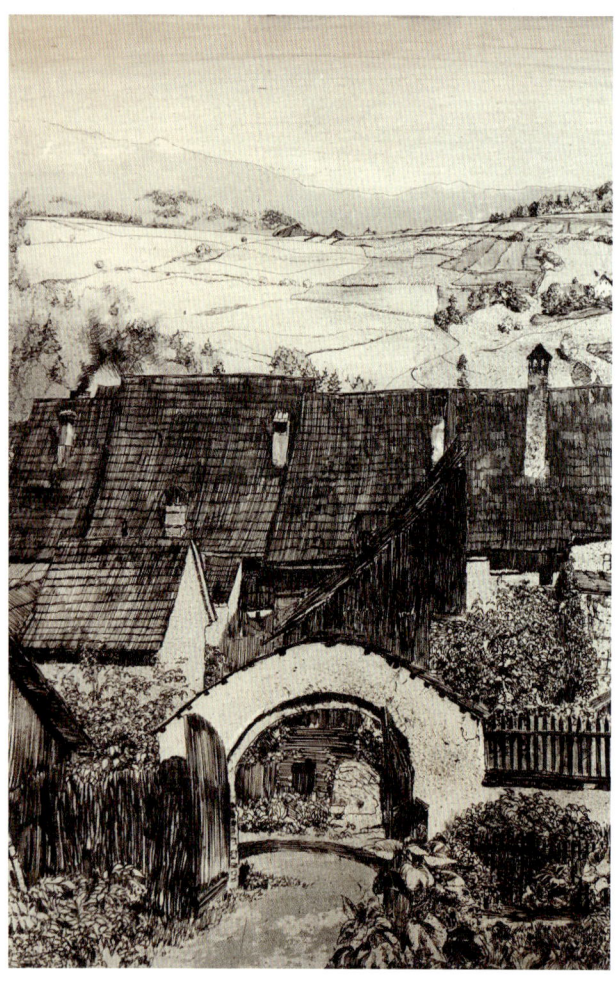

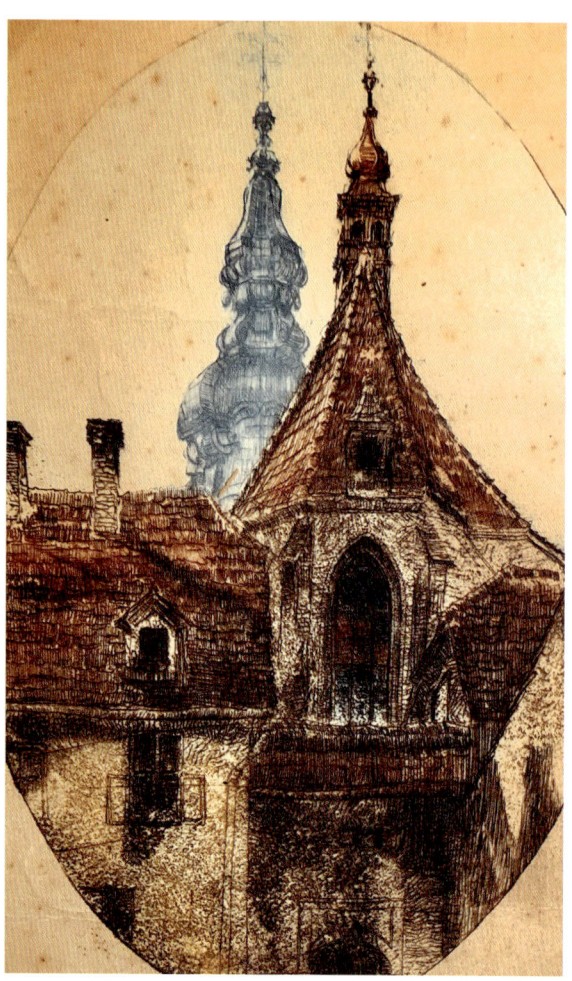

Oskar's "Scene in Neumarkt, Steiermark" (Styria, 1913)

Oskar's "View of the Choir of the Parish Church" (Graz, 1922)

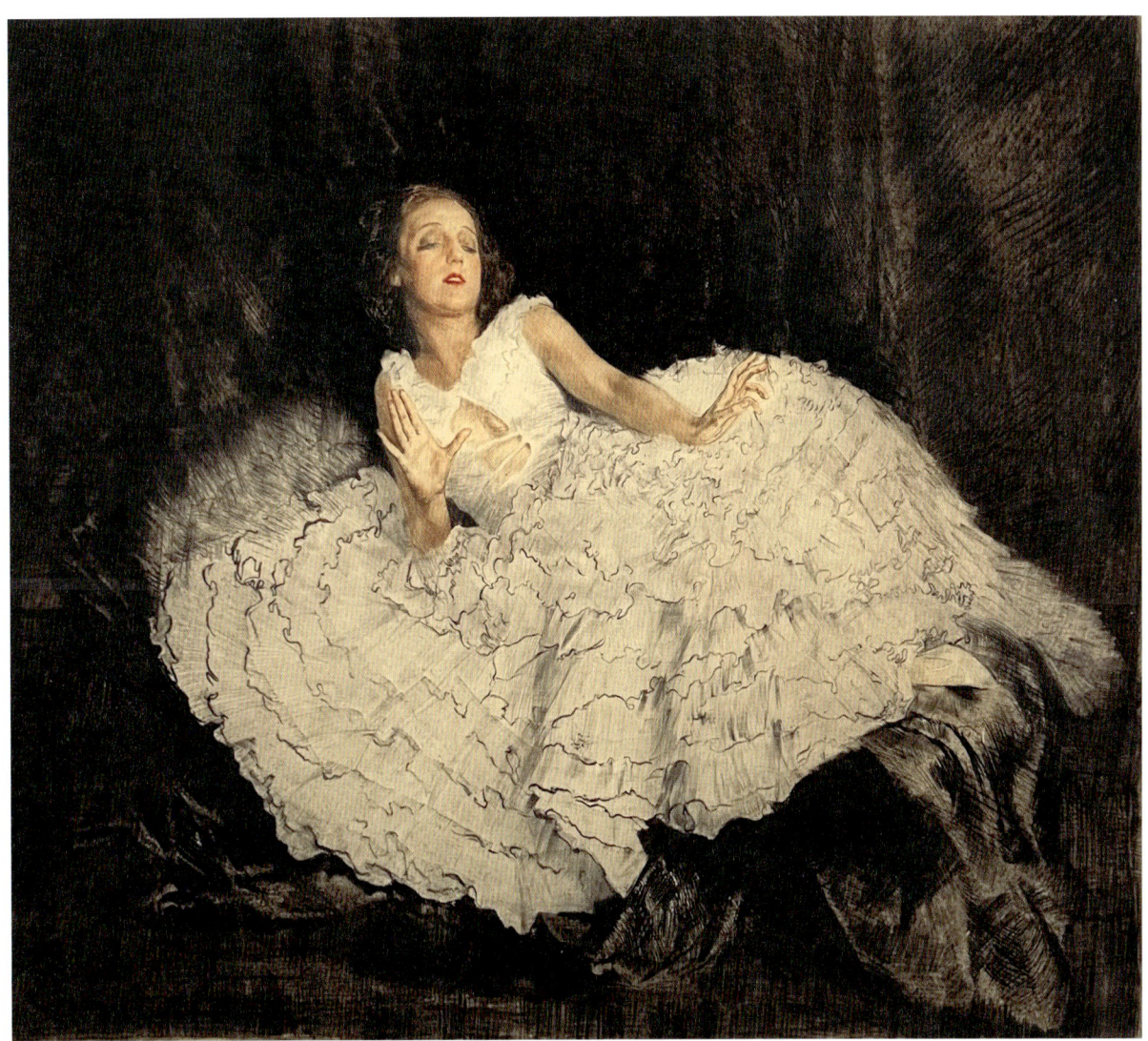

Oskar's 1924 color etching of the dancer Edmonde Guy in her role in the pantomime "The Shade." The scene depicts the last moment before she surrenders to the Shade. Here is what Bruno Binder wrote about this etching: "This big sheet is the apotheosis of the model, in the grace and movement of pose. One marvels at the smoothness of the skin and the fluffy, black-edged ruffles of her dress that billow out while she reclines on her dark bed, her hands outstretched in a slightly defensive position." Bruno Binder, "Der österreichische Maler und Radierer Oskar Stössel," Westermann's Monatshefte *(Berlin), Apr. 1931, 105, 110—11.*

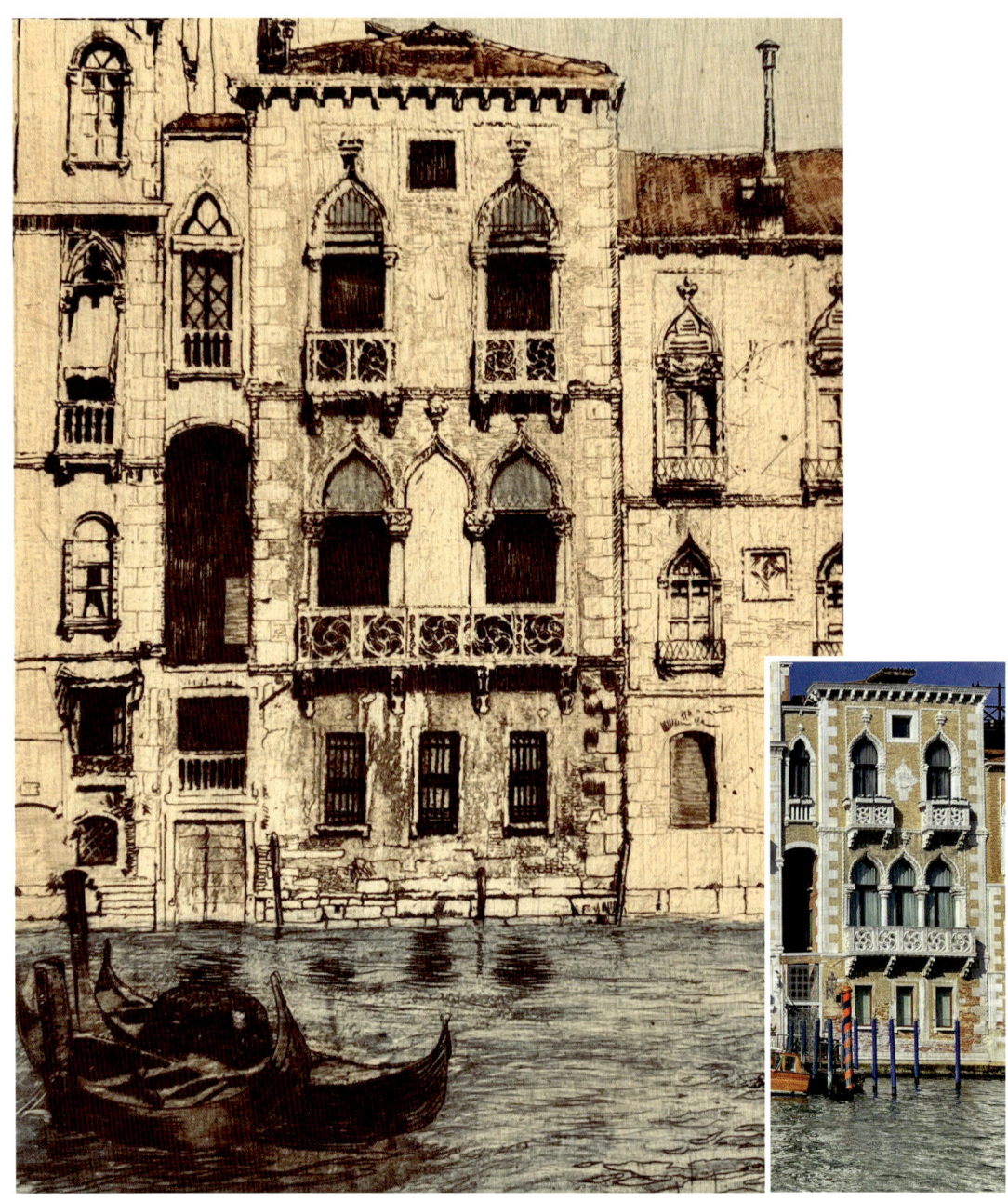

Oskar's 1911 etching of Palazzo Contarini Fasan in Venice. Built in Venetian—Gothic style about 1475, the palazzo is also known, for no discernible historical reason, as the House of Desdemona.
INSET: *How the house looks today*

CHAPTER 3

Oskar's Master Teacher

Ferdinand Schmutzer (1870–1928) reputedly came from a long line of Viennese artists, including possibly Jakob Matthias Schmutzer (1733–1811), who founded the Vienna Copperplate Engraving Academy. (The genealogy is disputed.) Ferdinand's father, also named Ferdinand Schmutzer, was a sculptor who specialized in animals. At 16, Schmutzer studied sculpture, but by his twenties his interests had shifted to painting. In the 1890s, he attended two schools for painters, and in 1894 he won the Rome Prize, which gave him a government travel stipend for two years' travel in Holland, where he grew dissatisfied with painting and turned to etching.

When Schmutzer returned to Vienna in 1896, he studied etching with William Unger, who held a professorship at the Imperial Academy of Fine Arts. Unger was an important art teacher in Munich for American artists William Merritt Chase, Frank Duveneck, and others. By 1897, Schmutzer was exhibiting his etchings at the Künstlerhaus, and that year he won the Great Gold State Medal. Soon he was exhibiting in Dresden (1899, 1901), Paris (1900), Munich (1903), Berlin (1905), London (1906), and Saint Petersburg (1907). In many of these places, he won gold medals.

Though a serious student of the Old Masters—especially Rembrandt and Vermeer—Schmutzer wasn't much influenced by them: he developed his own distinctive manner of portraiture, with characteristic uses of light and shade, as well as soft tones, to depict the subtle features of his subjects. In some of his work, he tinted his etchings. But his black-and-white portraits were generally thought to represent his best work, and Schmutzer himself preferred untinted images. As he grew in stature and in his mastery of etching, he began working with larger and larger copperplates, until they reached unprecedented dimensions—in the case of

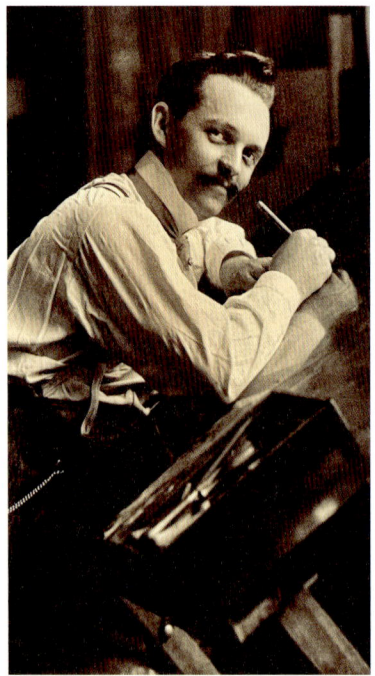

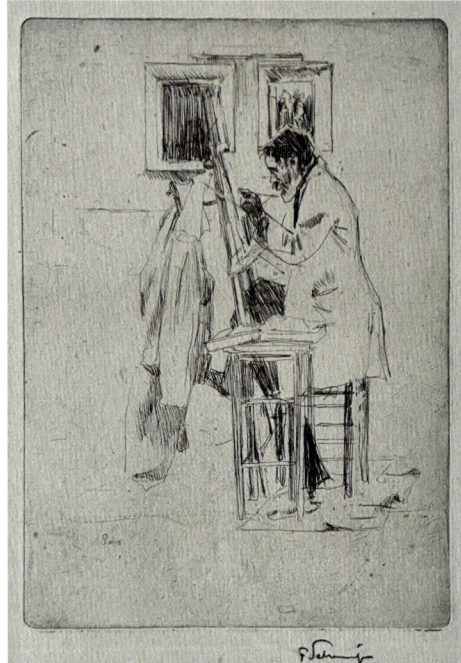

Ferdinand Schmutzer   *Schmutzer's "The Copyist at the Louvre" (1900)*

the *Joachim Quartet*, 36 inches high by 48 inches wide. Such enormous plates were thought by many to be exercises in ostentation, but the critical consensus was that his work showed virtuosity with the oversized plates.

Schmutzer typically photographed his subjects, then made pencil drawings in a separate sitting, and then began to create his etchings. Perhaps because he un-apologetically made use of photography, his portraits were ordinarily much more realistic and lifelike than those of his teacher, Unger.

In 1908, just as Oskar was preparing to enter the Academy, Schmutzer was chosen to succeed the retiring Unger as professor of art. Shortly after, he built a mansion in the Währing Cottage district of Vienna, where he housed his studio and printing press, as well as a darkroom. He kept his electrified press in an alcove within the studio. Its vibrations, he said, gave him a peculiar pleasure: they energized him in his work. The motor left him with both hands free to carry out his art. When not in use, the press was kept hidden from visitors by a drawn curtain.

From the turn of the 20th century, Schmutzer belonged to the Vienna Secession, which was a movement of artists, designers, and architects who reacted against the conservative artistic establishment. The Secessionists, started by Gustav Klimt and others, embraced modernism. Their motto was "To every age its art, to every art its freedom." From 1899 to the mid-1920s, Schmutzer frequently exhibited his work at the Vienna Secession headquarters. From 1914 to 1917, he served as its president.

The Schmutzers' upper-middle-class, nominally Catholic household bustled with activity and excitement. Oskar became a part of this world when he was Schmutzer's student, and afterward he—more than anyone else—took on the mantle of Schmutzer's chief protégé. Over time, Max Pollak's fame grew to such an extent that he might have rivaled Oskar for this title. In the 1920s, though, it was Oskar who was always listed first among Schmutzer's several famous students.[1]

With his wife Alice (1887–1949), Schmutzer made his large home into a salon for artists, musicians, and intellectuals. They were a Viennese "power couple": Alice wrote occasional reviews for *Neue Freie Presse*, Vienna's leading liberal newspaper, while Schmutzer was "generally recognized to be the most important Austrian etcher."[2] Schmutzer's remarkable personality and career made it possible for him to introduce Oskar to Vienna's high society. Oskar probably visited the house with some frequency, together with his contemporaries such as Max Pollak and their

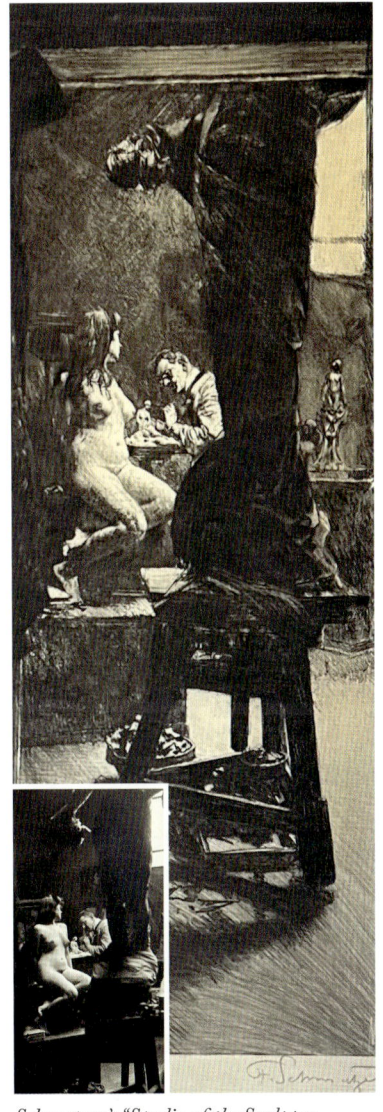

Schmutzer's "Studio of the Sculptor Charles Korschann" (1900)—photo inset

1. See, e.g., Arpad Weixlgärtner, *Das radierte Werk von Ferdinand Schmutzer 1896–1921* (Fritz Mandel Kunstverlag, 1922), xii.

2. Martin Birnbaum, *Catalogue of an Exhibition of Contemporary Graphic Art in Hungary, Bohemia, and Austria, Buffalo Fine Arts Academy, Jan. 4–Feb. 1st (1913–1914)* (De Vinne, 1913), 24.

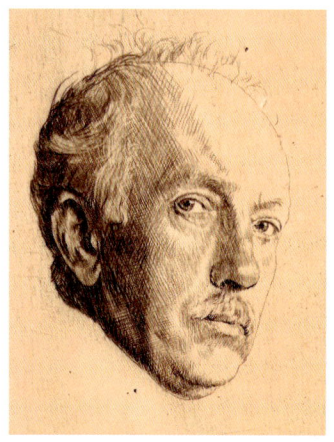

Schmutzer's portrait of the composer Richard Strauss

friend Gustinus Ambrosi, the sculptor. Among others who had associations with Schmutzer were the composers Arnold Schoenberg, Richard Strauss, and Hugo Wolf; the conductor Felix Weingartner of the Vienna Philharmonic; the violinist Arnold Rosé; the writers Felix Salten and Arthur Schnitzler; the poets Paul Heyse (a Nobel laureate) and Anton Wildgans; the actors Josef Kainz, Alexander Girardi, and Maria Carmi-Vollmöller; the painters Rudolf von Alt, Gustav Klimt, and Egon Schiele; the operatic singer Leo Slezak; the philosophers of the Vienna Circle, such as Moritz Schlick and Ernst Mach; and the Wittgenstein family, including the steel tycoon Karl Wittgenstein and his philosopher son, Ludwig.

It's probable, too, that Albert Einstein and Sigmund Freud were part of the circle. Schmutzer photographed and etched portraits of Einstein in 1921, the year that he won the Nobel Prize for Physics, and of Freud in 1926 in time for his 70th birthday. Freud proclaimed the etching "excellent," adding: "Others find its expression too severe, almost angry. Inwardly this is probably what I am."[3]

Early in 1914, Schmutzer received a commission to etch the portrait of Archduke Franz Ferdinand (1863–1914). It may well be the last portrait ever made of Ferdinand, who on June 24 was assassinated in Sarajevo. Shortly after, Austria-Hungary declared war against Serbia. Other nations declared war against Austria-Hungary or each other. The Archduke's death had sparked World War I. Although Schmutzer's photograph of the Archduke is well known, the etching is quite rare.

So similar are the techniques in Schmutzer's and Stoessel's early portraiture that it can be difficult, without looking at the penciled signature, to distinguish a Schmutzer from a Stoessel—at least a pre-1920 Stoessel. This suggests that Stoessel began with methods much like his mentor's: sketching the subject by

---

3. Sigmund Freud to the Members of the B'nai B'rith Lodge, May 6, 1926, in *Letters of Sigmund Freud*, ed. Ernst L. Freud (Basic Books, 1960), Letter 221, 369.

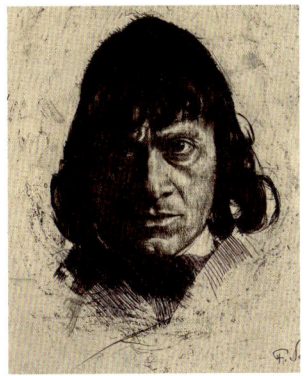 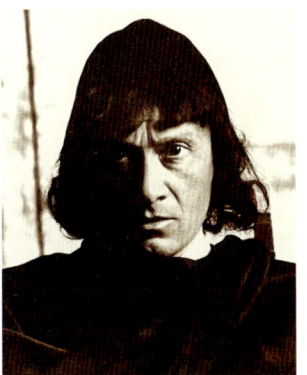 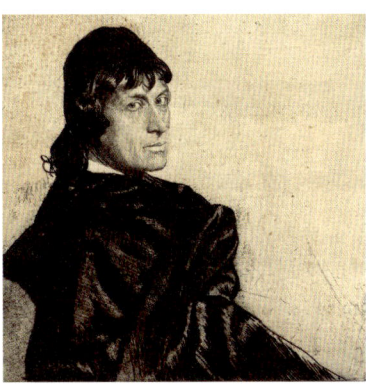

Two versions of the actor Josef Kainz (1858–1910) portraying Hamlet, plus the photo used in making the etching at left

pencil as well as taking photographs; working exclusively with copper, not steel or zinc; developing the plate from the simple to the complex; scratching lines into the base of the varnish with a needle, and then applying acid; beginning with the darkest areas, deepening them more and more through repeated "bitings" or applications of acid; using a roulette (a toothy, textured wheel attached to a handle) for delicate tones, such as skin; using a file for silky hair and soft fabrics; making two or three passes with a diamond engraver for thick lines;

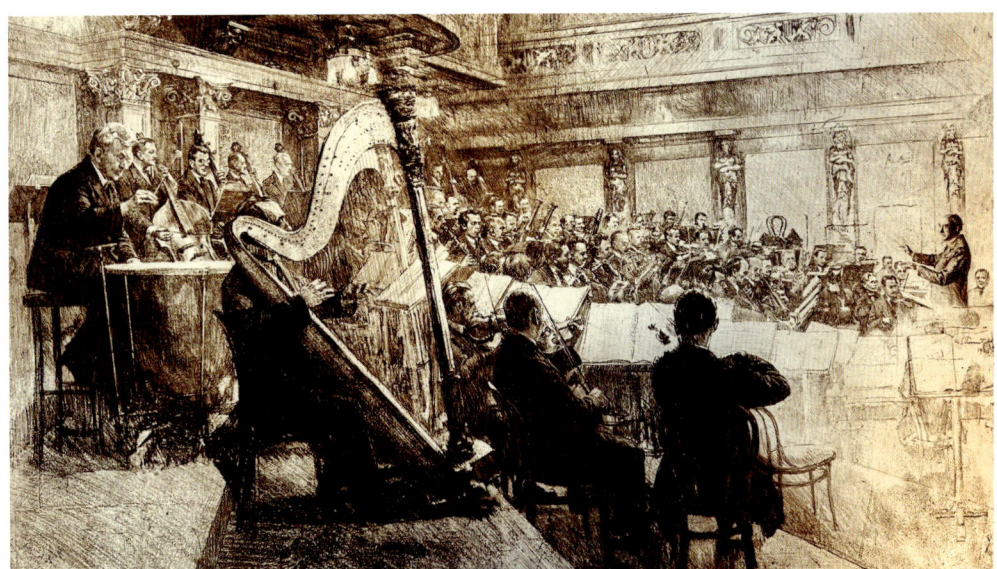

Schmutzer's "Vienna Philharmonic," conducted by Felix Weingartner (1926)

Schmutzer's 1914 photograph of Archduke Franz Ferdinand

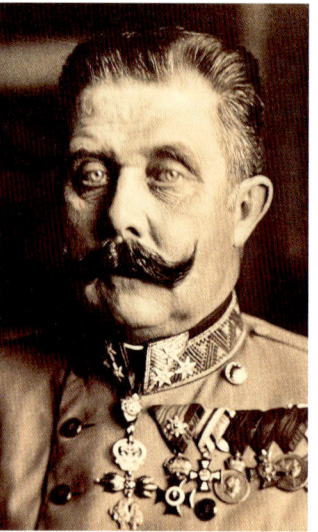

Schmutzer's "almost angry" Freud (1926)

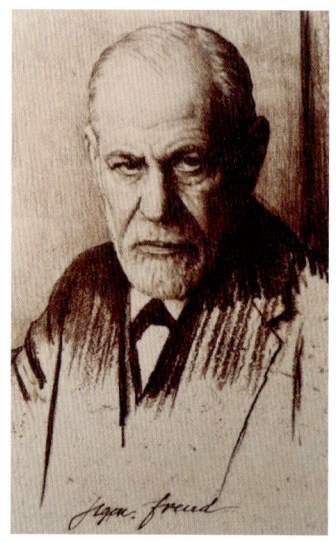

Einstein in 1921, the year of his Nobel Prize. Note the similarities and differences with the photograph.

using a file again, followed by a drypoint needle and scraper; sometimes polishing parts of the plate with steel wool; printing with his own press within his own studio; and if tinting was desired, completing some elements by watercolor gently brushed in. Then, of course, proofs would be sent to the subject for approval; after comments, the artist might either rework the plate or, if necessary, start anew. It might aptly be said of both Schmutzer and Stoessel that despite the iterative process of improving the plate, they had a knack for preserving in the final etching the liveliness of their first impressions.

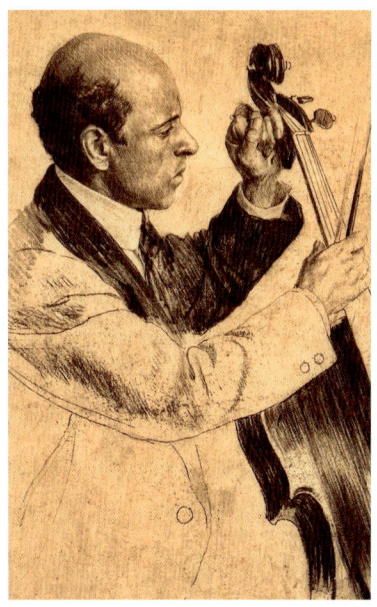

One of several etchings Schmutzer made of the cellist Pablo Casals in 1914

The process, understandably, was time-consuming and work-intensive. In their most productive periods, they might produce as many as 18 or 19 etchings a year. Schmutzer achieved that number only in 1912. Over the course of his most productive years as an etcher—from 1897 to 1921—Schmutzer averaged 10 etchings a year, including small pieces such as bookplates and greeting cards. This pace continued up until his sudden death in 1928 from a heart attack.

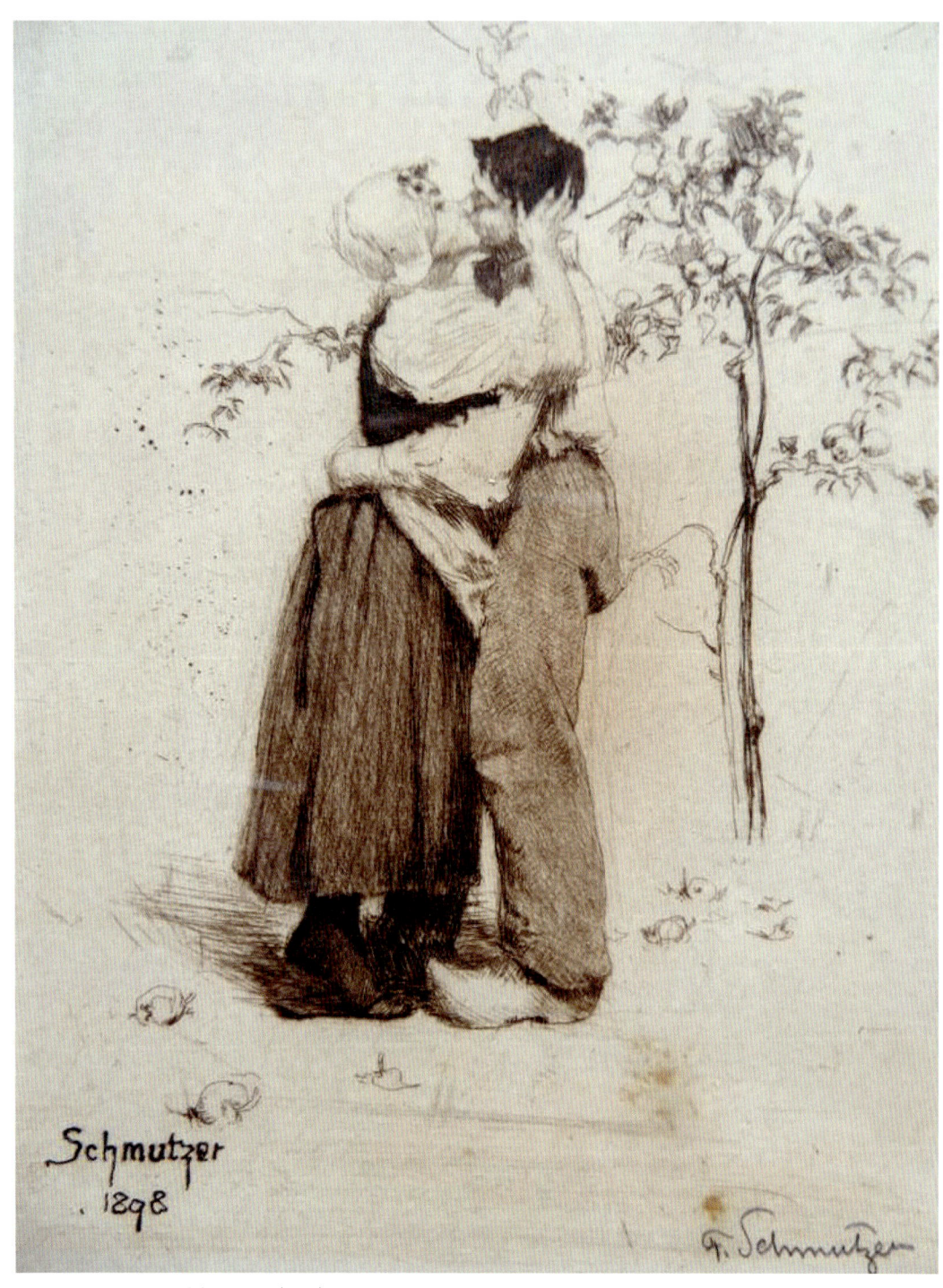

Schmutzer's version of "The Kiss" (1898)

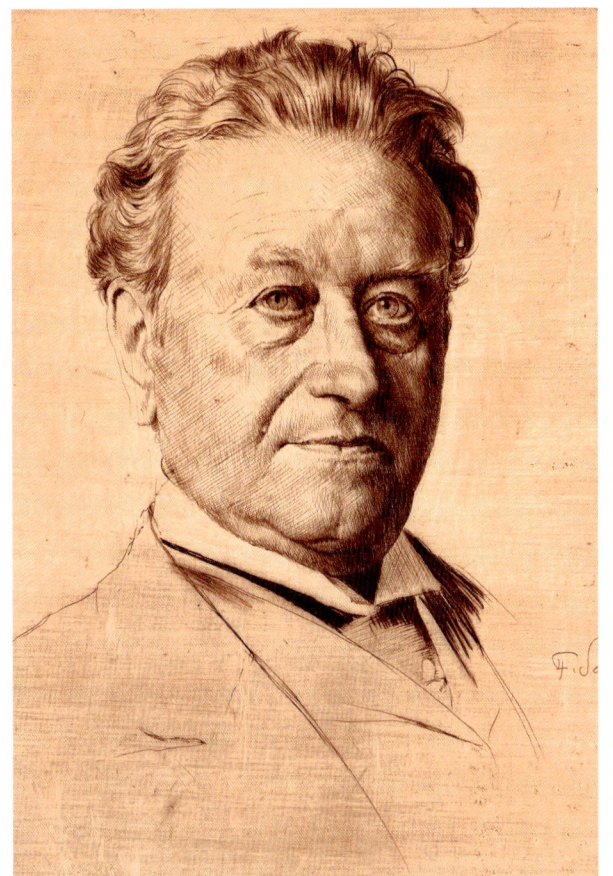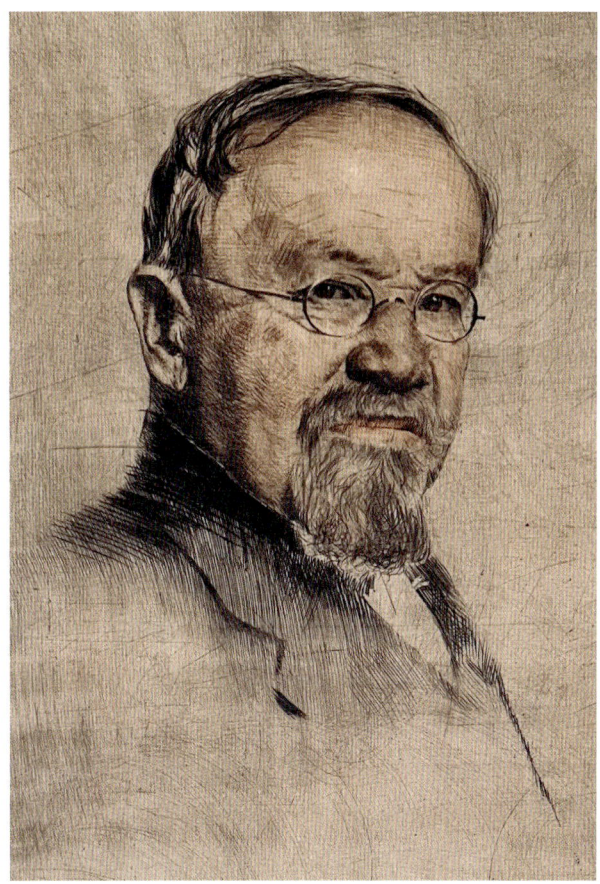

These two superbly executed portraits show some of the similarity in technique between Schmutzer (left) and Stoessel (right). Both are highly realistic, not impressionistic. Both convey the character and essence of the subject. With an economy of lines, Schmutzer captures the contours of the face, the fine details of the hair, and the shadows on the left side of the face; the wrinkles are tastefully emphasized to suggest wisdom and life. Stoessel's is more lifelike (perhaps from the subtle tinting), and the reserved gaze behind the glasses evokes complexity and vulnerability; all in all, it conveys discomfort, depth, and personality.

The subject at left is Ernst Hartmann, the stage actor at the Burgtheater in Vienna, one of the most famous theaters in Europe. Schmutzer's portrait, dated 1915, was made three to four years after Hartmann's death and is known to exist in an unprecedented ten different states or stages. (Arpad Weixlgärtner, Das radierte Werk von Ferdinand Schmutzer 1896—1921 *[Fritz Mandel Kunstverlag, 1922], no. 185.) In short, Schmutzer worked especially hard on this one, from both photographs and memory.*

The two works are both excellent. Yet in a poll of a few hundred art aficionados in March 2023, a strong majority of respondents expressed the view that the Stoessel portrait at right is the superior work of art. It might illustrate what was said of Stoessel in 1968: that he "harmonized elegant strokes with modern psychology."[1]

---

1.   Alfred Holzinger, *Das Buch von der Steiermark* (Forum Verlag, 1968), 164.

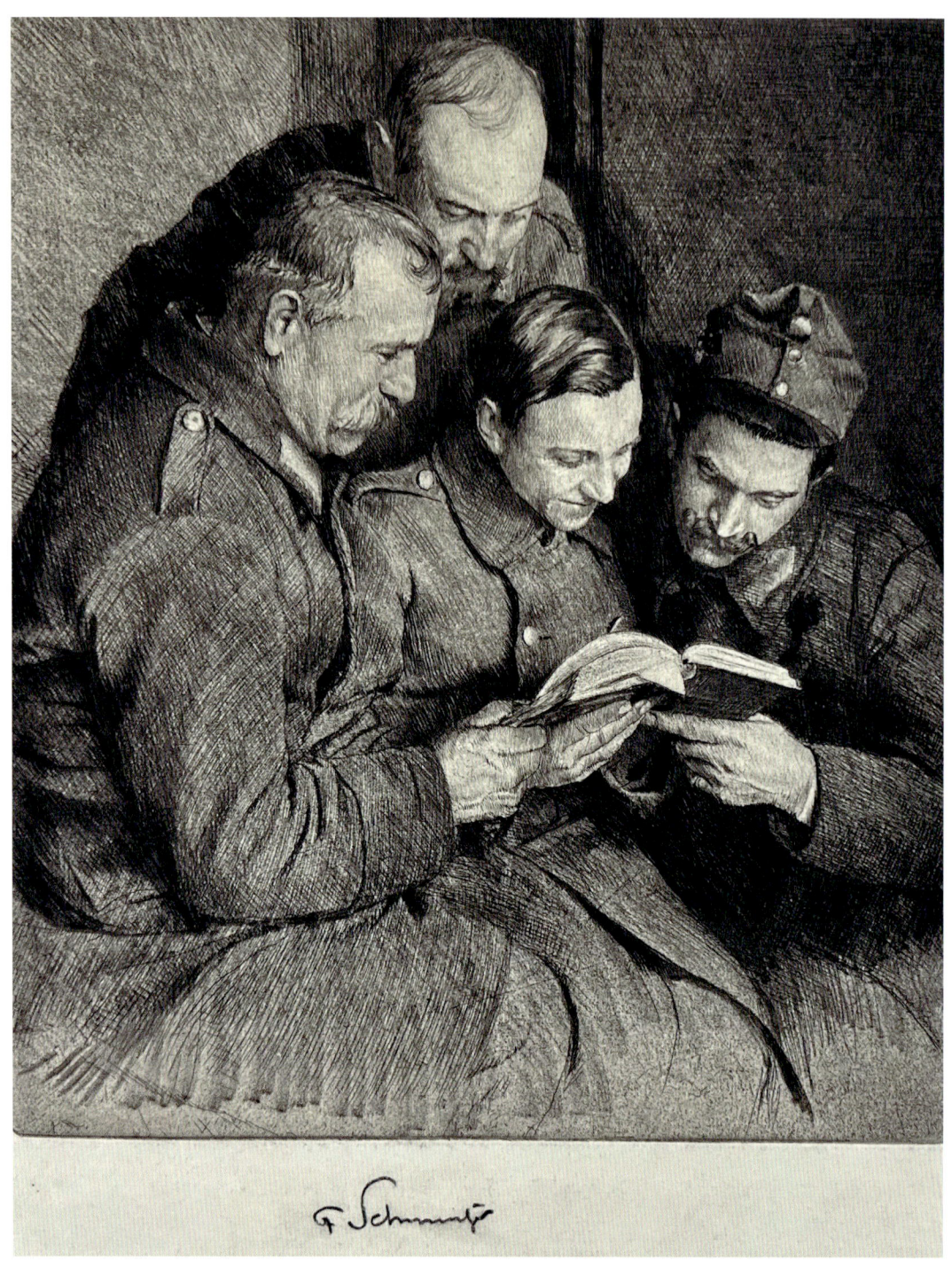

Schmutzer's cheery depiction of Austro-Hungarian soldiers during World War I

CHAPTER 4

The Not-So-Great War

Both Schmutzer and Stoessel created artwork depicting the Austro-Hungarian Army in World War I, but their experiences were entirely different. Having recently (1913) created a portrait of the German Emperor and King of Prussia, Wilhelm II, Professor Schmutzer made an idealized image of four Austro-Hungarian soldiers enthusiastically reading a book (opposite). It was made for a "Books for the Battlefield" campaign promoted by the Red Cross. Whatever they're reading, it seems to be engrossing. The ravages of warfare seem distant.

For Oskar, things were quite different. True, he was becoming known for his "extraordinarily beautiful portraits."[1] One of them had just been shown at an exhibition in Berlin.[2] Although he was 36 years old, he was drafted into service in the Austro-Hungarian Army, as were many other men in their 30s. Universal conscription was thought to be necessary to ensure the availability of soldiers.[3] But it stirred consternation, as a November 1914 letter from a Bavarian soldier on the Western Front suggests: "I am right in front of the enemy. In such a situation, one doesn't know if one survives the next hour. . . . There is something wrong here, otherwise they would not have sent these old soldiers of 36 years to the foremost front line."[4]

Oskar applied to become a war painter, but his request was denied. He was instead assigned to the 76th Regiment in the First Austro-Hungarian Army, which

1. "Wiener Herbstausstellungen," *Die christliche Kunst* (Munich, 1911/1912), 168.
2. *Grosse Berliner Kunst-Ausstellung* (Berlin, 1914), 78.
3. Bernd Ulrich and Benjamin Ziemann, *German Soldiers in the Great War: Letter and Eyewitness Accounts* (Pen & Sword Military, 2010), 43–44.
4. Ulrich and Ziemann, 85.

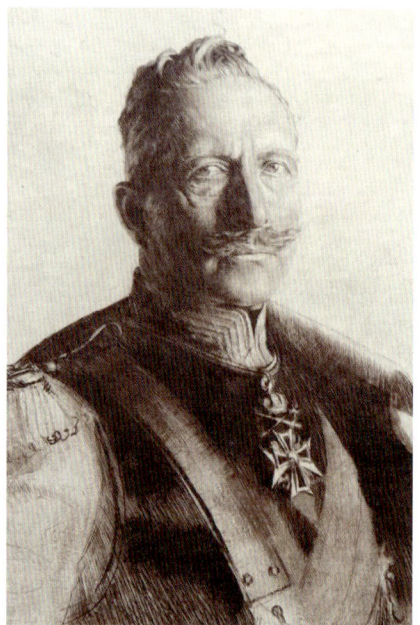

Schmutzer's "Kaiser Wilhelm II" (1913)

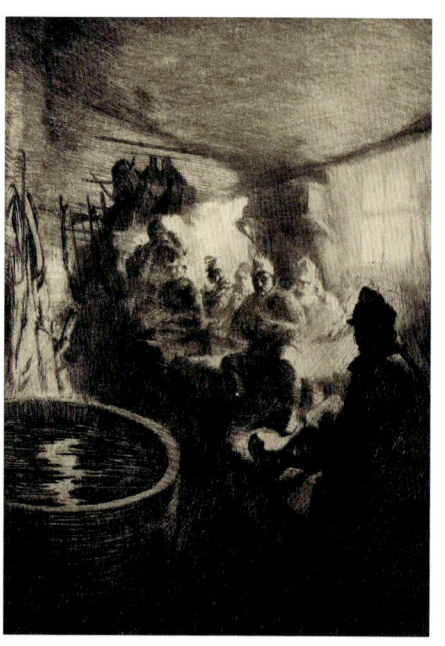

Oskar's portrayal of his fellow 76ers in their dismal barracks at Schafberg, just outside Vienna (1915)

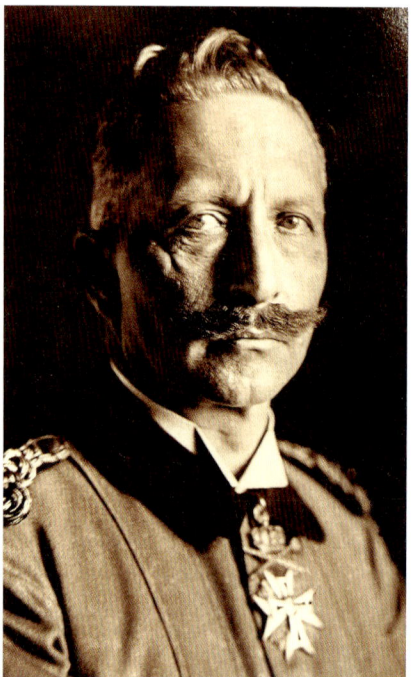

Schmutzer's photograph of the subject

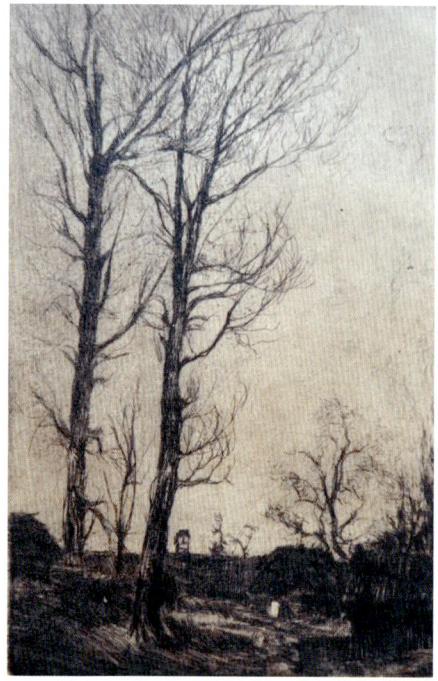

Oskar's "Scene in Krasnik" (1916)

fought against the Russian army on the Eastern Front, from Krasnik (now in Poland) to Halych (now in Ukraine). In contrast with the west, trench warfare was never established. Troops were more mobile and more thinly spread out on the longer front lines.

Life in an Austro-Hungarian unit was wretched. A German soldier from Berlin wrote in June 1915: "The term 'comradeship' has a special meaning in the Austro-Hungarian Army. If it were just that they had stolen my things and that I had to clean up my NCO's boots, I would not have complained. . . . But it was something different that I was always at risk of being beaten up by the guys and by my superior. The lieutenant does not care about absolutely anything, and the sergeant feels called to make the life of the one-year volunteers a misery in every possible and impossible way."[5]

Soldiers on the Eastern Front saw themselves as civilizing or protecting Germans living in occupied Russia-Poland—rescuing them from the oppressive tsarist regime.[6] But the jingoist attitude toward the Russian army was hard to sustain. No army on the Eastern Front was well prepared for war. An Eastern Front–stationed infantry brigade's official war diary noted on a day in November 1914 that "casualties were high while advancing."[7] In his private diary, the brigade's commander described how poorly prepared the troops were: "If the officers were not as unskillful and the men not as badly trained in modern infantry combat as they are, casualties like these could be avoided. But nobody has a clue about battling: everybody was running in broad lines right into the Russian artillery and machine gun fire. . . . Company and brigade commanders just give orders like Deploy! And then everybody starts running and everything is dispersed. . . . It makes me furious!"[8]

Weariness of the war had set in within a year. An Eastern Front soldier noted in November 1915, "The long period of wartime wears down several former hurrah

5. Ulrich and Ziemann, 81–82; see ibid., 102, 104.
6. Ulrich and Ziemann, 74, 98–99.
7. Ulrich and Ziemann, 113.
8. Ulrich and Ziemann, 113.

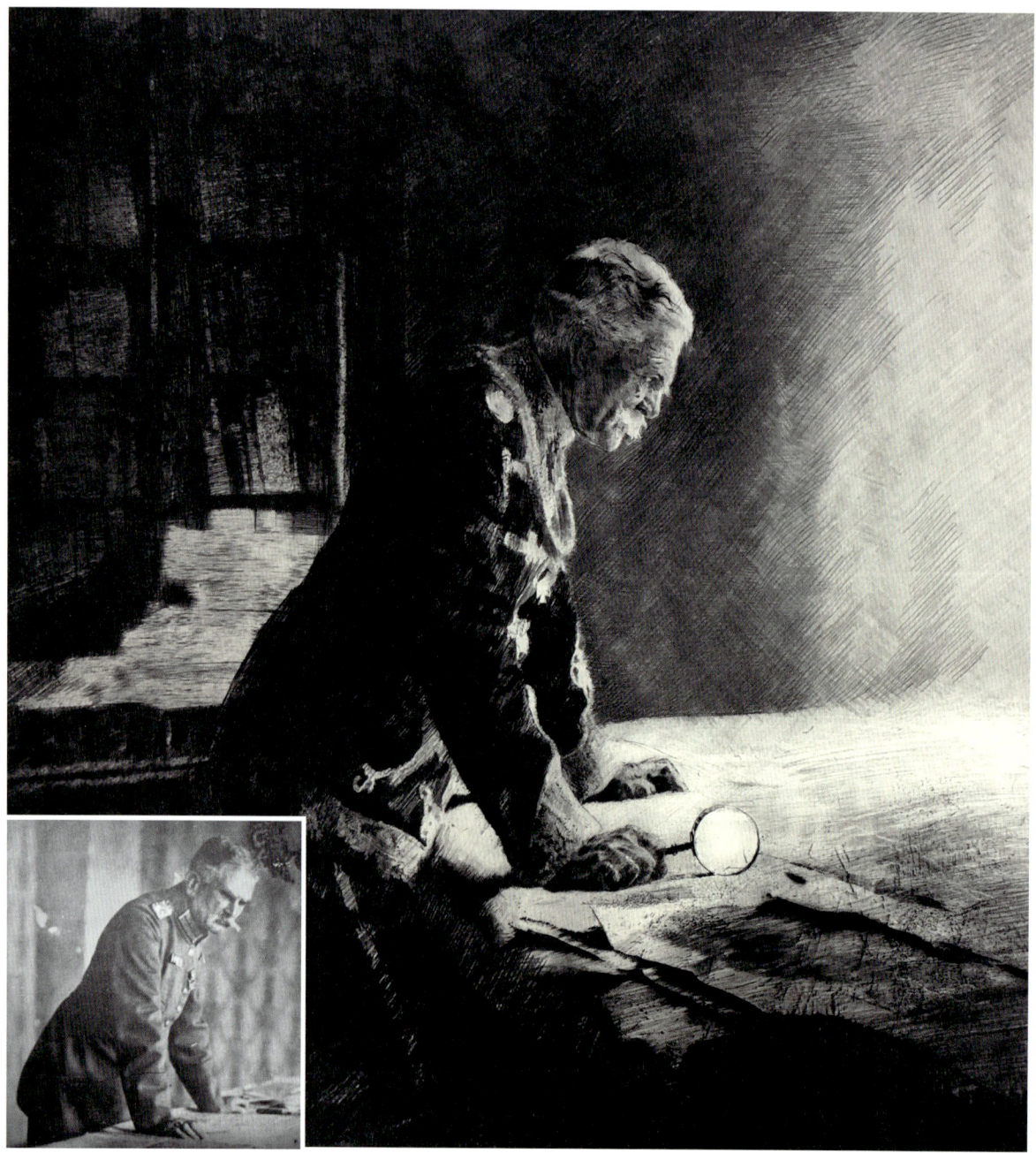

Oskar's etching of Field Marshal August von Mackensen (1918), who was one of Germany's most prominent military leaders during World War I
INSET: *A similar photo*

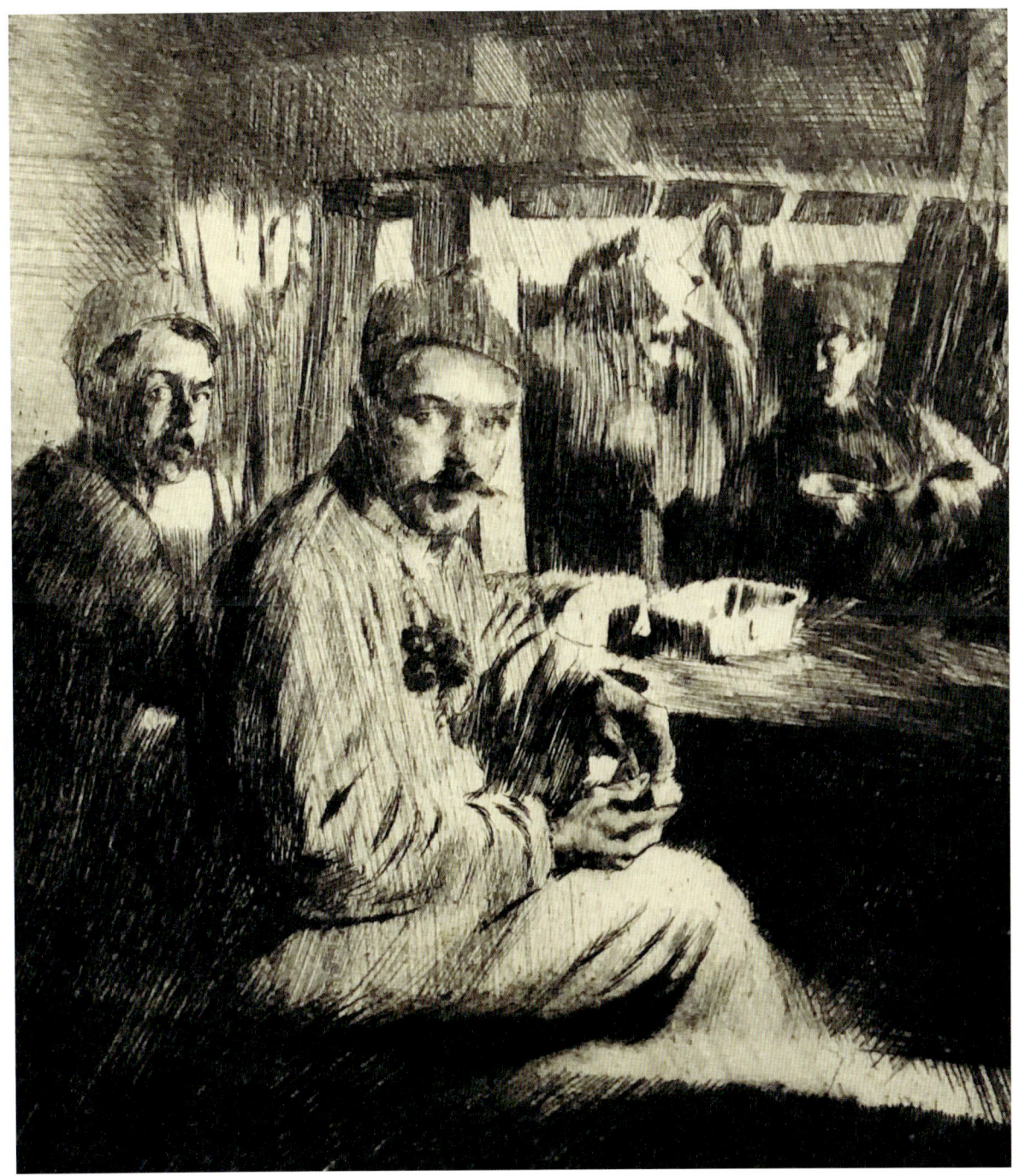

One of Oskar's lugubrious depictions of the Austro-Hungarian Army in a camp at Schafberg, outside Vienna (1916)

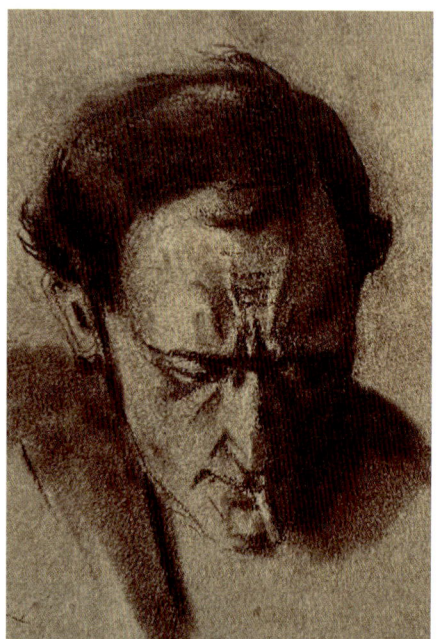

Oskar as he looked in 1912—as drawn by Fritz Silberbauer, a fellow student of Schmutzer's at the Vienna Academy of Fine Arts

jingoists."[9] Disheartening letters from home spoke of how the hard times were affecting families dealing with food shortages and soaring inflation. Hunger was a serious problem in the army, as another Eastern Front soldier reported that same month: "We had to march for 22 to 25 kilometers every day, in heavy marching order. Our weak condition was getting worse due to 'good' food provision day by day. When we arrived at the regiment after 8 days, 200 (out of 600) men were missing. . . . [The battalion commander] requested we pull ourselves up straight. The troops answered with hundreds of voices: 'Hunger, bread, eating' . . . ."[10]

When he could, Oskar made sketches (probably without photographs) for future etchings. As early as 1915, hardly a year into the war, his depictions of his comrades in their barracks were unsurprisingly dark and gloomy, and rather impressionistic. These etchings would likely not have pleased the military censors and certainly wouldn't have been suitable for war propaganda.

Beginning in 1916, Oskar's regiment participated in the Romanian Campaign. He was wounded or injured sometime in 1917 and sent to a hospital in Bucharest. There he met the German general Field Marshal August von Mackensen, later to become known as "The Last Hussar." At the time, Mackensen was in command of a multinational army of Bulgarians, Ottomans, Austro-Hungarians, and Germans. After capturing Bucharest in December 1916, Mackensen took the royal palace there as his residence. He was the most consistently successful military

9.   Ulrich and Ziemann, 84.
10.   Ulrich and Ziemann, 152–53.

commander on either side of World War I—even though, after the German loss, he ended up a prisoner of war for a few years outside Budapest.

In any event, at the height of Mackensen's power, someone recommended to him that Oskar be allowed to make his portrait, as a result of which Oskar made both an etching and a painting. The 1917 etched portrait of Mackensen—a sharp, naturalistic, and heroic image—is doubtless the best wartime portrait he created. Mackensen liked it so much that four years later, when he had become an even bigger public figure within Germany, he wrote to Oskar ("Dear Herr Stössel!"), requesting more copies to satisfy the demand from his friends and family.

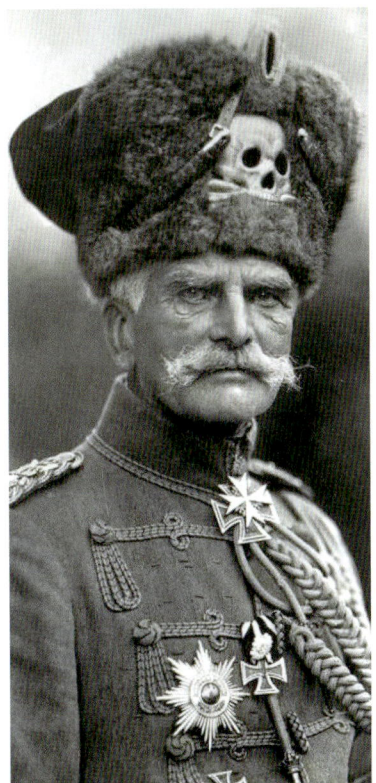

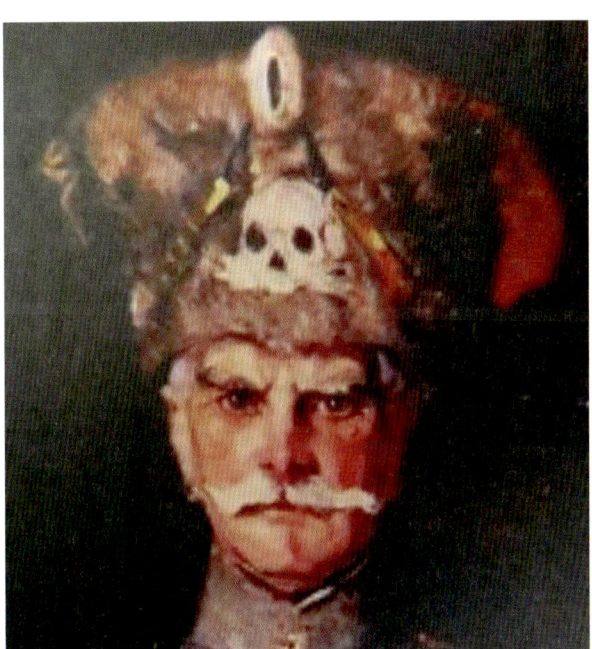

Oskar's painting of Mackensen (cropped). The painting's location today is unknown.

General Field Marshal Mackensen: The Last Hussar. As his shako declares, he was a member of the Skull-and-Crossbones Hussars, a Prussian regiment he led.

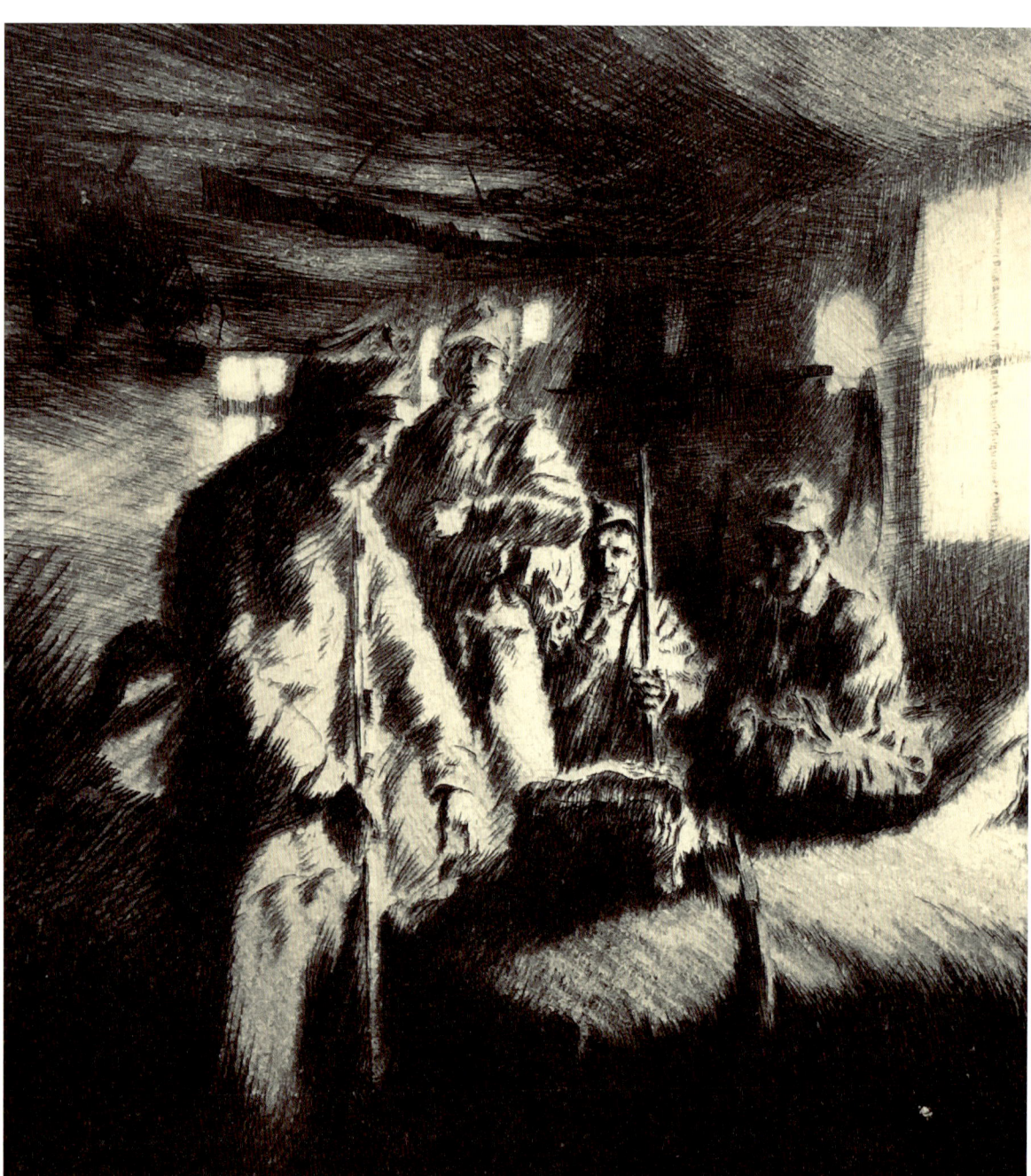

Without photographs, Oskar was relying entirely on sketches and memory.

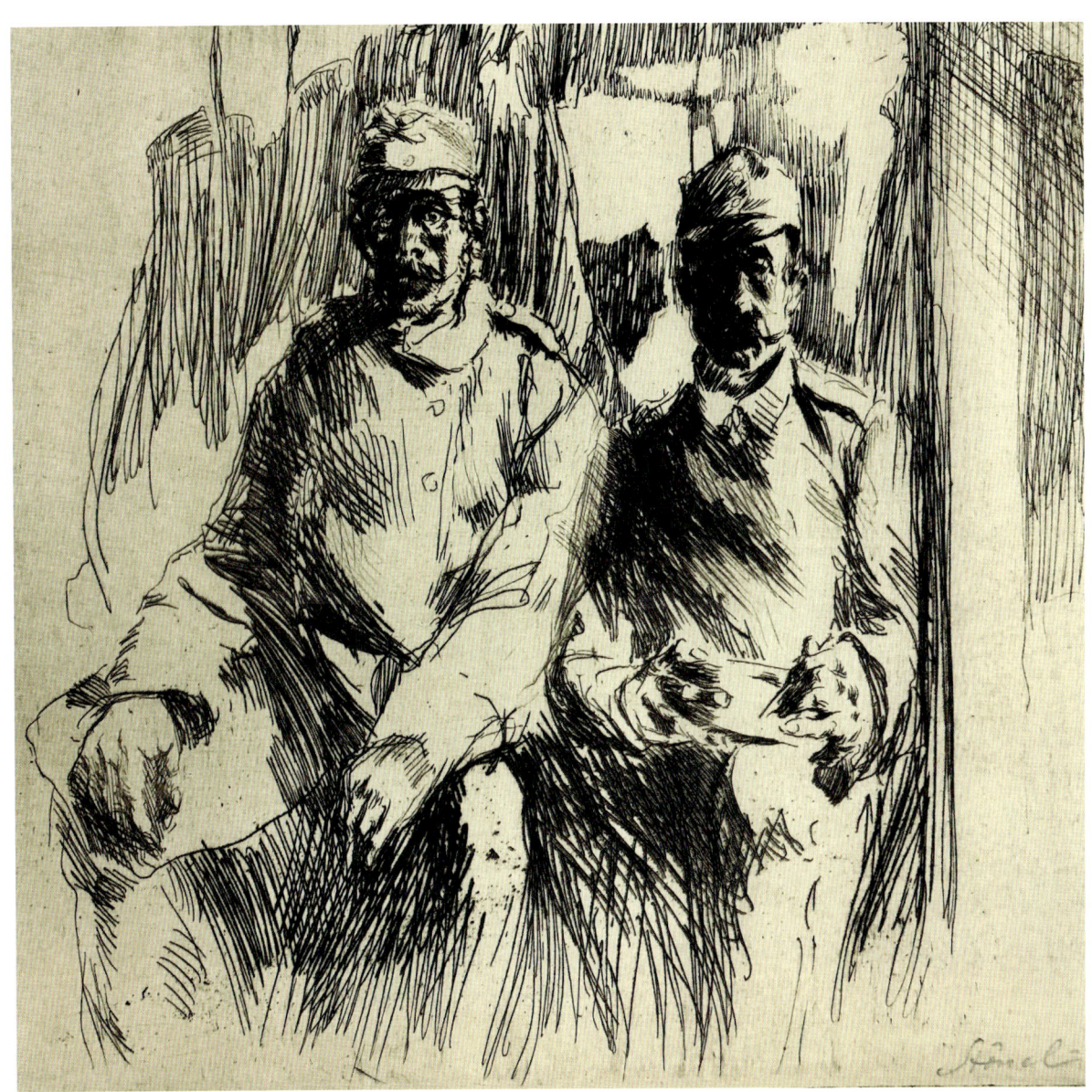

"Two Soldiers" (1916)

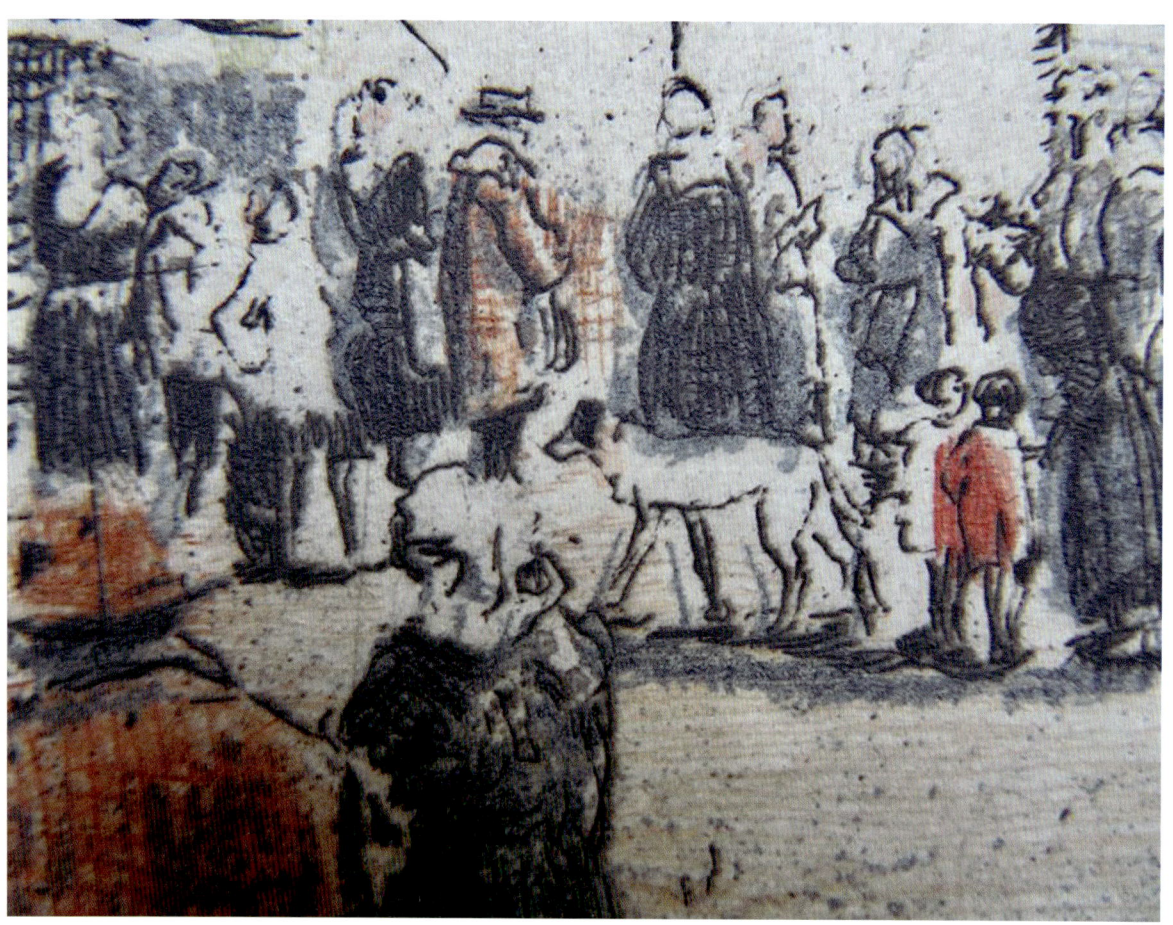

In the 1920s, Oskar once experimented with an impressionistic style of aquatinting. The only such piece known to be in his oeuvre, it is evocatively modernist in a way that makes it unrecognizably Oskar's work.

CHAPTER 5

Oskar's Growing Fame

EFORE and after the war, Oskar's work was widely admired. While still a student in 1911, he had won two nationwide prizes—one awarded in Graz, the other in Salzburg—for his portrait of Lotte Brociner, the daughter of the Viennese drama critic Marco Brociner. With this piece Oskar was thought to have mastered every important technique in the graphic arts. In congratulating him, Schmutzer reportedly remarked to his student: "Now you need only practice."[1]

By 1917, it was said that Oskar "knew how to capture the most interesting of what he saw to astonishing perfection."[2] Oskar's most notable early works were portraits made in Graz just after the war: of the novelist Emil Ertl (see page 38), Professor Josef Schumpeter, and Count Charles Bardeau and Countess Eleonara Bardeau. But he was also known for his landscapes and architectural prints, most notably *The Ruins* (1916) and *View of Graz* (1921) (see pages 40, 36). The latter was exhibited by the Medici Society of London to significant acclaim.[3]

How close Schmutzer and Stoessel stayed over the years isn't known. After the war, Oskar moved back to Graz for a time and then—for health reasons—to a health resort ten kilometers away: Lassnitzhöhe. The nature of his war injuries isn't known. Still, he traveled a fair amount and surely saw Schmutzer from time to time. In 1926, he moved back to Vienna. Meanwhile, Schmutzer's health might have been in decline during the 1920s as a result of heart disease. If so, he might have recommended Oskar in his place. That may well have helped Oskar

---

1. Bruno Binder, "Oskar Stoessel and His Graphic Art," *Print Collector's Q.* 22 (July 1935): 249.
2. Theodor von Frimmel, ed., *Studien und Skizzen zur Gemäldekunde* 3 (1917): 58.
3. The Medici Society Ltd. was founded in 1908 to create and sell reproductions of artists' works, originally by subscription. Today it maintains a gallery in South Kensington.

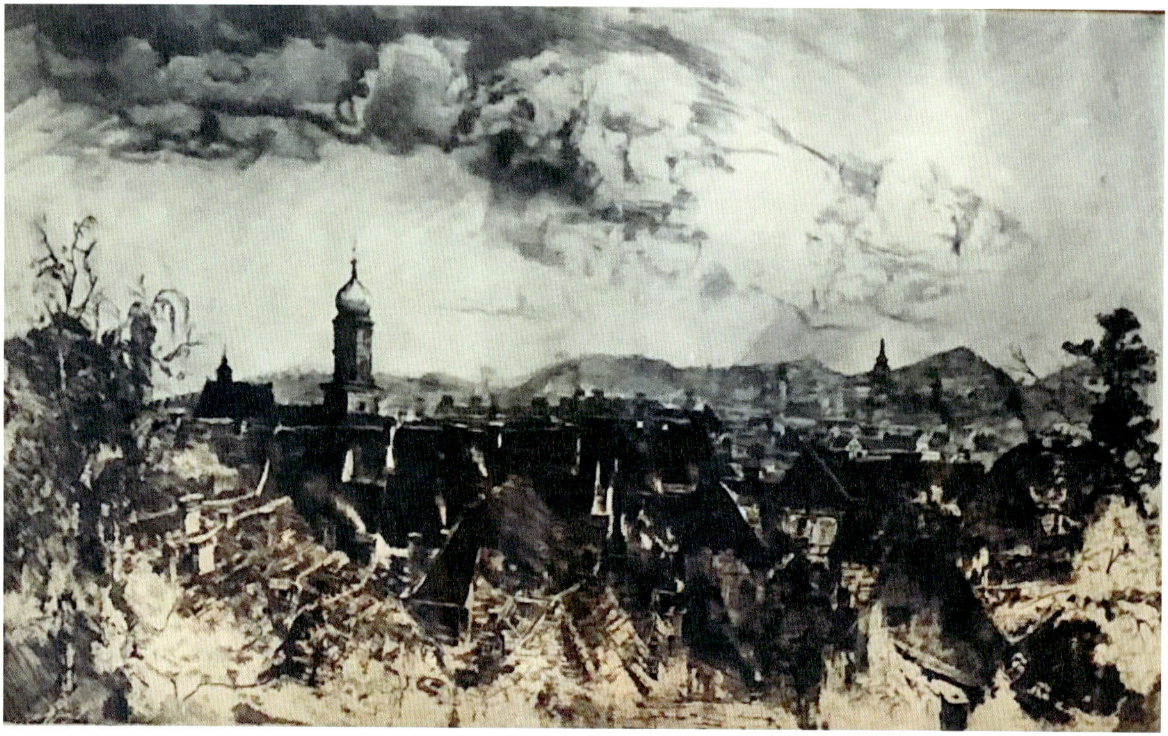

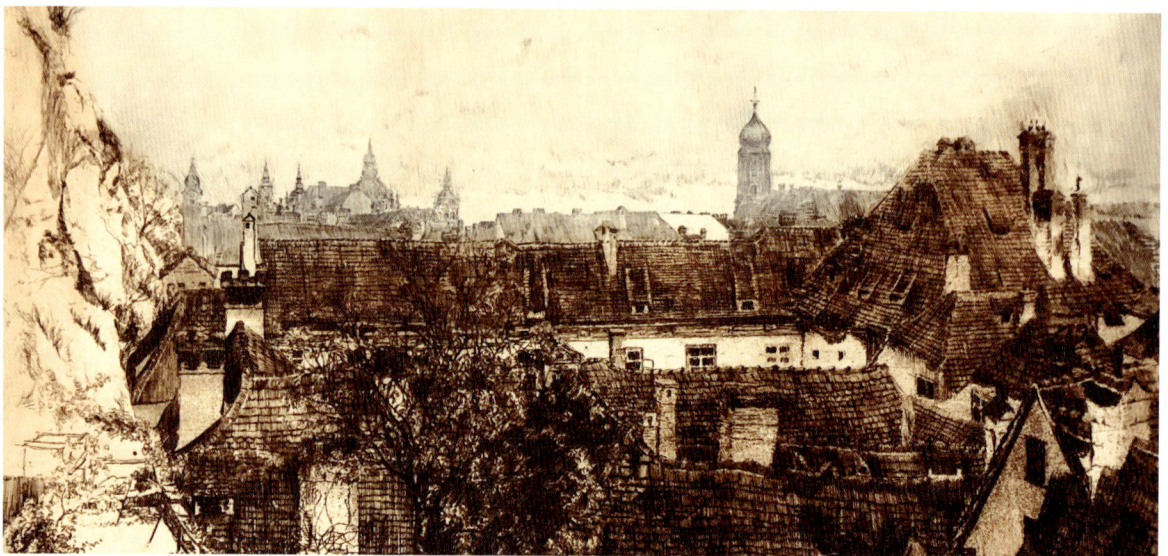

"View of Graz" (1921)

"View of the City from the Schlossberg" (1914)

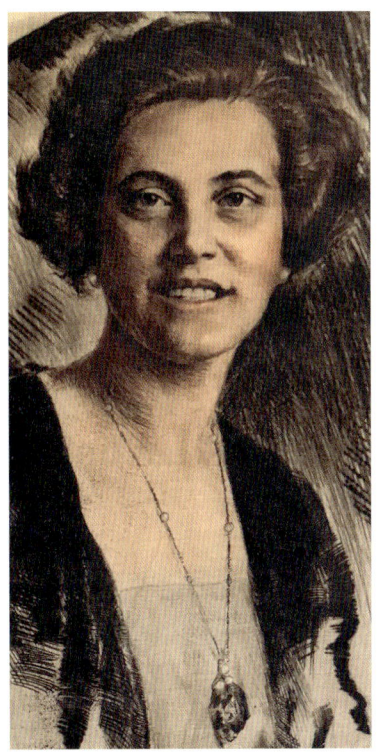

Unknown subject (ca. 1920)

receive commissions to etch the portraits of the royal families of Austria, Hungary, and Liechtenstein. Yet Oskar's own spreading fame must have been at least equally responsible. In 1924, he won a national prize for his portrait of Francis, Prince of Liechtenstein.

If Schmutzer was comfortable in recommending his erstwhile student to royal families, that would have been because Oskar had acquired a fair degree of savoir faire—partly through upbringing and partly through observing his mentor at work. Through just a little experience, Oskar became comfortable interacting with nobles. He had learned what to say and what not to say. He knew how to set expectations for a sitter and how to request a given gesture or pose—all with a gracious but firm politesse. Oskar had also come to know that successfully producing commissioned portraits meant gladdening the subject, whatever the person's station in life: achieving the right degree of verisimilitude, but in a flattering light. Not everyone was a Freud, who might be satisfied with an unduly stern countenance. Both teacher and pupil possessed Old World suavity. They were pleasant and refined. They were never overbearing, temperamental, or self-important. Otherwise, they couldn't have flourished as they did.

The ever-friendly relations between Schmutzer and Stoessel—for that's what the record strongly suggests—meant that the two men kept their egos in check. The teacher warmly congratulated the pupil without resenting his swift ascendancy. Schmutzer was genuinely proud of Oskar's accomplishments. At the same time, the pupil realized all that he owed to his teacher. Oskar's masterly skill and extensive know-how were acquired at the feet of a generous and nurturing

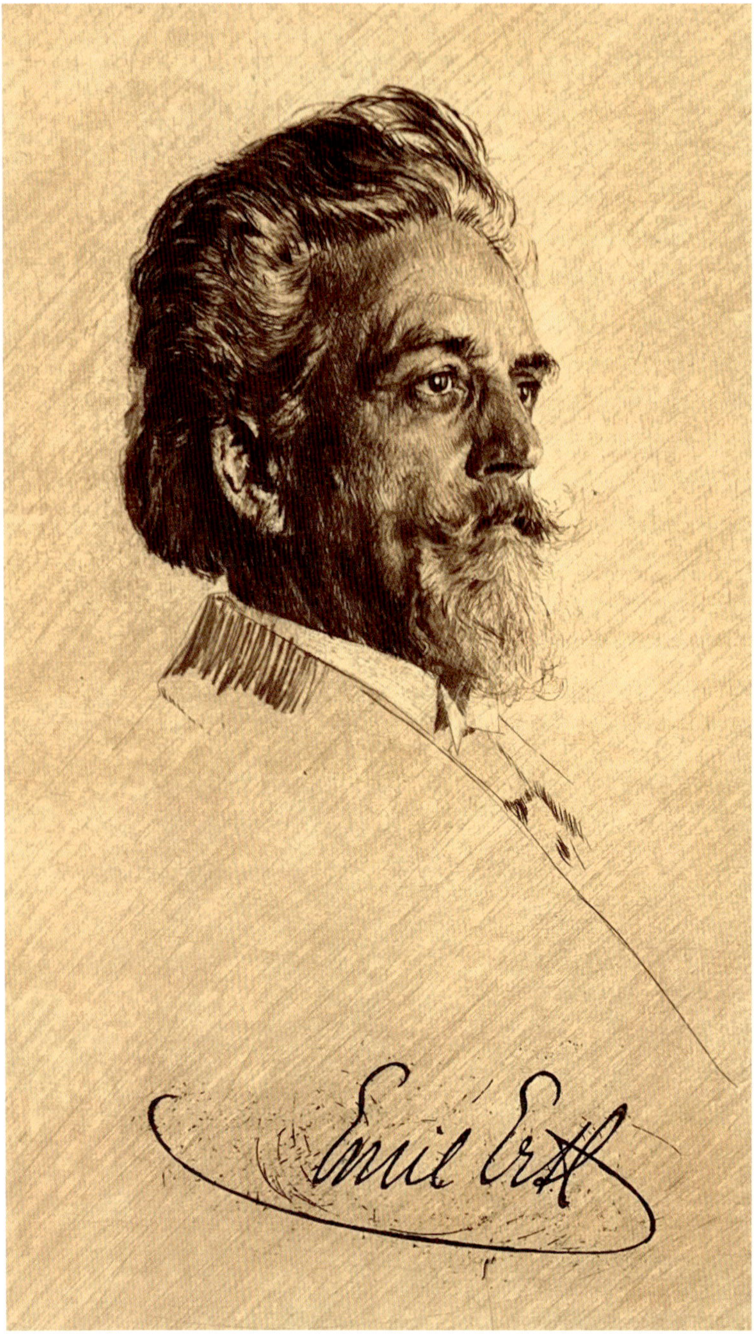

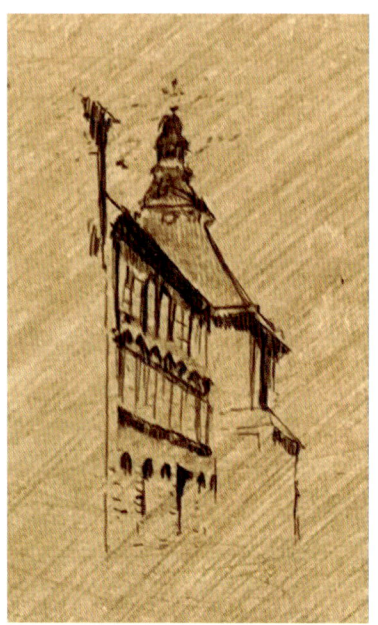

The remarque (enlarged) that Oskar made for this piece—Ertl's home at Ziegler-gasse 33 in Vienna

Oskar's 1919 etching of the Viennese novelist and poet Emil Ertl (1860—1935), whose work was much read between the two World Wars. Ertl studied philosophy in both Graz and Vienna, ultimately earning a PhD. He spent much of his working life as a librarian at the Graz University of Technology. He died in Vienna at the age of 75.

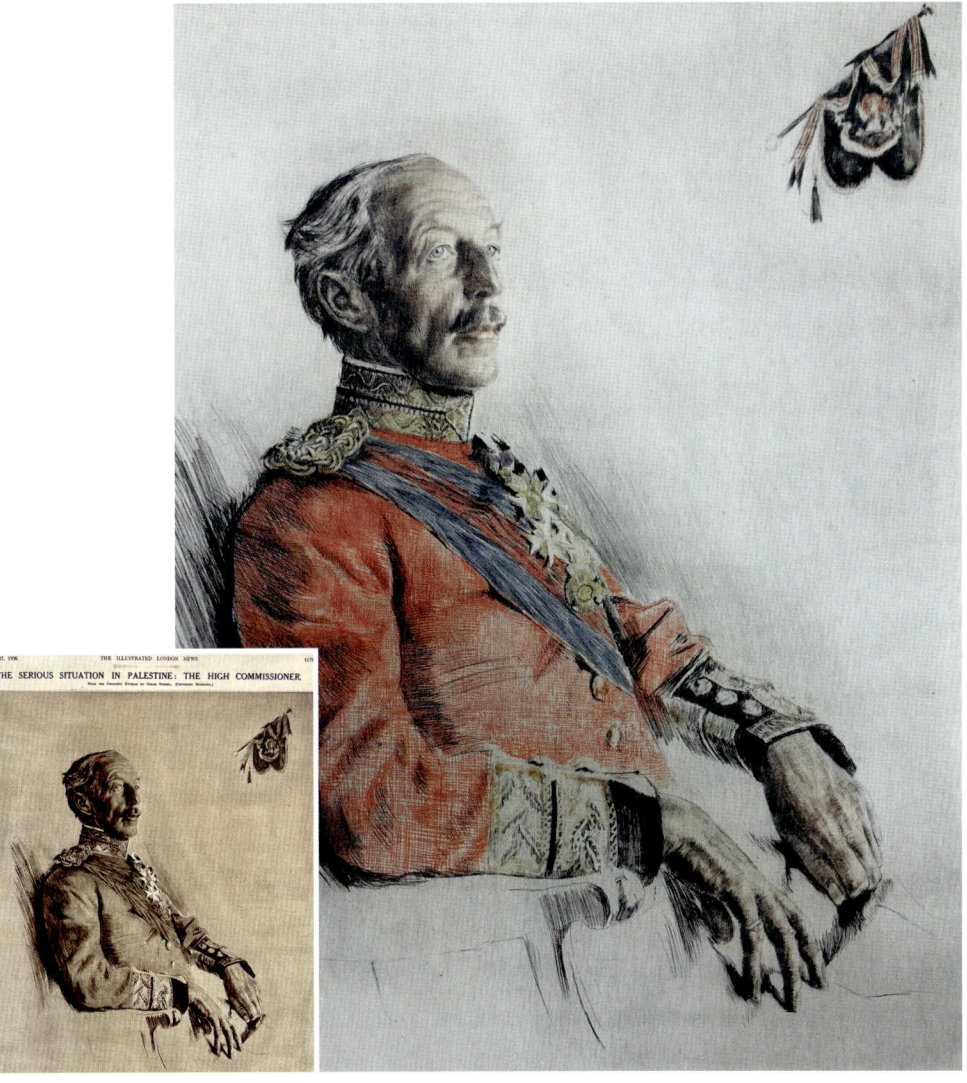

Sir Arthur Grenfell Wauchope (1935), dressed in his regalia as high commissioner in Palestine. Serving in that post from 1931 to 1938, Wauchope was viewed as sympathetic to Zionism. Born in Edinburgh in 1874, he served in the Second Boer War and World War I; he died in London in 1947. Oskar used two plates for this etching.

INSET: *On June 27, 1936, this etching appeared in* The Illustrated London News *(p. 29), which reported that Wauchope had instituted the death penalty and life imprisonment as penalties for using firearms against the police or British armed forces in Palestine. Having first been appointed high commissioner and commander-in-chief of Palestine in 1931 for a five-year term, he was reappointed to another five years in November 1935.*

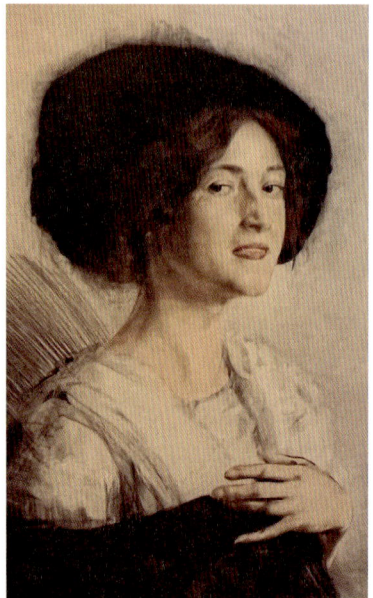

Lotte Brociner (1911)

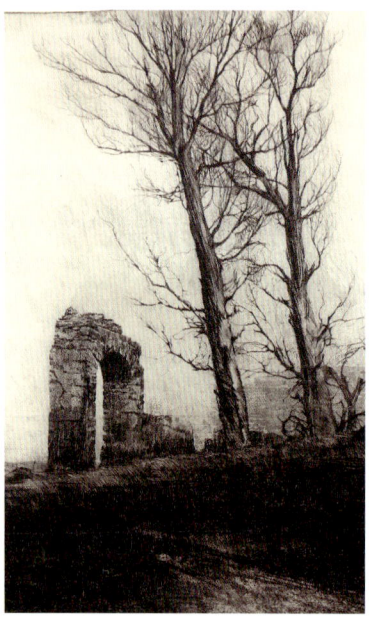

"The Ruins" (1916)

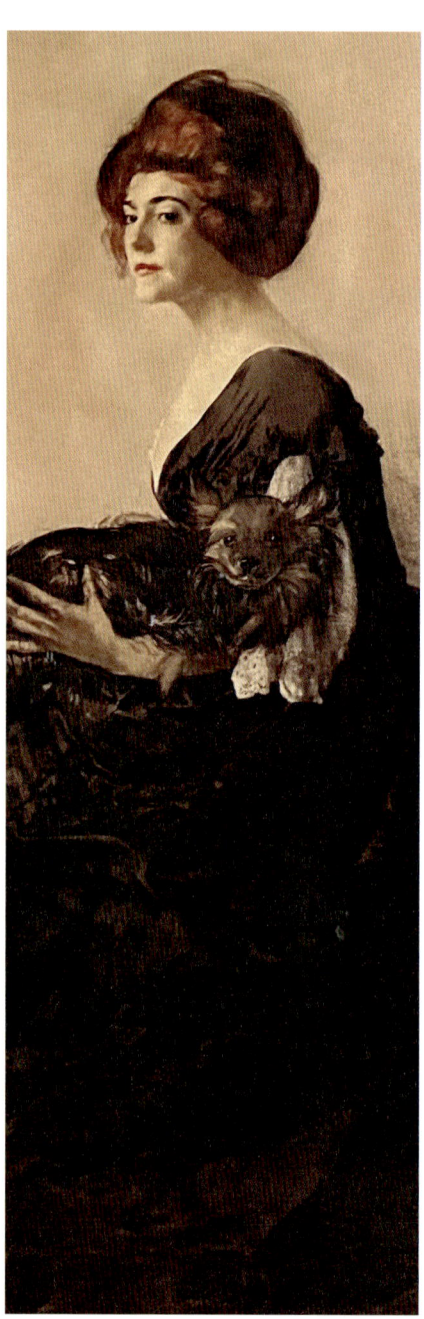

"Hilde Radnay" (1919), also named "The Large Dancer"

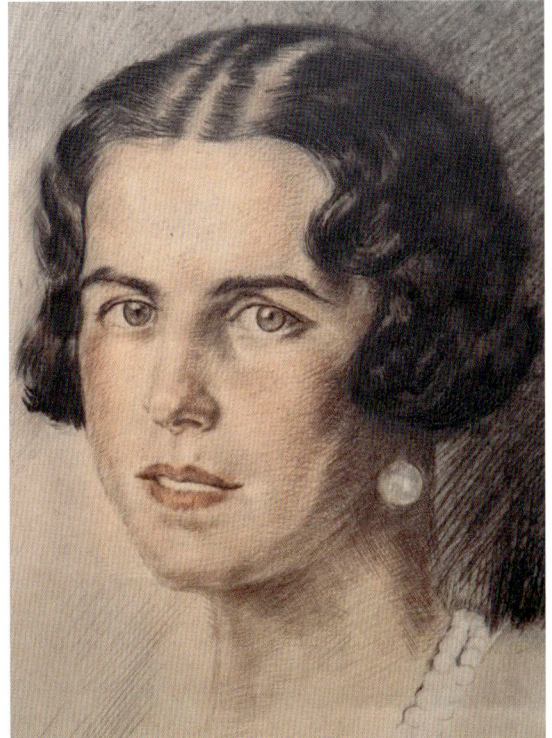

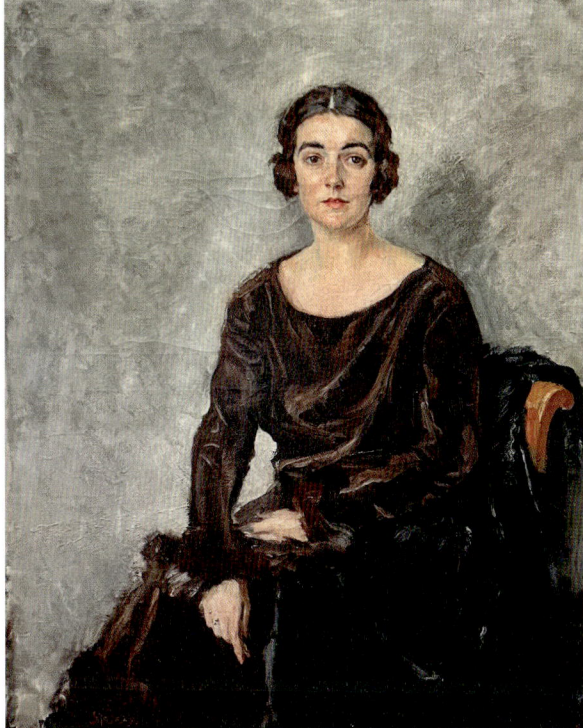

Oskar's etched portrait of Princess Irene of Greece and Denmark (1928) (etching)

Oskar's painting of Princess Irene

master, for whom he would always maintain the deepest respect, appreciation, and (one imagines) even affection.

One of Oskar's most notable and successful European etchings came in 1919—in the oversized manner made famous by Schmutzer. The plate was a square meter in size. The subject was the glamorous Hilde Radnay, a Viennese stage actress who also appeared in silent films. (See page 40.) She is shown in a crinoline dress holding a small dog with piercing eyes—her "figure, placed in an equilateral triangle, [being] one of monumental dignity."[4] Radnay would become famous for something she did at a Paris charity ball in July 1922: raising the equivalent of $150,000 (in current money) for a charity hospital by selling kisses to male patrons for $750 per kiss.

---

4.   Binder, "Stoessel and His Graphic Art," 249.

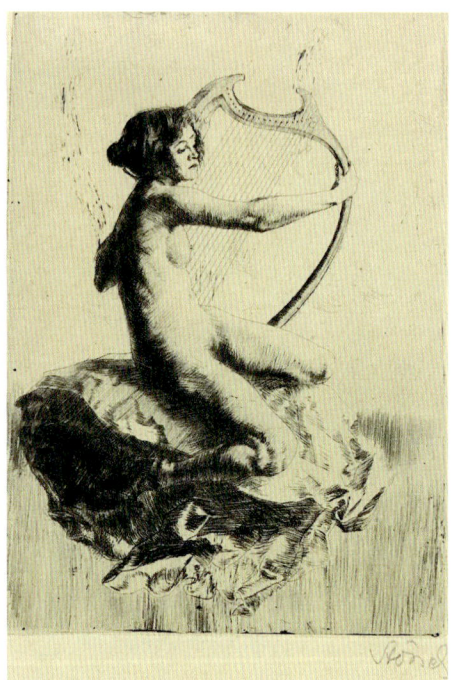

"Woman with a Lyre" (1919)

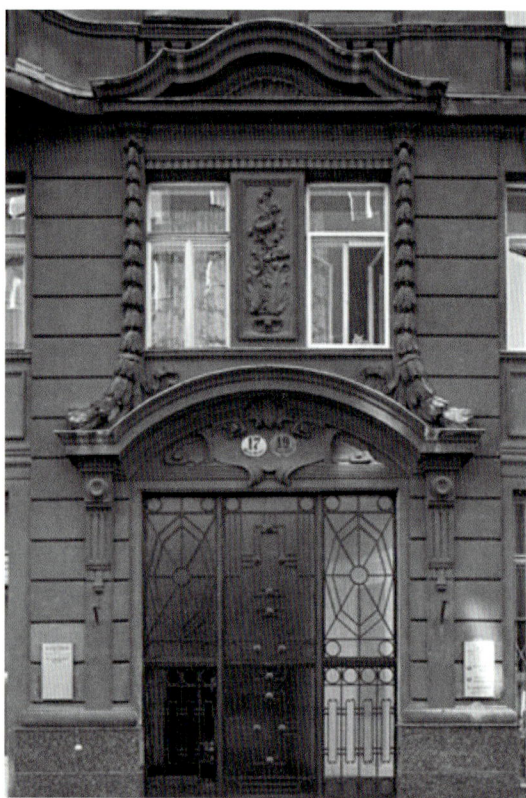

The facade of Oskar's home in Vienna from 1915 to 1938

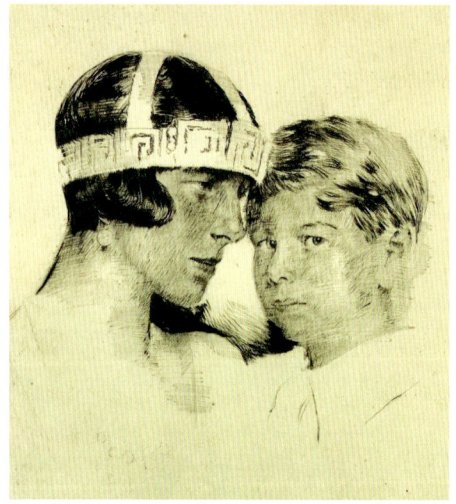

Oskar's etching of Princess Helen of Greece and Denmark, with her son, King Michael (ca. 1929). Michael would reign as King of Romania from 1927 to 1930 and again from 1940 to 1947.

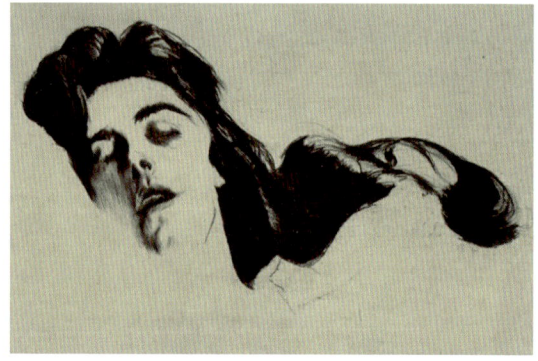

"Sleeping Girl" (1915)

In 1928, the year of Schmutzer's death, Oskar was summoned to the court of
Albania, and a year later to the court of Romania. While in Romania, he is known
to have made portraits of Princess Helen of Greece and Denmark; Helen's son
King Michael of Romania; Helen's sister, Princess Irene of Greece and Denmark,
daughter of King Konstantin II of Greece; and Princess Ileana of Romania. In
addition to all the etched portraits, he painted a portrait of Irene (page 41).

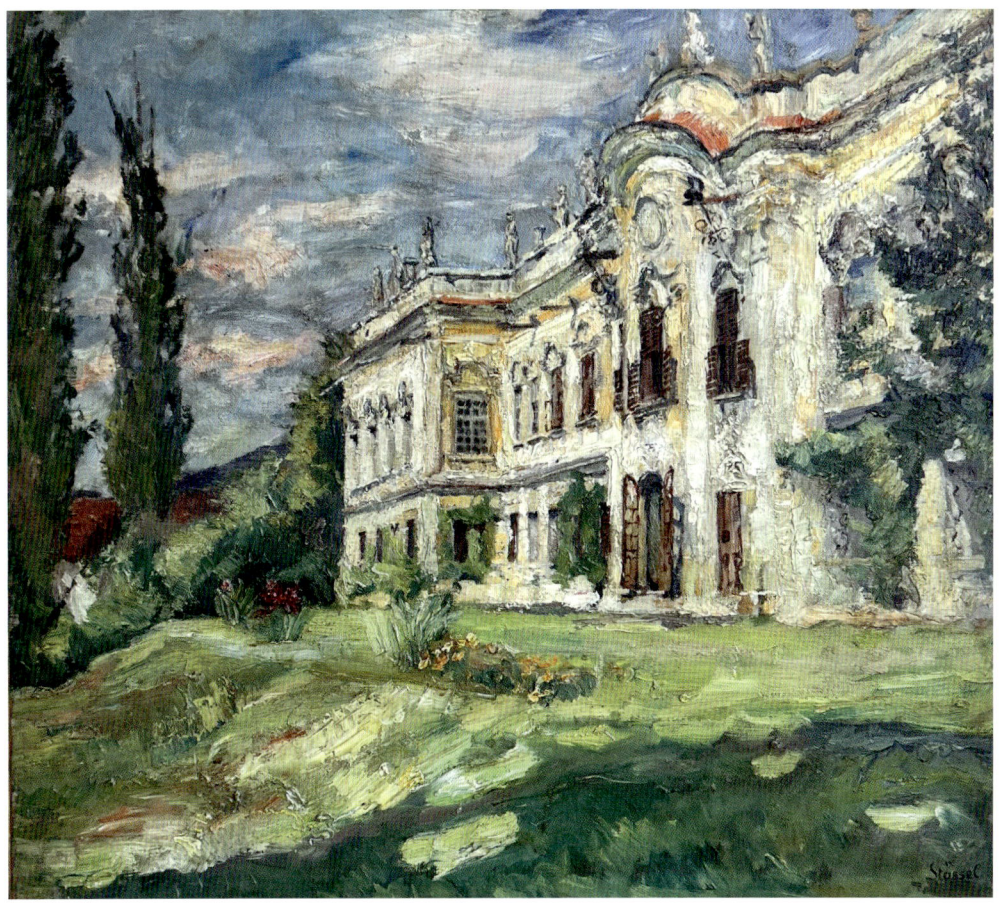

*Oskar's painting of Schielleiten Castle, near Stubenberg, Styria (about 37 miles from Graz). Built in the early 18th
century, it is the second-largest baroque palace in Austria. The painting dates from ca. 1925.*

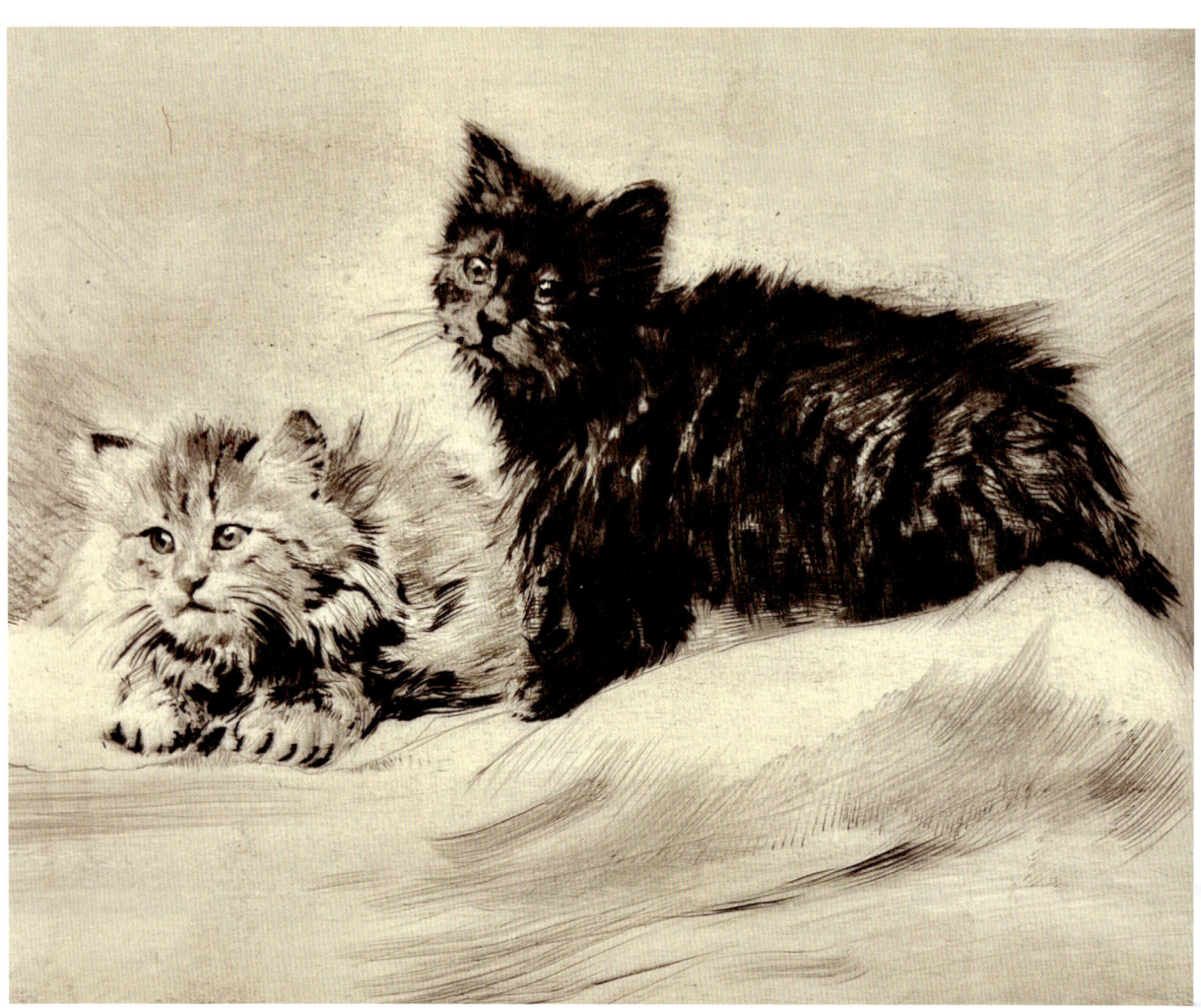

"Two Kittens" (ca. 1927)

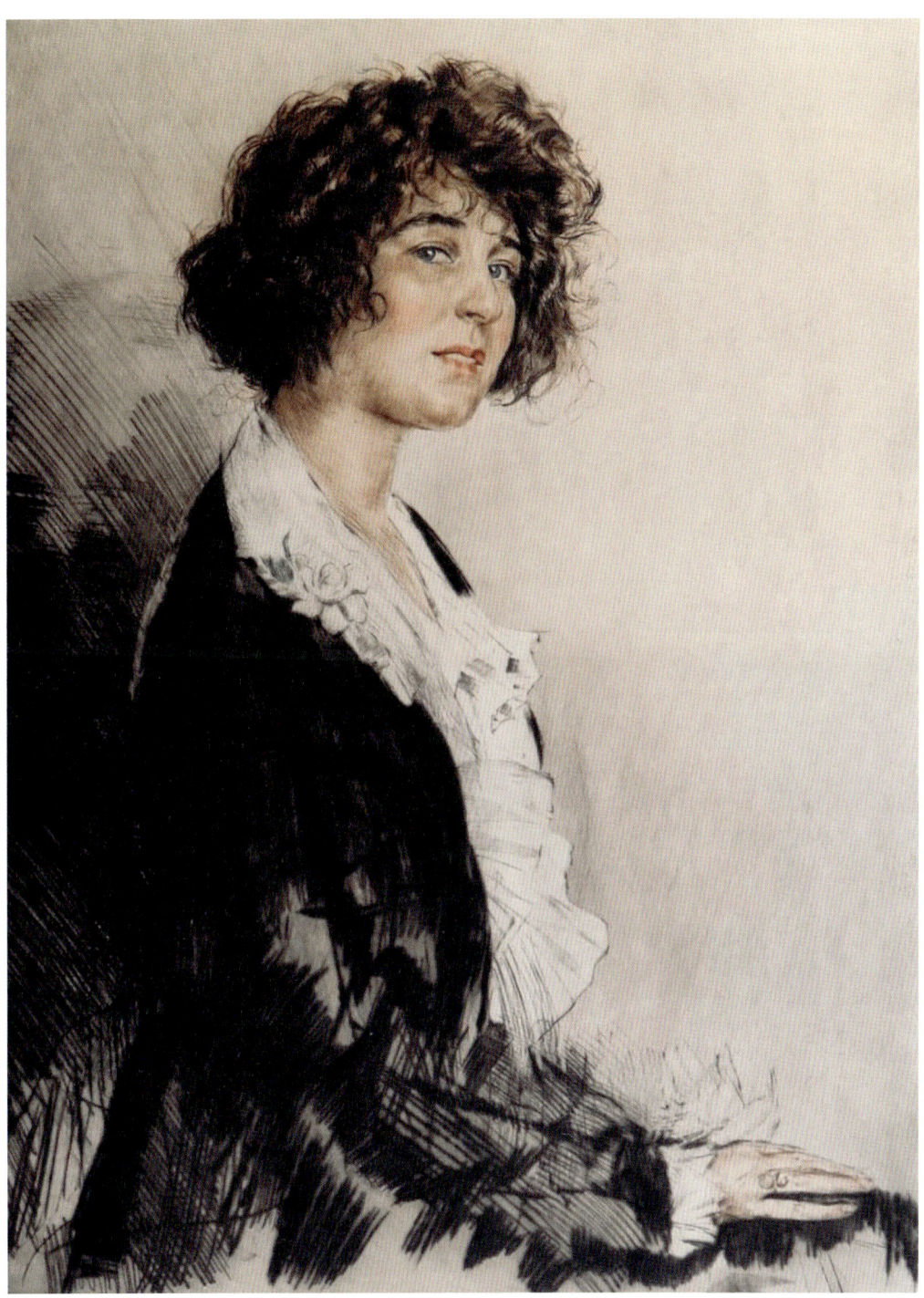

"Betty Stein" (1924)

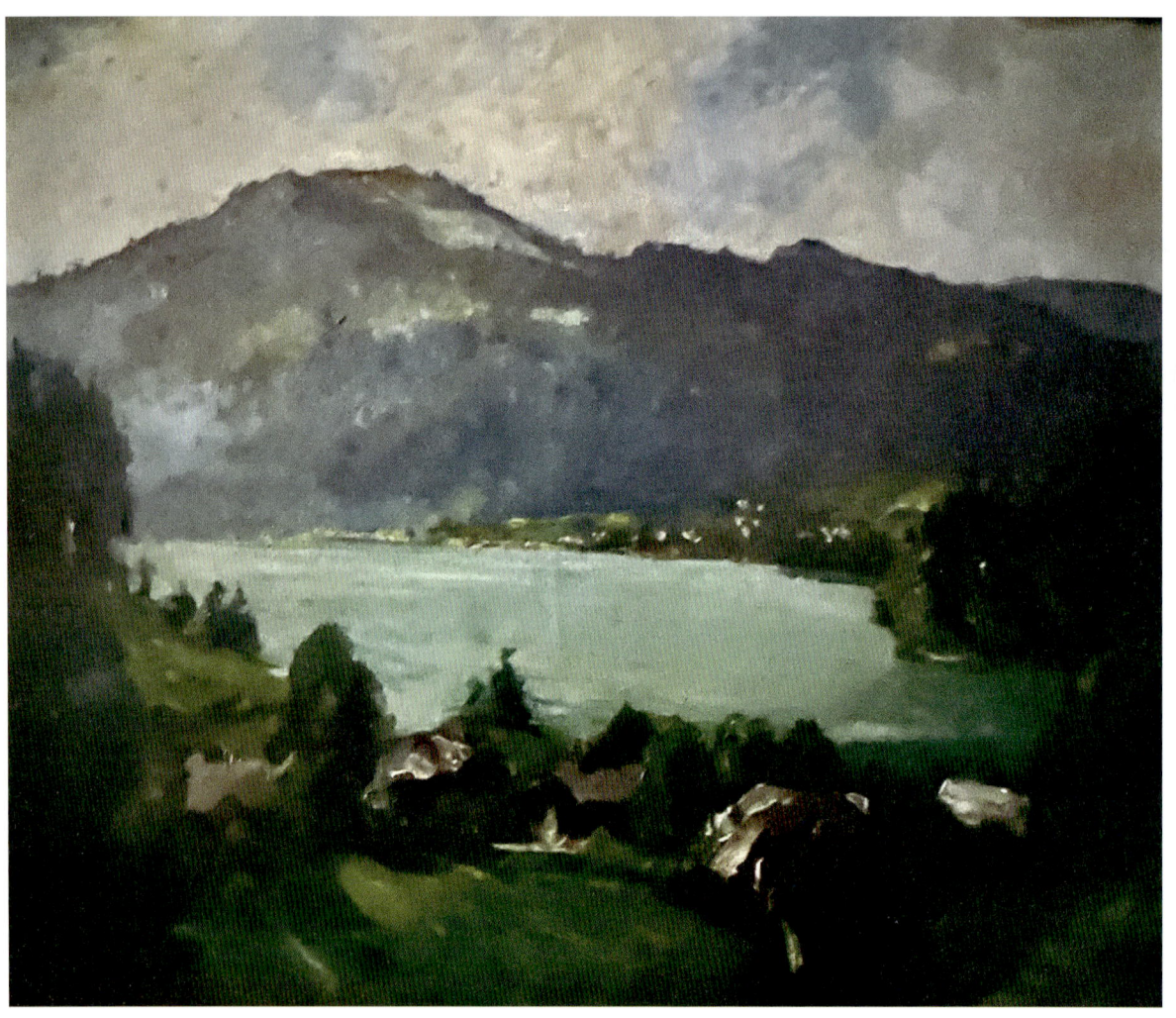

Oskar's mid-1920s painting of Lake Wolfgang, outside Salzburg. The vantage looks toward Abersee and St. Gilgen. Note the fog at the base of the mountain.

CHAPTER 6

Adolf Hitler's Artistic Anguish

A TANTALIZING question remains seemingly unanswerable: Did Oskar Stoessel cross paths with a young nobody named Adolf Hitler anytime from 1907 to 1913? They were both aspiring artists who arrived in Vienna in 1907. They both hoped to become students at the Imperial Academy of Fine Arts. Both young men were struggling artists, but only Oskar struggled successfully.

Held only once a year, the exam for admission to the painting school at the Academy was an ordeal designed to winnow the field radically. The first part of the exam required a three-hour painting session on each of two consecutive days. Some 112 candidates attended the first phase of the exam in October 1907. In each session, the applicants had to paint two subjects of their choice from a list of Christian, classical, and mythical themes. Hitler was not among the 33 applicants dismissed after the initial session was over. He was confident that despite being self-taught and never having received formal training, his portfolio would impress the examiners in the next phase. It did not. The official judgment was curt: "Sample drawings inadequate, few heads."[1] Angry and disappointed, Hitler sought and obtained answers from the Academy's director: he lacked aptitude for painting, but his work showed some promise for architecture. So the director urged him to apply to the Academy's school of architecture. But because Hitler lacked the required secondary-school education and diploma, he didn't apply. The fact that only 28 candidates had been admitted to the Academy during that year did not soften his conviction that he'd been wrongly excluded.[2]

---

1. J. Sydney Jones, *Hitler in Vienna, 1907 to 1913* (Stein and Day, 1983), 12.
2. Jones, 12.

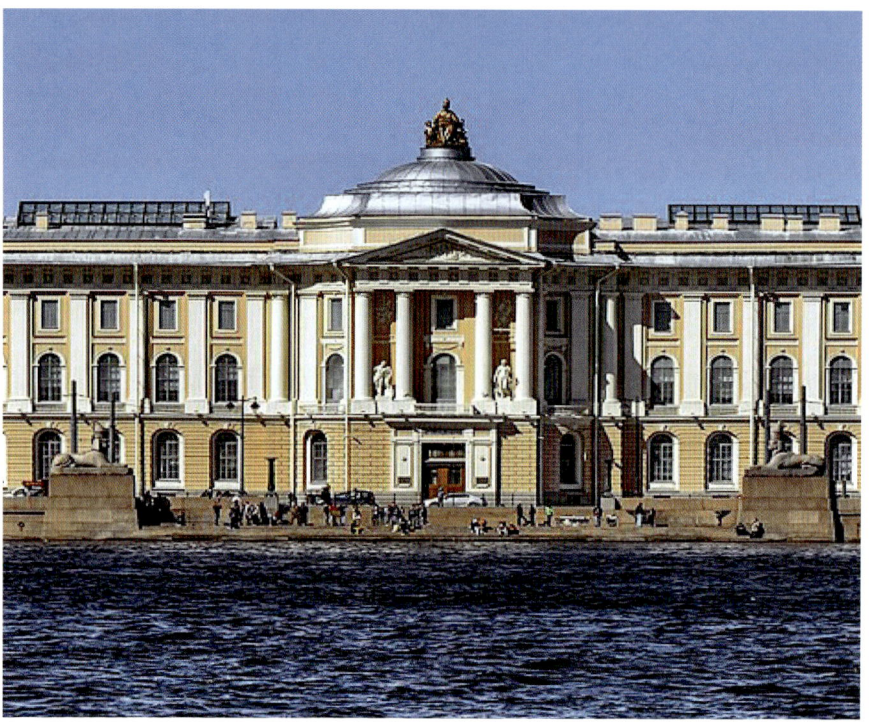

Despite the setback, Hitler spent some time over the next year studying art with a private teacher, Professor Rudolf Panholzer, who was a master artist and sculptor.[3] Although Hitler's studies were interrupted by his mother's illness and death in late 1907, he seems to have developed more confidence in his skill as a painter. In September 1908, he submitted some pieces needed to qualify to take the exam a second time. He was convinced that the professors would now see the error of their ways with his new submissions. The results came as a crushing blow: "Not admitted to the test."[4] Only 25% of the applicants that year were admitted to the Academy's painting school, Oskar being among the select few.

Hitler's rejection was among the most traumatic experiences of his life. He was angry, alienated, and lonely.

---

3.   Jones, 14.

4.   Robert Payne, *The Life and Death of Adolf Hitler* (Barnes and Noble, 1973), 77.

Did Hitler and Oskar ever interact? Possibly. It might have happened around the examinations, or it might have happened beyond the Academy. Over the six-year period, they might well have attended some of the same cultural events. They might have even spoken to each other. We can't know for sure. Although Hitler had few friends, he "would strike up a conversation with a virtual stranger passing in the street, no matter how many times they passed each other."[5] Before and after Hitler was rejected by the Academy, his interests in architecture, art museums, and music, particularly opera, persisted. Oskar likewise had a keen interest in music and art.

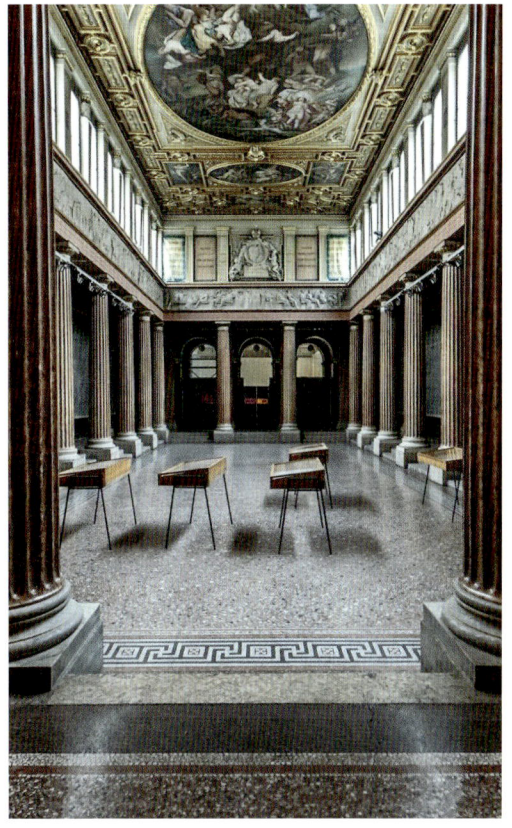

Inside the Imperial Academy of Fine Arts in Vienna

But the Academy would also have divided them. Hitler's friend August Kubizek (1888–1956) recalled that Hitler had uttered with rage: "This Academy ought to be blown up. A lot of old-fashioned fossilized civil servants, bureaucrats, devoid of understanding. Stupid lumps of officials. They rejected me. They threw me out. They turned me down."[6] This was probably the first ground for Hitler's hatred of Vienna: "He had to find the enemies who were keeping him from success. There were the stupid teachers at the Academy; the corrupt bureaucracy; even the Habsburgs themselves. The landlords were out to get him as well as the shallow-minded [military] officers who took his standing room at the

5.   Jones, *Hitler in Vienna*, 114.
6.   August Kubizek, *The Young Hitler I Knew* (Houghton Mifflin, 1955), 157.

Opera."[7] The Academy's rejections also played a role in fanning his antisemitism. Hitler believed that at least four of the Academy's seven examiners were Jews and claimed that he wrote a letter to the Academy after his second rejection, declaring: "The Jews will pay for this!"[8] After becoming Führer, his early artwork sold for what Hitler admitted were exorbitant prices for an artist who had been merely a "dilettante."[9] But he must also have enjoyed a sense that the Academy had misjudged his talent after all.[10]

During this period, Hitler was already steeped in antisemitism,[11] which was common throughout Austria. But he found additional reasons to hate Jews in general and in Vienna in particular. In the minds of Viennese antisemites, all Jews were affluent and flourishing despite the significant number of Jewish people living in the city's poor districts. But as an American journalist had observed in 1900, "the number of men of Jewish blood occupying positions in which intelligence is the chief requisite is astounding."[12] Indeed, by 1907, Vienna's intellectual, theatrical, and artistic circles included many prominent Jews. One authoritative biography describes Hitler during his years in Vienna as "a nobody struggling to survive day by day, who from time to time sounded off about politics, coping with his frustrations by believing that the Vienna that was treating him so badly was the capital of an empire that was doomed to destruction."[13] Chronically at the periphery of society, Hitler was even, for a time, dependent on aid for the homeless in the Asylum for the Shelterless in the Meidling district—which was largely underwritten by a wealthy Jewish family.[14] The humiliations of poverty must have cut deeply.

He continued pursuing art with paintings and picture postcards of famous Viennese buildings intended for tourists. At first, he sold these through a busi-

---

7.   Jones, *Hitler in Vienna*, 54.
8.   George Victor, *Hitler: The Pathology of Evil* (Brassey's 2000), n.p.; Jones, 227–28.
9.   Jones, *Hitler in Vienna*, 228.
10.   Jones, 228.
11.   Kubizek, *Young Hitler*, 79.
12.   L.T. Damon, "Austrian Antisemitism," *The Nation*, June 14, 1900, 455.
13.   Peter Longerich, *Hitler: A Biography* (Oxford Univ. Press, 2019), 30.
14.   Jones, *Hitler in Vienna*, 133.

ness associate, but after a dispute he sold them through two Jewish picture-framers, Jacob Altenberg and Samuel Morgenstern.[15] These works never brought him notice and earned him barely enough money for food, shelter, and clothing.

Even though Oskar was a part of the illustrious society that Hitler yearned to belong to, it's hard to believe that they wouldn't have seen each other and perhaps exchanged words at some point. They might even have known each other by name. We'll never know.

In any event, Hitler's deep hatred of Vienna and of Jews developed and began to surge during his years in the city. Eventually it would affect the course of Oskar's life and career.

---

15. Longerich, *Hitler*, 27.

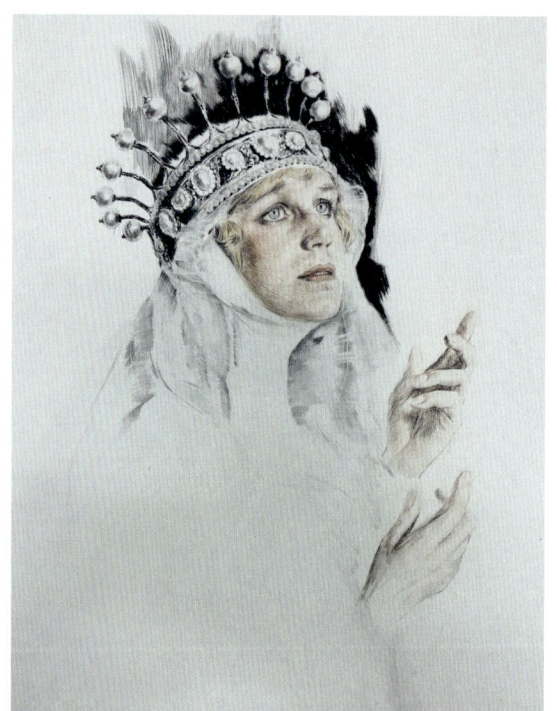
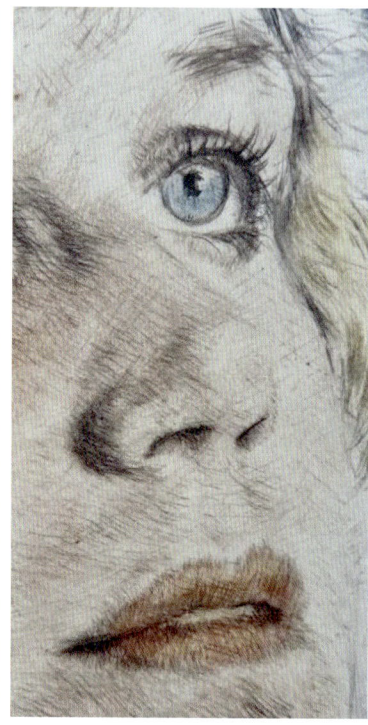

Maria Jeritza (1887—1982), the Austrian-Czech soprano, as Elisabeth in Wagner's Tannhäuser

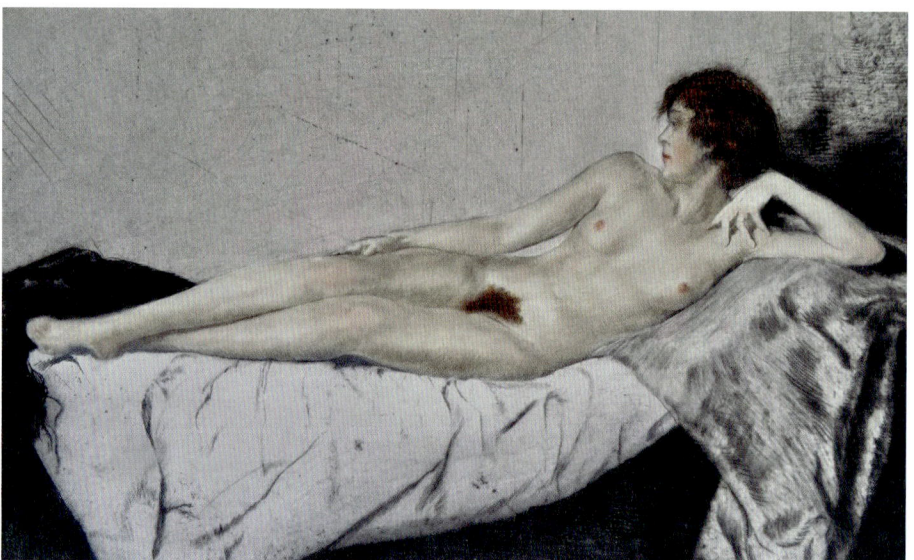

"Female Nude" (1924) is among very few nonmetaphorical nudes found in Oskar's oeuvre. The piece was specially dedicated to Bruno Binder.

CHAPTER 7

Assessing Oskar

B Y the 1930s, Oskar Stoessel's art was attracting enough international acclaim to warrant major critical attention. Three articles—two in German
(1922, 1931) and one in English (1935)—were published by Bruno Binder,
a highly accomplished museum curator and art critic in Graz. They were undoubtedly written from personal knowledge and with Oskar's cooperation, given
that the 1931 piece quotes from a private letter received by Oskar from Field
Marshal Mackensen.

The 1922 piece, reproducing seven etchings, reported on a major exhibition of
the Styrian Artists' Cooperative in Graz.[1] "Oskar Stössel's graphic work," it announced, "was on view in its entirety for the first time."[2] Consisting of portraits
and nature studies, Oskar's etchings showed the palpable influence of the Old
Masters and "surpassed everything else in the exhibition."[3] Even in retrospect,
Binder's laudatory assessment seems just:

> It is characterized by the most accurate possible rendering of form and pictorial
> effect of both the whole and the details. He knows how to animate portraits, he
> depicts landscapes in the finest and most convincing way, and he captures the
> patina of old architecture. The artist achieves this strong painterly effect in black-
> and-white etchings. . . . He never becomes sensational, and he doesn't seek to
> amaze either formally or with technical refinements. His model is Rembrandt,
> who was the first to recognize that one can also paint on the plate, whereas his
> predecessors did not really get beyond etched engravings. The artist's way of
> working is also that of the true, old craftsmen: the most exacting observation

---

1. Bruno Binder, "Der Radierer Oskar Stössel," *Gesellschaft für vervielfältigende graphische
    Künste*, 45 (1922): 99–105.
2. Binder, "Der Radierer," 99.
3. Binder, "Der Radierer," 99.

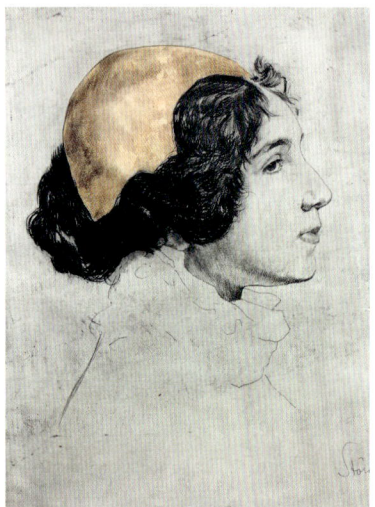

Portrait of Heidi Strasser (ca. 1909)

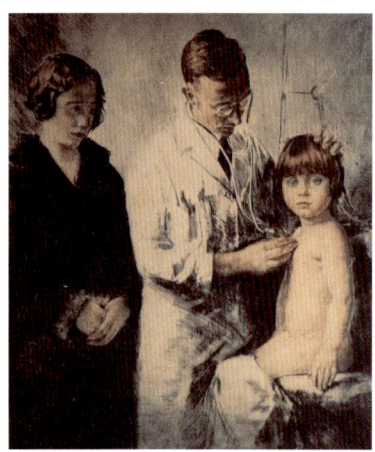

"Pediatric Care" (1931)

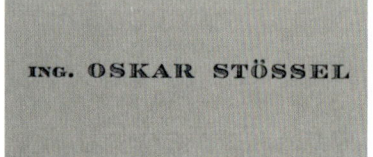

Oskar's 1920s calling card

of what is to be represented and conscientious draw-ing, which always grasps the whole and subordinates the details.[4]

Binder wrote that Oskar had matured remarkably from 1911 to 1921, moving from objective representations to a much greater mood-inducing kind of art. He cited the difference between the portrait of Alexander Girardi (see page 2) and that of Emil Ertl (see page 38). The lat-ter "captures a psychological moment" and "comes closer to the attitude and personality of the sitter."[5]

So hard had Oskar worked to achieve technical fluency that he could "be counted among the strongest talents in Austria."[6] Yet even in this early review, Binder recognized that Oskar might tend to be overlooked: "In our time, which largely judges artists by their shocking effects, Stös-sel may not mean much. He's not a revolutionary. His goal has been to develop in the modern era the precious legacy of past centuries, without renouncing it."[7]

Even if we're inclined to agree that "his portraits of glamorous women can be seen as spiritual profiles," Binder was overexuberant in asserting that Oskar "reveals each woman's innermost thoughts and feelings."[8]

Binder seemed to believe, as many portraitists believed and still believe, in the study of physiognomy—the idea that features of the face, or of the form of the body gen-erally, indicate character and intelligence. It's the idea re-flected in Georg Lichtenberg's aphorism: "Everyone at 50

---

4.   Binder, "Der Radierer," 99.
5.   Binder, "Der Radierer," 102.
6.   Binder, "Der Radierer," 104.
7.   Binder, "Der Radierer," 105.
8.   Binder, "Der Radierer," 99.

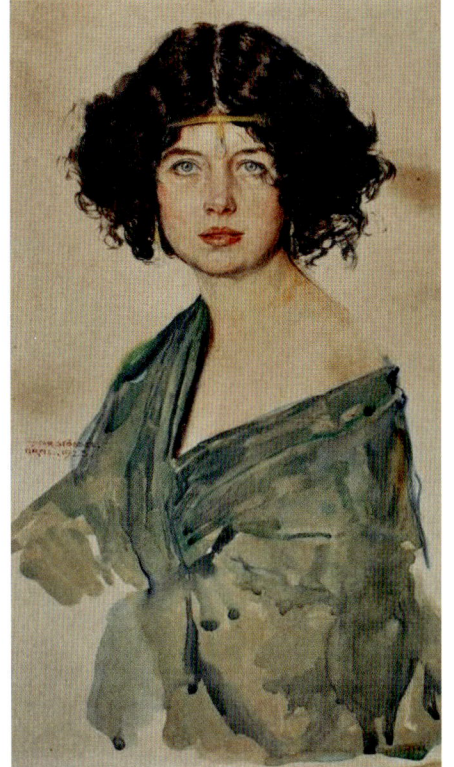

Unknown subject (Graz, 1923)

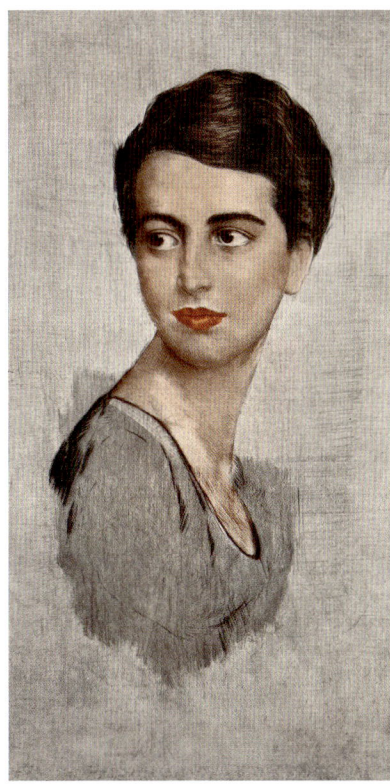

"Portrait of a Woman" (1920s)

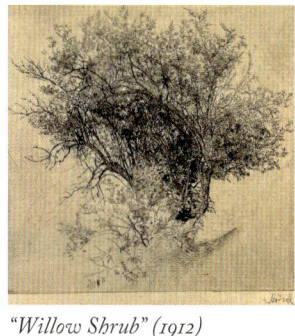

"Willow Shrub" (1912)

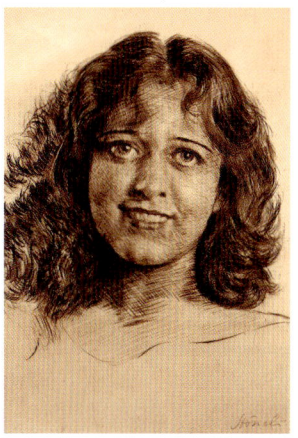

Unknown subject (1920s)

has the face that he deserves."[9] Your physicality comes to match your character and intellectual capacity. This now-discredited theory, which gained support in the late 18th century,[10] placed a great responsibility on portrait artists. It was severely tested when European expeditionary artists encountered unknown peoples and races as they explored the world, and perhaps led some of the artists to make the natives look more Caucasian.[11] What might be more safely said, in modern terms, is that a portrait can suggest something about the *personality* of the sitter—

9. Georg Christoph Lichtenberg (1742–1799), in *The Lichtenberg Reader: Selected Writings of Georg Christoph Lichtenberg*, trans. Franz H. Mautner and Henry Hatfield (Beacon, 1959) (a sentiment popularized in the 20th century by George Orwell).

10. See Johann Caspar Lavater, *Essays on Physiognomy: Designed to Promote the Knowledge and the Love of Mankind*, trans. Henry Hunter, 3 vols. in 5 (London, 1789–1798).

11. See Ron Tyler, *Western Art, Western History: Collected Essays* (Univ. of Okla. Press, 2019), 19–20.

and little more. Certainly it wouldn't reveal "innermost thoughts and feelings." If that were so, what might we say was the sitter for the *Mona Lisa* thinking?

As we will see, Binder attributed to Oskar an active interest in physiognomy—and it's a running theme among those who comment on Oskar's art and portraiture in general. Hence this cautionary note.

Binder's second piece appeared as the lead article in the April 1931 issue of *Westermann's Monatshefte* (*Westermann's Monthly Journal*). It reproduced 11 Stoessel etchings, with brief comments. More important, though, Binder vividly described Oskar's personality and interests:

> Anyone who knows the artist is enchanted by his kindness, by the charm of his spirit. Stössel is a brilliant companion, full of apt bon mots. He is thoroughly familiar with music, theater, and literature. He has had family ties with the theater world ever since his brother Ludwig, who is currently with [Viktor] Barnowsky in Berlin, has been on the stage. He particularly appreciates classical music. Only an artist who values this art would twice undertake to etch, for his own pleasure, a subject as challenging as the Rosé Quartet. An immersion into the

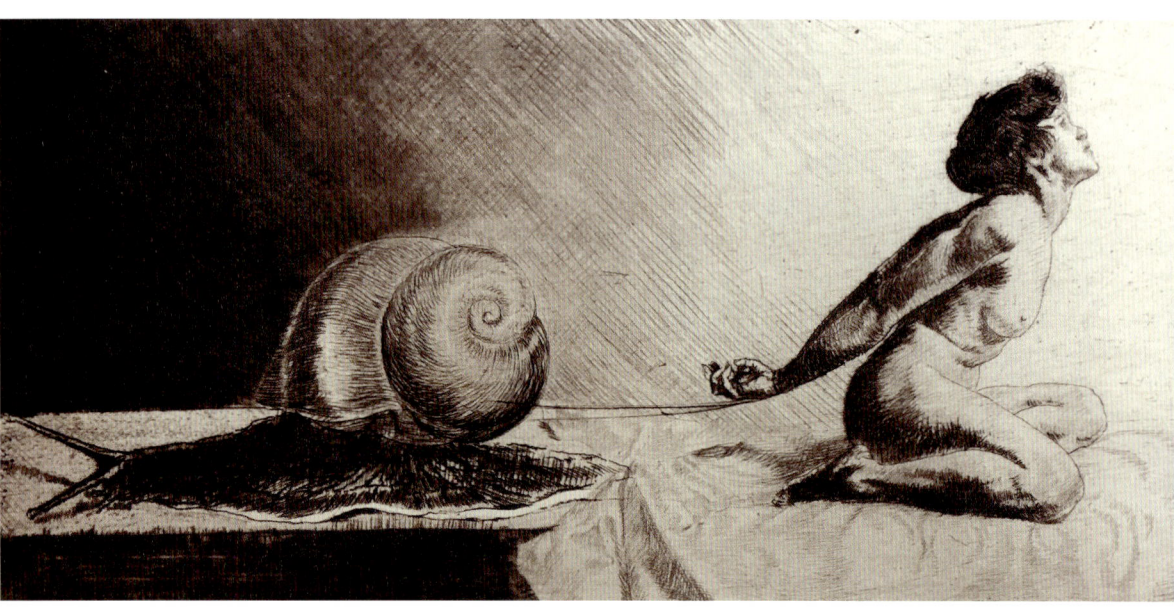

Oskar's "Unequal Pair" (1921)

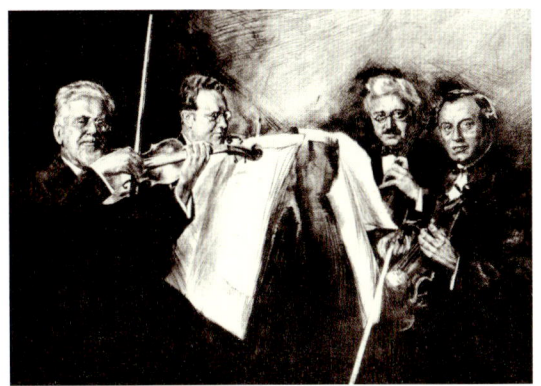

"Rosé Quartet" (ca. 1929)

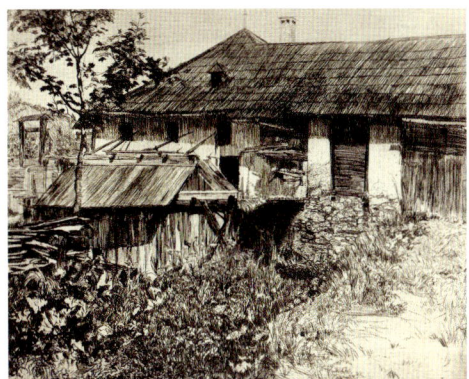

"Farm Homestead" (1912)

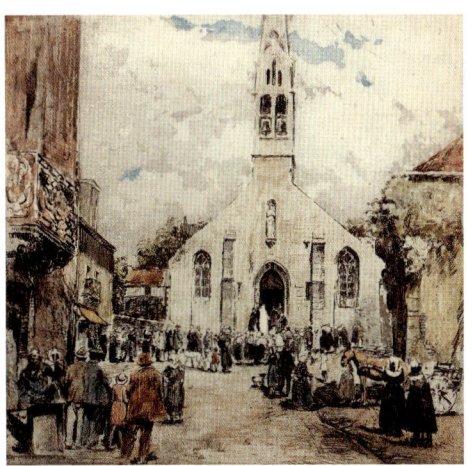

"Wedding in Bretagne" (1930), depicting St. Joseph Church of Port-Aren

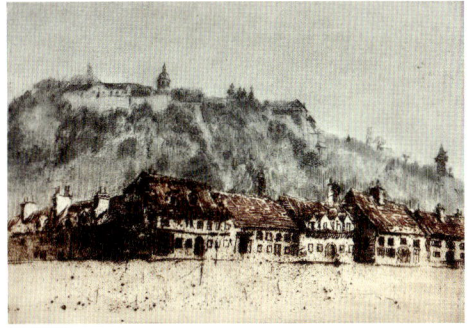

"View of the Schlossberg and Clock Tower" (Graz ca. 1919)

Vol. 22, No. 3.   July 1935.   17/6
$4.50 } a Year

(Single copies 5/– each)

THE PRINT COLLECTOR'S QUARTERLY

EDITED BY
CAMPBELL DODGSON, C.B.E., D.Litt.

CONTENTS

CATALOGUE OF ENGRAVINGS AND
ETCHINGS OF FRANS CRABBE
BY A. E. POPHAM

"THE SULTAN AND HIS MISTRESS," BY
ALBRECHT DÜRER
BY HANS TIETZE AND E. TIETZE-CONRAT

THE ETCHINGS OF GIOVANNI FATTORI
BY ANTONY DE WITT

OSKAR STOESSEL AND HIS GRAPHIC ART
BY BRUNO BINDER

THE DRYPOINTS OF LUIS QUINTANILLA
BY BASIL BURDETT

———

J. M. DENT & SONS LTD.
10-13 BEDFORD STREET, LONDON, W.C. 2

(FOR AMERICAN AGENTS, *vide* p. xvi)

personality of the artist reveals how subtly fine and unproblematic he is both as an artist and as a person. His work is uplifting and reassuringly certain.[12]

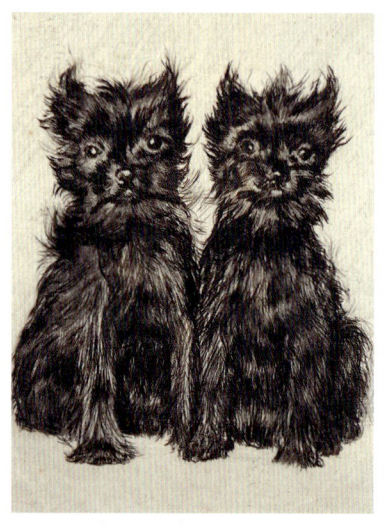

Untitled (ca. 1920s)

Binder also explained in this piece that when Oskar first saw Ferdinand Schmutzer's etchings, he was fascinated by the rigorous realism, which was "completely unknown" to the Impressionists of the time.[13] Binder again cited Rembrandt as one of Oskar's primary influences.

Four years later, a third Binder essay appeared in *The Print Collector's Quarterly*, a London journal. Titled "Oskar Stoessel and His Graphic Art," this piece criticized Stoessel's more-famous contemporaries—Gustav Klimt, Oskar Kokoschka, and Egon Schiele—as unrepresentative of modern Austrian art. (Binder himself obviously preferred realism.) Instead, he wrote, "the real Austrian spirit expresses itself with particular distinctness in the prints of Oskar Stoessel, whose graphic work contains more than 300 prints."[14] In Binder's view, Stoessel had surpassed Schmutzer even before graduating in 1913.[15] The 20-page article includes 11 full-page reproductions of Oskar's etchings—two of which had also been shown in the 1931 article (Mackensen and Prince Francis of Liechtenstein).

Here Binder observed that Oskar's landscapes and architectural renderings mostly depicted Graz, Venice, Paris, Quimper (Bretagne), Vienna, and Wachau (lower Austria). He was drawn to town squares, traditional spires, belvederes, rooftops, and city river views. When depicting rustic settings, he emphasized trees—both individual ones and those clumped in coppices.

---

12. Bruno Binder, "Der österreichische Maler und Radierer Oskar Stössel," *Westermann's Monatshefte* (Berlin), Apr. 1931, 112.

13. Binder, "Der österreichische Maler," 106.

14. Bruno Binder, "Oskar Stoessel and His Graphic Art," *Print Collector's Q.* 22 (July 1935): 245.

15. Binder, "Stoessel and His Graphic Art," 249 ("How great has the difference already become between master and pupil. . . .").

Oskar's print editions were "very small, generally limited to 20 impressions."[16] Binder said that what made Oskar a significant portrait etcher was "the great interest in the physiognomy as an image of the intellectual capacity of the sitter."[17] Although Oskar generally made his portraits from one plate, even for tinted etchings, there was a notable exception: the portrait of Sir Arthur Wauchope, the British High Commissioner and Commander in Chief for Palestine, whose boldly colored uniform made a second plate necessary (see page 39).[18]

But it was in faces, figures, and hands that Oskar chiefly excelled. In the various portraits he discussed, Binder praised Oskar's portrayals with such phrases as

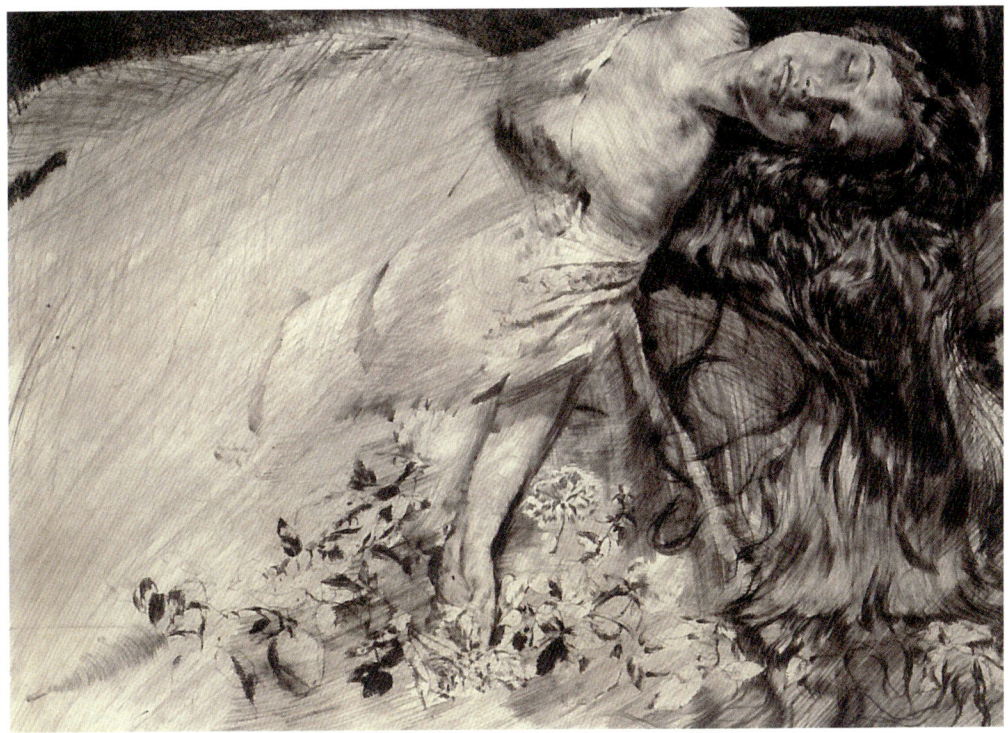

"Sleeping Beauty" (1921)

---

16. Binder, "Stoessel and His Graphic Art," 259.
17. Binder, "Stoessel and His Graphic Art," 254.
18. Oskar Stoessel, "Special Exhibition: Etchings by Oskar Stoessel," Corcoran Gallery of Art, Washington, D.C., Apr. 5–27, 1941.

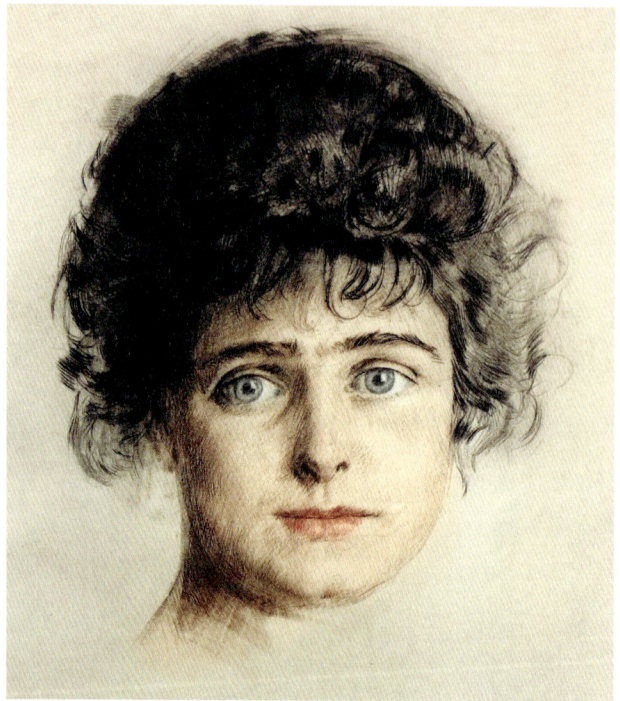

Oskar's portrait of Fräulein Rupprecht (1922). It was said of Oskar that "he may cover up your weaknesses, but he will never flatter you by lying."

"feminine charm and elegance," "certainty of profile-lines," "silky gloss of the hair," "curves of a dress swinging in large lines," "charming idylls of the model's grace and beauty," "the rich scale of tones," "fine taste in treatment of colour," "conscientious, precise, and sure drawing," and "the rich scale of reflexes of light and air." He noted that Oskar had been influenced not just by Schmutzer but also quite perceptibly by Dürer and Rembrandt.[19]

Binder's English-language article enhanced Oskar's international fame. Shortly after it appeared, Lord Wimborne,[20] Winston Churchill's cousin, sat with his family for portraits in Vienna and brought Stoessel into contact with George S. Messersmith, the United States minister to Austria from April 1934 to July 1937.

Oskar's acquaintance with Messersmith would perhaps save his life. At the very least, Messersmith opened doors to meetings with many of the most powerful Americans of the time. But Messersmith might never have met Oskar if his own career hadn't taken an unexpected turn.

---

19. Binder, "Stoessel and His Graphic Art," 249.
20. Lord Wimborne was Ivor Churchill Guest (1873–1939). See *Oxford Dictionary of National Biography* (Oxford Univ. Press, 2004), 24:174–76 (describing how Winston Churchill pressed his cousin's claim to become lord lieutenant of Ireland [1914–1918]; and how the unpopular Lord Wimborne was the subject of a derisive ditty: "One must suppose that God knew best / When He created Ivor Guest.").

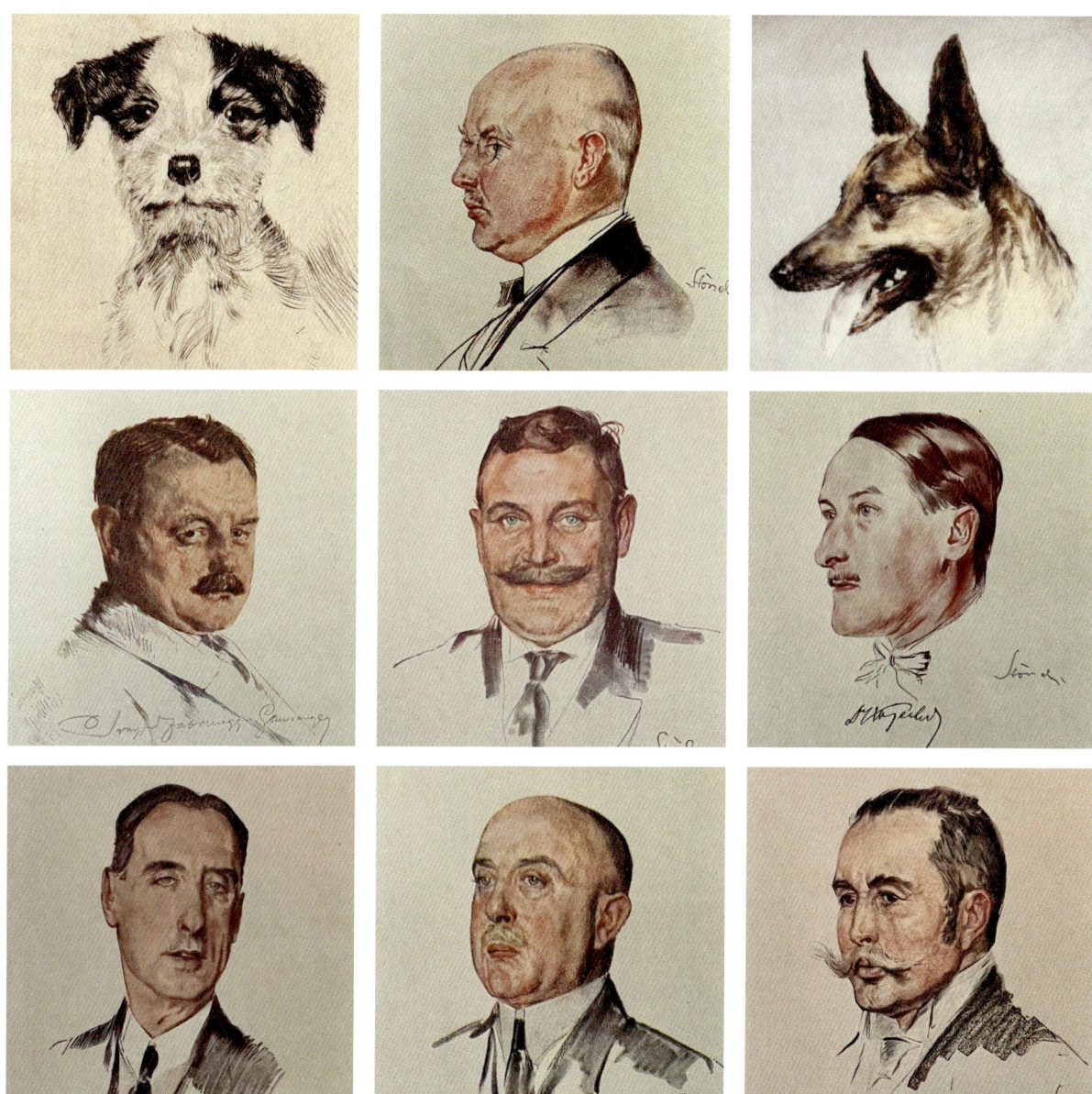

In 1925, Oskar was commissioned to make seven men's portraits for the Kynologisches Jahrbuch, *published by the Styrian Society for the Promotion of Purebred Dogs. In English,* cynology *is a rare word denoting the natural history of dogs. These portraits illustrate what Bruno Binder said of Oskar in 1931: "his strength is the unique, never-repeated personality." The two dogs also date from the mid-1920s— Oskar's cynological phase.*

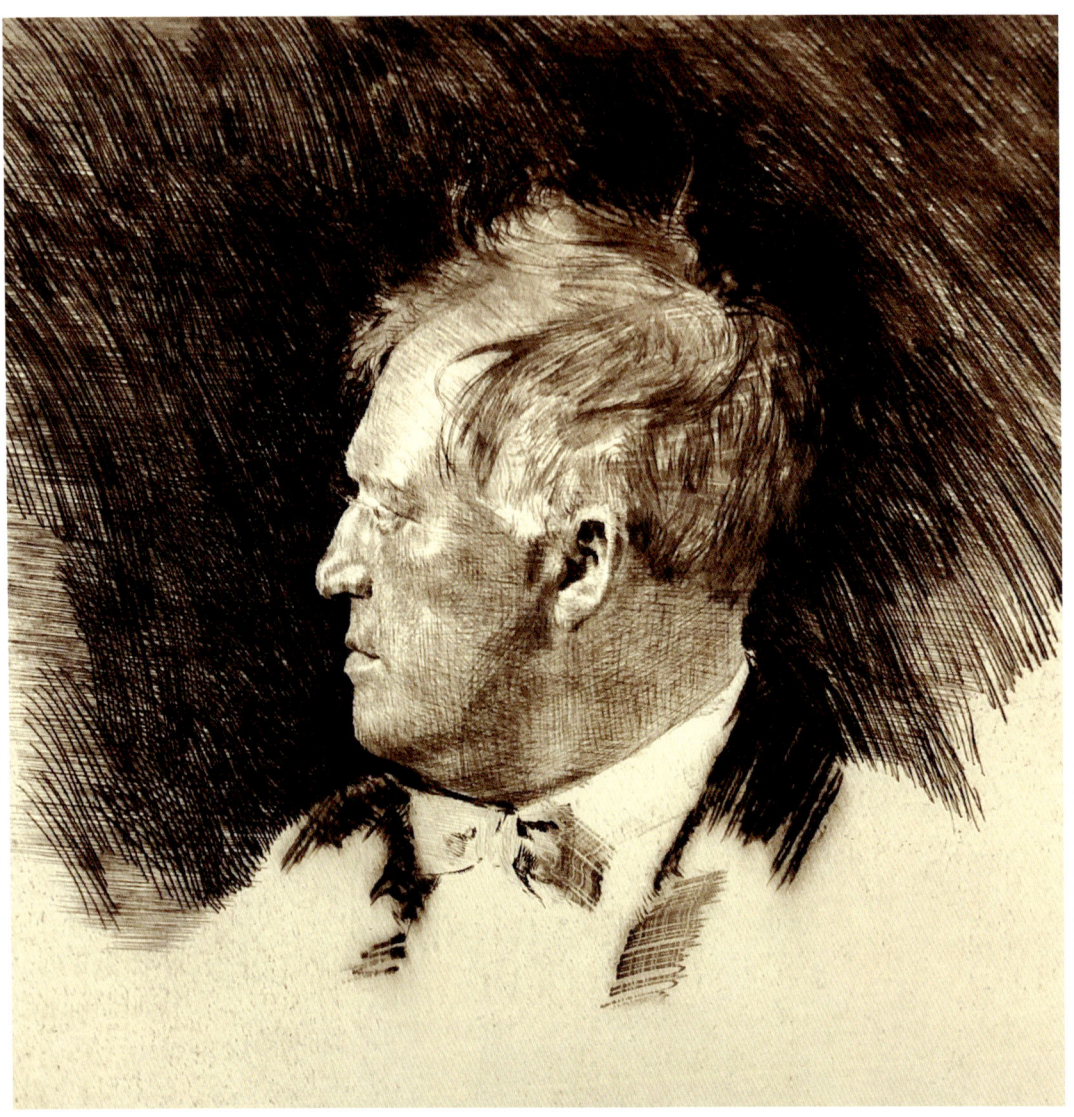

Oskar's portrait of Werner Krauss (ca. 1928). This portrait was considered important enough to be included in the London/New York anthology titled Etchings of Today *(1929), edited by G. Geoffrey Holme (commending Oskar's "vivid portraiture"). As an actor, Krauss was long a dominating presence in German films, as well as on stage. At the time of the portrait, Oskar was probably unaware of Krauss's intense antisemitism. Krauss would become a supporter of the Nazi Party: in a key supporting role, he participated in the Goebbels-backed propaganda film* Süss the Jew *(1940), one of the most antisemitic films of all time, in which Krauss prejudicially played six stereotypical Jewish characters. After World War II, he remained controversial. He underwent a denazification program and was somewhat rehabilitated in the public mind. In 1958, his autobiography,* The Play of My Life, *was released. He died the following year in Vienna.*

CHAPTER 8

The Humane Diplomat

A PENNSYLVANIAN by birth, George S. Messersmith (1883–1960) was home-schooled by his mother and then undertook a two-year course of study at Keystone Normal School (a teachers' college). Although he never received a college degree, he had enough schooling by 1900 to become a teacher and school administrator. He lived and taught in Delaware. Soon he published a textbook on Delaware state government[1] and coauthored another on English composition.[2] Deciding to shift his career in 1914, he entered the Foreign Service, becoming a consul successively in Fort Erie, Ontario (1914–1916); Curaçao, off the Venezuelan coast (1916–1919); Antwerp, Belgium (1919–1925), where he was promoted to consul general; Buenos Aires, Argentina (1928–1930); and Berlin (1930–1934).

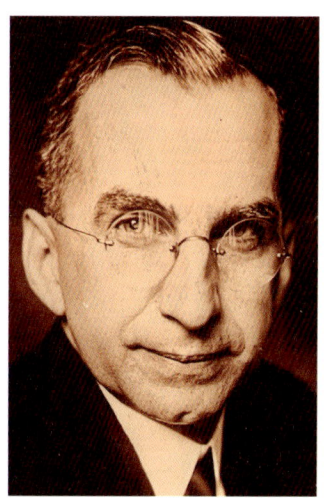

George Messersmith upon being named minister to Austria (March 1934)

Photographs of Messersmith suggest that he was a natty dresser and a formal man. He wore three-piece suits and fedora hats with deep crowns. In 1937, one newspaper described him as "wearing a gray suit of conservative check design, a starched collar, a maroon four-in-hand tie, and oxfords of a heavy tan leather," with "hair beginning to gray."[3] Having no hobbies, he was known as a workaholic. He also earned a reputation in the Foreign Service as a pedant and martinet. He was a deep-voiced traditionalist who steadfastly insisted on doing what he could, within the rules, to

---

1. George S. Messersmith, *The Government of Delaware* (American Book, 1908).
2. W. Owen Sypherd & G.S. Messersmith, *The High-School Course in English* (Del. College, 1908).
3. "Sees Austria Forging Ahead," *Reading Times* (Reading, Pa.), Apr. 19, 1937, 1.

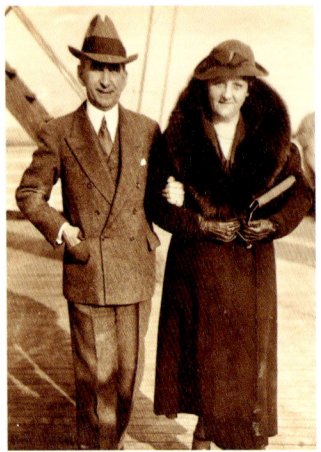

George and Marion Messersmith in 1935, probably not long before Oskar came to know the U.S. minister to Austria. The couple had just disembarked in New York for a short vacation from Vienna.

right wrongs—and to reform the rules if they seemed unfair. George Kennan, a fellow diplomat, called him "a dry, drawing, peppery man, his eyes always glinting with the readiness to accept combat, . . . stern and incorruptible in his fight for what he considered right and decent."[4]

While serving in Berlin, Messersmith witnessed perhaps as closely as anyone else in American government the rise of Adolf Hitler and Nazism, both of which he came to despise. When he discovered that his phones were being tapped, he misled the Nazis with elaborate disinformation.[5] Twice, as a pedestrian in Berlin, he was nearly run down by paramilitary sedans driven by Nazi stormtroopers.[6] Even though the Nazis often proclaimed their political moderation during those early years, Messersmith astutely saw that Hitler was implacable on two points: the exclusion of Jews and the annexation of Austria.

Messersmith often negotiated on behalf of Americans who were being badgered by Hitler's paramilitary—beaten, arrested, and subjected to extortion, usually for refusing to salute the German flag. In September 1933, for example, Messersmith managed to obtain the pardon and release of an American sailor who, at a bar, had called Hitler a "Czech Jew."[7] When Messersmith was called on to negotiate, the German ministers with whom he had to deal engaged in "Nazi harangues" with what he described as maniacal facial expressions.[8] By September 1933, the State Department was warning Americans to stay out of Germany for

4.   George Kennan, *Memoirs, 1925–1950* (Bantam Books, 1969), 66.
5.   Jesse H. Stiller, *George S. Messersmith: Diplomat of Democracy* (Univ. of N.C. Press, 1987), 40.
6.   Stiller, 40.
7.   "Prussia Frees U.S. Sailor," *Spokesman-Rev.* (Spokane, Wash.), Sept. 12, 1933, 5.
8.   Stiller, *George S. Messersmith*, 44.

their own safety. On October 10, an American named Roland Velz was severely beaten for failing to salute a passing Nazi procession.[9] About this time, Ambassador William Edward Dodd, Messersmith's immediate superior, claimed a case of flu and asked that Messersmith take his place in a meeting with Hitler. When Messersmith refused, Dodd's symptoms miraculously vanished.[10] Although Hitler promised that attacks on Americans would be "punished to the limit of the law,"[11] Messersmith came to believe that the Nazis were in fact staging well-publicized arrests of innocent Germans while allowing the true mischief-makers to continue wreaking havoc at the Nazis' bidding.

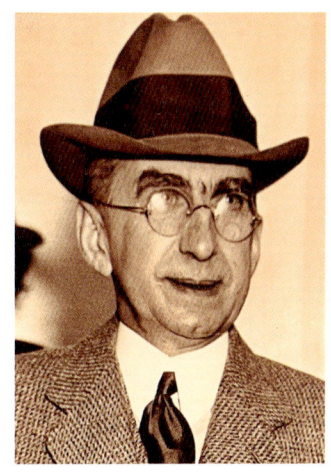

Messersmith in 1935

In one of his long missives to the State Department, Messersmith said that predicting Germany's future was no more possible than it would be for "the keeper of a madhouse . . . to tell what his inmates will do in the next hour."[12] He did opine, however, that Hitler's aim was "to make Germany the most capable instrument of war that . . . has ever existed."[13] Nazi propaganda had spread the idea that Germany was in danger of being bombed at any moment by enemies; in a matter of months, formerly apathetic Germans had been transformed into hawkish zealots "ready to follow the Führer wherever he led them."[14]

Some Americans, including Ambassador Dodd, believed Hitler when he professed wishes for peace. But Messersmith was convinced that these claims were intended only to confuse world opinion: "Judge Germany," he wrote to his colleagues in October 1933, "by her actions rather than by the declarations of her

---

9. Frederick T. Birchal, "Another American Beaten by a Nazi," *N.Y. Times*, Oct. 11, 1933, 1.
10. Stiller, *George S. Messersmith*, 45.
11. Stiller, 45.
12. Stiller, 46.
13. Stiller, 46.
14. Stiller, 46–47.

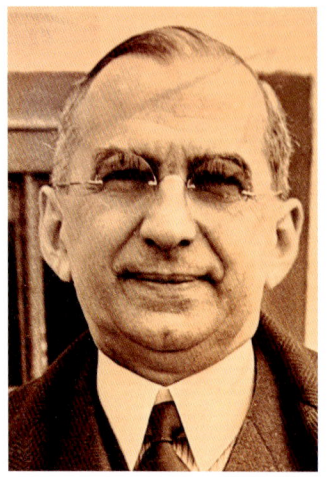

George Messersmith in Vienna, 1937

leaders."[15] Hitler's desired peace would be only "at the expense of complete compliance with German desires and ambitions."[16]

In fact, that same month, Hitler pulled Germany out of both the League of Nations and the World Disarmament Conference on the pretext of being dissatisfied with how slowly general disarmament was proceeding.[17] Yet Messersmith understood that Hitler in reality wanted to rearm Germany without constraint. Within weeks, German munitions factories were in full production.

In all his dealings with Nazi officials, Messersmith came to see Reich Marshal Hermann Göring, creator of the Gestapo, as one of the few top Nazis capable of "normal conversation."[18] But it was Göring who, in Messersmith's home, said matter-of-factly that Germany would eventually control all the land south of the Rio Grande (i.e., Latin America).[19]

Messersmith's long, rambling dispatches earned him the moniker "Forty-Page George" in Washington. Repeatedly, he mused that only Germans could reverse their bellicosity and recapture a sense of moderation. He posited but dismissed a "forcible intervention" or "preventive war."[20] He hoped that "basic human instincts, moral and economic, would reassert themselves."[21] Most of his letters were so detailed that they had to be summarized by functionaries at the State Department.

Within the Foreign Service, Messersmith became known as "the Jews' man."[22] In September 1933, he wrote privately that "there is no greater crime in history

---

15. Stiller, 47.
16. Stiller, 47.
17. "Germany Quits League and Arms Parley," *N.Y. Times*, Oct. 15, 1933, 1.
18. Stiller, *George S. Messersmith*, 48.
19. Stiller, 48.
20. Stiller, 48.
21. Stiller, 48.
22. Stiller, 50.

than that which the German government is committing against the Jews."[23] In conversation, when Göring asserted to Messersmith that Jews were also discriminated against in America, Messersmith responded that although there might be social prejudices, no responsible American advocated "any interference with their completely equal rights in Government, in the professions, in business, and before the law."[24] This came at a time when the Germans were actively divesting Jews of those very rights.[25] Göring even pressed the idea that President and Mrs. Roosevelt were surrounded by "practically nothing but Jews." Messersmith replied, "If the President ha[s] Jewish friends or Jewish advisers, it must be because they are fine people and good citizens of our country."[26]

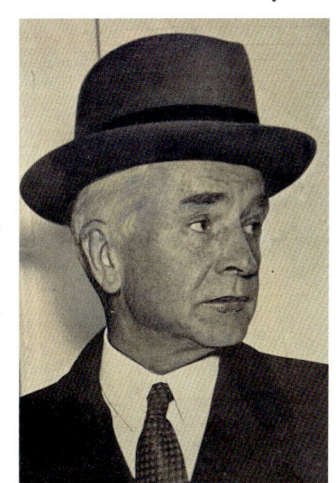

Although Supreme Court Justice Louis Brandeis and other prominent Jewish Americans came to see Messersmith as a champion of European Jewry,[27] his record was not unblemished. As a consul general in Berlin, Messersmith was personally in charge of issuing U.S. visas. Under a 1924 law, only 25,957 visas a year could be granted. Despite a waiting list of 82,787 applicants, mostly Jewish, only 1,241 visas were granted in 1933—not even 5% of the allotment.[28] Messersmith was under pressure within Cordell Hull's

Secretary of State Cordell Hull

23. Stiller, 50.

24. Stiller, 50.

25. Karl A. Schleunes, *The Twisted Road to Auschwitz* (Univ. of Ill. Press, 1970), 102–13; "Anti-Jewish Legislation in Prewar Germany," in *Holocaust Encyclopedia*, United States Holocaust Memorial Museum, accessed Dec. 3, 2024, https://encyclopedia.ushmm.org/content/en/article/anti-jewish-legislation-in-prewar-Germany.

26. Stiller, *George S. Messersmith*, 50.

27. See, e.g., "Named Minister to Austria: George S. Messersmith," *Am. Israelite* (Cincinnati), Apr. 5, 1934, 1 (noting, upon Messersmith's appointment as minister to Austria, that he, "it is believed, . . . will continue his friendly offices to improve the treatment of Jews").

28. *How Many Refugees Came to the United States from 1933–1945?*, United States Holocaust Memorial Museum: Americans and the Holocaust, accessed Dec. 3, 2024, https://exhibitions.ushmm.org/americans-and-the-holocaust/how-many-refugees-came-to-the-united-states-from-1933-1945.

State Department to keep the number low, and he did so. He had been instructed to reduce the number of visas granted to no more than 10% of the German quota, and he "complied promptly and efficiently."[29] Sadly, from his office in Berlin, he advised applicants "not to run away but stay here and adopt a policy of watchful waiting."[30] It is also said that Messersmith "never favored relaxing or altering immigration restrictions,"[31] possibly because he was sensitive to widespread American unemployment at the height of the Great Depression.[32]

The bureaucratic red tape for visa applications was burdensome. The law required each applicant to submit, "if available," two copies of his or her police dossier, prison record, and military record, together with two certified copies of a birth certificate and two copies of all other available government records concerning each applicant.[33] It was hard to extract this kind of material from German officials. Equally thorny was the requirement of two affidavits from American citizens vouching for the financial security of the applicant so that there would be no question of becoming a burden on the welfare system.[34] And of course, receiving that kind of guarantee while forfeiting all one's property to the German government was all but impossible. As an informal adviser to President Roosevelt, Felix Frankfurter worked to relax what became known as the "LPC" barrier (likely public charge). But his draft proposals to help German Jewish refugees ended up, after much wrangling, being rejected.[35]

The immigration quota for Austrians was a mere 1,413 a year. After the German annexation of Austria in 1938, the Roosevelt administration combined the two quotas for a total of 27,370 available visas. Even at that late date, the State Department left almost one-third of these spots unfilled. Not until 1939 would all

---

29. Richard Breitman and Alan M. Kraut, *American Refugee Policy and European Jewry* (Ind. Univ. Press, 1987), 43.
30. Stiller, *George S. Messersmith*, 51.
31. *American National Biography* (1999), "Messersmith, George Strausser [3 Oct. 1883–29 Jan. 1960]."
32. Breitman and Kraut, *American Refugee Policy*, 44.
33. Breitman and Kraut, 17.
34. Breitman and Kraut, 17.
35. Breitman and Kraut, 14–15.

27,370 available visas be issued. The quota wasn't quite filled in 1940 (15 visas went unissued), and in 1941—once the United States entered the war—the waiting list was canceled and immigration became impossible.

But returning to 1934: one of Messersmith's dispatches caught the eye of President Roosevelt—probably the one relating to Messersmith's defense of the First Family in conversation with Göring. When the American minister to Austria, George Earle, resigned to run (successfully) for governor of Pennsylvania, his post became open. Despite intense jockeying for the job among career diplomats, President Roosevelt appointed Messersmith, who was approved by the Austrian government on March 20.[36]

The promotion was a major step up in rank for Messersmith: he had moved from being a consul-level member of the diplomatic corps to the highest official in Austria—which did not have an ambassador (the highest diplomatic rank) but a minister (the second-highest). In an interview with the *Chicago Daily News*, President Roosevelt sounded impishly exultant about the appointment: "It was a good joke on the State Department, wasn't it! Just think what the career boys will say! I've put a lowly consul into a diplomatic post. Ha, ha, ha!"[37]

By 1935, Messersmith had had only two 15-minute meetings with President Roosevelt—one on the eve of his appointment and one in April 1935 on a visit to Washington.[38] But Roosevelt assured Messersmith that his letters were "the ones in which he placed the greatest dependence concerning developments in Central Europe."[39] In a 1935 letter to a mutual friend, Roosevelt wrote about Messersmith: "I count greatly on his judgment."[40]

Yet during this period, Messersmith remained an outlier at the State Department. Though others sought peace with Germany, Messersmith kept making the case that a confrontation involving the United States was inevitable.

---

36. "Berlin Consul, Fleetwood Man, Wins Promotion," *Reading Times* (Reading, Pa.), Mar. 21, 1934, 1.
37. Stiller, *George S. Messersmith*, 55.
38. Stiller, 82.
39. Stiller, 83.
40. Stiller, 83.

In Vienna, George and Marion Messersmith led an active social life, hosting soirees and attending many more at the imperial palaces and museums throughout that resplendent city. Although his biographer has said that Messersmith had an underdeveloped sense of the arts, he and his wife became heavily involved in the cultural events of Vienna—and Marion liked parties. They attended concerts of the Vienna Philharmonic when conducted by maestros Bruno Walter and Wilhelm Furtwängler, as well as the Vienna State Opera. Messersmith himself wrote in his unpublished memoir that "to be a good reporter from the field for the Department of State," it was important for him to develop familiarity with, among other things, Vienna's "cultural circles," including writers, musicians, actors, and artists.[41]

In late 1936, the Messersmiths became socially acquainted with the Duke of Windsor, who had just abdicated as King Edward VIII, and his bride, Wallis Simpson. Having recently become the Duke and Duchess of Windsor, they were staying in Vienna at the time, and Messersmith came to believe they were Nazi sympathizers. Messersmith knew that the Duke was untrustworthy. At a dinner party in 1937, Messersmith received a sealed letter from the Austrian Chancellor containing proof that Germany was illegally sending munitions to Italy. When the Duke inquired about the letter, Messersmith shared its contents but stressed that he was doing so in the strictest confidence. Almost immediately afterward, Messersmith saw the Duke speaking with the Italian attaché. And the next day, the Italian ambassador reported to Rome what the Duke had told him about the letter.[42] Messersmith arranged to have the Duke and Duchess followed at various points and reported on their associations. Even so, the Messersmiths and the Windsors became friends.

It was in this environment that the Messersmiths first crossed paths with Oskar Stoessel, whose etchings Messersmith had begun to collect soon after arriv-

41. George S. Messersmith, "Vol. I—Scope of Memoirs," 7 (unpublished notes), Messersmith Papers, University of Delaware, accessed Dec. 3, 2024, http://udspace.udel.edu/handle/19716 /7900.

42. Martin Allen, *Hidden Agenda: How the Duke of Windsor Betrayed the Allies* (M. Evans, 2002), 74–75.

ing in Vienna. In late 1935 or early 1936—well before the Windsors' arrival—Messersmith commissioned Oskar to make his own portrait. It required four or five sittings, and the work was finished in May 1936. It isn't known how many prints were made, but Messersmith had one earmarked for President Roosevelt. Emboldened by the president's sponsorship and encouragement, Messersmith inscribed it "with sincere admiration and gratitude," adding the notation "Vienna May 1936."

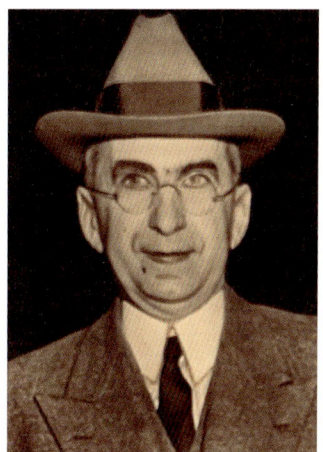

The portrait arrived in the Oval Office in the midst of international turmoil. Just two months before, German troops had marched into the Rhineland, which had been demilitarized at Versailles in 1919 and in the Locarno Pact of 1925. Austrians were feeling less secure than ever. In a dispatch to the State Department, Messersmith asked pointedly: "Who can blame the German people for believing that after all Germany is invincible and has a mission to carry through by the domination of Europe."[43] Tellingly, he punctuated that statement with a period, not a question mark.

Messersmith in 1937

---

43. Allen, 87.

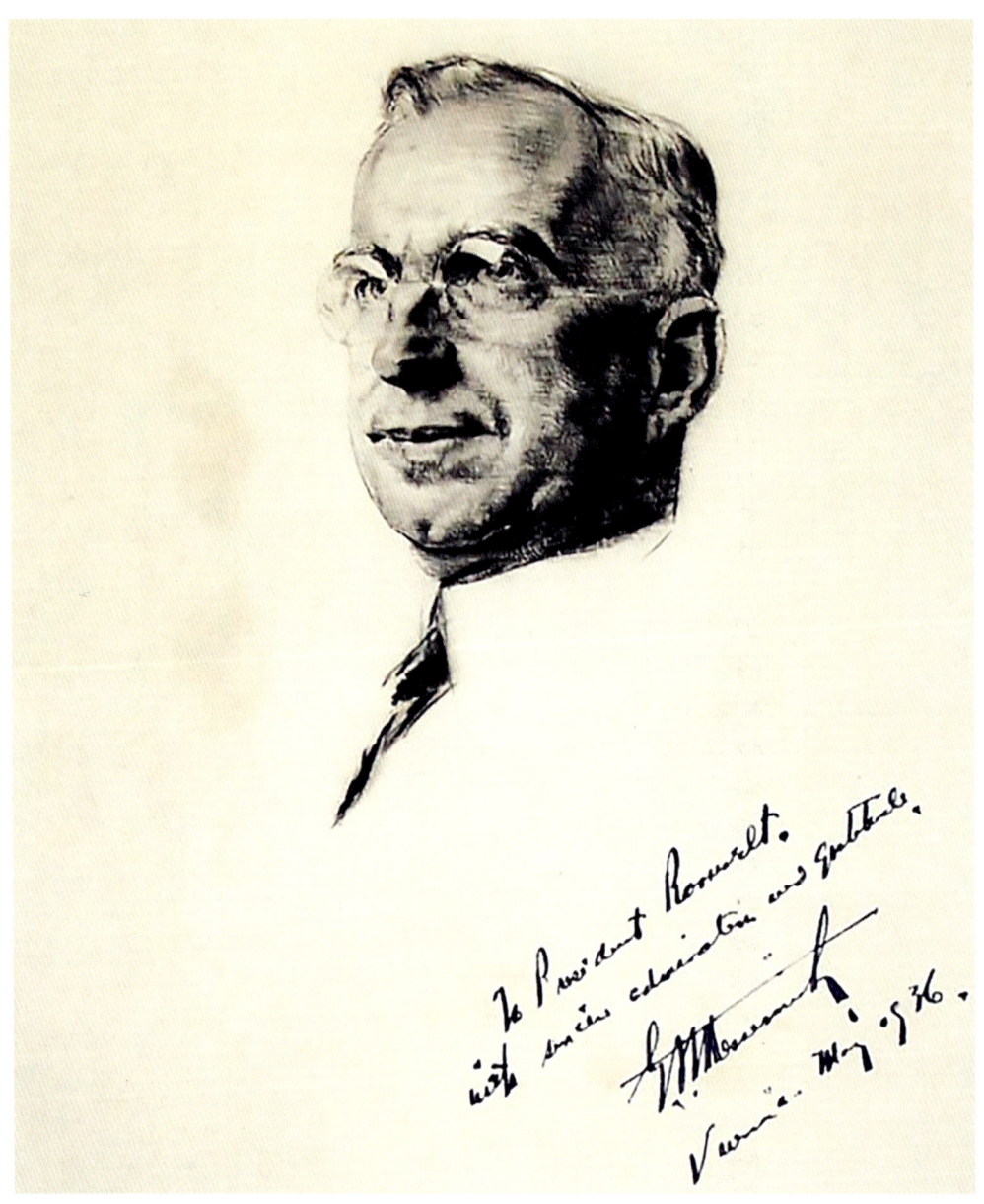

Oskar's etching of Ambassador George S. Messersmith (1936) as the United States minister to Austria. In May 1936, Messersmith sent this inscribed etching to President Roosevelt "with sincere admiration and gratitude." In July 1937, he was re-called to Washington, D.C., where he served as assistant secretary of state until February 1940, when he became ambassador to Cuba. While in Washington, in mid-January 1940, he met with the president in the Oval Office. Discussions at these meetings led to FDR's sitting for Oskar on January 29, 1940.

CHAPTER 9

Flight from the Anschluss

WITH the rise of Adolf Hitler and the German Nazi Party in 1933, Oskar's brother Ludwig had left Berlin to return to Austria, where he appeared on the stages of the Raimund Theater and the Theater in der Josefstadt. Little is known of the two brothers in Vienna during this time. Oskar was approaching the age—60—at which, in the words of Lord Lytton, "a man learns how to value home."[1] Yet suddenly he had no real home—no sense of belonging. The "homeland" had come to represent a place of alienation and of widespread hatred directed at people with Oskar's lineage, even if they were secular Jews.

In *Mein Kampf,* Hitler wrote that "the safety of Germany first required the destruction of Austria."[2] Hitler sought to unify Germany and Austria in various ways—monetarily, militarily, and politically—through a series of proposals, threats, and encroachments throughout the 1930s. A majority of Austrians wanted to merge with Germany—yet this move had been forbidden by the Allies in the Treaty of Versailles. Nevertheless, in 1938, he formally embarked on the "annexation" of Austria (the Anschluss Österreichs). Austria stopped making its own coinage, which was replaced by German coins and currency. All sorts of repressive measures were taken against people of Jewish descent, and antisemitic gangs were a constant threat. The Nazis arrested Ludwig Stössel three times during this period. He was released each time. Oskar may well have experienced similar cruel indignities.

---

1. Lytton died just 16 days after turning 60. The quotation is attributed to Lytton in many places. My immediate source is Desmond Morris, *The Book of Ages* (Viking, 1983), under "60."
2. Adolf Hitler, *Mein Kampf* (1925), trans. Ludwig Lore (Stackpole Sons, 1939), 30 ("[D]ie Sicherung des Deutschtums die Vernichtung Österreichs vorausetzte."). The Nazis approved an official translation in which the words were substantially altered: "The dissolution of the Austrian Empire is a preliminary condition for the defence of Germany." Adolf Hitler, *Mein Kampf* (1925), trans. James Murphy (Hurst and Blackett, 1939), 30.

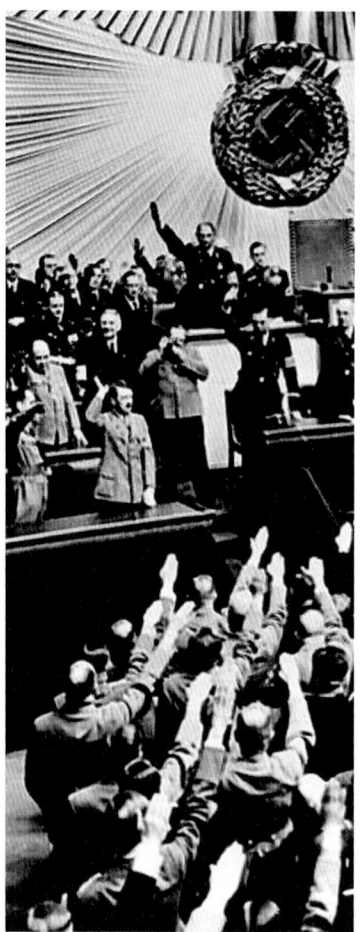

Hitler receiving an ovation from the Reichstag for the Anschluss (March 1938)

The annexation of Austria came on March 13, 1938. It marked a turning point for Austrian Jews. Those who fled were abandoning their homes, their heirlooms and other possessions, and typically their family members. Jewish émigrés were allowed one suitcase when leaving, and only ten Reichsmarks. Many Jews were forced to sell their possessions at a fraction of their true value in order to finance their escape. They had to cross multiple borders and navigate their way through hostile neighboring countries, which had their own restrictive immigration policies.

Among Viennese Jews who remained for a time, life was torturous from March 1938. In April, the Nazis' "Decree for the Reporting of Jewish-Owned Property" took effect. All Jews had to register their assets valued at more than 5,000 Reichsmarks (about USD $2,000). Nothing was exempt. By August 1, nearly 700,000 German and Austrian Jews had registered property worth 7 billion Reichsmarks, most of which would be confiscated.[3] Another law placed all Jews in the highest tax bracket, regardless of their actual income.[4]

Every public bench had a sign that warned, "Jews strictly forbidden." Public transportation bore huge posters that declared, "Jewry is criminality." From March to August, 9,000 Viennese Jews committed suicide. Their doors were decorated by the Nazis with placards that said things like this: "Five Jews who have killed themselves. Course of action highly recommended to others."[5]

3.   Lorraine Boissoneault, "A 1938 Nazi Law Forced Jews to Register Their Wealth—Making It Easier to Steal," *Smithsonian*, Apr. 26, 2018, https://www.smithsonianmag.com/history/1938 -nazi-law-forced-jews-register-their-wealthmaking-it-easier-steal-180968894/.

4.   Boissoneault, "1938 Nazi Law."

5.   Moriz Scheyer, *Asylum: A Survivor's Flight from Nazi-Occupied Vienna Through Wartime France*, trans. and ed. P.N. Singer (Little, Brown, 2016), 9–10.

Things got even worse after the pogrom known as Kristallnacht (the Night of Broken Glass), November 9–10, 1938, when a violent riot against Jews, organized by the Nazis, resulted in the torching of 267 synagogues (over 90 of them in Vienna alone) and untold thousands of Jewish-owned businesses and homes in Germany, Austria, and the Sudetenland. The event's name comes from the shards of broken glass that, in its aftermath, littered the streets.

Kristallnacht proved to be the major turning point toward the beginning of the Holocaust in Europe. More than 30,000 Jewish men were arrested throughout Germany, Austria, and the Sudetenland and taken to concentration camps. The German government confiscated insurance proceeds for the damage done by the Kristallnacht rioters, leaving homeowners and businesses struggling to repair the damage and replace stolen goods. Worse, quickly enacted laws allowed "Aryan" buyers to seize Jewish businesses' goods and property. Jews were barred from many forms of employment, expelled from public schools, forbidden to drive, restricted from using public transportation, and barred from entering most theaters, cinemas, and concert halls.

The odds are that Oskar and Ludwig fled Austria sometime after the Anschluss but before Kristallnacht. First Lady Eleanor Roosevelt specifically wrote that Oskar left "after the Anschluss."[6] Further, Oskar's art had been accepted for an exhibition in the spring of 1938. Suddenly, though, after the Anschluss, the acceptance was withdrawn—doubtless because the Nazi authorities had learned that his etchings were the creation of a Jew.

The Austrian borders were busy beyond capacity after March 1938, as thousands tried to escape persecution and violence. Before emigrating, Jews had to convert their property to Reichsmarks and exchange them for the currency of their destination. By the end of the year, the Nazis were exchanging Reichsmarks for only 8% of their actual value.[7] Despite facing hordes of desperate people, border security was tightly controlled, and severe travel restrictions included the necessity for an exit visa and exorbitant fees for transportation. Some organizations, such as

6.   Eleanor Roosevelt, "My Day," Apr. 5, 1956, distributed by United Feature Syndicate (printed in dozens if not hundreds of newspapers).

7.   Boissoneault, "1938 Nazi Law."

the International Red Cross and the Joint Distribution Committee, helped Jews escape from Austria. There were also sympathetic individuals who did so.

Although Messersmith had already been gone from Vienna for nine months, he continued to work on German and Austrian issues in Washington, D.C. From there he could have ensured that Oskar and Ludwig received their visas from the U.S. Consulate, which had been downgraded after the Anschluss from its earlier status as a legation. Oskar and Ludwig were certainly in the select category of what Messersmith called "useful people" who ought to be allowed to enter the United States. Similarly, the United Kingdom allowed only a narrow class of "Jews whom it deemed likely to be an asset" to the country.

To a small percentage of applicants, America's consulate in Vienna would issue visas that were good for 12 months for "all United States ports." Messersmith was doubtless in touch with the new consul.

But an American visa wasn't enough. Émigrés needed other documentation for the German authorities. One account describes how refugees had to go to their alma maters and employers "to beg for a copy of a diploma or testimonial and to be called a filthy Jew and left standing, once, twice, three times, before the document—on which was pinned the hope of any future—was finally, with fresh insults, produced."[8] A consular endorsement of these papers was required, but this, too, entailed hazards because those waiting in line were often attacked by Nazis. Further, they needed a preposterous document from the head of the Viennese police stating that their departure was entirely voluntary. All this paperwork was valid for only one month, and often by the time it had all been assembled—after interminable waits and declinations—some of it would have expired. For someone in this predicament, the process would start anew.

In whatever way, Oskar and Ludwig obtained the necessary papers.

But how did refugees—and Oskar and Ludwig in particular—transfer wealth outside Austria? Smuggling is an age-old problem, of course, but this was a special type: righteous smuggling. There are three possible scenarios for how it happened.

One is that Messersmith and Oskar together made plans for Oskar's future residence in the United States. As of April 1940, Messersmith knew that Oskar

---

8.   Tim Bonyhady, *Good Living Street: Portrait of a Patron Family, Vienna 1900* (Pantheon Books, 2011), 233.

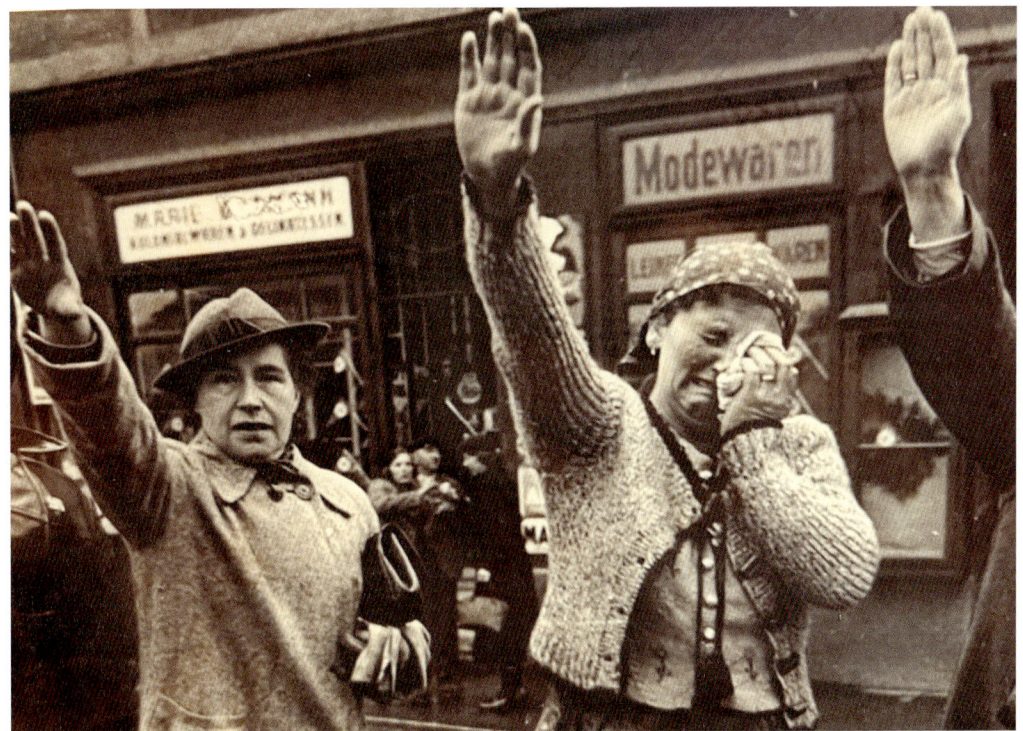

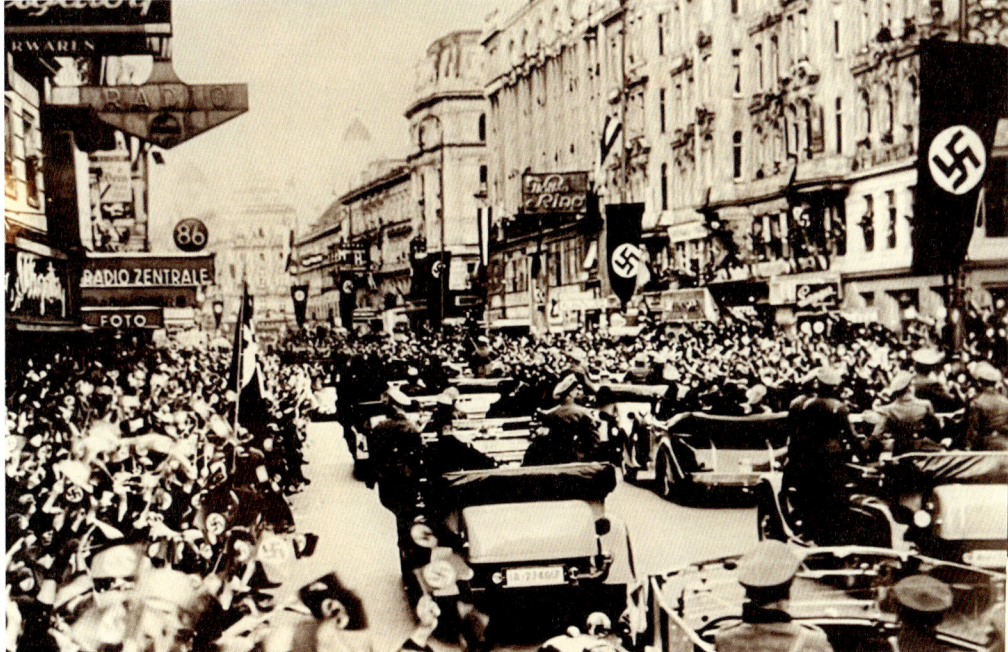

Vienna during the Anschluss (March 13, 1938)

already had "some modest means." Could it be that before leaving, Messersmith had ensured that this would be so? Had he used diplomatic pouches or cargo containers to convey to Zurich or to Washington Oskar's valuables, such as Old Master etchings of great worth? Had he helped Oskar establish a Swiss bank account? After fleeing, the brothers would need wherewithal.

Messersmith would have had to satisfy his State Department colleagues that Oskar and Ludwig would not be "likely public charges." He might have done this in the two ways just suggested: helping Oskar establish a Swiss bank account and sending out, by diplomatic pouch, Oskar's collection of valuable art, whatever jewelry the family had, and any other portable valuables. Perhaps Messersmith helped Oskar to evade the confiscation of his collection of valuable art—and even to avoid having to report it. Messersmith probably foresaw the possibility that the wealth-reporting forms would be used to ensure against smuggling.

The minuscule amount of cash that the Nazis would have allowed Oskar and Ludwig to retain upon leaving Austria wouldn't have been adequate to allow them to get much farther than the Swiss border. Hence it seems likely that Oskar had access to a bank account and retrieved the family's valuables in Switzerland so that he and Ludwig could get their mother established and pay for their travels through France and beyond.

The other two scenarios would have been riskier.

One would have been secreting valuables within a suitcase or clothing and smuggling them out. Oskar might have put dozens of valuable etchings—such as those by Dürer and Rembrandt—in a secret compartment of his suitcase to elude confiscation. This seems unlikely because it was so dangerous. He would have faced immediate imprisonment and probably deportation to a concentration camp. Or the outcome might have been even worse: in May 1938, Sigmund Freud's son Martin was told that when a Jew had recently been found with stamps in his pocketbook, he was taken from a train and summarily shot.

The third possible scenario would have involved confederates. It's possible that Oskar and Ludwig had one or more gentile allies take valuable property to Switzerland for safekeeping sometime before they left. This would have required detailed planning and coordination. It's even possible that a gentile friend carried the valuables and boarded the same train, all the while pretending not to know Oskar and Ludwig. But then the handoff at the end of the line, even with elaborate subterfuge, might have been risky for the ally returning to Austria. Witnesses entailed danger.

All in all, the likelihood is that Messersmith was the low-key liberator who ensured that Oskar and Ludwig would come to America with sufficient means. Whatever methods he might have used were off the record: his papers at the University of Delaware are devoid of evidence.

It is now well known that several embassies were engaging in this type of activity. Before Sigmund Freud left Austria in June 1938, one of his admirers had his collection of gold coins taken across the border in a diplomatic pouch of the Greek Embassy. And the Bulgarian Embassy transported the Gallias family's jewelry to a trusted friend in Switzerland.[9] For anyone who had access to them, these diplomatic bags were the best conduit available.

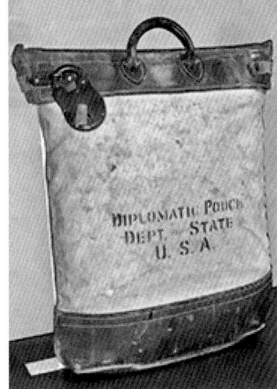

We know nothing of Oskar and Ludwig's actual experience of leaving with their mother. But other accounts are illuminating. Take the example of Moriz Scheyer, a Viennese journalist who escaped in August 1938. He stopped by the house of a well-known architect, Dr. Hans Berger, to say goodbye. Scheyer knew he was being thrust into the position of the poor relative who would need handouts—the very concept of "refugee." As he paid for his tram ticket and bade adieu to his friend, he said: "Look at this. This is the last time I'll be able to buy a ticket out of my own pocket. From the moment I cross the border, I'll have to live on charity."[10]

On the train bound for Switzerland, Scheyer was in a compartment with three Swiss citizens. A German stormtrooper walked up, took Scheyer's passport in hand, and said, "So you're the Jew Scheyer. Fifty-one years old."

Scheyer said nothing.

---

9.   Bonyhady, 246.
10.   Scheyer, *Asylum*, 14 (cleaned up).

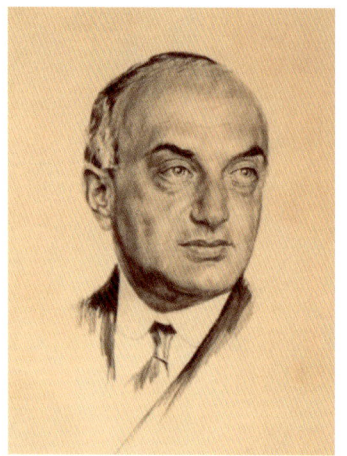

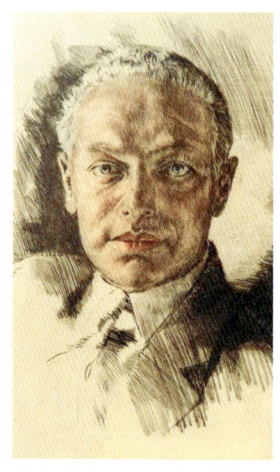

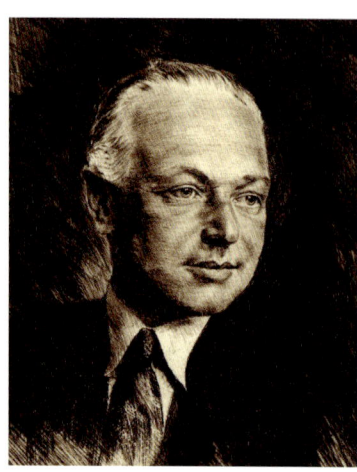

Oskar's portrait of Paul Khuner (1933)

Oskar's first portrait of Georg Khuner (ca. 1930)

Oskar's second portrait of Georg Khuner (1932)

"Fifty-one. Not as old as all that. And ten marks in your pocket. So—how are you going to live, now, with your ten marks? Can you tell me that?"

Again Scheyer stayed silent.

"These Jews," the stormtrooper shouted, "these Jewish pigs! You can take everything away from them and they'll still find someone to take them in." Then he threw the passport on the floor as the train started.

In his memoir, Scheyer called these "the last words of comfort—the provisions with which my homeland sent me off into the unknown."[11]

* * *

WHO was Oskar's contact in Switzerland? It might well have been someone affiliated with the Jewish industrialist Georg Khuner, for whom Oskar made two portraits in the early 1930s (see above). Oskar also made a posthumous portrait of Khuner's older brother Paul, who had died in Vienna in late 1932. From 1923 until 1935, Georg Khuner served as Austria's honorary general consul in Zurich. He was also president of Kunerolwerke A-G, a producer of coconut oil. Viennese by birth, Khuner was a serious art collector: in 1925, he had acquired a major collection of etchings from the Albertina Museum in Vienna—possibly with Oskar's advice and assistance—and presented it to the city of Zurich. So he was predisposed to appreciate Oskar's artistic brilliance. As an industrial magnate,

---

11.   Scheyer, 15.

Khuner had a broad network of connections in Switzerland. In 1935, though, he left Zurich to live in Paris, where he stayed until 1939. Then he found his way to California.[12]

Given that Khuner was already in Paris when Oskar and Ludwig needed to cross, they might have been helped by Khuner's Swiss connections—with communications facilitated by Messersmith. But even with these well-positioned people, the entry into Swiss territory was hardly easy.

Since 1933, Switzerland had been inhospitable to the refugees inundating its border. Some political refugees were placed in internment camps, where life was severely regimented and many were forced to work at manual labor. All others were expelled as soon as possible. Then in August 1938, the borders were closed to Jews. Switzerland and Germany agreed that Austrian and German passports would be marked with a large red J to make it easy to identify and reject Jews.[13] Oskar and his family nevertheless managed to enter Switzerland. As nonpolitical refugees, they needed help to stay.

They may have been helped by Paul Grüninger, the commander of the Swiss border police in St. Gallen, the canton that borders Austria. After Switzerland closed its borders,[14] Grüninger continued to admit Jewish refugees. He used many different methods, including backdating visas, making false reports about the number of refugees who arrived and what their status was, and encouraging theatrics to justify a decision not to expel a refugee. When Swiss border guards under Grüninger's command intercepted Jewish refugees, they instructed them that when Grüninger appeared, they were to beg him to shoot them immediately rather than force them to return to Austria. This type of frenzied desperation

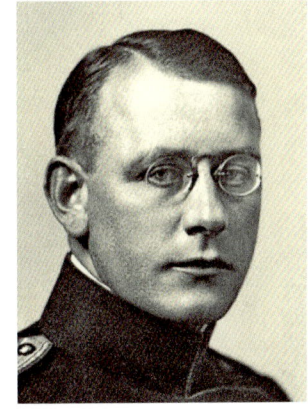

Paul Grüninger

12. He died in Beverly Hills in 1952. Ultimately, his widow Marianne would bequeath the George Khuner Collection (so spelled) to the Metropolitan Museum of Art in New York.

13. Mary Williams Walsh, "Swiss Finally Clear Rescuer of WWII Jews," *L.A. Times*, Dec. 1, 1995, A1.

14. "Circular of the Swiss Police Department, Sept. 7, 1938," in the collection of Vad Yashem, The World Holocaust Remembrance Center, accessed Dec. 9, 2024, https://www.yadvashem.org /righteous/stories/grueninger/swiss-police-circular.html.

enabled Grüninger to announce that they could stay in Switzerland.[15] Before he was dismissed from the police force in March 1939 and charged with crimes related to illegally helping Jews, Grüninger had allowed at least 3,600 Jews to escape from Austria.[16]

Oskar and Ludwig seem to have parted with their mother in Switzerland. Maybe she didn't want to travel any farther. Maybe, in the relative safety of Switzerland, her sons had made arrangements for her to stay with friends. She would live there for the rest of her life.

Oskar and Ludwig reached France perhaps in late 1938, and perhaps together. Those who arrived by that time often felt a sense of relief. The guards there would frequently say to people at the checkpoint, "Now you can breathe again." Refugees were not yet greeted with resentment, as they would be about a year later, when the Nazis encroached directly on France. Still, the French wished to avoid hearing unpleasant stories. In 1938, it was common to hear them exclaim, "Pas d'histoires!" ("No stories!") They wanted to hear nothing that would trouble their minds. They just wanted to continue their epicurean habits in relative prosperity.

As Oskar made his way to Le Havre, France, Ludwig traveled to London, where he stayed and acted in British films for a year—daily perfecting his English in London pubs.[17] Oskar, meanwhile, sailed from Le Havre, on February 23, 1939, on the S.S. *Manhattan* bound for New York.[18]

This was Oskar's first trip out of Europe. The eldest son in his family, he was leaving behind his mother, his younger sister and brother-in-law, his niece, and

---

15. Walsh, "Swiss Finally Clear Rescuer," A1.

16. "The Policeman Who Lifted the Border Barrier," in the collection of Vad Yashem, The World Holocaust Remembrance Center, accessed Dec. 9, 2024, https://www.yadvashem.org /righteous/stories/grueninger.html.

17. See Don MacLean, "Meet Ludwig Stossel" (widely syndicated piece), *Fitchburg Sentinel* (Mass.), Sept. 27, 1971, 4 (arrested and released three times; British pubs); "Veteran Actor Plays Role of Anton Kovac," *Honolulu Star–Bulletin*, Feb. 28, 1959, 15 (left Austria in 1938 and spent a year acting in British films).

18. List or Manifest of Alien Passengers for the United States Inspector at Port of Arrival, List 7, U.S. Department of Labor Form, departing Feb. 23, 1939, and arriving in N.Y.C. Mar. 3, 1939 (listing Stoessel's occupation as "Artist Painter," the languages he could read as "German, English," and his immigration visa number as QIV 27124). The manifest lists Ludwig Stössel as his nearest relative, with the address of 59 Queens Gate, London, SW7 England.

other family members. For years he had been experiencing fear. Like everyone else in his situation, he had felt displacement, desperation, and anger. Although a few friends had helped—most notably, George Messersmith—others from whom he might have expected support had suddenly shown indifference and even hostility. That was a common experience. The Austria he had known in the 1920s, a society in which he thought he'd gained full acceptance, had somehow vanished. A savage mob had taken over. The streets were overrun with an elaborate festival of tastelessness and barbarity.

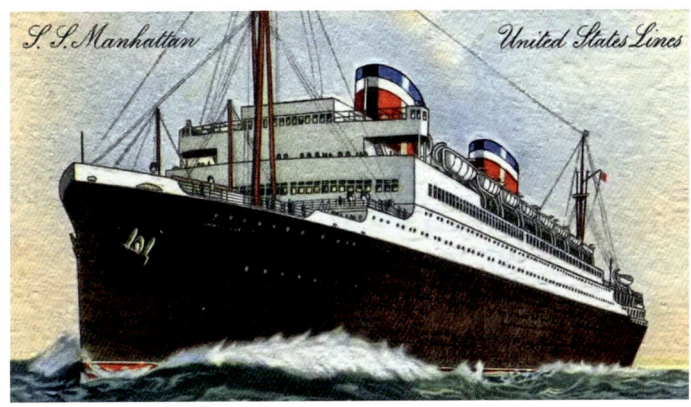

The S.S. Manhattan, *the luxury liner on which Oskar crossed the Atlantic, could carry up to 1,239 passengers in three classes of service (cabin, tourist, and third class). When it was completed in 1932, it was the largest ocean liner ever built in the United States. In 1936, the ship carried the U.S. Olympic team to the Summer Olympics in Berlin. In 1938, she carried most of the Kennedys to England after Joseph P. Kennedy was appointed U.S. ambassador to the United Kingdom. In to-day's money, the cheapest room available—on a one-way off-season trip—cost about $1,800. In June 1941, the ship was commissioned as the U.S.S.* Wakefield *and became the largest ship ever operated by the U.S. Coast Guard.*

Although Oskar doubtless hoped for a better life, he was, in the words of one historian, one of the "Austrian refugees [among whom were] many of the most gifted individuals Austria has ever produced."[19] Indeed, he was "among the most Austrian" of all émigrés, and he "represented that Vienna which [was] the epitome of Austrian culture"[20]—a culture that had vanished.

19. Wilhelm Schlag, "A Survey of Austrian Emigration to the United States," in *Österreich und die Angelsächsische Welt*, ed. Otto Hietsch (Wilhelm Braumüller, 1961), 181 (listing Oskar alongside Otto Preminger, Max Reinhardt, Arnold Schoenberg, Rudolf Serkin, Bruno Walter, and others).

20. Schlag, 182.

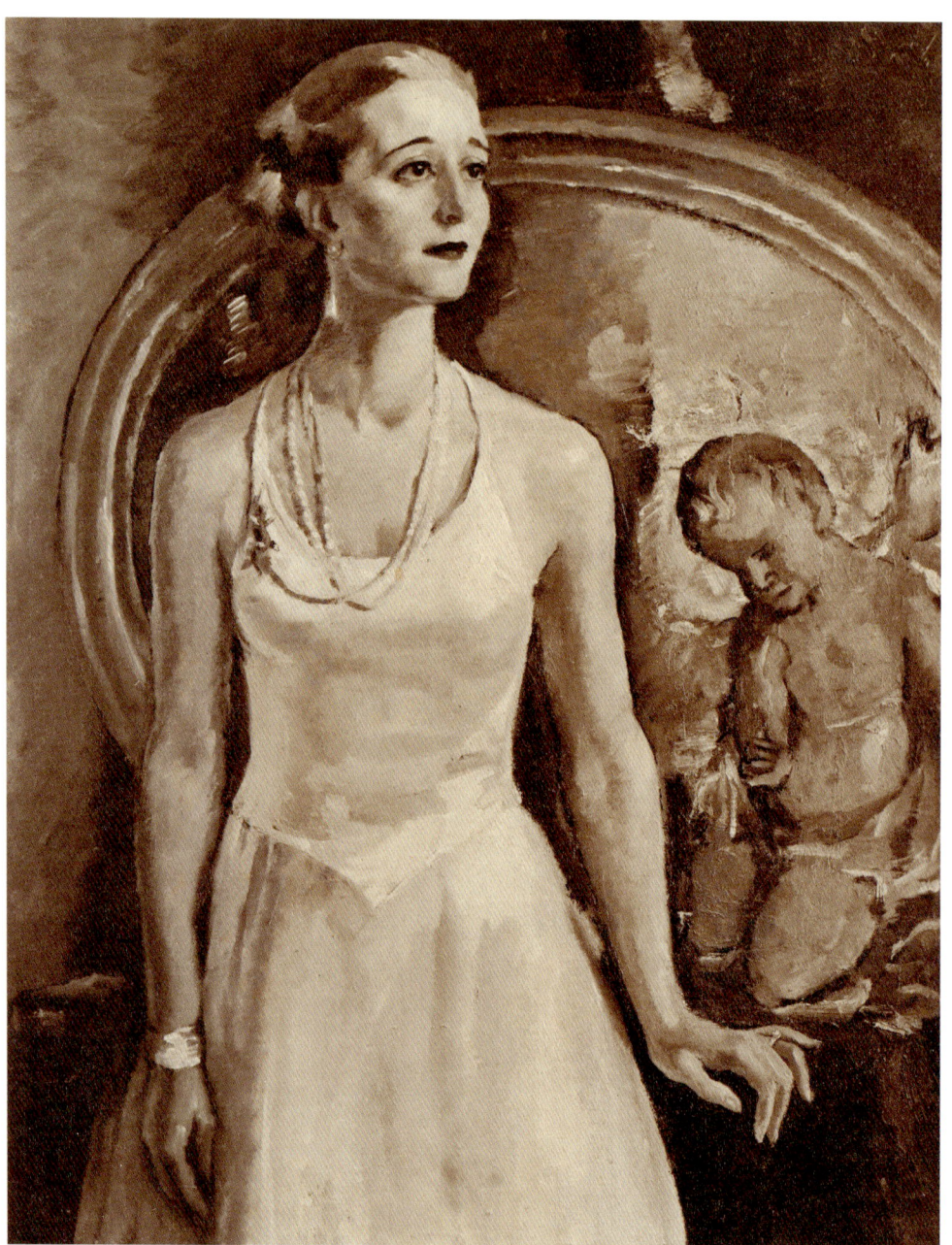

Hildegarde Hofmann, about age 23 (ca. 1938), as portrayed by Oskar before he left Vienna. The location of the portrait isn't known today. This photograph of it is the only known image.

CHAPTER 10

The Beatific Hildegarde

WHEN departing Austria, Oskar left behind a special student with whom he had developed a close friendship. Her name was Hildegarde (or "Hilde") Hofmann. He had made a large portrait of her. Who was she? Born November 26, 1915, in Tamsweg, a small village in Upper Styria, Hilde moved to Graz and later to Vienna, where she studied painting and perhaps etching at the Imperial Academy of Fine Arts from 1937 to 1939. She missed the 1939 classes because of an illness that apparently began about the time Oskar fled. One might wonder whether heartbreak over Oskar's departure contributed to her temporary withdrawal from school. Hilde agreed to be caretaker of Oskar's many heavy copperplates in his absence. It's conceivable that she played a role in removing Oskar's valuable Old Master etchings from Austria, perhaps by accompanying him to Switzerland while posing as a stranger.

Sometime during the war, she married a Mr. Winnar—for in 1947 she requested a transcript from the Academy and signed as a married woman under the name Winnar.[1] The marriage appears to have ended in or before 1947, by either widowhood or divorce. Throughout the turmoil of the war, Hilde remained steadfast in her loyalty to Oskar.

---

1. Dr. Peter Peer, email message to author, April 23, 2019.

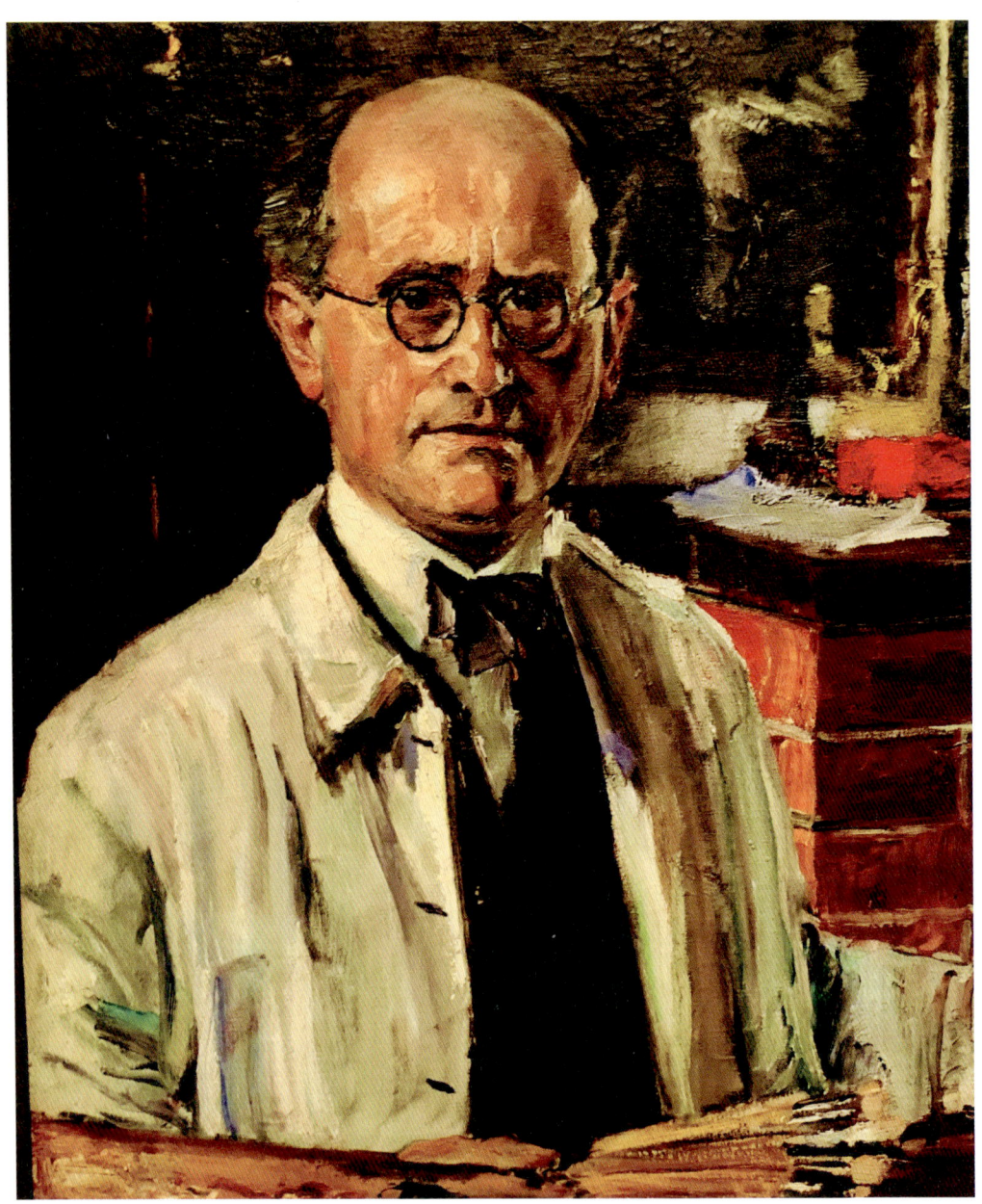

Oskar's 1926 self-portrait in oil

CHAPTER 11

Alighting in New York

For an Austrian Jew, entering the United States was no easy feat. President Franklin Roosevelt had set up the Intergovernmental Committee on Refugees,[1] an initiative that focused on German émigrés, not those of other nationalities. In October 1938, Assistant Secretary of State George Messersmith answered a query from Justice Louis Brandeis, a noted proponent of Zionism, who was worried about European Jewry: "All of us in this Department [the State Department] are deeply concerned over the desperate plight of so many of these people in Europe."[2] In answering Justice Brandeis, Messersmith defended his colleagues in the State Department: "I am sure that if you have all the facts, you will agree with me that we are doing all that we humanly can under our existing law and that the law is being carried through in a most sympathetic and understanding way."[3] He laid blame at the feet of Congress, arguing that the mood in the United States favored "further limiting immigration rather than in liberalizing our present practice."[4]

---

1. *Encyclopedia Britannica, International Committee on Refugees*, accessed Dec. 9, 2024, https://www.britannica.com/topic/Intergovernmental-Committee-on-Refugees.

2. George S. Messersmith to Justice Louis Brandeis, Oct. 24, 1938, Brandeis Papers, Library of Congress.

3. Messersmith to Brandeis, Oct. 24, 1938, p. 3. Cf. *American National Biography* (1999), "Messersmith, George Strausser [3 Oct. 1883–29 Jan. 1960]": "Messersmith clearly held that Germany's Jewish population was mistreated, but this did not translate into a welcome for the persecuted minority into the United States. Those who met the legal requirements to come to American shores were accepted, but he never favored relaxing or altering immigration practices."

4. Messersmith to Brandeis, Oct. 24, 1938. Cf. Anthony Heilbut, *Exiled in Paradise: German Refugee Artists and Intellectuals in America from the 1930s to the Present* (Viking, 1983), 39 ("The obstacles to Jewish emigration set up by officers of the U.S. foreign service constituted a scandal that has tarnished this country's history. These civil servants were as callous as any

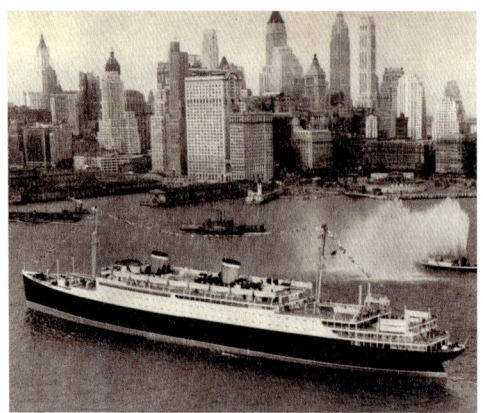

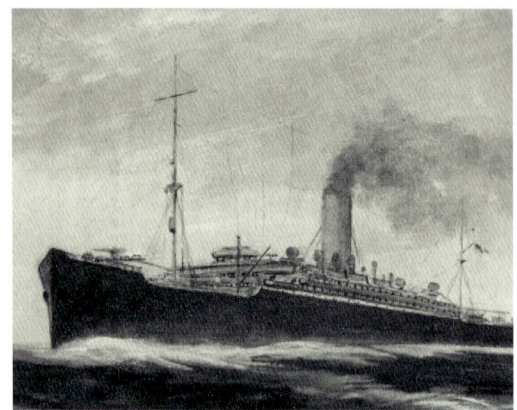

The S.S. Manhattan, *Oskar's transport, approaches New York City.*

The S.S. Van Dyck, *the commercial liner on which Ludwig sailed, was the third British ship to be so named. Soon after Ludwig's trip, it was converted into an armed vessel in the British Navy and, in June 1940, was sunk by a German bomber off the coast of Norway.*

Given this restrictiveness, Oskar and Ludwig were among the most fortunate refugees. Oskar's transatlantic trip took eight days. His immediate destination was the Murray Hill Hotel,[5] on Park Avenue near the Grand Central Depot. Soon, perhaps with Messersmith's help, he would be living in a studio at Carnegie Hall.

Ludwig stayed in London for a time before coming to America via Liverpool.[6] He arrived in the United States aboard the S.S. *Van Dyck* on September 13, 1939, a little more than six months after Oskar. Soon, with his background in Austrian, German, and English movies, he ended up in Hollywood.

The brothers' names then diverged. Unlike Ludwig, Oskar immediately decided to anglicize the spelling of his surname, changing it from *Stössel* to *Stoessel.*

European bureaucrats. No matter how fervent the gratitude expressed by émigrés, they all knew that their entrance was a matter of luck, not principle. Up to 1940, Breckinridge Long of the State Department went out of his way to inhibit their arrival with a series of obstacles in the form of visa regulations and affidavit requirements.").

5. List or Manifest of Alien Passengers for the United States Inspector at Port of Arrival, List 7, U.S. Department of Labor Form, departing Feb. 23, 1939, and arriving in N.Y.C. Mar. 3, 1939.

6. Ludwig Stössel's Declaration of Intention (no. 97737) upon entering the United States, in the California, Federal Naturalization Records, 1843–1999.

Why? The straightforward answer might seem to be that the German-language umlaut wouldn't have served Oskar well during and after World War II. Ludwig, by contrast, might have thought he could benefit from retaining the umlaut because, as soon as he arrived in the United States, he was playing German roles as a character actor: he wanted to be recognized as a Germanophone. It might have been as simple as that.

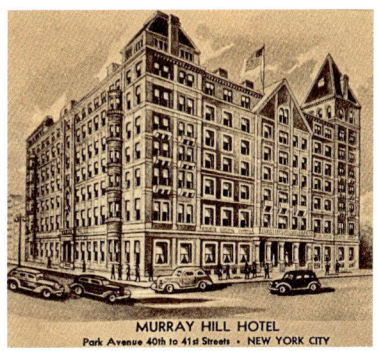

Oskar's initial destination in New York City as it looked at the time

But rarely in life are things so clear-cut. In fact, Oskar had been very occasionally using the *Stoessel* spelling in the 1920s and 1930s. In the 1920s, he had an autograph stamp that he used on a few etchings—a stamp with the spelling *Oskar Stoessel*. So he was already somewhat accustomed to eliminating the umlaut.

In uniformly adopting the spelling *Stoessel* during his American phase, Oskar was following the pattern of Ferdinand Schmutzer's friend Arnold Schoenberg, the composer, who upon arriving in the United States in 1933 dropped the umlaut and added the first *e* to his name. Schoenberg saw this as part of the "key to successful acculturation to America."[7] With Oskar, there is a fairly decisive demarcation: with few exceptions, his pre-1939

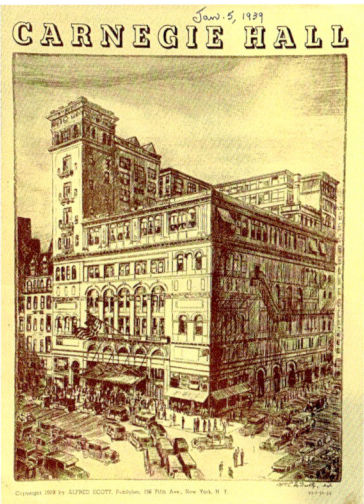

Carnegie Hall as it looked when Oskar arrived there. He lived in a studio in the tower to the left—at first on the tenth floor and later on the eleventh.

(European) etchings are signed *Stössel*, while his post-1939 (American) etchings consistently show the switch to *Stoessel*. At 61, he was adjusting to his adoptive home.

Oskar was also getting used to his new environment on Seventh Avenue between 56th and 57th Streets. Carnegie Hall studios were home to some of New York's most creative and colorful people. Between 1894 and 1986, hundreds of

---

7.   Sabine Feisst, *Schoenberg's New World* (Oxford Univ. Press, 2011), 113.

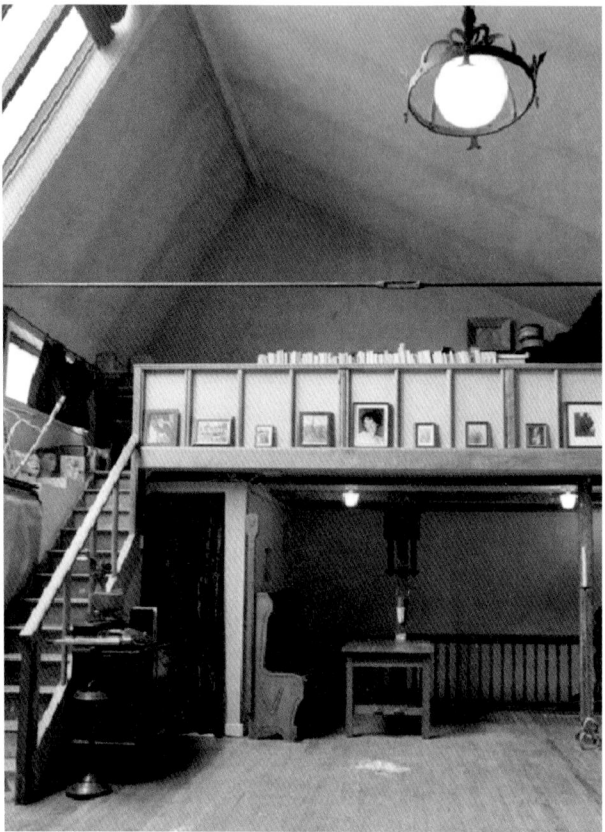

An artist studio in Carnegie Hall

important artists were among the more than 1,100 tenants who lived or worked in the 150 studios in the tower. Some stayed for as long as 50 years. Oskar would live there throughout the 1940s and 1950s. In 1940, Oskar paid a mere $900 a year for studio 1008. Two years later he upgraded to studio 1111, for which he paid $1,500 a year over the next 18 years. That studio had previously been occupied by the portrait painter Christine Marie Voss Lumsdon (1870–1937).

The artistic opulence of the place must have been unique in the world. Carnegie Hall was the zenith of Manhattan concert life. It was the premier venue for classical music, with its luxurious seating, its plush red curtains, and its impeccable acoustics. During the 1940s and 1950s, Carnegie Hall hosted many of the world's most famous conductors, soloists, and orchestras. Tickets cost as little as 25 cents. Oskar doubtless saw performers he had encountered years before in Vienna, and various friends of his teacher Ferdinand Schmutzer. In 1947, Oskar's near-contemporary, the Austrian-American pianist Arthur Schnabel, performed the complete Beethoven piano sonata cycle. And in 1952, the conductor Hermann Scherchen led the Vienna State Opera Orchestra there. When Oskar spoke with performers, as he doubtless occasionally did, they would have had many friends in common.

As an aficionado of music and the arts, Oskar was surely a regular at performances. In the great Hall adjoining his studio, he had the opportunity to see orchestras conducted by Arturo Toscanini and Leopold Stokowski; by the pianists Leonard Bernstein, Vladimir Horowitz, Sergei Rachmaninoff, Arthur Rubinstein, and Rudolf Serkin; by the violinists Isaac Stern and Yehudi Menuhin; and by countless others. If Oskar liked jazz, he would also have had the opportunity during these years to see performances by Louis Armstrong, Duke Ellington, Ella Fitzgerald, Benny Goodman, Billie Holiday, Lena Horne, Glenn Miller, and Frank Sinatra. In April 1946, Oskar surely attended the concert given by Maria Jeritza, whose portrait he had made in 1932 (see page 52).

Yet he didn't confine himself to Carnegie Hall. He seems to have painted at least one portrait of Maria Callas, the operatic soprano, long before she first appeared at the Hall in 1959. He may have seen her at the Metropolitan Opera, where she began performing in 1945.

Oskar's daily life amid the 150 Carnegie Hall studios teemed with activity. Painters, sculptors, writers, composers, musicians, and actors were living there. Oskar overlapped with the tenancies of Leonard Bernstein, Marlon Brando, Martha Graham, Marilyn Monroe, and Isamu Noguchi. Living there wasn't like being in a normal apartment. In the words of one former resident, "Life was lived in the hallways, with people clattering up and down the stairs, singing, rehearsing lines, doing their exercises, like one woman who would come out in her ballet clothes."[8]

Oskar's portrait of Maria Callas (putatively)

Despite the artistic excitement of his surroundings, and the enjoyment of social activities in the émigré community, Oskar found he couldn't wholly escape the age-old scourge of antisemitism.

---

8.   Billie Tsien, quoted in Michael Kimmelman, *The Intimate City: Walking New York* (Penguin, 2022), 78.

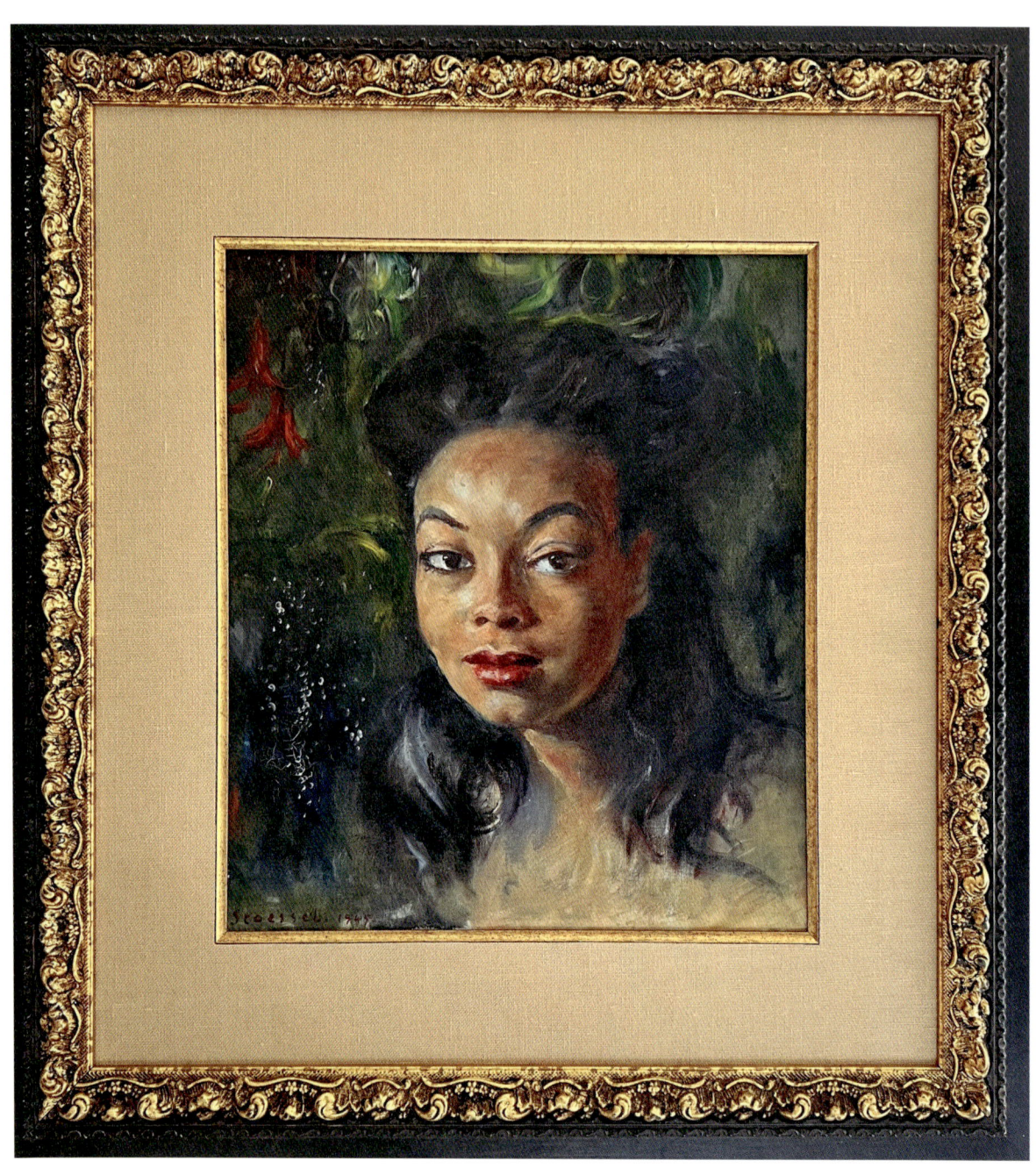

Oil portrait of a woman Oskar painted in New York, dated 1945. It might be the acclaimed jazz singer Billie Holiday (1915—1959), who at the age of 29 had made her Carnegie Hall debut the previous year. Oskar took the painting back to Vienna in 1960.

CHAPTER 12

American Prejudice and Indifference

Antisemitism—a thought pattern rife with fallacies, non sequiturs, illogical inconsistencies, and credulity toward elaborate smear campaigns—was not mild in the United States in the mid-20th century. Thought to be largely a byproduct of Christian teachings about the Crucifixion, it was exacerbated by American policies of isolationism after World War I and antipathy to immigration. Because of these policies, combined with the economic hardships of the Great Depression, American Christians often stereotyped Jewish immigrants as greedy, aggressive, and clannish. They were sometimes branded as left-wing anarchists or communists. A 1940 survey showed that 63% of Americans believed that Jewish immigrants had "objectionable qualities," such as "a lack of culture or good breeding."[1] Assimilation into American culture was difficult because the popular mind equated "American" with "Christian." No matter how highly cultured individual Jewish immigrants might be, their foreign birth and different religion made them "un-American" to the general population. Discrimination in employment was widespread.

The threat of war, and then its onset, put significant strains on the self-image of American Jews: although some reaffirmed their Jewish identity, many others accelerated their assimilation. Artists and the art world weren't immune from discrimination. The acclaimed artist Mark Rothko changed his surname in 1938 from Rothkovitz so that he could "disguise his Jewish identity," a change that seemed to hasten his success as an artist. The incentive came from J.B. Neumann, a prominent art dealer, who told the artist, "I have so many Jewish painters, why don't you make your name Rothko?" The implication was that "Rothkovitz" would

---

1. Andrea Pappas, "Mark Rothko and the Politics of Jewish Identity" (PhD diss., Univ. of S. Calif., 1997), 182.

be perceived as "just another Jewish painter" and that his gallery represented too many Jewish artists, which could damage his gallery's image and Neumann's professional reputation. This attitude appears to have been the norm.

World War II aggravated American antisemitism. When Oskar arrived before America's involvement, nearly 60% of Americans who responded to a poll agreed that "the persecution of Jews in Europe [was] their own fault."[2] Six years later, in 1945, most Americans still agreed with that proposition. In 1942, 15% of Americans thought that Jews were "a great threat to the United States," and 18% thought the same thing of the Germans. The "threats," people thought, were almost equal. By June 1944, during the height of the war, 24% said Jews were the greatest menace to the country—while only 9% said the Japanese and only 5% the Germans.[3]

Some 40% of American Jews lived in New York City, and they made up more than a quarter of the population of that city.[4] But Oskar could not escape antisemitism even there—or the Nazis. The German-American Bund, a Nazi-affiliated organization with between 20,000 and 25,000 members, was concentrated in the New York metropolitan area.[5] So was the far-right group known as the Christian Front. Members of these groups committed crimes throughout the metropolis but particularly focused on the Manhattan neighborhood of Washington Heights, where synagogues were desecrated and Jewish youngsters physically attacked. About 70% of the time, the police didn't bother investigating.[6]

Coverage of the Holocaust in mainstream American news media—even in New York City and Washington, D.C.—was poor. In newspapers that reported anything, it was typically placed where it would get little attention. Only Jewish

2.   Charles Herbert Stember et al., *Jews in the Mind of America* (Basic Books, 1966), 138.
3.   Leonard Dinnerstein, *Antisemitism in America* (Oxford Univ. Press, 1994), 131.
4.   See Stember et al., *Jews*, 54; Deborah Dash Moore, *At Home in America: Second Generation New York Jews* (Columbia Univ. Press, 1981), 21–23.
5.   See "Fascism in America: Like Communism, It Masquerades as Americanism," *Life*, Mar. 6, 1939, 57 (describing German-American Bund rally at Madison Square Garden attended by 17,000 people); Ronald H. Bayor, *Neighbors in Conflict: The Irish, Germans, Jews, and Italians of New York City, 1929–1941* (Johns Hopkins Univ. Press, 1978), 61.
6.   David S. Wyman, *The Abandonment of the Jews: America and the Holocaust 1941–1945* (Pantheon Books, 1984), 10.

newspapers, which Oskar very likely read, contained frequent and detailed accounts. Americans generally shrugged.

Politicians, of course, were acutely aware of popular prejudice. It stifled any courage they might have possessed. Consider the crisis that occurred in May 1939, at a time between Oskar's arrival in the United States and his brother Ludwig's. The private German liner *St. Louis* sailed from Hamburg to Cuba with 1,000 Jewish refugees aboard. While they were in transit, the Cuban government invalidated their visas. The ship then turned toward Florida, as various passengers cabled President Roosevelt and other administration officials, pleading for immigration visas to be issued on a humanitarian basis. A few brave Americans tried negotiating on their behalf. Roosevelt never responded, and the ship was denied access to an American port—as a result of which it had to turn back to Europe and cross the Atlantic again. In the end, 254 of its passengers perished in the Holocaust.[7]

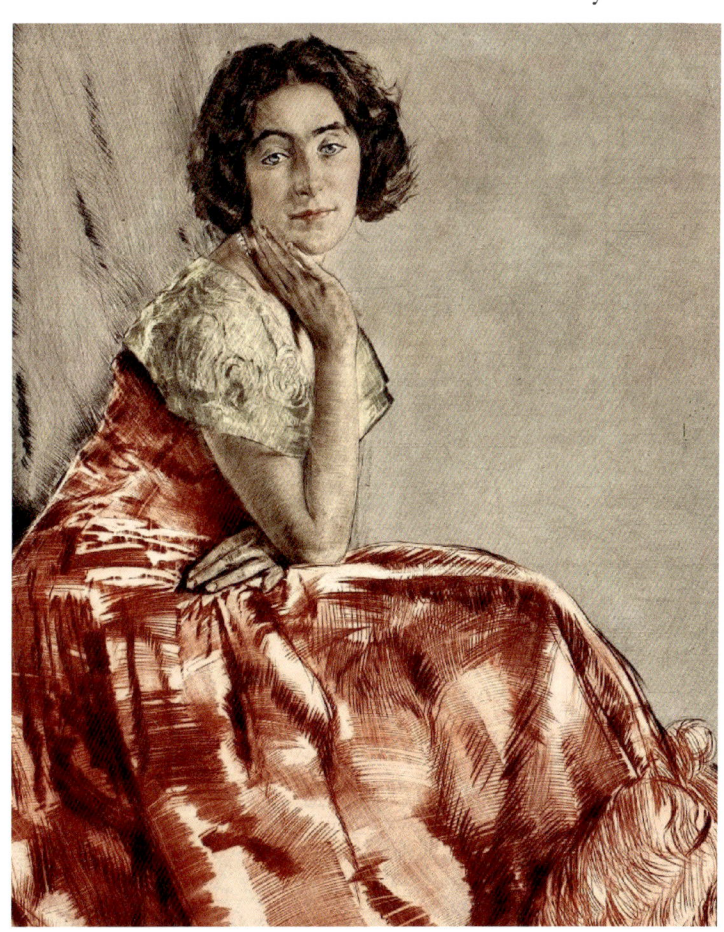

The lovely Helene Benisch, wife of a Viennese banker, portrayed in 1922 by Oskar in a moment of contemplation. Note her striking blue eyes, the pearls around her neck, and the flowing red dress. Just after the Anschluss, in late March 1938, Helene and her husband Franz sent their only child, Anne Marie, to England. Twelve years later, Anne Marie learned the fate of her parents: in 1941, Helene and Franz had been deported to Auschwitz and murdered there.

---

7.   Sarah A. Ogilvie and Scott Miller, *Refuge Denied: The St. Louis Passengers and the Holocaust* (Univ. of Wis. Press, 2006), 15.

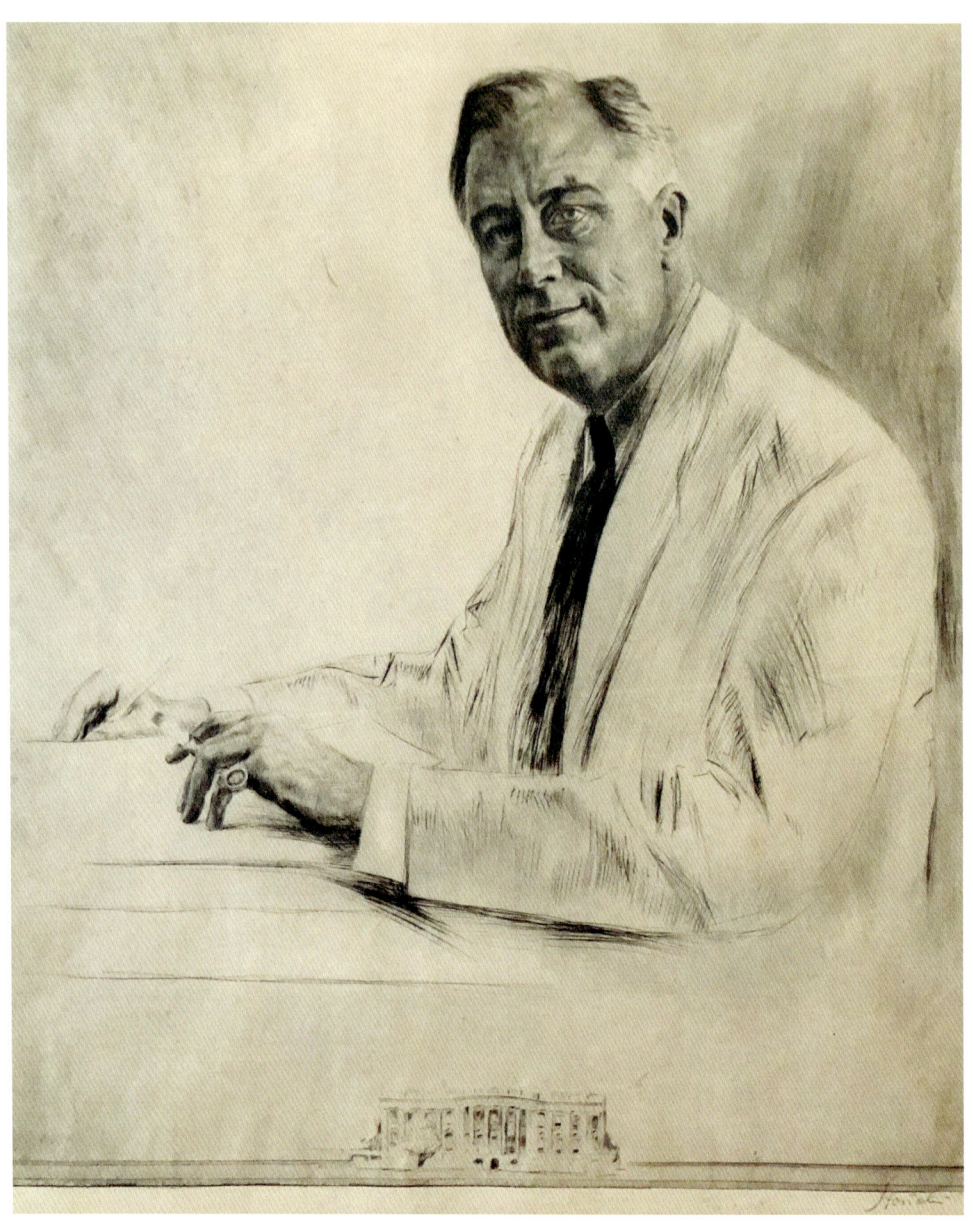

Oskar Stoessel's finished etching of President Franklin D. Roosevelt (1940), said to have been Eleanor Roosevelt's favorite portrait of her husband. Some versions, presumably earlier ones, lack the White House remarque at the bottom. Prominent in all versions is FDR's pinky ring, which he inherited from his father in 1900 and wore until he gave it to his son James at his fourth inaugural. The bloodstone center of the gold ring was engraved with the Roosevelt family crest; inside the band was the date 1853, the year in which FDR's parents married. Also featured in the etching is FDR's famous cigarette holder: it was white ceramic with an enamel tip.

CHAPTER 13

An Hour with the President

ALTHOUGH George Messersmith had been reassigned in 1937 to Washington, D.C., as assistant secretary of state—and would soon be reassigned to Havana, Cuba, as the American ambassador—he had maintained his interest in Oskar and his art. Hoping to help his talented émigré friend establish himself as an artist in America, Messersmith provided Oskar's entrée into the corridors of American power by writing letters to President Roosevelt, the justices of the Supreme Court, and others. Through his professional ties with Secretary of State Cordell Hull and Assistant Secretary of State Breckinridge Long, Messersmith persuaded them to sit for a Stoessel portrait. Probably no arm-twisting was required.

Messersmith's letter to the president reached the Oval Office in January 1939, a little more than a year before the president would sit for his portrait. Written on Messersmith's letterhead as assistant secretary of state, the letter reveals a great deal about both its author and its subject:

January 5, 1939.

Dear Mr. President:

You may recall that about a year ago I brought to your attention[1] an etching of myself made by Oskar Stössel who was the best known portrait etcher in Austria and who is known in Europe as one of the leading etchers in that field. He is, I believe, without question unexcelled at present in the field of portrait etching. Through the events in Austria he has been obliged to leave and is now in Paris. He will shortly be arriving in this country on an immigration visa.

He is a man of about 60 and his one desire is to secure a position in one of our schools where he may have an opportunity to pass on his art as a portrait etcher to

---

1. "Brought to your attention" is a severe understatement. Messersmith had sent to the president an inscribed etching of himself nearly three years before this letter was sent. See page 72.

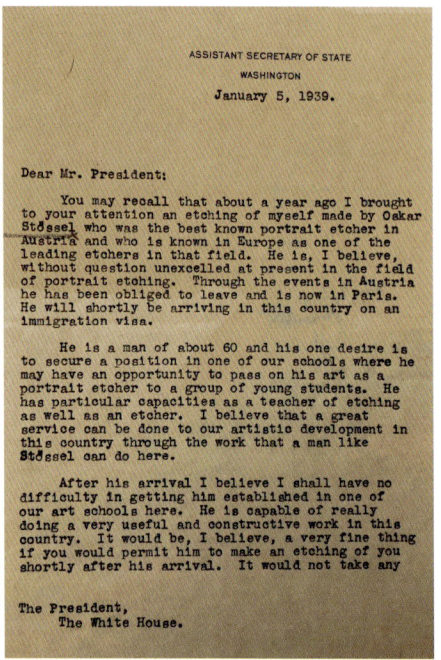

ASSISTANT SECRETARY OF STATE
WASHINGTON
January 5, 1939.

Dear Mr. President:

You may recall that about a year ago I brought to your attention an etching of myself made by Oskar Stössel who was the best known portrait etcher in Austria and who is known in Europe as one of the leading etchers in that field. He is, I believe, without question unexcelled at present in the field of portrait etching. Through the events in Austria he has been obliged to leave and is now in Paris. He will shortly be arriving in this country on an immigration visa.

He is a man of about 60 and his one desire is to secure a position in one of our schools where he may have an opportunity to pass on his art as a portrait etcher to a group of young students. He has particular capacities as a teacher of etching as well as an etcher. I believe that a great service can be done to our artistic development in this country through the work that a man like Stössel can do here.

After his arrival I believe I shall have no difficulty in getting him established in one of our art schools here. He is capable of really doing a very useful and constructive work in this country. It would be, I believe, a very fine thing if you would permit him to make an etching of you shortly after his arrival. It would not take any

The President,
   The White House.

of your time as he could do the necessary work while you are engaged at your desk and he would not need more than four or five sittings at the most. I am sure too that he would make a more acceptable and finer portrait etching of you than any that is now available.

I am sending with this letter a few etchings of his which I have which show his extraordinary capacities.

Believe me, with every good wish,

   Faithfully yours,

a group of young students. He has particular capacities as a teacher of etching as well as an etcher. I believe that a great service can be done to our artistic development in this country through the work that a man like Stössel can do here.

After his arrival I believe I shall have no difficulty in getting him established in one of our art schools here. He is capable of really doing very useful and constructive work in this country. It would be, I believe, a very fine thing if you would permit him to make an etching of you shortly after his arrival. It would not take any of your time as he could do the necessary work while you are engaged at your desk and he would not need more than four or five sittings at the most. I am sure too that he would make a more acceptable and finer portrait etching of you than any that is now available.

I am sending with this letter a few etchings of his which I have which show his extraordinary capacities.

Believe me, with every good wish,
   Faithfully yours,
   G.S. Messersmith[2]

We don't know what sample etchings Messersmith enclosed. Perhaps he had collected them, or perhaps he had borrowed them from Oskar. Unsurprisingly, they seem to have been returned once they had served their purpose of convincing the president of Oskar's worthiness.

Oskar's red-letter day would come on Monday, January 29, 1940, when President Roosevelt sat for his portrait. In retrospect, it all seems most unlikely: within 11 months of reaching American shores, a European refugee—an asylum-seeker—

---

2. Assistant Secretary of State George S. Messersmith to President Franklin Delano Roosevelt, Jan. 5, 1939, Roosevelt Papers, Franklin D. Roosevelt Presidential Library and Museum, Hyde Park, New York.

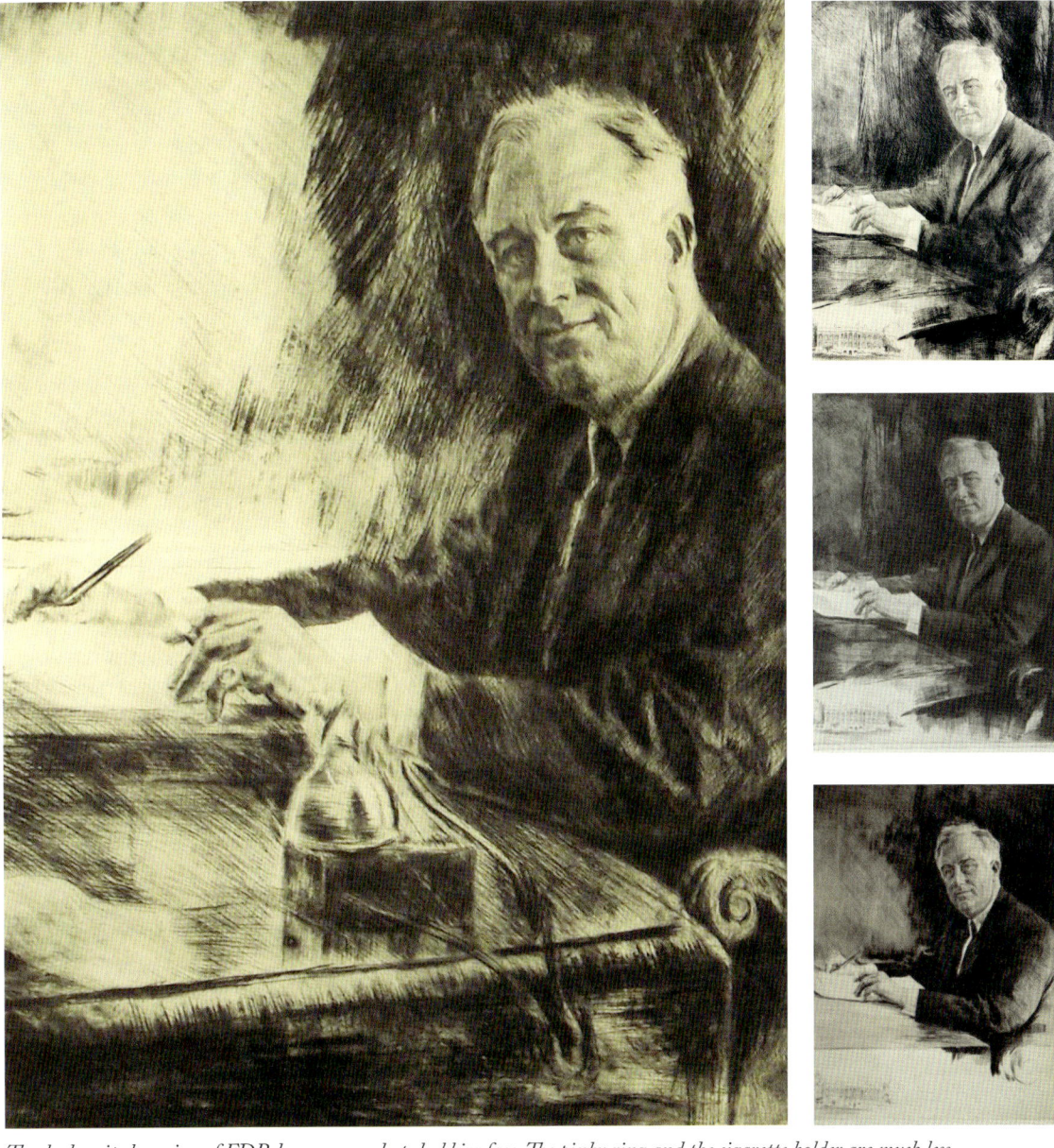

The dark-suited version of FDR has a somewhat chubbier face. The pinky ring and the cigarette holder are much less prominent in these versions. Notice the differences in the materials depicted on the desktop (especially the telephone in the foreground of the larger photo) as well as the differing backgrounds. The version in the FDR Presidential Library bears not only Stoessel's signature (as is usual) but also a pencil notation on the lower left corner of the mat: "Oskar Stoessel : Original dry-point. Edition limited to 100 impressions."

spent an hour in the Oval Office. The event has a remarkable backstory that shows just how difficult it was to procure a sitting of the country's chief executive.

In the first half of the 20th century, Presidents were fairly deluged with artists' requests to make portraits. Among the voluminous papers housed at the Franklin D. Roosevelt Presidential Library and Museum in Hyde Park, New York, are three sizable archival boxes labeled "Requests for President to Sit for Portrait." Throughout the 1930s and 1940s, a steady stream of requests came to the White House, seeking the opportunity to paint, draw, or sculpt an image of the president. An early one, dating from 1933, prompted a reply from FDR with what had become fairly standard language denying access: "My time is so fully taken up . . . that it would not be possible to arrange for sittings for a portrait."[3] Most requests prompted such a response.

Of course, Messersmith's intervention on Oskar's behalf made his case different. Still, though, the arrangements were no easy matter—and in the end, Oskar would end up piggybacking on a sitting arranged for another artist: Esteban Valderrama of Cuba.[4] In June 1939, the Cuban Embassy began communicating with the White House about whether Valderrama might paint a portrait to be hung in the Cuban Senate, which had recently passed a resolution naming President Roosevelt "Eminent Son of America."[5] The Chief of Staff, Brigadier General Edwin ("Pa") Watson, commented internally that "the President did not have time to sit for a portrait."[6] But the Cuban Embassy persisted, renewing its efforts the following December: Dr. Jose T. Barón, chargé d'affaires at the Em-

---

3.   FDR to Samuel Salko of Philadelphia, Mar. 28, 1933, official file 116, box 1, Franklin D. Roosevelt Presidential Library and Museum. Salko was not an insignificant artist: the Smithsonian's Archives of American Art has a collection of the Samuel Salko papers.

4.   Esteban Valderrama y Peña (1892–1964) was a native Cuban who studied at art academies in Spain and France. Unlike Stoessel, Valderrama does not have an entry in the 14-volume *Benezit Dictionary of Artists* (Gründ, 2006). His finished FDR portrait was featured on Cuban postcards and Cuban stamps in 1947.

5.   Department of State, Division of Protocol, to FDR, memo, June 26, 1939, official file 116, box 2, Franklin D. Roosevelt Presidential Library and Museum.

6.   State Department, memo of meeting between Henry C. Spruks of the Division of Protocol and Dr. Jose T. Barón, Counselor of the Cuban Embassy, Dec. 5, 1939, Franklin D. Roosevelt Presidential Library and Museum, official file 116, box 2 (recounting June statement of Watson).

bassy, was dispatched to the State Department, where Henry C. Spruks told him that the president "is frightfully busy because of the pressure of official business."[7] Dr. Barón countered that "although it was desired to have the portrait in oil, if the President's time is limited the portrait could be done in pastel which could be done very quickly."[8] He added that the daughters of Governor James Cox of Ohio—a prominent Democrat who had been Roosevelt's presidential running mate in 1920—had "recommended this artist to Mrs. Roosevelt."[9]

The matter was immediately treated as a diplomatic one, and the assistant secretary of state assigned to handle the matter in the Division of Protocol at the State Department was none other than George Messersmith, to whom Henry Spruks reported. On December 5, 1939, Messersmith wrote a letter to General Watson, asking to "know the President's wishes in the matter."[10] General Watson responded not to Messersmith but to the chief of protocol, G. T. Summerlin: "The President says okay if we can arrange it so that this man will not bother him in making the portrait. You and I will have to go into this thing a little further between us."[11]

What followed was a letter directly to the president from the Cuban ambassador, Dr. Pedro Martinez Fraga—whose formal title was Ambassador Extraordinary and Plenipotentiary. He pressed Valderrama's claim, explaining that the Senate of Cuba had passed a resolution to place an oil portrait of FDR in the Senate Building.[12] He reminded the president that an oral request had been made the previous June but that "no reply was received," and "the Embassy has reiterated its previous request."[13] He then closed: "I fully realize that the present tremendous pressure of work would make it very difficult to give any of your

---

7. Memo of meeting between Spruks and Barón.
8. Memo of meeting between Spruks and Barón.
9. Memo of meeting between Spruks and Barón.
10. Messersmith to Edwin Watson, memo, Dec. 5, 1939, official file 116, box 2, Franklin D. Roosevelt Presidential Library and Museum.
11. Watson to G. T. Summerlin, typed letter, Dec. 8, 1939, official file 116, box 2, Franklin D. Roosevelt Presidential Library and Museum.
12. Dr. Pedro Martinez Fraga to FDR, typed letter, Dec. 15, 1939, official file 116, box 2, Franklin D. Roosevelt Presidential Library and Museum.
13. Fraga to FDR, Dec. 15, 1939.

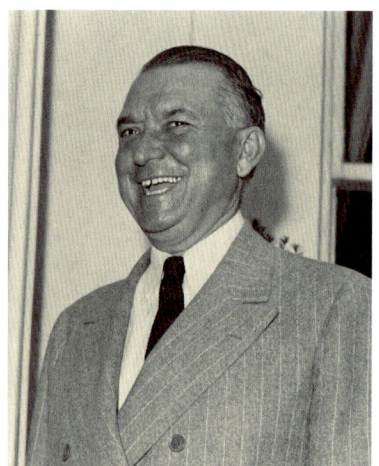

General Edwin "Pa" Watson

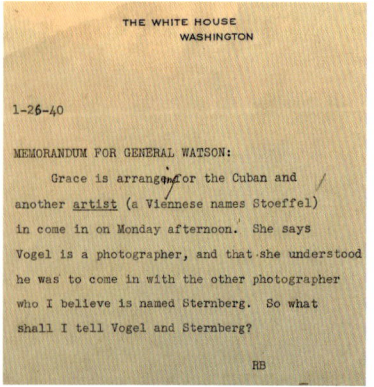

valuable time to matters of this kind, but in order that I may be able to inform the President of the Cuban Senate of this matter, I am taking the liberty of requesting the kindness of your reply as to whether such sittings could be arranged."[14]

On December 19, 1939, four days after receiving the ambassador's letter, President Roosevelt himself prepared a memo for General Watson: "Will you arrange for him [Valderrama] to come in after the holidays and tell him that I cannot give him any formal sittings? He will have to work while I dictate mail and see visitors. Toward the end I will give him one sitting of a half hour sitting absolutely quiet."[15] Note that the final sentence retreats from the initial statement that Valderrama would have no formal sittings.

In the end, it took no fewer than 17 memos and letters back and forth, and internally within the State Department and the White House, to arrange the time for Valderrama's sitting. The Cuban Embassy asked for photographs in advance of the sitting.[16] General Watson obliged, sending eight and asking that they be returned when Valderrama's work was finished.[17] The final memo in the file, dated January 26, 1940—just three days before the sitting was to occur—notes that "Grace [Tully, private secretary to FDR,] is arranging for the Cuban and another artist (a Viennese named Stoeffel) to come

14. Fraga to FDR, Dec. 15, 1939.

15. FDR to Watson, typed White House memo, Dec. 19, 1939, official file 116, box 2, Franklin D. Roosevelt Presidential Library and Museum.

16. Senor Don Carlos Tornes, Cuban Embassy, to Watson, typed letter, Jan. 12, 1940, official file 116, box 2, Franklin D. Roosevelt Presidential Library and Museum.

17. Watson to Tornes, typed letter, Jan. 13, 1940, official file 116, box 2, Franklin D. Roosevelt Presidential Library and Museum.

in on Monday afternoon."[18] The misspelling doubtless arose from something Os-kar had signed with his old-fashioned long esses (*s*'s), which looked like efs (*f*'s). We can infer that George Messersmith, having witnessed the many hurdles to be overcome in arranging a sitting, intervened on Oskar's behalf and suggested that the two artists could work simultaneously without disturbing the president.

When the afternoon of the appointment came, President Roosevelt was deal-ing with grave matters. His calendar shows that shortly before the scheduled sit-ting, Winston Churchill—who was then serving as first lord of the admiralty—had sent the president a telegram[19] giving an assurance that the president had requested: Churchill had ordered that no American ship would, in any circum-stances, be diverted into the combat zone around the British Islands.[20] He would soon forswear himself, though, insisting that the United States must ensure that its ships contained no objectionable cargo—and that suspect ships might be sub-ject to diversion. Roosevelt responded that "the benefits [to the U.K.] of a block-ade hardly offset the development of anti-British feelings in America."[21] U.S. involvement in the war loomed. As Hitler's naval forces threatened both English and American shipping, a refugee from Hitler's invasion of Austria was about to enter the Oval Office.

The appointed time arrived. Uncannily, a newspaper account of the beginning of the sitting appeared—doubtless with the cooperation of the White House. A popular syndicated column, "The Washington Merry-Go-Round," by journal-ists Drew Pearson and Robert Allen, ran a piece that appeared in dozens if not hundreds of American newspapers. Here's what happened just outside the Oval Office:

PAINTING ROOSEVELT

A Cuban artist sat in a White House anteroom, waiting for his appointment to see the president. He was animated and eager. The president was to sit for a

18. R.B. (staffer) to Watson, typed White House memo, Jan. 26, 1940, official file 116, box 2, Franklin D. Roosevelt Presidential Library and Museum.

19. FDR's calendar for Jan. 29, 1940, Franklin D. Roosevelt Presidential Library and Museum.

20. Warren F. Kimball, ed., *Churchill and Roosevelt: The Complete Correspondence* (Princeton Univ. Press, 2016), 1:33.

21. Kimball, 1:33.

portrait, and the portrait would be placed in the senate chamber in Havana. It was the opportunity of a lifetime.

Across the room sat another man. He too was waiting eagerly.

Presently General Watson, presidential secretary, entered the room. "All right," he said, "are you men ready? Now which one is the Cuban?"

Dr. Esteban Valderrama rose. Watson greeted him and turned to the other man. "And you are Dr. . . . ?" Up rose Oscar [sic] Stoessel of Vienna, presenting his card.

"All right," said Watson, "now you gentlemen can have an hour with the president. He'll be working at his desk, and you mustn't ask any questions. Just go ahead with your drawing, and make the most of it."

The two men stared at each other. Each had been given an appointment separately, each had supposed he would be alone with the president.

"What is your medium?" said Stoessel to Valderrama.

"I work in oil," said the Cuban. "And you?"

"Etching," said the Viennese.

"Come along," interposed Watson. "The president is ready."

So the two artists shook hands, picked up their portfolios, and marched into the president's office together.[22]

This vignette offers some insights into the making of the famous FDR portrait. One is that Oskar had a full hour for FDR's first sitting. (Although the appointment on the president's calendar was from 3:00 to 3:30 p.m., the artists were given an hour—if the newspaper report is to be trusted.) Another is that perhaps no words passed between Roosevelt and Oskar during the sitting. Valderrama completed his portrait in 1940; it was displayed in Cuba's Senate

A page from the president's 1940 appointments calendar. Note that the next appointment is with the surgeon general.

---

22. Drew Pearson and Robert Allen, "The Washington Merry-Go-Round," *Santa Fe New Mexican*, Feb. 1, 1940, 4; *Star Press* (Muncie, Ind.), Feb. 1, 1940, 4; and many others.

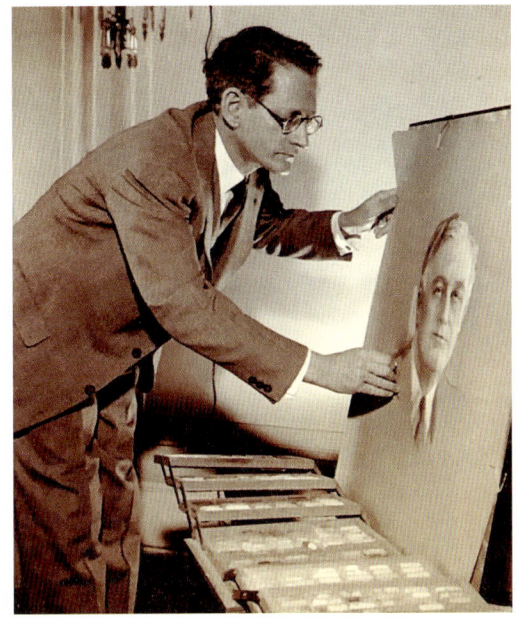

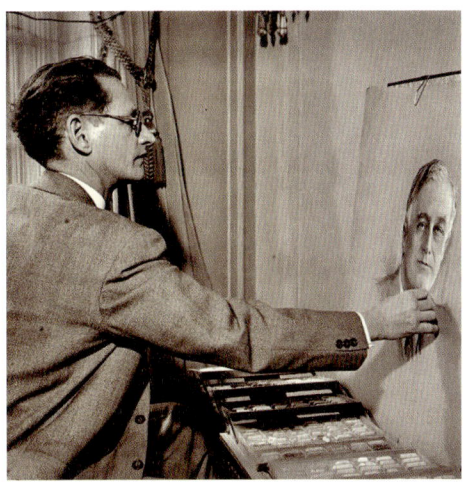

Esteban Valderrama puts the finishing touches on his FDR portrait, which was begun in the Oval Office at the same time as Oskar's. The two artists were instructed that they'd have an hour with the president but not to speak unless spoken to.

Presidency Hall in Havana until at least 1952.[23] Its whereabouts since then are unknown.

The same cannot be said of Oskar's portrait of President Roosevelt. We know that there are two versions: a relatively rare one with Roosevelt in a black suit (in which he looks heavier-set, in face as well as in body); and one with Roosevelt in a white suit (in which he looks leaner and handsomer). The white-suited version became the official version, of which there are many prints. Some of these, probably those of later pressings, have a miniature White House as a remarque at the bottom center. All the known black-suited versions depict the White House at the bottom left.

We also know that Eleanor Roosevelt felt a strong attachment to Oskar's white-suited etching of her husband. In April 1956, when Oskar's portrait was used as a magazine cover, Eleanor used her daily "My Day" newspaper column to comment on it: "*The Nation* magazine has used on its cover one of my favorite etchings of my husband, done by Oskar Stoessel, a Viennese who fled Austria after the Anschluss. Mr. Messersmith gave him a letter to my husband, who sat

---

23. See *La Pintura y Escultura en Cuba* (Los Talleres Tipográficos, 1952), 90–92.

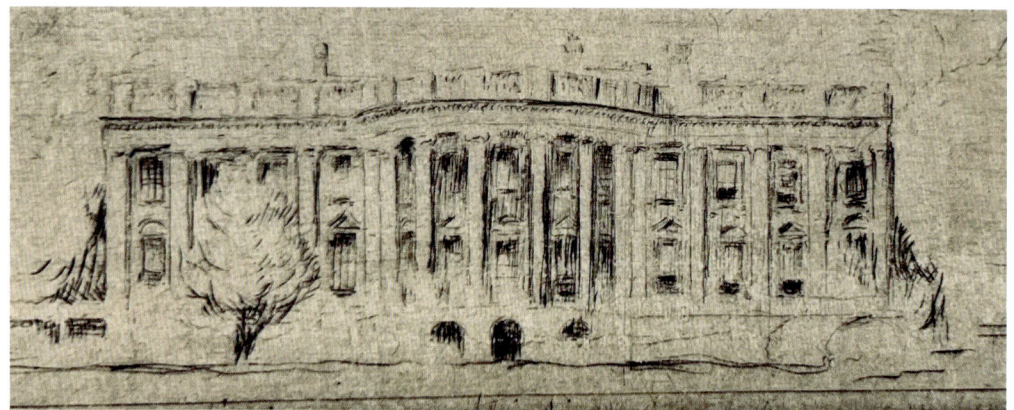

Oskar used this scene as his remarque at the base of President Roosevelt's portrait. It's the back of the White House as viewed from the South Lawn.

for this portrait in 1940."[24] This might suggest that the former First Lady was quite familiar with Oskar, with Messersmith's suggestion on his behalf, and with the making of the portrait. But the truth is otherwise. Correspondence from the managing editor of *The Nation* magazine leading up to the issue featuring Oskar's portrait as cover art shows that neither Mrs. Roosevelt nor her secretary knew "anything about the artist."[25] The managing editor, when writing to the FDR Library in 1956, couldn't even discern the artist's name: "The original bears a scrawl which reads something like Arthur Howard or Secord. The handwriting is almost illegible."[26] But he did know that "an original is now hanging in Mrs. Roosevelt's bedroom in her New York apartment."[27]

24. Eleanor Roosevelt, "My Day," Apr. 5, 1956, distributed by United Feature Syndicate (printed in dozens if not hundreds of newspapers). Cf. *N.Y. Times*, Apr. 5, 1947, 4 (advertisement for the weekend edition of a newspaper called *PM*: "Mrs. Roosevelt's Favorite Sketch of F.D.R.: Above her desk in the study of Mrs. Roosevelt's apartment hangs a hitherto unpublished etching of F.D.R. Only 60 prints of this famous etching were made from the original plate by Oskar Stoessel. NOW—On a full page in the picture News section of PM's week-end edition, this etching is published for the first time.").

25. Victor H. Bernstein to FDR Library, typed letter, Mar. 5, 1956, Franklin D. Roosevelt Presidential Library and Museum).

26. Bernstein to FDR Library, Mar. 5, 1956.

27. Bernstein to FDR Library, Mar. 5, 1956.

After Mrs. Roosevelt's death in 1962, the world learned that the Stoessel etching was one of the few pieces of art she specifically bequeathed in her will. She left it to her personal doctor, A. David Gurewitsch, with whom she had had a close platonic relationship in her later years.[28] She had said of him: "I loved him as I . . . never loved anyone else."[29]

In both its versions, the Roosevelt portrait shows something about the sitter that may be historically important. There is a pigmented lesion over the president's left eyebrow. First seen in the early 1920s, it continued to grow and darken through January 1940. The height of its darkening was about the time of this portrait. In fact, four days before Roosevelt's sitting with Oskar, the physician to the president privately acknowledged the lesion in a letter to a concerned cancer specialist: "The pigmented area above the President's eye is very superficial and has never shown any sign of an inflammatory nature."[30] Soon it was covered up cosmetically and treated surgically. By December 1940, it was a mere shadow, and by the time of Pearl Harbor (December 7, 1941), it was essentially gone. A distinguished neurologist has credibly theorized that Roosevelt ended up dying in April 1945 from a hemorrhage resulting from a metastasis of the lesion.[31]

Mrs. Roosevelt's largest single cash bequest was to her long-time physician, Dr. a. David Gurewitsch of New York. She left him $10,000 "in gratitude for his devoted care for which he would not accept compensation during my lifetime." She also gave Dr. Gurewitsch an etching of her late husband by Oskar Stossel.

"Mrs. Roosevelt Left Mementos to Many," New York Times, *Nov. 16, 1962, 1*

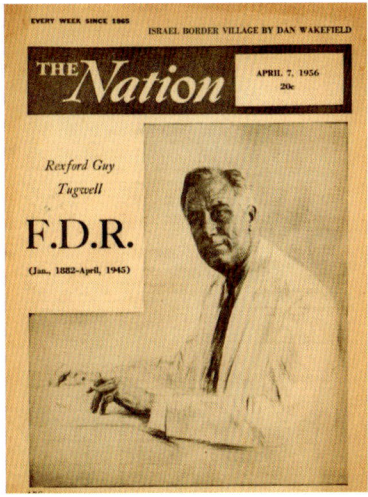

Front cover of The Nation *(Apr. 7, 1956)*

28. "Many Persons Receive Mrs. FDR's Mementoes," *Free Lance-Star* (Fredericksburg, Va.), Nov. 17, 1962, 3 ("Dr. Gurewitsch also was left an etching of President Roosevelt by Oskar Stoessel."). See A. David Gurewitsch, *Eleanor Roosevelt: Her Day* (Quadrangle, 1974).

29. Edna P. Gurewitsch, *Kindred Souls: The Friendship of Eleanor Roosevelt and David Gurewitsch* (St. Martin's, 2002) (in which Geoffrey C. Ward, in the introduction, recounts "the complicated relationship between Mrs. Roosevelt and the man [Dr. Gurewitsch], 18 years her junior, whom she herself said she loved 'as I . . . have never loved anyone else'").

30. Dr. Ross McIntire to Dr. Ruben Peterson, Jan. 25, 1940 (quoted in Steven Lomazow MD, *FDR Unmasked: 73 Years of Medical Cover-ups That Rewrote History* [Kugler Pubs., 2023], 149).

31. See Steven Lomazow MD and Eric Fettmann, *FDR's Deadly Secret* (PublicAffairs, 2010), x.

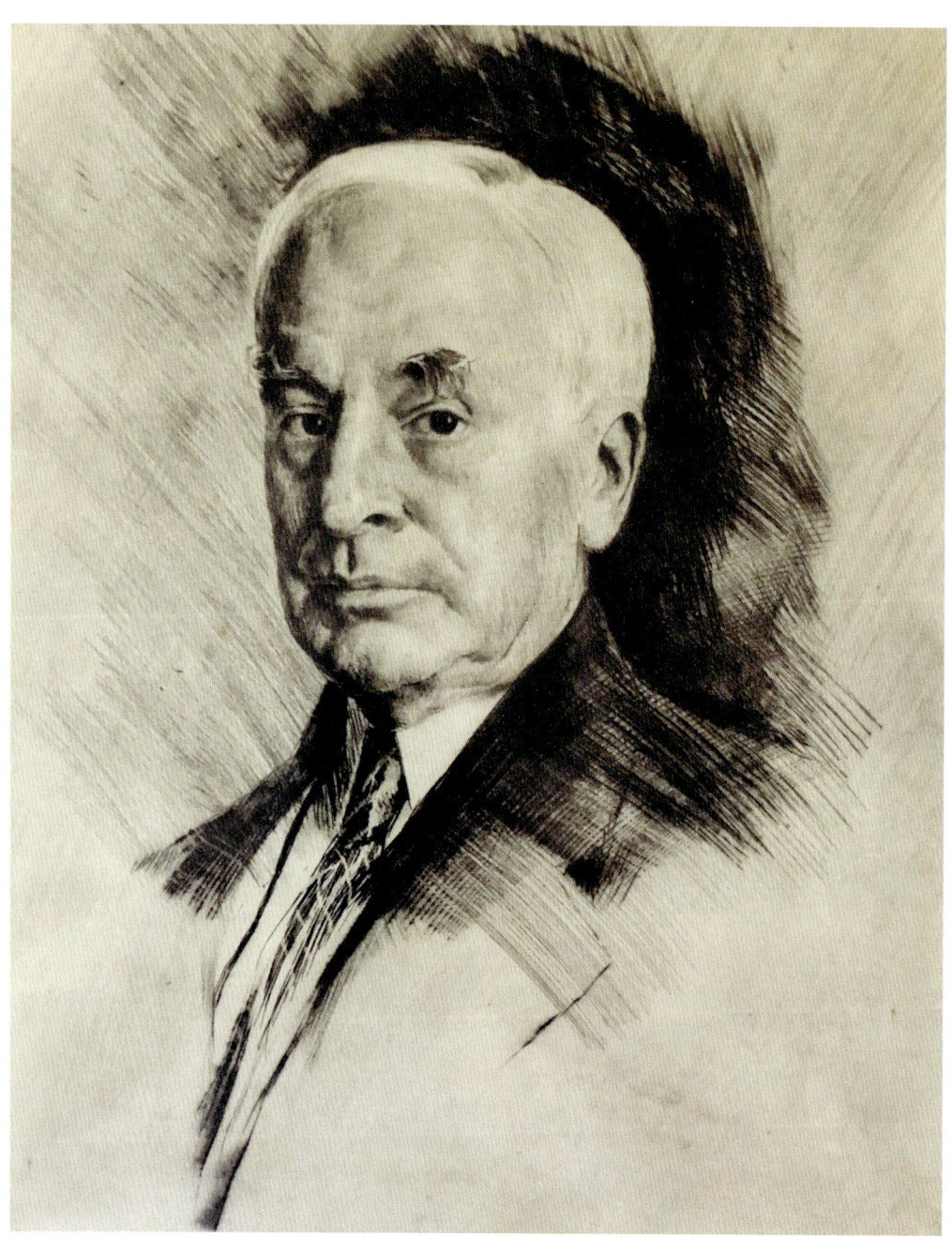

Oskar's etching of Secretary of State Cordell Hull (ca. 1940)

CHAPTER 14

Hull's Callous State Department

ABOUT the same time as Oskar made the Roosevelt portraits, he also made one of Secretary of State Cordell Hull (opposite)—undoubtedly in Hull's office at the Department of State. A lifelong Democrat from Tennessee, Hull served in the U.S. House of Representatives from 1906 to 1920, when he lost in a Republican landslide. He then became head of the Democratic National Committee, returning to Congress in 1922 and then running (unsuccessfully) for Vice President alongside Al Smith on the 1928 Democratic ticket, with Franklin Delano Roosevelt's support. After Hull supported Roosevelt in the 1932 election, the new President rewarded him with the post of secretary of state. He held that position for 11 years and became the longest-serving secretary of state in U.S. history.

Although Hull was said to have an "attractive appearance," this apparently masked several deficiencies: lack of managerial experience, hypersensitivity to criticism, indecisiveness, fear of insubordination among his ranks, and pettiness.[1] This tetchiness leaps off the page in Oskar's portrait of Hull.

Secretary Hull's mother, raised an Episcopalian, had a Jewish father. Hull went to great lengths during his political career "to forestall the potentially harmful effects of her background on his career."[2] He steadfastly "refused to address Jewish issues."[3] In his memoirs, written mostly by a ghostwriter but reviewed closely by Hull, he "avoided his mother's Jewish ancestry and even applauded his department's role in the Holocaust."[4]

---

1. *American National Biography* (1999), "Hull, Cordell [2 Oct. 1871–23 July 1955]."
2. "Hull, Cordell."
3. "Hull, Cordell."
4. "Hull, Cordell."

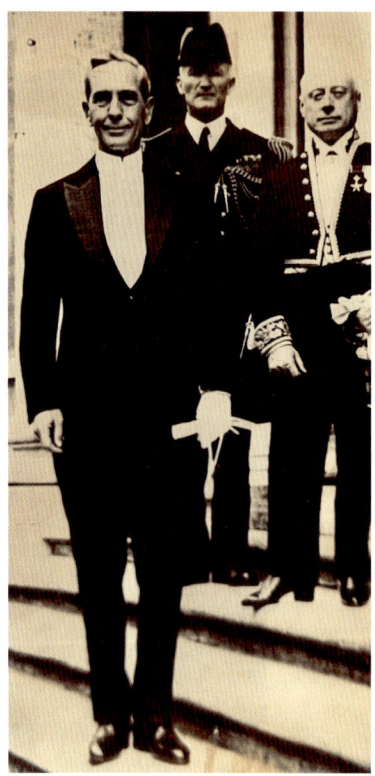

Breckinridge Long as U.S. ambassador to Italy (1933)

Hull knew in 1933 that the Nazis considered someone with a Jewish grandfather "non-Aryan."[5] He knew that German Jews were being brutally persecuted. Yet he continually called descriptions of the Nazis' actions "exaggerated," and he opposed American protests against the Nazis on grounds that these concerned internal matters for Germany. Hull played an important role in appeasing and emboldening Hitler.[6] In his self-aggrandizing memoirs, Hull applauded his department's controversial role in severely limiting the number of Jewish refugees who were allowed into the United States.

Oskar also etched a portrait of the assistant secretary of state, Breckinridge Long, who would later be seen as the American official more responsible than any other for preventing Jewish refugees from finding refuge in the United States. Long's actions resulted in thousands of European Jews' being sent to the death camps. His private diary contained a February 1938 entry in which he praised Hitler's *Mein Kampf* as being "eloquent in opposition to Jewry and to Jews as exponents of Communism and chaos." Many modern Holocaust scholars "hold Long and his associates responsible for preventing European Jews from finding safe haven in the United States during their time of gravest peril."[7]

---

5.   Arthur D. Morse, *While Six Million Died: A Chronicle of American Apathy* (Random House, 1968), 113.

6.   Morse, 113.

7.   *American National Biography* (1999), "Long, Breckinridge [16 May 1881–26 Sept. 1958]." See also Shlomo Shafir, "George S. Messersmith: An Anti-Nazi Diplomat's View of the German–Jewish Crisis," *Jewish Social Studs.* 35 (1973): 32 (stating that "the rescue of many thousands of Jewish refugees was prevented [by] the antisemitic, nativist, and deep-seated conservative prejudices of Breckinridge Long").

But when Oskar made Long's portrait, neither he nor anyone else outside the Roosevelt administration knew about Long's actions or proclivities. In a 1938 diary entry, Long wrote: "My estimate of Hitler as a man rises with the reading of his book." This was the man whom Cordell Hull had put in charge of all matters relating to European Jews. More than anyone else, he foreclosed the United States as a safe haven for Jews in their time of most imminent danger. Yet perhaps from vanity, he willingly posed for Oskar and may well have been personally responsible for approving his visa.

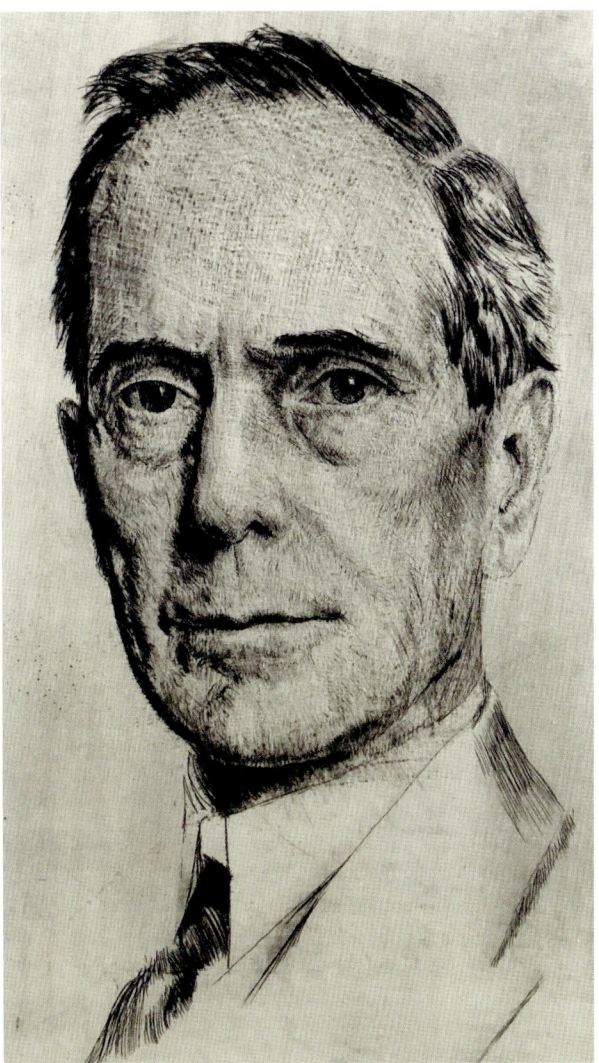

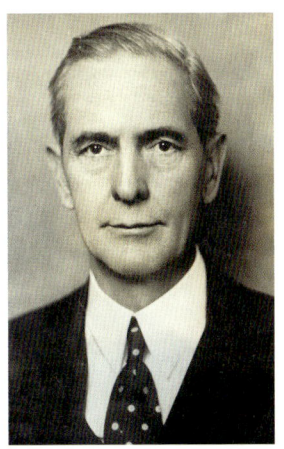

Oskar's portrait of Breckinridge Long (ca. 1940). The assistant secretary of state is thought to be more directly responsible than any other American official for low quotas on the number of Jewish refugees who could enter the United States before and during World War II.
LEFT: *Long as he appeared in 1933, when he was named American ambassador to Italy*

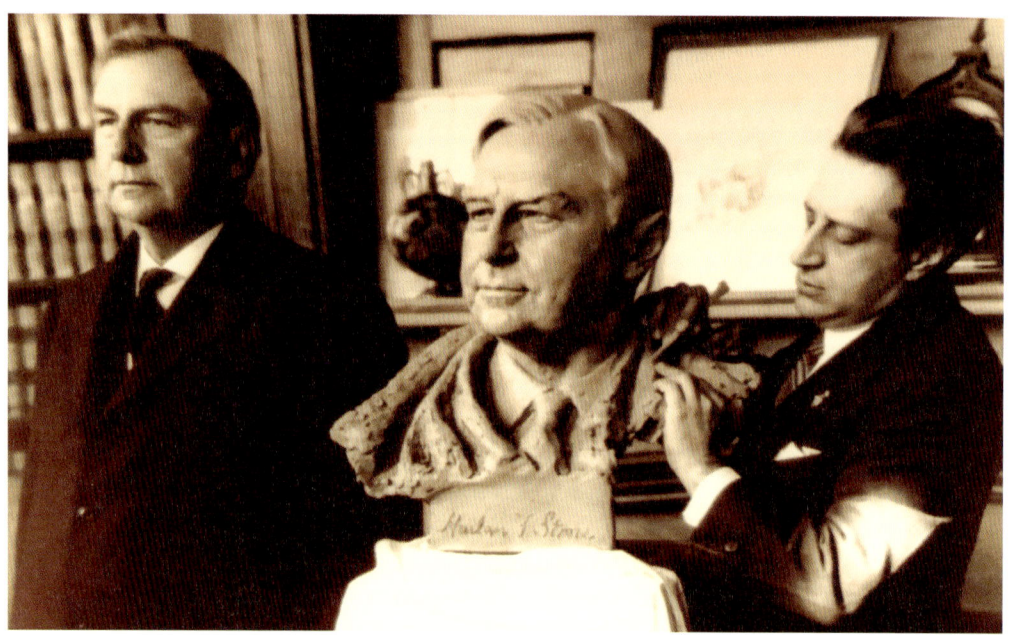

Justice Stone was no stranger to portraiture. Here he stands in March 1930 as the noted Italian sculptor Edgardo Simone (1890—1948) puts finishing touches on a bust.

CHAPTER 15

All Rise for the Supreme Court

THE Roosevelt portrait was undoubtedly Oskar Stoessel's most famous etching. But how does one transition from refugee to presidential portraitist? The letter from Messersmith to Roosevelt provides only part of the answer. There also seem to have been in-person conversations with the president. A hint of what Messersmith might have said to Roosevelt can be found in correspondence with Supreme Court Justice William O. Douglas. In a persuasive letter dated April 26, 1940, Messersmith expressed fervent support for Oskar:

26 April 1940

My dear Friend:

You may recall that before I left Washington, I mentioned to you one evening[1] my friend, Dr. Oscar [sic] Stoessel, the well-known Austrian etcher who is now living in the United States. Dr. Stoessel was not only the best known etcher in Austria, but I think I am right in saying that he was considered the leading portrait etcher in Europe. I knew him very well in Austria and found him a delightful person, as well as a great artist. He is well known to collectors in the United States as he was the principal authority on the old etchings in the Albertina Museum in Vienna, which had, as you may know, the finest collections of old etchings in existence.

As a result of events in Austria, Dr. Stoessel was obliged to leave and he has established himself in the United States. I encouraged him in coming to our country, as I felt sure that he would be able to pass on his art to some young people there. I have been endeavoring to try to get him placed in one of our art schools in the United States but, so far, have not had any success. Dr. Stoessel is not himself interested in any considerable income because he has some modest

---

1. The event seems to have been a dinner at the house of Barney Nover (1899–1973), who was a columnist and editorial writer for the *Washington Post* from 1936 to 1947.

means and is a real artist in this respect. His great desire is to pass on his art to a group of young people in our country and it would, of course, be a very fine contribution to our artistic life.

In the meantime, he is beginning to make some etchings and he has recently made one of the President and of Secretary Hull. Both of them, I understand, are excellent. It has occurred to me that it would be a really fine thing to have, through him, etchings of the members of the Supreme Court. The etchings which have been made of some high officials of our Government in the past have usually been the work of etchers from the Bureau of Engraving and, while excellent in some ways, most of these did not have any artistic merit. I am convinced that there are many people in our country who would be delighted if first-class etchings of the members of the Court were available and I have, therefore, encouraged Dr. Stoessel to see what he can do in this direction. I took the liberty of speaking to Justice Stone and Justice Frankfurter, and I have recently written to Dr. Stoessel not to hesitate to get in touch with you. I am sure that you will find that he is not interested in this matter from any point of view of pecuniary gain, and I believe if you have seen some of his etchings you will wish one from his hand of yourself. I know, of course, that such a modest person as yourself is not much interested in this sort of thing from a personal point of view, but I am sure that if Mrs. Douglas sees any of the specimens of Dr. Stoessel's work she will not give you any rest until you have sat for him.

I am writing you so fully about this as I took the liberty of suggesting to Dr. Stoessel not to hesitate to get in touch with you. . . .

My wife joins in very good wishes to you and Mrs. Douglas.

Cordially and faithfully yours,

George Messersmith[2]

Less than two weeks later came Justice Douglas's reply: "I have been extremely interested in [Stoessel's] work ever since you mentioned him to me one night out at Barney Nover's before you left for Cuba. I should be delighted to see Dr. Stoessel and to sit for him. I think it would be a splendid idea if he could get at least a majority of the Court."[3]

---

2. George S. Messersmith to Justice William O. Douglas, Apr. 26, 1940, Douglas Papers, Library of Congress.
3. Douglas to Messersmith, May 7, 1940, Douglas Papers, Library of Congress.

Meanwhile, in March 1940, Oskar had already met with Justice Harlan Fiske Stone at the Supreme Court.[4] (The precise impetus for that first visit is unknown—apart from the certainty that it involved Messersmith.) Justice Stone's acquaintances knew him as an art connoisseur who was particularly "interested in fine etchings, to which he was introduced as a law student."[5] In 1931, Stone had written to a friend: "The intellectual appeal of the etcher's art is emphasized more than in other forms, and . . . good examples of it are within reach of most devotees."[6] Stone particularly admired the etchings of Charles A. Platt (1861–1933),[7] and he owned two of them.[8] "Even after etchings and engravings of eminent lawyers covered the walls of his huge library-study," wrote his biographer, "he was constantly on the alert for more."[9]

In short, Justice Stone was primed to befriend Oskar Stoessel, who had already set up residence in New York at Carnegie Hall, in studio 1008. In a letter that presages what is to follow, Justice Stone wrote to Oskar in late March 1940:

28 March 1940

Dear Mr. Stoessel:

After you called here I was afflicted with grippe [the flu] and became quite unfit as a subject for an artist.

As I told you when you called, I was quite pleased with your etchings and would be glad to sit for you if a mutually convenient time could be found, and if the result is good I shall be glad to show it to my associates and that might perhaps induce them to do likewise.

---

4. Justice Stone may have first met Oskar in 1939. Stone's letter to C. Powell Minnigerode of the Corcoran Art Gallery in November 1940 says: "Mr. Stoessel, who is a Viennese refugee, was introduced to me last year by Mr. Messersmith." Letter of Justice Harlan Fiske Stone to C. Powell Minnigerode, Nov. 25, 1940, Stone Papers, Library of Congress.

5. Alpheus Thomas Mason, *Harlan Fiske Stone: Pillar of the Law* (Viking, 1956), 751.

6. Mason, 751 (quoting letter to H.S. Latham, May 30, 1931).

7. See *American National Biography* (1999), "Platt, Charles Adams [16 Oct. 1861–12 Sept. 1933]" (explaining that late in life he became a noted landscape architect, but that early in life his etchings, begun in 1879, "earned him the epithet of 'the boy etcher,' critical acclaim, and financial success").

8. Mason, *Harlan Fiske Stone*, 751.

9. Mason, 751.

The best time for me to sit is in the forenoon of the days when the Court is in session. We probably will stop sitting about the middle of next week, and will then sit again the week of April 22nd. It is possible that I might have some time around the middle of the week of April 15th, but I am not yet certain of it. It is possible also that I may be in New York for a few days in early June, when I could sit for you there, if that were more convenient.

Yours sincerely,
Harlan F. Stone.[10]

Oskar's reply is his earliest known letter—in a characteristically flowery hand. It appears on letterhead, the top of which displays, in Old World font: "Oskar Stoessel • Carnegie Hall • Studio 1008 • New York City • Circle 5-8591." Then the brief handwritten missive:

April 11th 1940.

To His Honour, Justice Harlan F. Stone.

Sir:

I have your kind letter . . . and thank you very much and will be in Washington Tuesday, April 23rd 9:30 in the morning, to have the first sitting for the etching.[11]

I have the honour to be, Sir, your most obedient servant

Oskar Stoessel.[12]

Oskar took quite some time in finishing Justice Stone's etching: Stone wouldn't approve the final trial proof until after three sittings, receiving the final version on December 10, 1940.

---

10. Justice Harlan Fiske Stone to Oskar Stoessel, typed letter, Mar. 28, 1940, Stone Papers, Library of Congress. All the letters from Stone are typed carbons of his original letters.

11. The letter actually says, "I have your kind letter of April 9th," as opposed to March 28th. That's a little confusing. Either Oskar inexplicably got the date wrong, or Justice Stone wrote another letter on April 9, 1940, of which there is now no trace. The latter is more likely because the date of Stoessel's Washington appointment is long after those suggested in Stone's March letter.

12. Stoessel to Stone, handwritten letter, Apr. 11, 1940, Stone Papers, Library of Congress.

Meanwhile, both Messersmith and Stone were doing what they could to help Oskar, who must have had a magnetic personality to elicit so much ardent backing. On May 31, 1940, Messersmith wrote a letter to Justice Felix Frankfurter in which he said, toward the end: "I hope Stoessel is making an etching of you and understand that the ones he made of the President and of Secretary Hull are turning out very well."[13]

13. Messersmith to Justice Felix Frankfurter, typed letter, May 31, 1940, 11, Frankfurter Papers, Library of Congress.

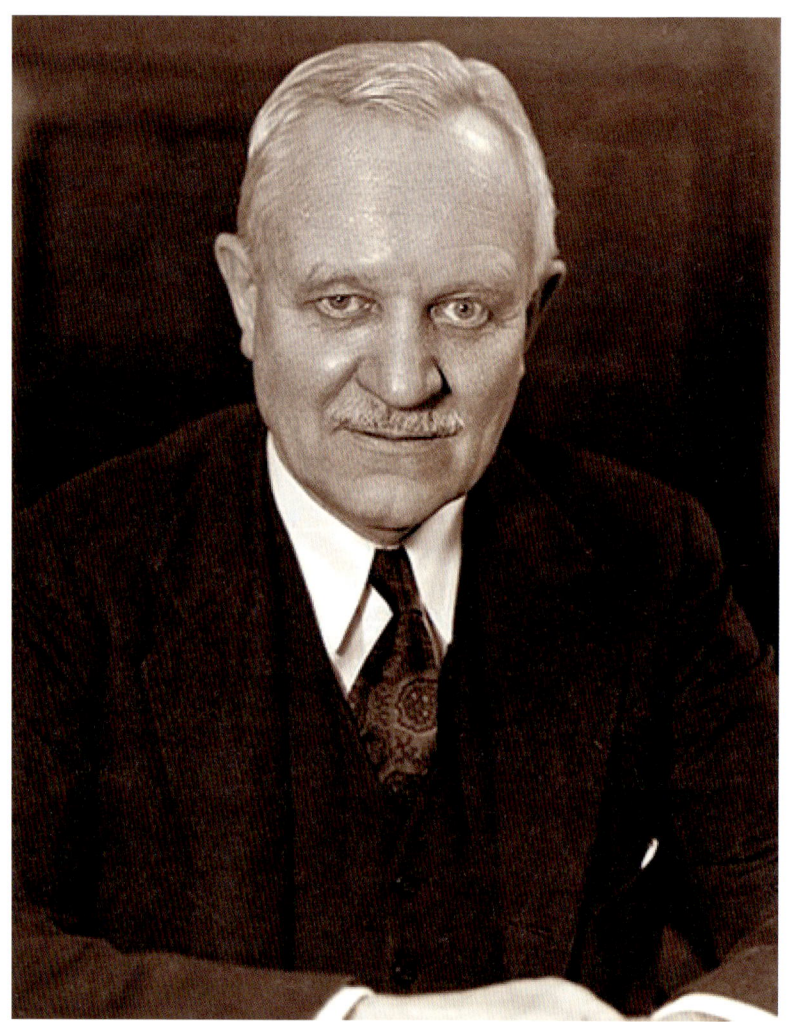

Frederick Paul Keppel

CHAPTER 16

That He Might Work

O SKAR earnestly wished to find a teaching position in America so that he could pass on his knowledge and skills to another generation, just as his mentor Schmutzer had done for him. His friends—especially Justice Harlan Fiske Stone—did their best to help him.

On October 4, 1940, more than two months before seeing any version of his portrait, Justice Stone wrote a letter to his friend Frederick Paul Keppel, president of the Carnegie Foundation and dean of Columbia College, where Stone had been a professor and dean of the law school. The letter may have been prompted by a second sitting with Oskar. Stone doubtless knew that Keppel's father, a prominent New York art dealer and scholar, had been a connoisseur of etchings, especially those of Evert van Muyden (1853–1922).[1] In 1911, the father had founded the publication *Print Collector's Quarterly*, which was devoted entirely to the subject of print collecting.

But Stone was writing to the son, whom he knew well. The younger Keppel was openly antisemitic. In 1914, as dean of Columbia College, Keppel had written a book titled *Columbia*, in which he complained about the number of Jews in his institution. He raised the question whether too many Jewish immigrants on campus would make Columbia "socially uninviting to students who come from homes of refinement."[2] Keppel thought he was soothing widespread concerns when he assured his readers that "the proportion of Jewish students is decreasing rather than increasing."[3]

---

1. See Atherton Curtis, *Catalogue of the Etched Work of Evert van Muyden* (Frederick Keppel, 1894), 12 ("I am also greatly indebted to Mr. Frederick Keppel of New York for permitting me to see many rare states [versions of etchings] unobtainable elsewhere.").
2. Frederick P. Keppel, *Columbia* (Oxford Univ. Press, 1914), 179.
3. Keppel, 180.

119

Whether Stone remembered this passage or knew about Keppel's antisemitism through personal interactions, he decided to mention what would doubtless be on Keppel's mind in the first sentence of the second paragraph:

October 4, 1940

Dear Keppel:

I am turning to you for a bit of information and a bit of assistance, which I think you can probably easily give by virtue of your interest in current art projects.

Mr. Messersmith, recently Assistant Secretary of State and formerly our Minister to Austria, introduced to me last year a Viennese refugee, Oskar Stoessel by name (not Jewish, I think), who does the most extraordinary etched portraits of any that I have seen by a modern artist. He has lately etched the President and some of my acquaintances, producing portraits which are both wonderful likenesses and artistic. He is more interested in his art and its perpetuation than he is in its financial returns, although he has to make a living. He lately said to me that he thought no one in this country was doing the sort of thing he does, and that it is an art which ought to be perpetuated, and inquired whether there was any place where he could get an opportunity to teach.

I pass this inquiry along to you with the suggestion that if you do not have the information at hand you refer me to the proper person to answer it. He would be glad to show to you, or to anyone else to whom I might send him, examples of his work. I am sure you would find them charming.

It was a pleasure to see you at The Century [Association].[4] I wish I could go there oftener.

With best regards, I am,

Yours sincerely,
Harlan F. Stone.[5]

---

4.   See *American National Biography* (1999), "Keppel, Frederick Paul [2 July 1875–8 Feb. 1943]" ("He was a member of many clubs and organizations and especially enjoyed the Century Association in New York City, where he usually met friends for lunch.").

5.   Justice Harlan Fiske Stone to Frederick Paul Keppel, typed letter, Oct. 4, 1940, Stone Papers, Library of Congress.

"Not Jewish, I think." The statement might seem in modern eyes to damn both Keppel and Stone. About Keppel, there seems no serious doubt about his invidious views.

But about Stone, we must consider carefully. He probably did know full well that Oskar was of Jewish descent. The two men had had long conversations in chambers and had come to know each other. If that's true, then Stone was not being entirely candid with Keppel. The other possibility is that he truly didn't know and didn't want to know—a kind of don't-ask-don't-tell policy that would give him deniability if anybody asked why he was promoting Oskar so enthusiastically. Either way, Stone seemed not to care that his friend was Jewish—that is, he didn't harbor a bias—but he knew that antisemitism was common enough among Americans. Regardless, he wanted to help his talented friend.

If indeed he was misleading Keppel and is therefore chargeable with a degree of dishonesty, he probably thought it was a justifiable lie. Why harm Oskar with a frank admission that would torpedo his chances with the influential man who might help him? The fact remains that Stone was doing all he could to bolster Oskar's career. But one could argue that whether Stone raised the issue of Jewishness or not, Oskar's chances of winning over Keppel were slim.

Keppel's initial response was warm and encouraging: "Thank you for telling me about Stoessel. I'll make some inquiry and see whether there's a chance of placing him as a resident artist in some good college."[6] Meanwhile, Keppel wanted to see two or three photographs of Oskar's portraits.[7]

Three days later, Justice Stone wrote to Oskar: "I enclose herewith a copy of a letter I received from Mr. Keppel, and a copy of my reply. If you do not hear from him in due course let me know and I will take the matter up again. Yours sincerely, Harlan F. Stone."[8]

The effort that Justice Stone exerted on Oskar's behalf was extraordinary. On the same day that Stone wrote to Oskar, he also replied to Keppel, suggesting

---

6.   Keppel to Stone, typed letter, Oct. 7, 1940, Stone Papers, Library of Congress.
7.   Keppel to Stone, Oct. 7, 1940.
8.   Stone to Oskar Stoessel, typed letter, Oct. 10, 1940, Stone Papers, Library of Congress.

that photos of etchings wouldn't do justice to Oskar's artistry: "I think it would be much better for him to leave at your office for inspection some of his original work."[9] Even though Stone hadn't yet seen the etched likeness of himself, he was eager to promote Oskar: "He has just done portraits of the President, Justice Douglas, and Assistant Secretary of State Breckinridge Long, which are superb examples of etched portraiture, and I should like very much to have you see them."[10] Stone sounded almost importunate: "May I suggest that you have your secretary write or telephone him suggesting a time when he can bring in some samples of his work?"[11]

On U.S. Supreme Court letterhead, these requests might have seemed more like mandates. Then came a pitch for a job for Oskar: "I think he would probably desire to teach in some center like New York or Washington where he could continue to devote some time to sitters."[12]

Justice Stone's efforts were evidently effective: less than two weeks later, Oskar gave an update with another handwritten letter, again with his usual flourishes:

<blockquote>

October 21st 1940

Honorable Harlan F. Stone.
Supreme Court of the United States of America.
Washington, D.C.

My dear Judge Stone.

I had been out of town for some days and got your kind letter only three days ago. I thank you very much for your kindness in taking so much interest in my work. I phoned to Mr. Keppel's office and was told by his Secretary to bring some of my etchings to the office, which of course I did. Mr. Keppel at present is out of town and he will inspect my work sometime before Thursday next. I shall be pleased to keep you informed of the further development. The first etching of the new plate of your etching is very good and I hope to finish the plate in about

</blockquote>

---

9.   Stone to Keppel, typed letter, Oct. 10, 1940, Stone Papers, Library of Congress.
10. Stone to Keppel, Oct. 10, 1940.
11. Stone to Keppel, Oct. 10, 1940.
12. Stone to Keppel, Oct. 10, 1940.

ten days. Then I will send the first trying-proof. The beginning of the plate is so good that I hope Mr. Justice will enjoy the work.

Thanking again, I am

Very respectfully yours,

Oskar Stoessel.[13]

Perhaps predictably, given that Keppel had probably now learned of Oskar's Jewish background, Keppel's response was unenthusiastic. It was typed on Carnegie Corporation letterhead: "We have been seeing Stoessel and his work, . . . but we really have not been successful accomplishing anything in his behalf."[14] He provided no encouragement: "Frankly, it is not likely that we can."[15] Despite his earlier optimism, he now did what he could to dash any hope: "If you have another talk with him, you might help him to realize that people in his circumstances have to start pretty low on the scale here."[16] There seemed to be no consideration of merit: "The big positions are in the big institutions where there are men who have been held back from promotion for ten years during the Depression, and naturally do not want an outsider to come in on equal terms."[17] It would be best, Keppel wrote, if Oskar set his sights on places "where the salaries and living expenses are low"[18]—perhaps hinting that he ought to leave New York. Although Keppel promised not to forget about Oskar, he said that "it would not be fair to let him think that anything might materialize."[19]

Justice Stone persisted in his efforts to secure a long-term teaching position for Oskar. But he seems to have realized that Keppel represented a dead end:

---

13. Stoessel to Stone, handwritten letter, Oct. 21, 1940, Stone Papers, Library of Congress.
14. Keppel to Stone, typed letter, Nov. 20, 1940, Stone Papers, Library of Congress.
15. Keppel to Stone, Nov. 20, 1940.
16. Keppel to Stone, Nov. 20, 1940.
17. Keppel to Stone, Nov. 20, 1940.
18. Keppel to Stone, Nov. 20, 1940.
19. Keppel to Stone, Nov. 20, 1940.

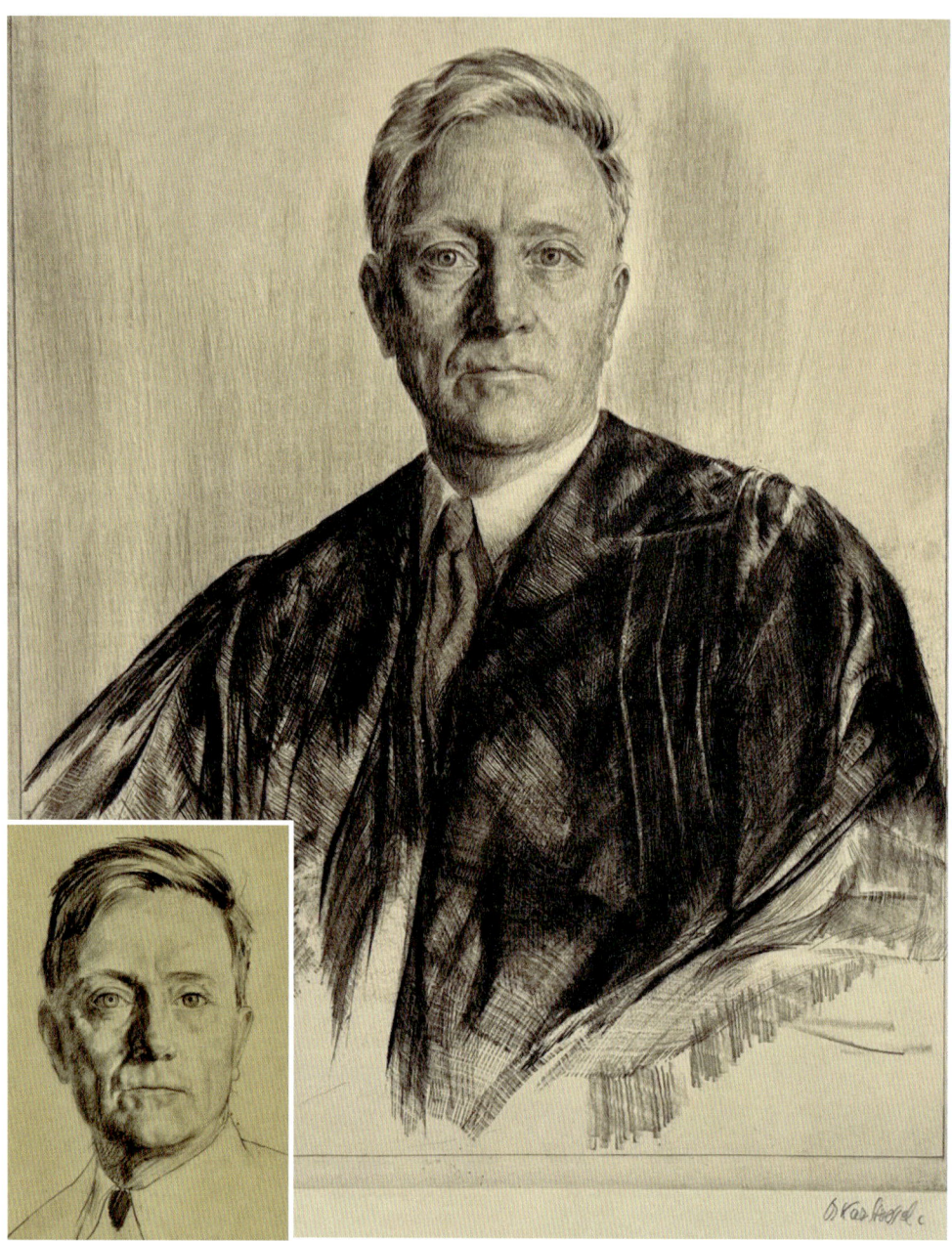

Oskar's 1940 etching of Justice William O. Douglas. (Inset: Oskar's preliminary pencil sketch.) Justice Douglas had been on the Court a little more than a year when the portrait was made. In a letter to George Messersmith, then the U.S. ambassador to Cuba, Justice Douglas said that this is a portrait that "critics say is tops" (see page 137). A strong civil libertarian, Justice Douglas would become the longest-serving justice at more than 36 years.

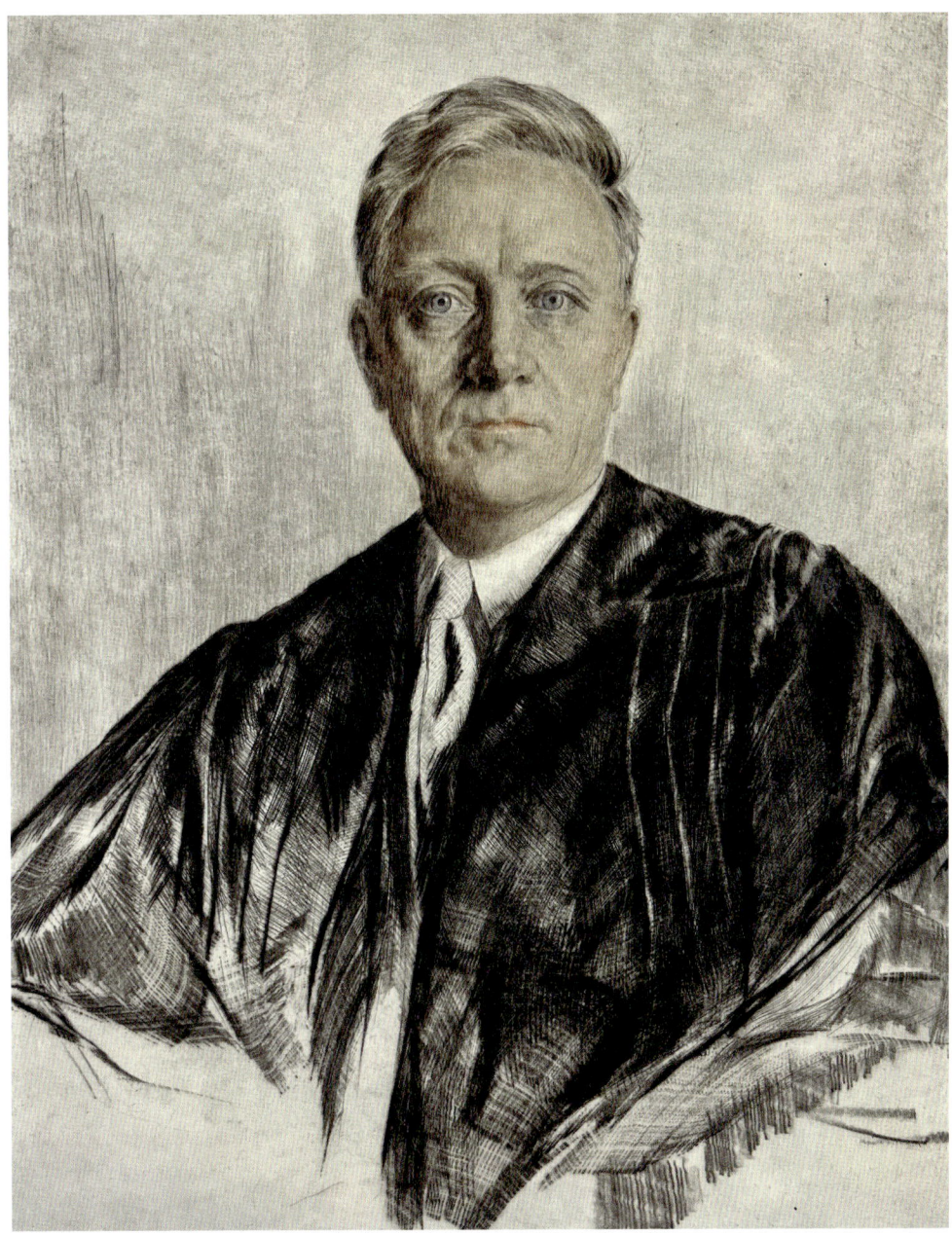

Justice Douglas is the only Supreme Court justice for whose portrait Oskar is known to have experimented with tinting. For the most part, Oskar abandoned tinting his etched portraits after arriving in the United States. This version is a proof that Oskar apparently rejected in favor of black and white.

November 25th 1940

Dear Keppel:

Thank you very much for your interest in Mr. Stoessel. I hope I did not give you too much trouble about this.

My thought was and is that he is a very talented man and that it would be desirable if he could pass his special skill on to satisfactory students wherever they may be found. I think it possible that I might find some opportunity for him here in Washington, but he really should be in New York where he would be likely to find more private patrons than he would here.

With kind regards, I am,

Yours sincerely,
Harlan F. Stone.[20]

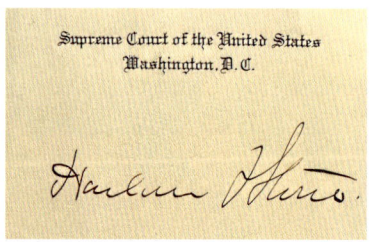

The same day, Justice Stone wrote to Cuthbert Powell Minnigerode, the director of the Corcoran Gallery of Art in Washington, D.C., and former president of the Association of Arts Museum Directors.[21] Again, Justice Stone was doing what he could to further Oskar's career:

November 25, 1940.

Dear Mr. Minnigerode:

I am much interested in Mr. Oskar Stoessel, who is an extremely competent portrait etcher, and who is desirous of securing an opportunity to teach the principles of his art.

Mr. Stoessel, who is a Viennese refugee, was introduced to me last year by Mr. Messersmith until recently Assistant Secretary of State and formerly our Minister to Austria, who had known Mr. Stoessel very favorably in Vienna. The latter has shown to me some very fine examples of his art done here and in Vienna. He has lately etched the President, Justice Douglas, one of my associates, and Assistant Secretary of State Breckinridge Long. All of the portraits are beautiful examples of the etcher's art and are living likenesses. I would like very

---

20. Stone to Keppel, typed letter, Nov. 25, 1940, Stone Papers, Library of Congress.
21. Minnigerode (1876–1951) spent his entire career at the Corcoran until retiring in 1947. He served as president of the Association of Arts Museum Directors in the late 1930s.

much to have you see some of his work and when he next comes to Washington I will, with your permission, give him a note to you and ask him to show you some examples.

If you should know, either now or later, of any opportunity for him to do some teaching, it would gratify me very much and you would do him a great service.

With kind regards, I am,

Yours sincerely,
Harlan F. Stone.[22]

The next day, November 26, Minnigerode answered Justice Stone: "Please accept my thanks for your note of the 25th instant with regard to Mr. Stoessel, which I have read with interest."[23] Minnigerode explained that he had had both correspondence and a conference with George Messersmith about Oskar and "would be glad to meet with him when he is next in Washington."[24] He expressed an enthusiastic willingness to help: "If there should be any way in which I could aid him, I would be most happy to do so and would be glad to have him call here at any time."[25]

22. Stone to Cuthbert Powell Minnigerode, typed letter, Nov. 25, 1940, Stone Papers, Library of Congress.
23. Minnigerode to Stone, typed letter, Nov. 26, 1940, Stone Papers, Library of Congress.
24. Minnigerode to Stone, Nov. 26, 1940.
25. Minnigerode to Stone, Nov. 26, 1940.

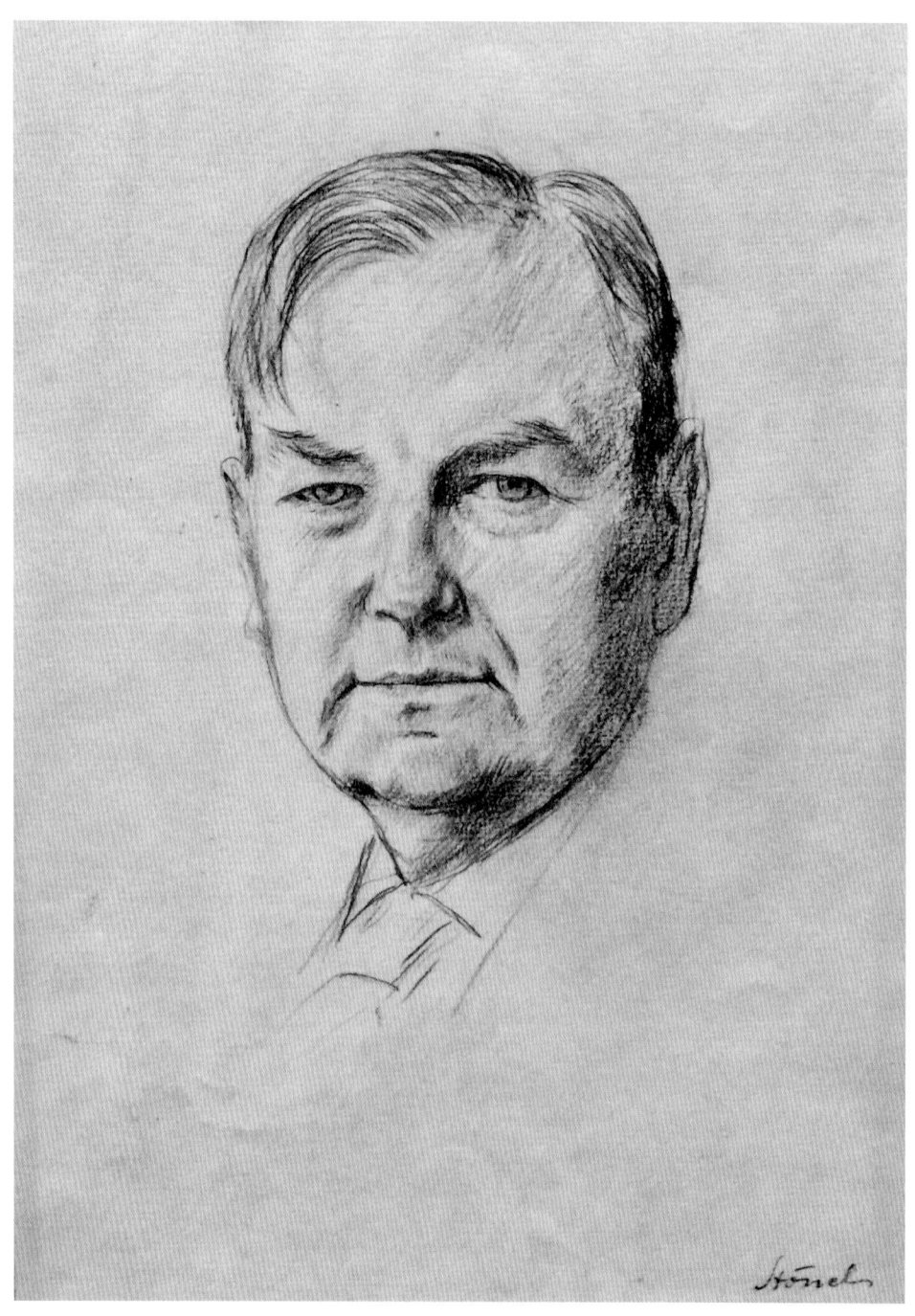

Oskar's pencil sketch of Chief Justice Stone, perhaps from April 23, 1940. Then again, it may date from the summer of 1940, given that it more closely resembles the thinned face of the second plate than it does the jowly first plate.

CHAPTER 17

Etched Stone

IN early December, Oskar had finished his trial proof of the Stone etching. He enclosed a two-page letter with the portrait:

December 6th 1940.

The honorable Mr. Justice Harlan F. Stone.
Washington, D.C.

Dear Mr. Justice.

I am pleased to send you the first trying proof of the etching of your portrait, and I hope you may like it. In case you should wish any alterations please let me know and I shall be able to do them.

Encouraged by the kind interest you have been taking in my work, I am taking the liberty of asking your support in a matter that is of utmost importance to me. Mr. Messersmith was kind enough to write to Mr. McBride, the administrative and business head of the newly founded State Museum [the National Gallery of Art] in Washington, and suggested that I may be employed in founding the graphic section of the Museum. May I mention to you that I have a wide experience in the judgement of the printing qualities of old engravings and etchings. I acquired this experience chiefly through my profession. (It is worth remembering that the great collections in Europe have always been arranged by professional etchers. Basan,[1] Bartsch,[2] and many more). And by gradually building up my own collection and as a matter of fact my opinion often was decisive at the acquisition of valuable prints with important collectors. I am by no means interested in a big salary but I should feel proud of being allowed to take part in the foundation of a collection that I expect will be the best in the world. I

---

1. Pierre François Basan [1723–1797], engraver active in Paris. *Benezit Dictionary of Artists* (Gründ, 2006), 1:1264.
2. Zacharias Bartsch [16c German], engraver active in Graz. *Benezit Dictionary of Artists*, 1:1255.

should be very grateful to you for any kind of support you may be able to give me in this regard.

Apologizing for troubling you so and thanking you in anticipation,

I am very respectfully

Yours

Oskar Stoessel.[3]

Justice Stone replied on December 10, in a letter that doesn't survive in his archive at the Library of Congress. In that letter, he seems to have been concerned primarily with Oskar's interest in a job at the National Gallery of Art, which was founded with a gift by Andrew Mellon and headed initially by Colonel Harry A. McBride. Justice Stone promptly wrote to Colonel McBride on Oskar's behalf. The National Gallery was slated to open on March 17, 1941.

On December 11, Justice Stone wrote a most interesting letter to Oskar about the proof portrait and the elements that he wanted Oskar to change:

December 11, 1940.

Dear Mr. Stoessel:

I have the trial proof of my etched portrait, which came yesterday.

Both Mrs. Stone and I think it a great improvement over the first one, but we are agreed that there are some things which you can probably do to it to make it more effective. If you are coming to Washington soon, I would be glad to talk with you about it. They are all things that can be easily corrected, I think. For example, the eyes should be a little more alert than they are, possibly by darkening them and then giving them a little more high light. Standing close to the picture the likeness is excellent, but at a distance it seems to be blurred as though the face were covered with blotches. The bridge of the nose appears wide, whereas the bridge of my nose is actually quite narrow. The robe seems somewhat full and "overstuffed," which can probably be reduced by high lights.

I do hope you do not think that I am over-critical. I am only trying to be helpful and I am quite sure that most of my criticisms are due to the fact that this is a trial proof and can easily be remedied.

---

3.   Oskar Stoessel to Justice Harlan Fiske Stone, handwritten letter, Dec. 6, 1940, Stone Papers, Library of Congress.

Whenever you come to Washington I have arranged to have you see my friend Mr. Minnigerode, who is Curator of the Corcoran Art Gallery here. He may know of teaching opportunities for you and in any case I would like to have him see some examples of your work.

With kind regards, I am,
Yours sincerely,
Harlan F. Stone.[4]

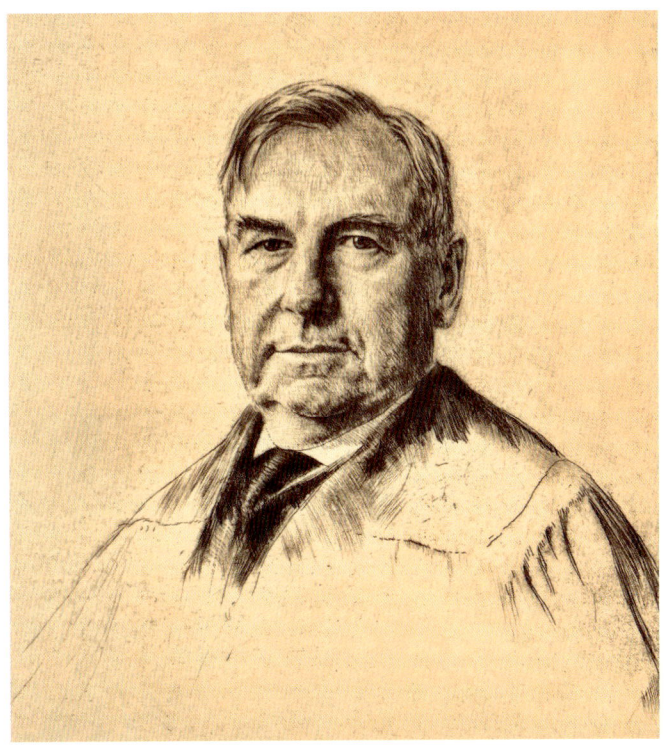

Oskar's first plate (probably summer 1940). Note the jowls, the saggy neck, and the broad bridge of the nose. The shoulders slope unflatteringly.

The meeting with Minnigerode, which finally took place on January 9, 1941, must have gone well. Things moved quickly with the Corcoran Gallery. By February, Oskar's personal collection of 18th-century French engravings was on display. That exhibition was replaced in April by Oskar's own etchings for nearly the entire month of April. (See chapter 20.)

Meanwhile, Oskar had high hopes for an opportunity at the National Gallery. He had received a copy of Justice Stone's letter of recommendation to Colonel McBride:

December 28th 1940.

The Honorable Mr. Justice Harlan F. Stone.
Dear Mr. Justice.
I have received your letter of December 10th and thank you so much for your great kindness and all you have been doing for me. I read the copy of the letter you wrote to Mr. McBride with great pleasure and I am sure it will influence

4.   Stone to Stoessel, typed letter, Dec. 11, 1940, Stone Papers, Library of Congress.

my chances a great deal. I quite realize that the main difficulty lies with the fact that I never had any institutional affiliation. I think, though, that I would be able to compensate this lack by experience in judging qualities of prints as well as craftsmanship and I also think that this might be of greater importance for the building up of a new collection. Anyhow, whatever the result may be you have been a wonderful help to me and I shall never be able to thank you enough I am sure.

Very respectfully,
Oskar Stoessel.[5]

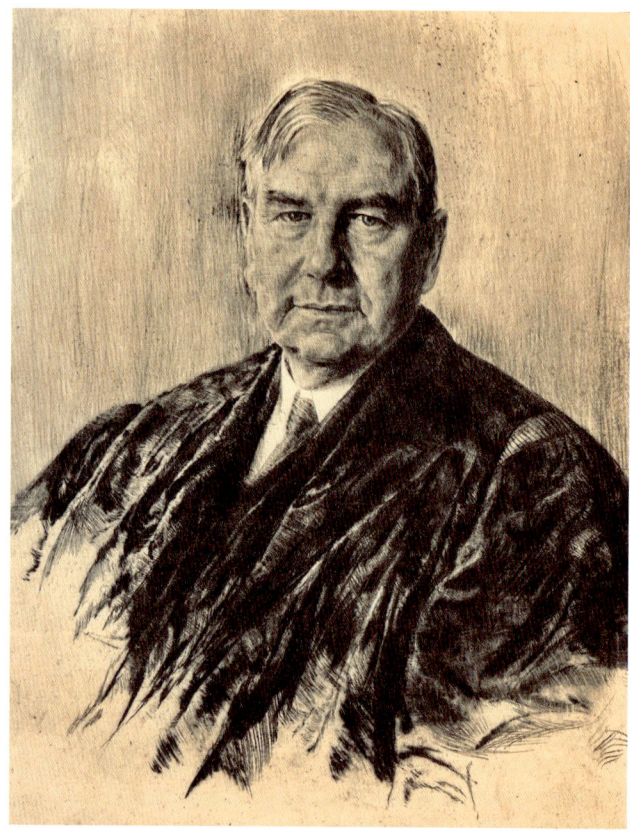

An early state of the second plate. The bridge of the nose is still broad. The chair back has not yet been added; the background strokes are vertical.

The following pages illustrate the progression of Justice Stone's portrait, from Oskar's initial sketch to the first plate to the new plate with gradual tweaks. Oskar worked exceedingly hard on Stone's portrait. There are at least a dozen known states of the plate.

---

5   Stoessel to Stone, handwritten letter, Dec. 28, 1940, Stone Papers, Library of Congress.

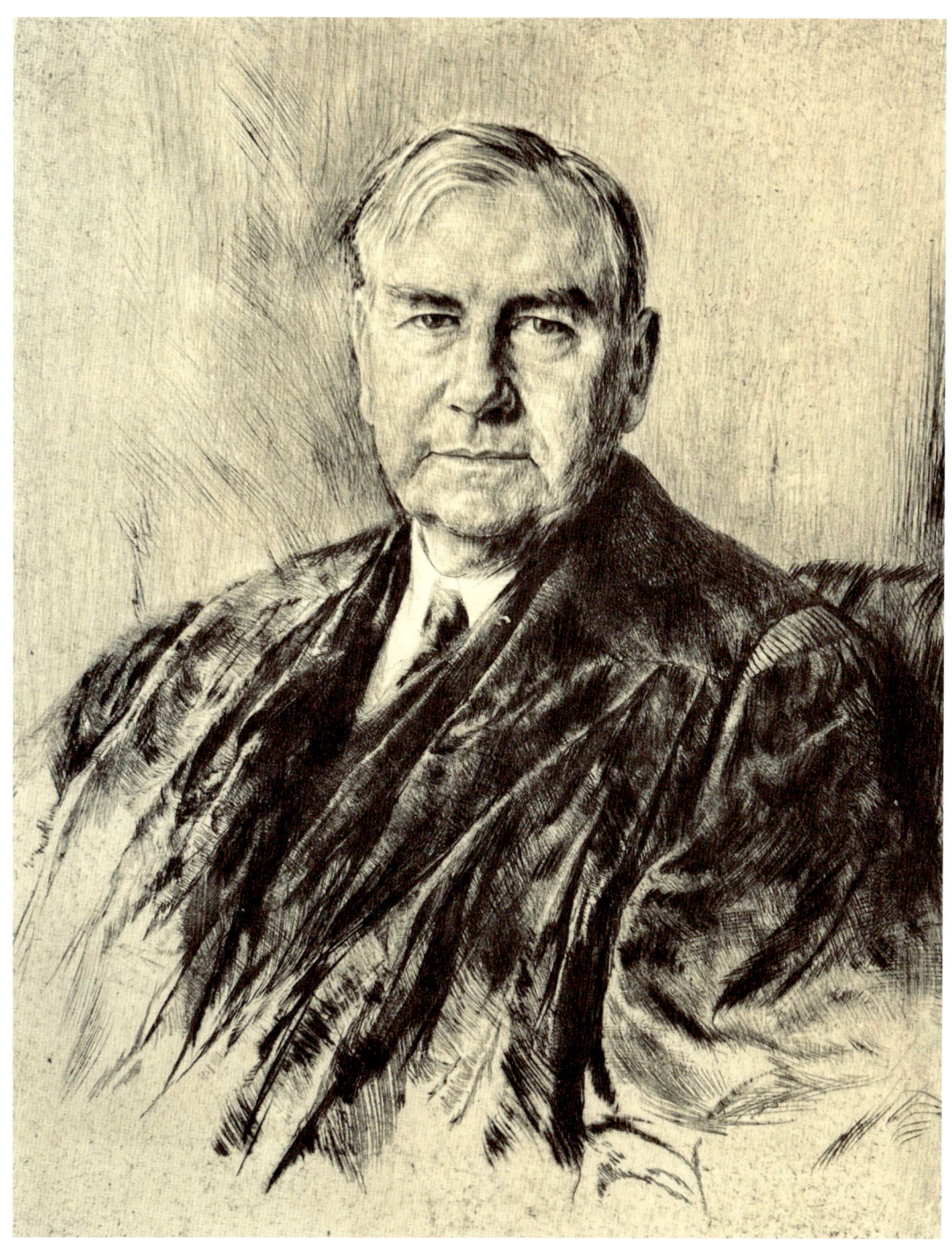

The chair back has been added. The bridge of the nose remains broad. The hair now appears whiter because Oskar has lightened the image.

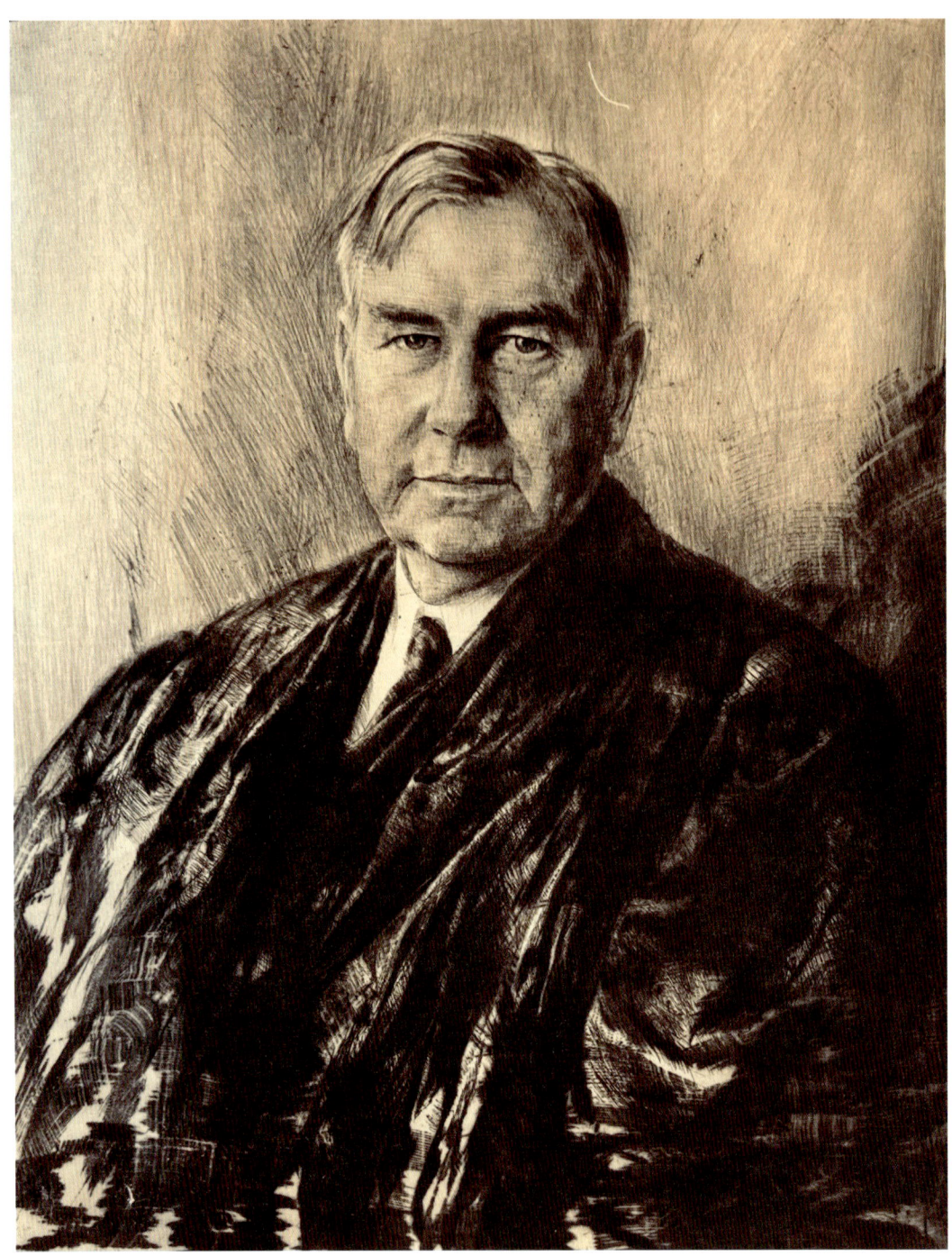

Oskar has given more definition to the bridge of the nose. The chair back has been obscured somewhat by enhancements to the background. Oskar appears to have responded to Stone's requests (page 130).

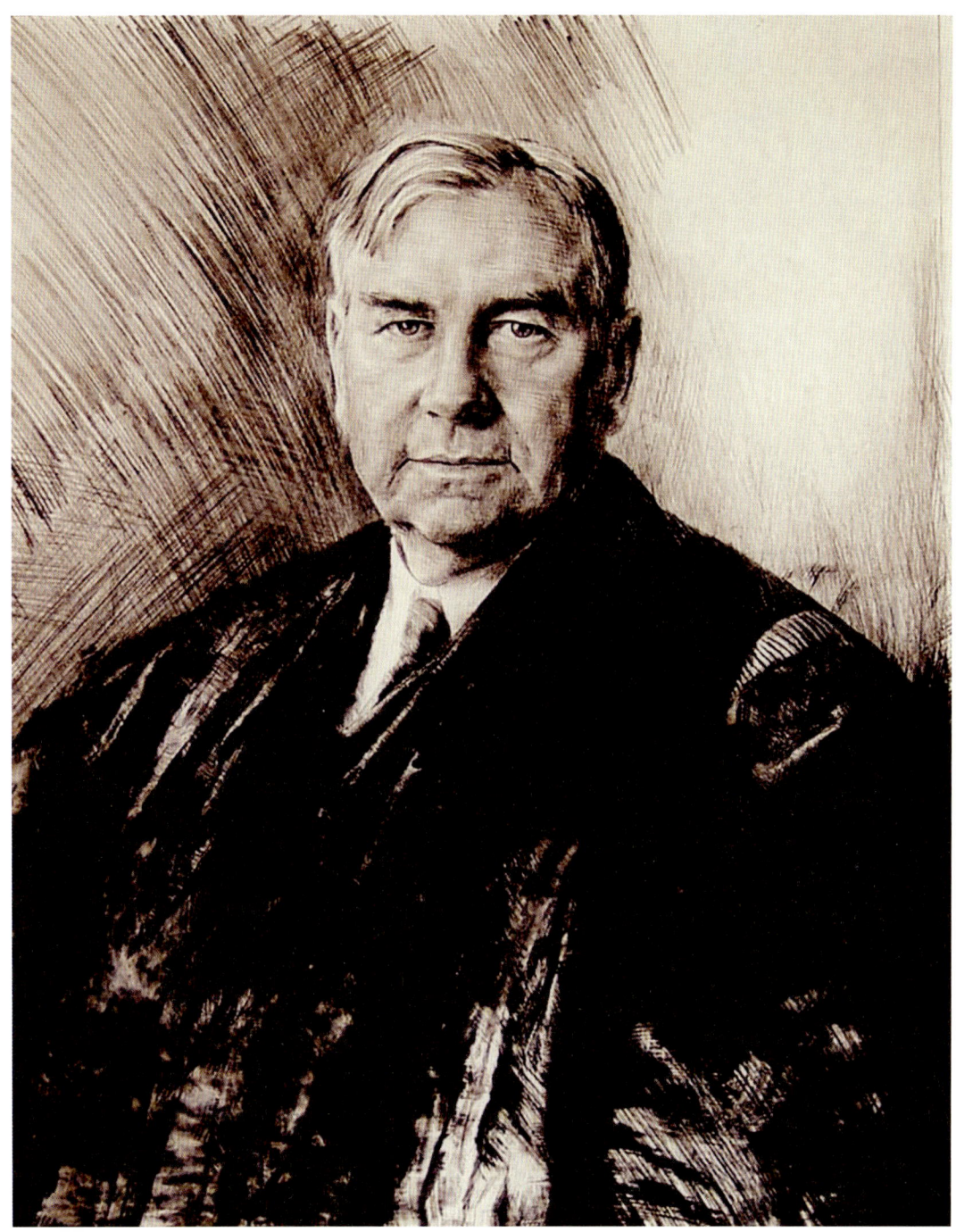

The Supreme Court's version of the Stone portrait, perhaps given to the archivist by Stone himself. There is now cross-hatching on the left side and a lightening of the background to the right; the chair back has been minimized.

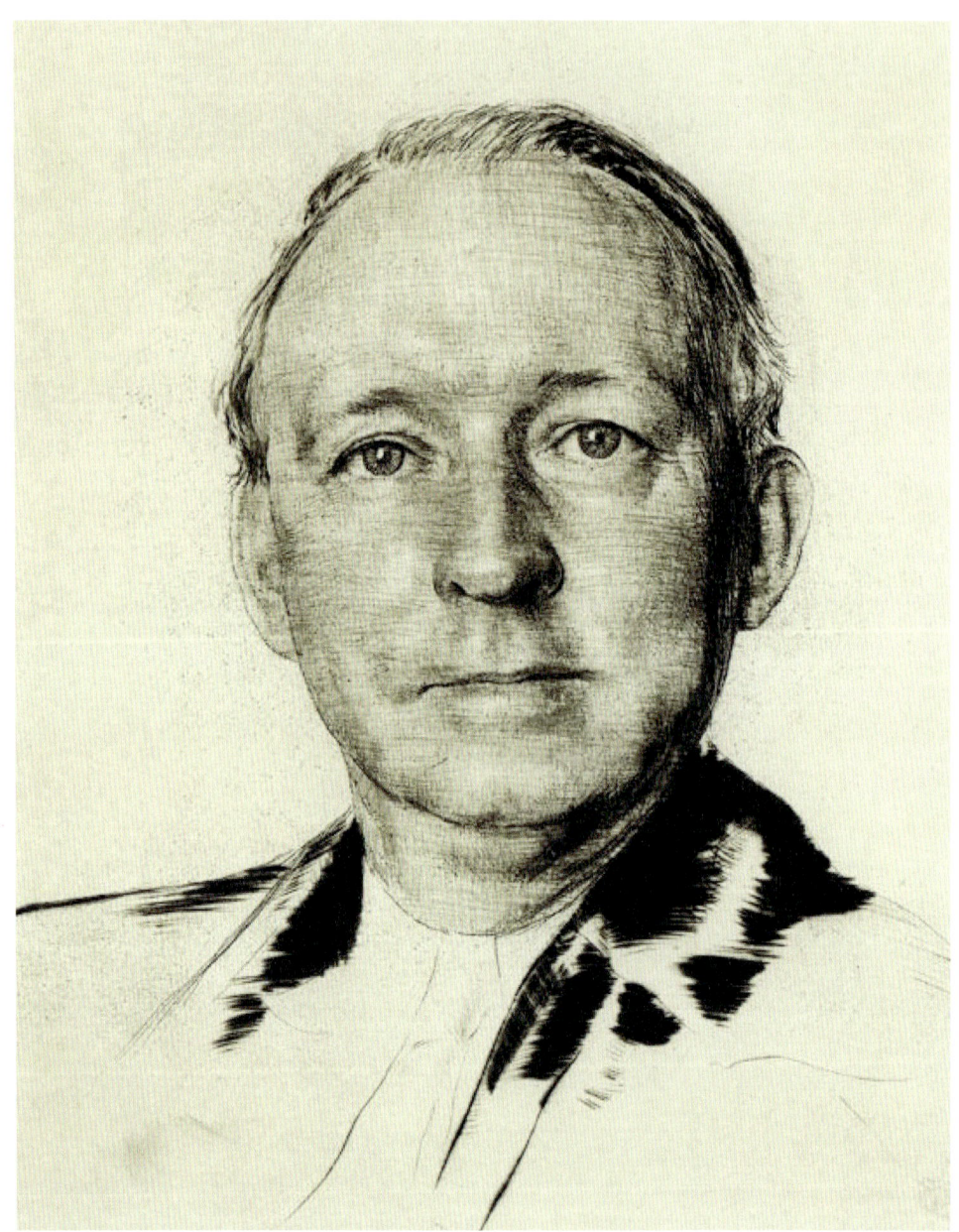

Oskar's 1941 etching of Justice Hugo Black, FDR's first appointee to the Supreme Court in 1937. Before that, Black had been a Senator from Alabama for more than a decade. As a justice, Black was a textualist and generally a civil libertarian. Yet until his mid-30s he had been a member of the Ku Klux Klan——a fact that dogged him later in life. Shortly after coming onto the Court, he insisted that he had long since disowned the Klan: "Before becoming a Senator, I dropped the Klan. I have had nothing to do with it since that time. I abandoned it."

CHAPTER 18

The Justices En Banc

Y now, Oskar Stoessel had generated a good deal of talk around the Supreme Court. On December 30, 1940, Justice William O. Douglas was thanking George Messersmith for his Christmas card and adding: "You will be interested to know that Stoessel continues his good work. He did one of me which critics say is tops. And the one of Stone is very good—at least to my untrained eye. I hope eventually he can make the rounds here at the Court."[1]

Oskar had corrected the deficiencies in Justice Stone's proof. He had narrowed the bridge of Stone's nose, made his face less blotchy, and trimmed the look of the "overstuffed" robe. Justice Stone was apparently pleased. He soon wrote to the artist, who at the time was staying at the Lee Sheraton Hotel at 15th and L Streets in Washington. Justice Stone was concerned with the practicalities of persuading his colleagues to sit:

February 5, 1941.

Dear Mr. Stoessel:

I showed Justice Douglas's portrait and mine to the other Justices today, and I think they like them very much, and I am quite sure that they, or some of them, will be glad to sit for you if they know the terms on which it is to be done.

You will understand that men in their position are often asked to sit for a portrait and that sometimes they have unpleasant experiences with artists who think they should take the portrait even though they do not care for it. That makes them hesitate to sit at all.

I suggest that the best way for you to proceed is to tell me exactly on what terms you would be willing to make an etched portrait of each Justice, and at what price you would be willing to let each one have a limited number of his own portrait,

---

1. Justice William O. Douglas to George S. Messersmith, typed letter, Dec. 30, 1940, Douglas Papers, Library of Congress.

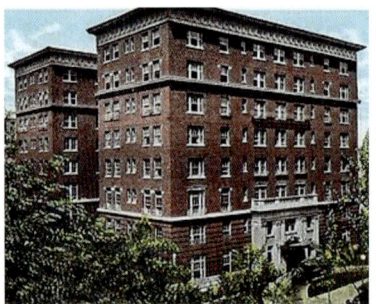

The Lee Sheraton Hotel was Oskar's usual accommodation in Washington, D.C. This postcard photo shows how it appeared in the 1940s.

say ten. I shall then be very glad to write to each Justice, telling him your terms, and suggesting that if he is willing to sit that he let you or me know, and invite you to come and make the portrait. If you will let me know sometime tomorrow I will get the letters out at once.

With kind regards, I am,

Yours sincerely,
Harlan F. Stone.

P.S. I am having inquiry made also of Justice McReynolds if you wish to do his portrait.[2]

The U.S. mail was extremely prompt. The following day, Oskar sent his handwritten answer:

February 6th 1941.

The Honorable Mr. Justice Harlan F. Stone.
Dear Mr. Justice.

I have received today your very kind letter and the enclosed letter of Mr. Minnigerode. I thank you very much indeed and I come tomorrow to Washington with a collection of my etchings, but I think it would be better to make the etchings of all members of the Supreme High Court before making an exhibition [at the Corcoran]. I think this set would be of greater interest than my portraits of European people, and I hope to be able to finish this set in the next few weeks. Thanking once more for your kindness.

I am respectfully,
Yours,
Oskar Stoessel.[3]

Justice Stone's calling card that he gave to Oskar for an introduction to Justice Douglas, who accepted and kept the card. It now resides in the Douglas Papers at the Library of Congress.

Again the Postal Service proved reliable, and Justice Stone, as he had pledged to do, wrote to his colleagues the very next day. The Library of Congress's Stone Papers contain virtually identical letters from

2. Justice Harlan Fiske Stone to Oskar Stoessel, typed letter, Feb. 5, 1941, Stone Papers, Library of Congress. Justice McReynolds had retired on Jan. 31, 1941.
3. Stoessel to Stone, handwritten letter, Feb. 6, 1941, Stone Papers, Library of Congress.

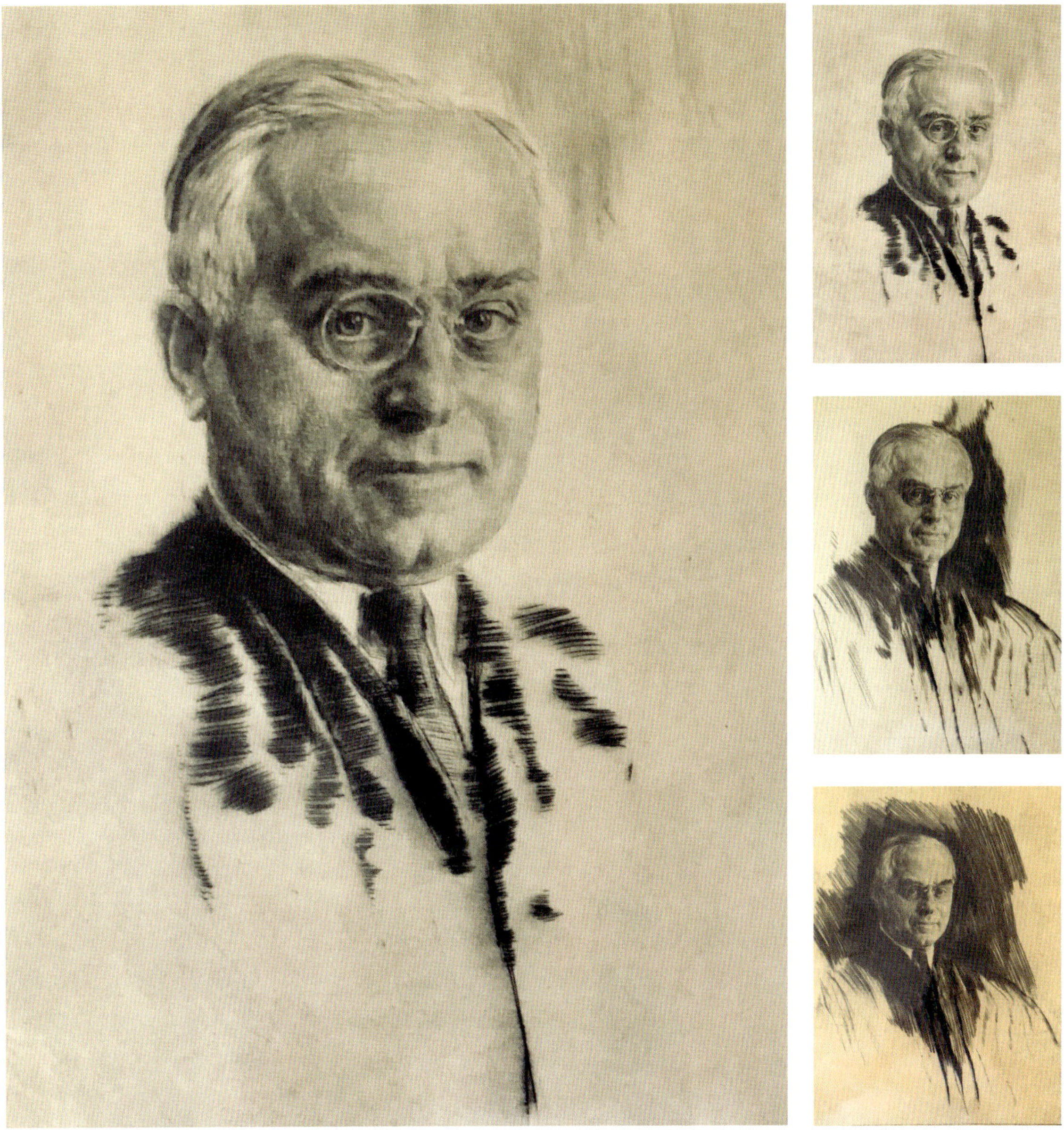

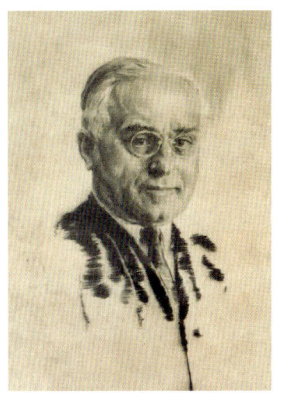

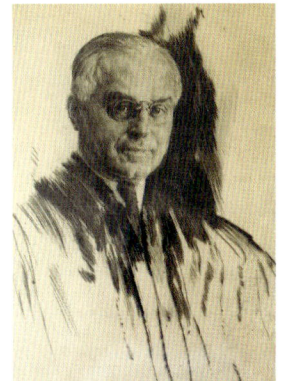

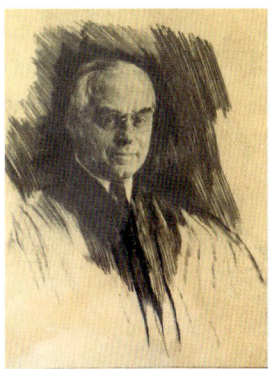

Oskar's etching of Justice Felix Frankfurter. (Insets: variant prints.) Despite superficial similarities with Oskar——the two being Jewish men born in Austria within three years of each other——no record of close ties between the two exists. The Frankfurter family immigrated to New York City in 1894, when Felix was 12. He went to Harvard Law School, served in various federal positions, and then became a professor at Harvard Law School——as well as a friend and adviser to FDR——before his appointment to the Court in 1939.

Stone to Chief Justice Charles Evans Hughes and to Justice Owen Roberts. Six others probably went out as well. Oskar might also have had a telephone conversation with Justice Stone—a fact deducible from the additional details about the financial terms on which Oskar would proceed:

February 7, 1941.

Dear Chief Justice:

Mr. Oskar Stoessel, who did the etched portraits of Justice Douglas and myself, proof of which you saw the other day, is very anxious to have the privilege of doing portraits of all the members of the Court, or as many of them as are willing to sit. I am very anxious to have him do them because I think a distinguished group of portraits would result.

As he asks the privilege he will be glad of the opportunity to do these portraits without any obligation of any kind on the part of the sitter. He will be glad to present one proof of the portrait to each sitter without charge and then if they desire additional proofs to supply them at $20 each.[4]

Fortunately he consumes very little of the time of the sitter. He came to me either three or four times, each time about three quarters of an hour. Much of the time he allowed me to move about freely so that it interfered with my work very little.[5]

If you are interested I will give Mr. Stoessel a card of introduction, when he can arrange for a sitting and also show you some of his work.

Yours faithfully,
Harlan F. Stone.

P.S. Mr. Stoessel is a very extensive collector of prints and engravings. His collection of Eighteenth Century colored prints is not [read *now*] on exhibition at the Corcoran Gallery.[6]

---

4. Equivalent to about $360 in 2024.
5. This method of allowing the sitter to work and move around freely is consistent with the known facts of the FDR sitting (see pages 102–04).
6. Stone to Chief Justice Charles Evans Hughes, typed letter, Feb. 7, 1941, Stone Papers, Library of Congress. The postscript suggests that C. Powell Minnigerode had moved quickly at Stone's suggestion: just nine weeks after Stone's initial contact with Minnigerode, the Corcoran Gallery was mounting an exhibition of Oskar's 18th-century prints. This exhibition may have already been in the works as a result of Messersmith's efforts.

The letter to Justice Owen Roberts was almost identical apart from the typo in the postscript (which was correct in the Roberts letter):[7]

> P.S.   Mr. Stoessel has a very extensive collection of prints and engravings. His collection of Eighteenth Century prints is now on exhibition at the Corcoran Gallery.

The corrected postscript to Justice Stone's letter suggesting that Justice Roberts sit for a Stoessel portrait. Identical letters were probably sent to all the justices.

The nationally syndicated column "The Washington Merry-Go-Round" ran an item about the portraits. It was the second time Oskar had been a subject in Drew Pearson's influential column (the first being the one about President Roosevelt's sitting). It said: "A Viennese artist named Oskar Stossel [sic] is making a set of etchings of the Supreme Court Justices. He has completed work on Stone and Douglas. Justice Stone, whose wife is an artist, helps arrange the sittings."[8] This is the only public mention of Mrs. Stone in relation to Oskar, and indeed the only mention at all of her helping to schedule the sittings. She was a considerable painter herself, and her works had many gallery exhibitions in Washington, D.C., and Virginia in the 1930s and 1940s.[9]

Apparently, and remarkably, within just six days of Justice Stone's letter to the other justices, they had all agreed to sit—which was something of a coup, given the general acrimony within the Court during this period.[10] Justice Frank Murphy's calendar shows that he had an appointment with Oskar on March 18, 1941, and then again two days later. These appointments were followed by yet another sitting on April 5, 1941. He had two more sittings, on April 21 and May 7.[11] It seems that Justice Murphy must have rejected the first proof, which depicted

---

7. Stone to Justice Owen Roberts, typed letter, Feb. 7, 1941, Stone Papers, Library of Congress.
8. Drew Pearson and Robert Allen, "The Washington Merry-Go-Round," *Indiana Gaz.* (Indiana, Pa.), Feb. 13, 1941, 4; *Sheboygan Press* (Sheboygan, Wis.), Feb. 13, 1941, 28; and dozens of others.
9. Alpheus Thomas Mason, *Harlan Fiske Stone: Pillar of the Law* (Viking, 1956), 757.
10. See generally Noah Feldman, *Scorpions: The Battles and Triumphs of FDR's Great Supreme Court Justices* (Twelve, 2010).
11. Justice Frank Murphy's calendars are on file at the Murphy Papers, University of Michigan.

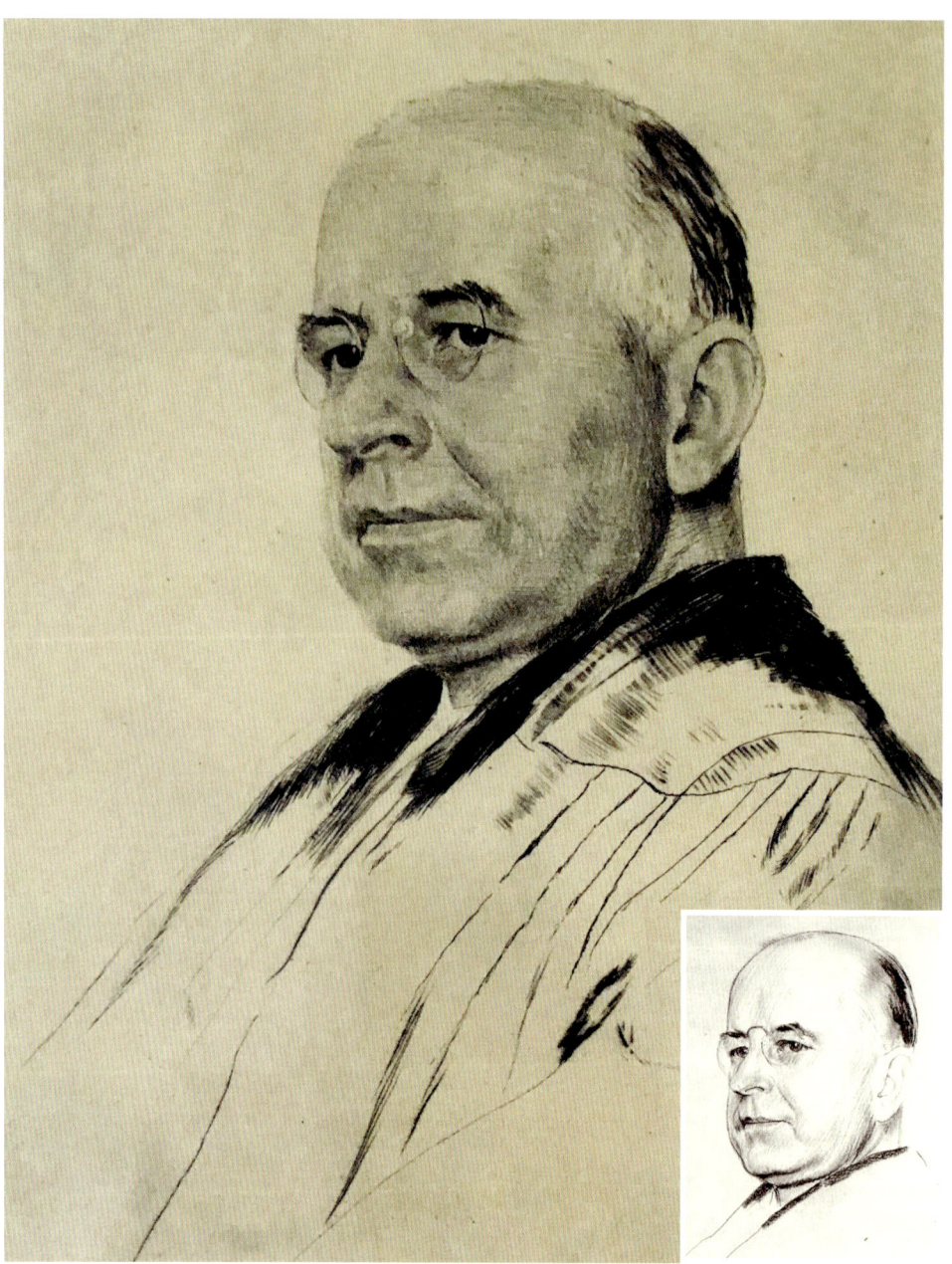

Oskar's 1941 etching of Justice Stanley Forman Reed. (Inset: Oskar's pencil sketch.) Justice Reed was the latest-serving justice not to have graduated from a law school. A native Kentuckian, he was expected by his colleagues to be the lone dissenter in Brown v. Board of Education *in 1954, but he switched and joined the majority before an opinion was issued. He is reported to have wept during the reading of the opinion in open court.*

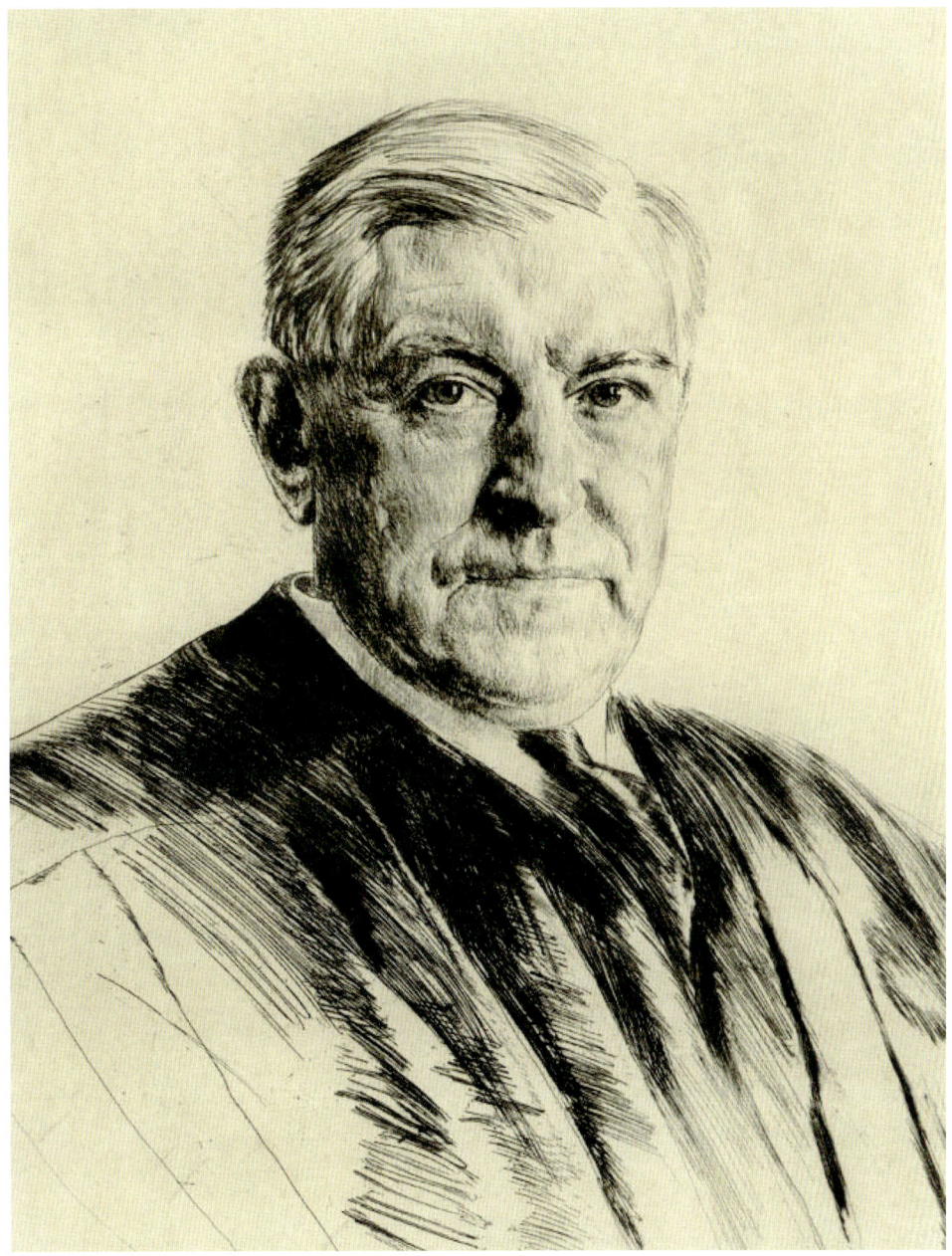

Oskar's 1941 etching of Justice Owen Roberts. By the time Chief Justice Stone succeeded Chief Justice Hughes, Justice Roberts was the only member of the Court appointed by a President other than FDR: he had been appointed by President Herbert Hoover in 1930. His relations with colleagues were so strained that the Court could not even agree on the wording of a farewell message to him. In the end, none was sent.

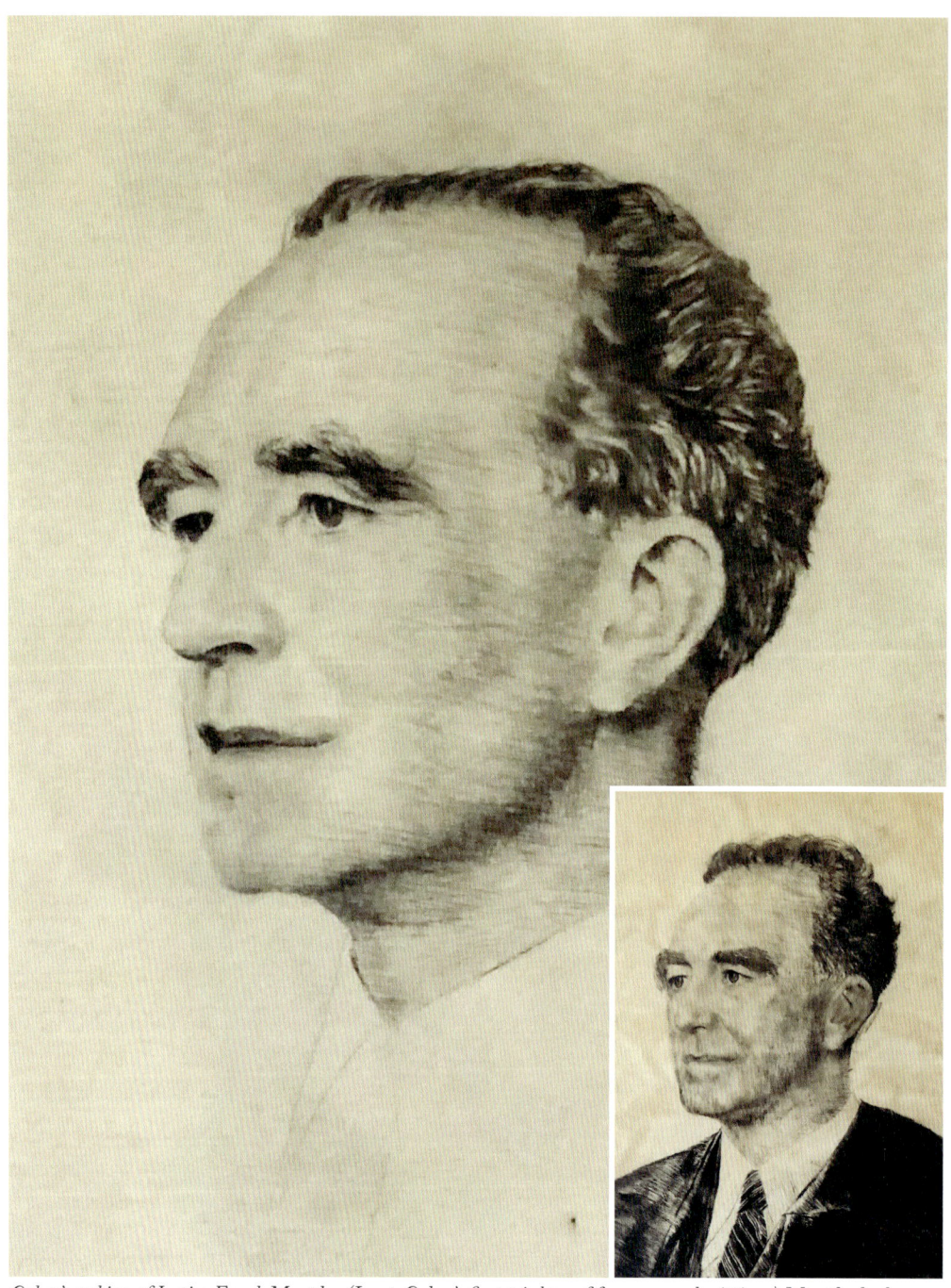

Oskar's etching of Justice Frank Murphy. (Inset: Oskar's first trial proof from an early sitting.) Murphy had a total of five sittings with Oskar from March to May 1941. Justice Murphy had a storied career as mayor of Detroit (1930–1933), governor general of the Philippine Islands (1933–1935), governor of Michigan (1937–1939), U.S. attorney general (1939–1940), and finally associate justice (1940–1949).

him as somewhat scruffy. A second version, from a different angle and doubtless another sitting, depicts him with hair more neatly combed (see page 144).

Given the timing of the Corcoran Gallery exhibition—most of April 1941—it was probably the initial etching of Justice Murphy that Oskar exhibited. After all, Murphy had three more sittings with Oskar after the exhibition began.

The brochure accompanying the exhibition stated that Oskar had made portraits of "all the justices of the United States Supreme Court, the only case, it is believed, in which one artist portrayed them all." Eight were listed: Hughes C.J. and Stone, Roberts, Reed, Douglas, Murphy, Frankfurter, and Black JJ. Only eight.

Who was the missing ninth? The famously antisemitic Justice James Clark McReynolds, who had resigned from the Court on January 31, 1941. Hence although the Court was without its full complement of nine, the brochure was accurate in saying that all the active justices had portraits.

Nothing seems to have resulted from Justice Stone's letter to McReynolds. That might have been just as well. McReynolds was gratuitously nasty to people: Chief Justice William Howard Taft called him "selfish to the last degree . . . fuller of prejudice than any man I have ever known."[12] He ostentatiously objected to having Jewish justices on the Court and for years refused to acknowledge the presence of Justices Brandeis, Cardozo, and Frankfurter. Opposing Cardozo's impending appointment in the early 1930s, McReynolds reportedly implored the president not to "afflict the Court with another Jew."

McReynolds didn't consider or care about whether his colleagues, over a quarter-century, felt afflicted by him.

---

12. Alpheus Thomas Mason, *William Howard Taft: Chief Justice* (Oldbourne, 1964), 217 (quoting a Taft letter dated June 11, 1923).

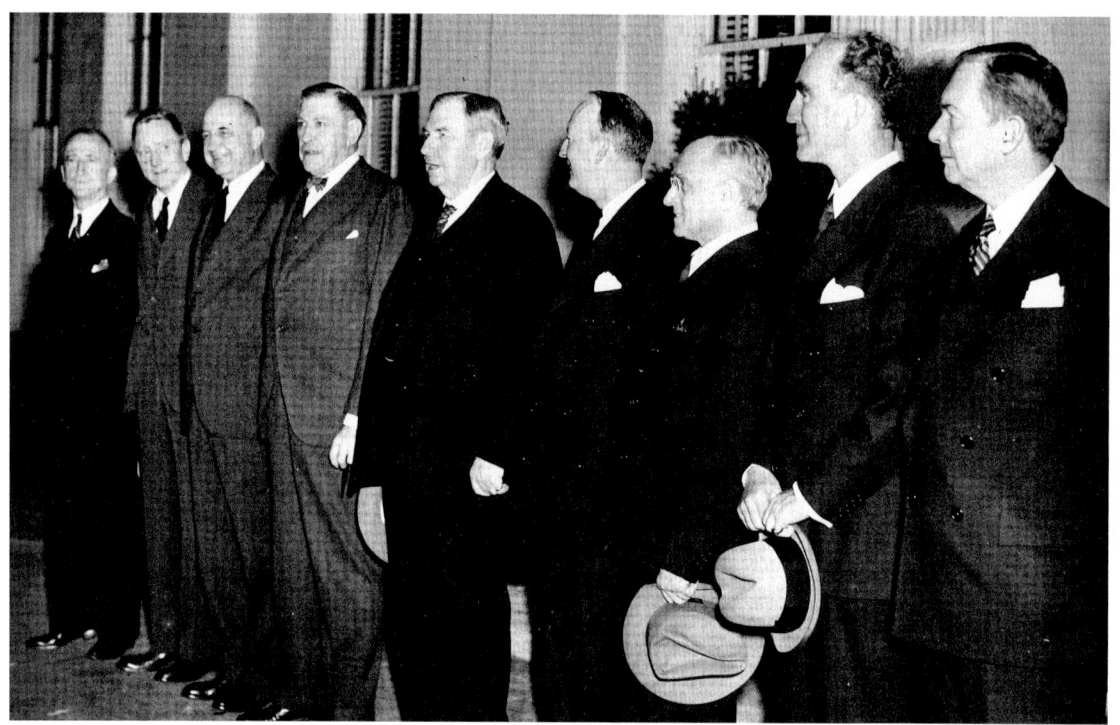

ABOVE: *The justices whose portraits Stoessel etched from 1940 to 1942*

BELOW: *The Court calls on the president on October 13, 1942: Jackson, Murphy, Douglas, Frankfurter, Reed, Black, Roberts, and Stone. Justice Byrnes has just resigned.*

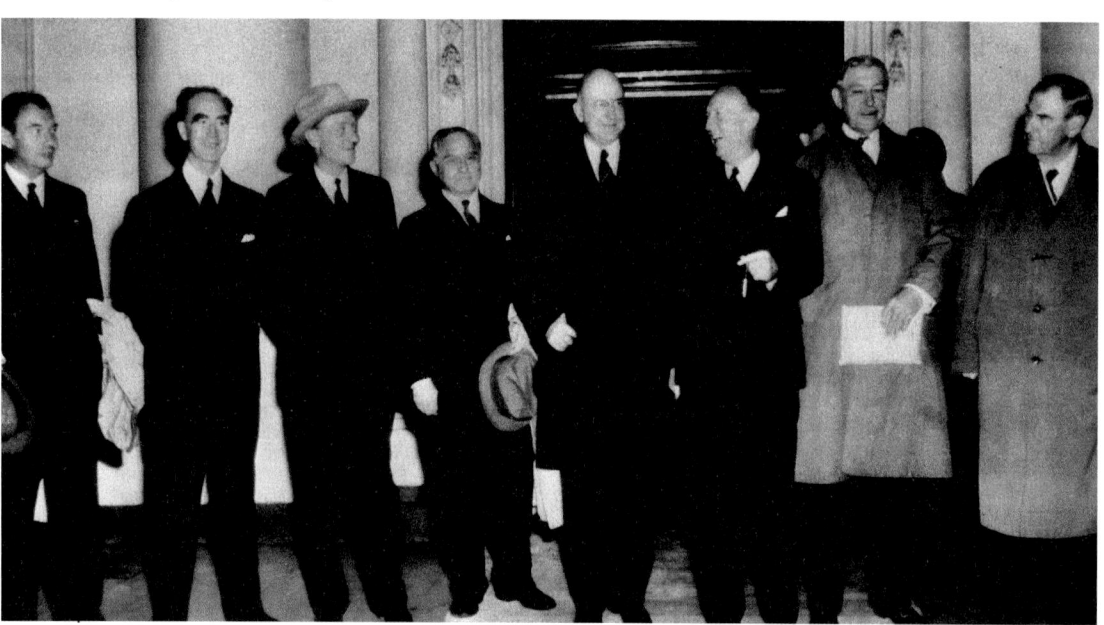

CHAPTER 19

Pretend Monarch

EARLY in 1941, Oskar connected with the 28-year-old crown prince of Austria-Hungary—Otto von Habsburg. Oskar had fought for the Austro-Hungarian Empire during World War I. Soon after the empire was dissolved in 1918, Otto became the pretender to the former kingdoms and head of the House of Habsburg-Lorraine. He would remain putative sovereign of the Imperial House into the 21st century, resigning in 2007.

The eldest son of Charles I (the last emperor of Austria and king of Hungary) and his wife Zita of Bourbon-Parma, Otto had 17 given names at birth: he was *Franz Joseph Otto Robert Maria Anton Karl Max Heinrich Sixtus Xaver Felix Renatus Ludwig Gaetan Pius Ignatius von Habsburg*. But he was known as Otto, and at birth he was third in line to the thrones of Austria, Hungary, Bohemia, and Croatia. With his father's accession to these thrones in 1916, he was likely to become emperor and king. His father, never having abdicated despite the Habsburgs' exile from Austria, died in 1922. From that point on, Otto was considered by many (including himself) to be the rightful emperor-king.

From the 1930s, Otto was active in Austrian and European political affairs by promoting both Habsburg restoration and European integration. He fiercely opposed Nazism, nationalism, and communism. Despite living in exile, he became a leader of the Austrian Resistance and helped thousands of Austrian Jews flee after the Anschluss. His efforts might even have helped Oskar in some way. After Hitler ordered the prince's execution, Otto fled Europe to the United States.

The two men had much in common, even if Otto's stage was much larger and grander. Otto was the urbane patrician; Oskar was the cultured but humble artist. Despite their different stations in life, the two bachelors would have had gossip to share. Oskar had spent time with European royals, especially in 1928–1929, and

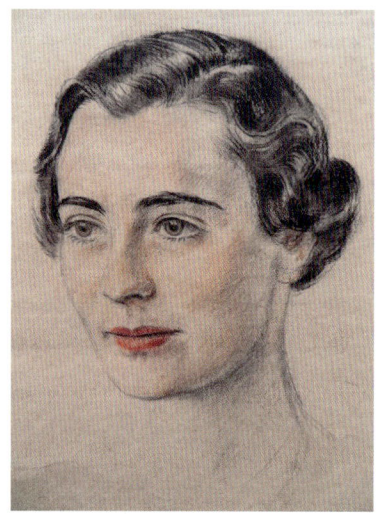

*Pencil and chalk of Princess Helen of
Greece and Denmark (1929)*

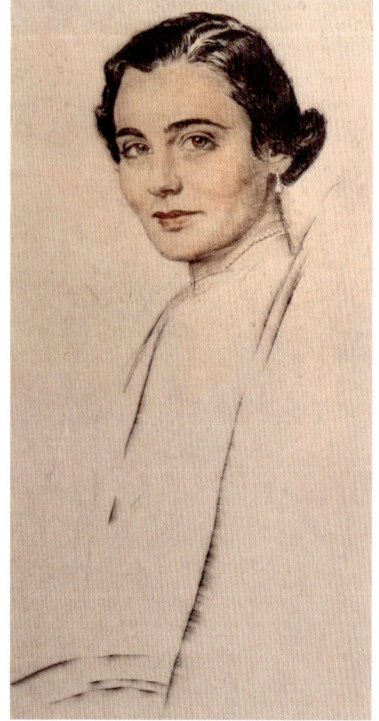

*Oskar's etching of Princess Helen of
Greece and Denmark (1929)*

Otto—if so inclined—could have filled in many titillating details about the people Oskar had encountered.

Not that Oskar needed a history lesson, but Otto was probably free in giving his account to a trusted and discreet countryman. One imagines the lively discussions that Otto and Oskar had during the sittings for Otto's portrait. They doubtless reminisced about their youth in the Old Empire, about the travails of World War I, and about Vienna's artistic heyday that had lasted until the nightmare of the late 1930s began to play out. They'd have recounted how each of them escaped the Nazis. Otto had fled to France in 1938, and then to Portugal in 1940, and then later that year to the United States. Both men had harrowing tales to tell.

The sittings took place in Otto's New York apartment. At the time, Otto was courting support from Justice Frank Murphy for his "Free Austria Movement," projected to be a conservative Catholic forum that would promote an antisocialist future for Austria. Otto was surely fascinated to learn of Oskar's exploits at the Supreme Court—and in particular his experiences with Otto's new acquaintances there. Equally, though, Otto and Oskar would have compared notes on President Roosevelt, who had warmly welcomed Otto upon his arrival in Washington. Since then, Otto had become a frequent guest at the White House and a principal adviser there on European affairs. Otto might well have purchased some of Oskar's Washington portraits, including that of Roosevelt.

Oskar and Otto may also have talked about King Michael of Romania, who had recently been restored to his throne. World War I had brought an end to many of the

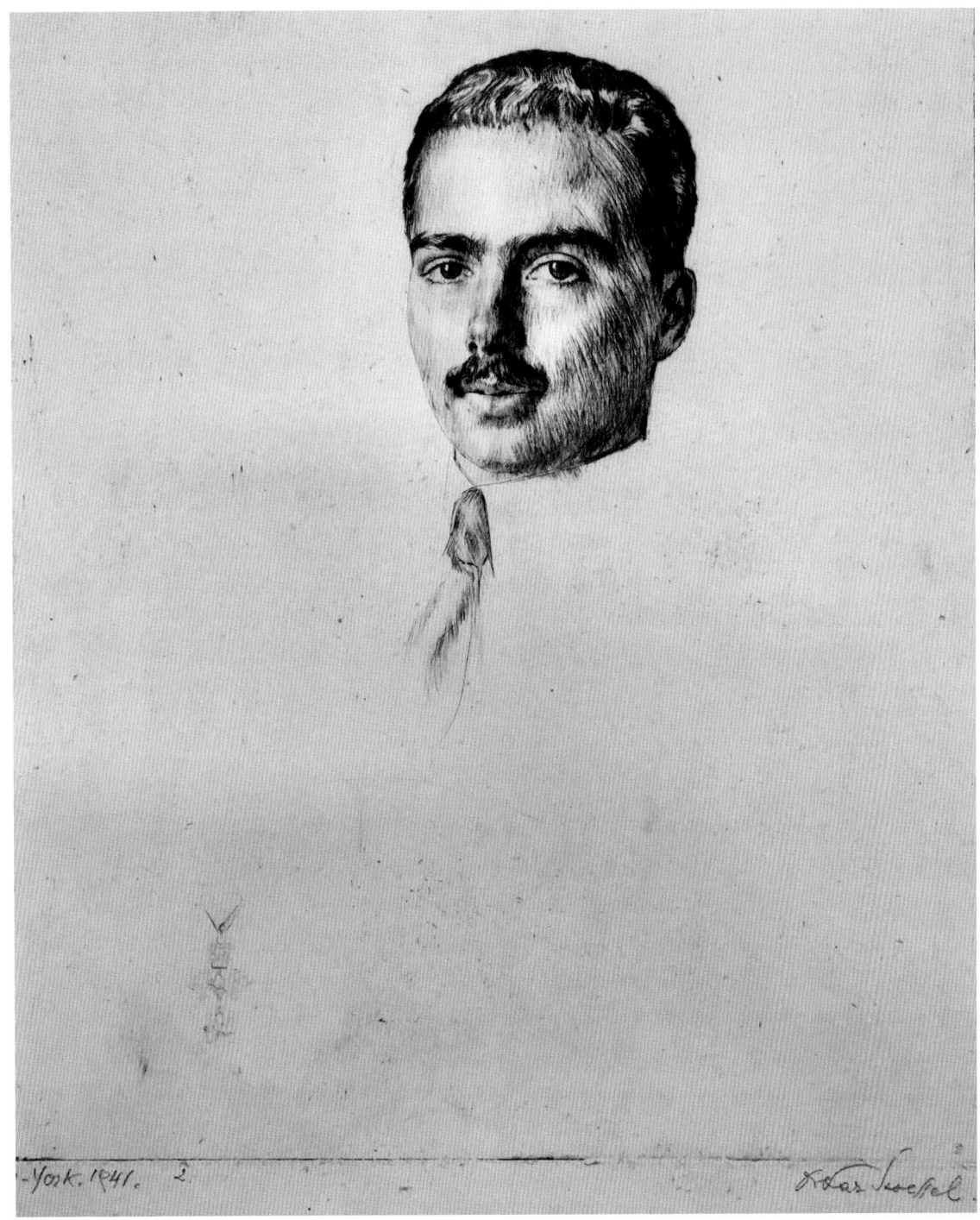

Oskar's 1941 portrait of Otto von Habsburg. The remarque (lower left) is Otto's badge for the Order of the Golden Fleece, for which he was grand master.

royal houses of Europe, from the Romanovs to the Habsburgs.[1] Romania was an exception; it was a young kingdom, created in 1880[2] and ruled by the Hohenzollern-Sigmaringens. At the beginning of World War I, when Ferdinand I became king, the royal family's primary seat was the Cotroceni Palace in Bucharest. But the king and his family had fled before the city fell in 1916 to the German Army led by Field Marshal August von Mackensen. During this time, as we've seen, Oskar etched Mackensen's portrait in the palace, where the Germans had established their headquarters. The royal family wouldn't return until after the war ended.

The Treaty of Versailles changed the map of Romania, expanding it to include Transylvania, Bukovina, and Bessarabia. In 1922, King Ferdinand I and Queen Marie were officially crowned as the rulers of Greater Romania. It was a tumultuous period for the Romanian royal family. Ferdinand's heir apparent, Carol, had deserted the Romanian Army during the war and, in 1918, secretly married a commoner.[3] After the Romanian Supreme Court annulled the marriage, Carol was forced in 1921 to marry Princess Helen of Greece and Denmark. She gave birth to their only child, Michael, that same year. Carol became a rebellious playboy and ignored his wife, son, and country, preferring to frolic openly with his mistress, even traveling across Europe with her. Faced with an ultimatum, Carol kept his mistress, renounced his right to the Romanian throne in 1925, and divorced Princess Helen in 1928.[4] When King Ferdinand died in 1927, his six-year-old grandson Michael became king.

Oskar had met them all.

Although photographic portraits of royalty were by then common, many royals still preferred etched portraits. Oskar had been invited to the newly established royal court of Albania in 1928 to make etchings of various royals. With many important portraits already to his credit (including the Prince of Liechtenstein)—and the tempestuous events of renunciation, infidelity, and divorce resolved—it's

---

1.   Gareth Russell, *The Emperors: How Europe's Rulers Were Destroyed by the First World War* (Amberly, 2015).

2.   Charles J. Vopicka, *Secrets of the Balkans* (Rand McNally, 1921), 15.

3.   Lily Marcou, *Le Roi Trahi: Carol II de Romanie* (Pygmalion/G. Watelet, 2002), 96–99.

4.   Ivor Porter, *Michael of Romania: The King and the Country* (History Press, 2005), 25.

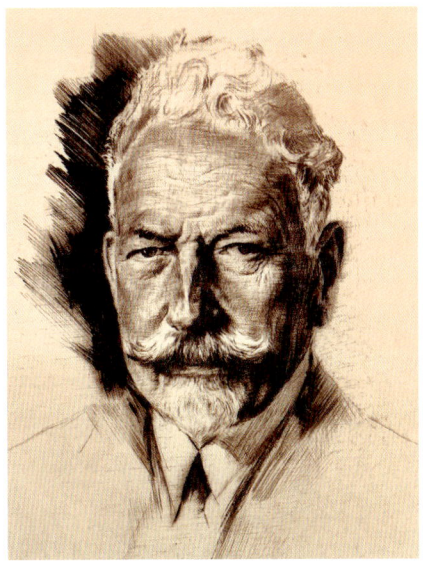

Archduke Eugen of Austria (1863—1954) was among the last of the Habsburg dynasty. Oskar etched his portrait in 1935, when he was living at the Teutonic Order's convent in Gumpolds-kirchen, near Vienna.

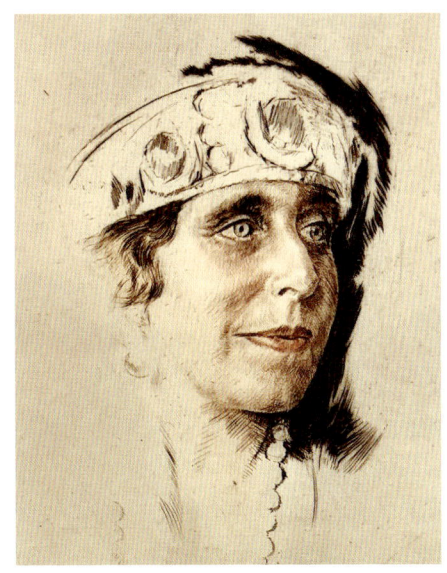

Queen Marie of Romania (1875—1938) was the last queen of her country as the wife of King Ferdinand I. Born a Briton, she declined a mar-riage proposal to the future George V of England; instead, she married the crown prince of Romania.

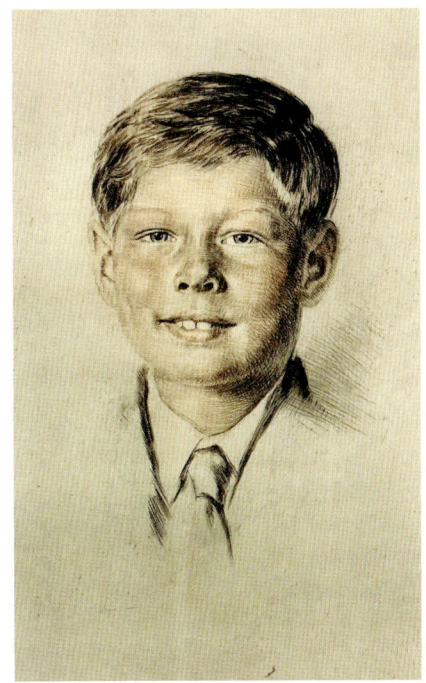

King Michael of Romania (ca. 1929)

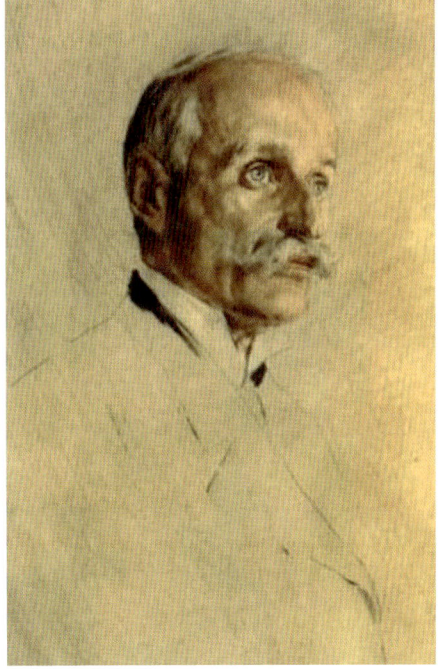

Francis, Prince of Liechtenstein (1924)

not surprising that the royal house of Romania engaged Oskar to immortalize them. It's conceivable that August von Mackensen recommended Oskar. Despite the events of World War I, Mackensen was a staunch monarchist who retained his connections with German royalty, including King Ferdinand and Queen Marie.

Oskar's clients in Romania probably sat for their portraits both in the Cotroceni Palace, Bucharest, and in Bran Castle, their summer residence. Oskar ultimately produced etchings of King Michael, the dowager Queen Marie, her daughter Princess Ileana, Michael's mother Princess Helen of Greece and Denmark, and her sister Princess Irene of Greece and Denmark. By the end of 1929, Michael would be deposed by his own father,[5] who would rule as Carol II until 1940, when Michael was reinstated.[6]

Oskar was surely the only man alive, other than Otto, who knew not only these people but also Mackensen, Roosevelt, Hull, and the justices of the Supreme Court. The conversations between the two men must have been animated, nostalgic, and touching—and perhaps, at times, mildly salacious.

By June 1942, Otto would meet Chief Justice Stone at the White House. Stone described him as "a very intelligent, attractive young chap" who was "profiting by his exile in America"—adding: "When the present war is over, if Austria gets her freedom she might do worse than to call the young man back."[7]

5. *Mihai, Mare Voievod de Alba Iulia*, in the collection of the Rumania Libere, accessed Dec. 9, 2024, https://romanialibera.ro/sport/atletism/fotodocument-mihai-mare-voievod-de-alba-iulia -316277/.

6. Julia P. Gelardi, *Born to Rule: Five Reigning Consorts, Granddaughters of Queen Victoria* (St. Martin's, 2005), 384.

7. Chief Justice Harlan Fiske Stone to Helen Stone Willard (his sister), typed letter, June 13, 1942, Stone Papers, Library of Congress.

CHAPTER 20

Exhibiting at the Corcoran

R EMARKABLY, Oskar had two consecutive exhibitions at the Corcoran Gallery of Art in Washington, D.C. Everything moved quickly. On January 9, 1941, Oskar met with C.P. Minnigerode and Emily P. Millard, the Corcoran's manager of special exhibitions. They offered first to exhibit Oskar's collection of 18th-century French prints in Gallery 40 beginning three days later, or as soon as he could have the items matted. The Corcoran would insure the collection for $8,000.

The prints were aquatints, engravings, and etchings that Oskar had somehow managed to move past the Nazis when he fled Austria. According to the typewritten catalogue that the Corcoran prepared with Oskar's help, there were 27 of them:

1. *Queen of France—Marie Antoinette d'Autriche*, by Jean François Janinet (1777).
2. *Foire de Village* ["Village Fair"], by Charles Melchior Descourtis.
3. *La Rixe* ["The Brawl"], by Descourtis.
4. *Le Tambourin*, by Descourtis.
5. *Noce de Village* ["Village Wedding"], by Descourtis.
6. *L'Amant Écouté* ["The Lover Heard"], by Louis-Marin Bonnet.
7. *The Pleasures of Education*, by Bonnet (1777).
8. *The Milk Woman*, by Bonnet (1774).
9. *Annette et Lubin*, by Philibert-Louis Debucourt (1789).
10. *La Cruche Cassée* ["The Broken Pitcher"], by Jean Massard (although Oskar misidentified the artist as "Eysen" [Louis Eysen of the 19th century?]).
11. *Le Dépit* ["Vexation"], by "Eysen" (perhaps actually *Le Dépit Amoureux* ["The Vexed Lovers"] by Jean Michel Moreau le Jeune).

12. *Charlotte Corday*, by Jean Pieter Tassaert-Anselin.
13. *La Sagesse et la Justice* ["Wisdom and Justice"], by Bonnet.
14. *Que vas tu faire?* ["What will you do?"], by Debucourt.
15. *Qu'as tu fait* ["What did you do?"], by Debucourt.
16. *L'Automne*, by Jean-Baptiste Huet.
17. *Le Baiser de l'Amour* ["The Kiss of Love"], by Janinet.
18. *Le Déjueuné* ["The Lunch"], by Bonnet.
19. *Le Gouter* ["Afternoon Tea"], by Bonnet.
20. *Le Diner*, by Bonnet.
21. *Le Souper*, by Bonnet.
22. *Le Concert*, by Augustin de Saint-Aubin
23. *L'Aveu difficile* ["The Difficult Confession"], by Janinet (1787).
24. *La Comparaison*, by Janinet (1786).
25. *L'Indiscretion*, by Janinet.
26. *Les Bouquets*, by Debucourt (1788).
27. *Le Compliment*, by Debucourt (1787).

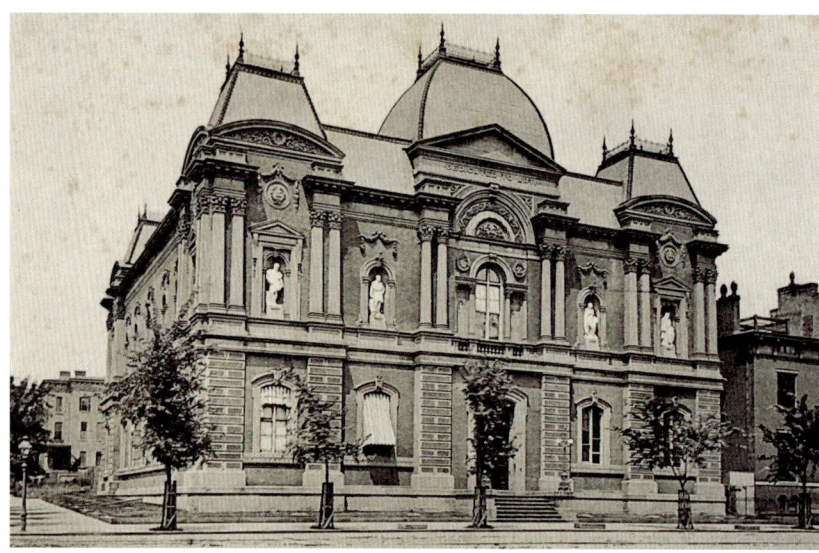

The Corcoran Gallery of Art, on Pennsylvania Avenue near the White House, as it appeared in the 1940s. Founded in 1878, the museum was a nonprofit institution that focused on American art. In 2014, after years of financial problems, the Corcoran was dissolved by court order and its $2 billion worth of holdings given to the National Gallery of Art. Today this building is known as the Renwick Gallery——a branch of the Smithsonian American Art Museum.

SPECIAL
EXHIBITION
ETCHINGS

BY
OSKAR STOESSEL

————

THE
CORCORAN GALLERY of ART
WASHINGTON, D. C.

FROM SATURDAY, APRIL 5th,
UNTIL
SUNDAY, APRIL 27th,
1941, Inclusive

LEFT: *Cover of the brochure for Oskar's second exhibition at the Corcoran Gallery. His previous exhibition, in the same room, was of his valuable collection of Old Master etchings.*
BELOW: *Inside the Corcoran Gallery brochure*

CATALOGUE

1. Archduke Eugen of Habsburg
2. Professor Ehrmann of the University of Vienna
3. Mrs. Lilian Koerner
4. Wedding in Bretagne
5. Portrait of a Girl
6. Portrait of My Mother
7. Edmonde Guy, French Dancer
8. Archduke Otto of Austria
9. Mrs. Sobotka
    Members of the United States Supreme Court
10. Chief Justice Hughes
11. Justice Stone
12. Justice Roberts
13. Justice Reed
14. Justice Douglas
15. Justice Murphy
16. Justice Frankfurter
17. Justice Black

18. Mr. George S. Messersmith, United States
        Ambassador to Cuba
19. The President of the United States
20. The Secretary of State, Cordell Hull
21. Assistant Secretary of State, Breckenridge Long
22. Prince Franz Liechtenstein
23. The British High Commissioner, Sir Arthur
        Wanchope
24. Portrait
25. Notre Dame, Paris
26. Study of a Tree
27. University Professor Tandler
28. Maria Jeritza as Elizabeth, Tannhauser
29. Miss Lotte Brociner
30. Queen Marie of Rumania

> The majority of these prints are for sale and no commission is charged by the Gallery. For prices and further information concerning portrait orders and other works by this artist, apply at the Office of the Director.

Oskar didn't have the prints mounted and displayed until February 7. He lent them to the Corcoran for nearly two months. While they were up, Millard wrote to Oskar that they were "being greatly enjoyed by our visitors."[1] Many of them seem to have been acquired from Oskar the following year by the Widener Collection and later given to the National Gallery of Art.

The main event, though, came in April: Oskar's exhibition of his own etchings. Minnigerode suggested that Oskar bring along more etchings than he would be able to display, so that the museum would "have a wider range of selection when arranging them in the cases."[2] Oskar was to bear the expense of exhibition brochures. In reply, he was characteristically gracious: "I am very pleased indeed to have the chance of exhibiting my work under so favorable circumstances in your famous museum."[3]

Millard then explained why April had been selected for Oskar's exhibition: "Mr. Minnigerode's wish to open the exhibition of your work either the latter part of March or early in April was with a view to selecting for that exhibition a particularly fine period. April is a month which is a particularly popular one with visitors to Washington."[4] Doubtless the annual Cherry Blossom Festival played a role in timing.

Oskar was under some pressure to complete his Supreme Court portraits, and possibly also that of Otto von Habsburg. Millard wrote to Oskar: "With a view to allowing you as much time as possible to complete the portraits you have in hand and to selecting the best possible part of the season, [Mr. Minnigerode] has authorized me to reserve the room (No. 40) from Friday, April 4th when the work will be installed, through Sunday, April 27th, the last day of the exhibition."[5]

Oskar might have rushed a few of the etchings, particularly that of Justice Frank Murphy, whose likeness appears to have been the scruffy-looking rough

---

1.   Emily P. Millard to Oskar Stoessel, typed letter, Feb. 8, 1941, Special Collections Research Center, George Washington University.

2.   Millard to Stoessel, typed letter, Jan. 10, 1941, Special Collections Research Center, George Washington University.

3.   Stoessel to C.P. Minnigerode, handwritten letter, Jan. 23, 1941, Special Collections Research Center, George Washington University.

4.   Millard to Stoessel, typed letter, Jan. 27, 1941, Special Collections Research Center, George Washington University.

5.   Millard to Stoessel, typed letter, Feb. 8, 1941, Special Collections Research Center, George Washington University.

draft (see page 144). After all, Oskar kept returning to Murphy's chambers for additional sittings well after the exhibition began. In any event, Oskar was able to mount 30 of his own etchings, all but 3 of which were portraits, mostly of distinguished people.

The critical commentary in the *Sunday Star* newspaper was the most extensive review that Oskar had attracted since arriving in the United States.[6] The reviewer, Leila Mechlin (1874–1949), was the first major female art critic in the country, and she had served as critic for the newspaper since 1900.[7] She introduced her review by saying that Oskar's work, "while a little uneven in merit, is, at its very best, very, very good, and his manner of working is pleasantly varied."[8] Mechlin continued:

> His portraits of men and of aged persons are perhaps his finest, delineating character very astutely and retaining vitality. In some instances, he uses color in almost flat tint effectively and skillfully. This, even in his very large plates, is, it is understood, accomplished with a single printing, which is quite remarkable.[9]

Mechlin thought that the "most successful [portrait] is that of Justice Harlan Fiske Stone, which is rendered in masterly fashion and is at the same time excellent as likeness."[10] The Stone portrait was reproduced alongside her review.

Mechlin's only negative words were about the Roosevelt portrait:

> Least satisfactory is that of President Roosevelt, which lacks, sadly, his expressive vitality and evident force of character through a rather forced and unnatural delicacy of handling—elongated face and very thin hands. But Presidents rarely have the good fortune of being satisfactorily portrayed by even the greatest of the great portraiturists [sic]. Possibly it is the hoodoo of the official portrait, doomed to failure before begun.[11]

---

6. Leila Mechlin, "Oskar Stoessel Demonstrates His Ability at Portraiture in Corcoran Presentation," Art Notes, *Sunday Star*, Apr. 13, 1941, F6.
7. "Mechlin, Leila (1874–1949)," *Encyclopedia.com*, accessed Dec. 9, 2024, https://www.encyclopedia.com/women/dictionaries-thesauruses-pictures-and-press-releases/mechlin-leila-1874-1949.
8. Mechlin, "Oskar Stoessel," F6.
9. Mechlin, F6.
10. Mechlin, F6.
11. Mechlin, F6.

Although this is speculation, the elongation of Roosevelt's face might have resulted from a rejection of the first trial proof—the one in which Roosevelt appears somewhat heavier in a black suit (see page 99)—as a result of which Oskar might have thinned up the president for the final portrait (see page 96). The leanness of Roosevelt in the final version might also explain Mrs. Roosevelt's partiality toward it. Like any other portraitist with an income at stake, Oskar was willing to gratify his subjects in rendering and reworking their portraits.

Mechlin concluded by saying that "there are comparatively few portrait etchers today—and fewer still so successful or accomplished as Oskar Stoessel."[12]

The *Washington Post* reviewer, Alice Graeme, was generally in agreement. She wrote that "Stoessel's work, which is highly realistic and conservative, shows a remarkable degree of craftsmanship and a command of the medium. The portraits have been drawn with a surprising exactness and discipline of technique which is seldom found in the work of the contemporary artist."[13]

Graeme added: "Of its kind, Stoessel's work must be ranked among the best."[14] But it wasn't unqualified praise: "There is . . . considerable unevenness in the success of the different portraits . . . . His portraits of women, which require feminine grace and delicacy, are far less interesting, and in certain cases quite mediocre."[15] And she agreed with Mechlin about the Roosevelt portrait: "While his study of the President is sentimentalized and by no means worthy of his best work, the series of the Justices is most interesting."[16] She closed by adding that Stoessel "is at present here in Washington"—perhaps for the duration of the exhibit—"and would be available for further portrait commissions."[17] A reproduction of the portrait of Breckinridge Long accompanied her review.

Of the 30 prints exhibited at the Corcoran, only 2 are unidentifiable from the catalogue's description: no. 5 (*Portrait of a Girl*) and no. 24 (*Portrait*). They might

---

12.   Mechlin, F6.
13.   Alice Graeme, "Stoessel's Etchings Show Force," *Wash. Post*, Apr. 13, 1941, L6.
14.   Graeme, L6.
15.   Graeme, L6.
16.   Graeme, L6.
17.   Graeme, L6.

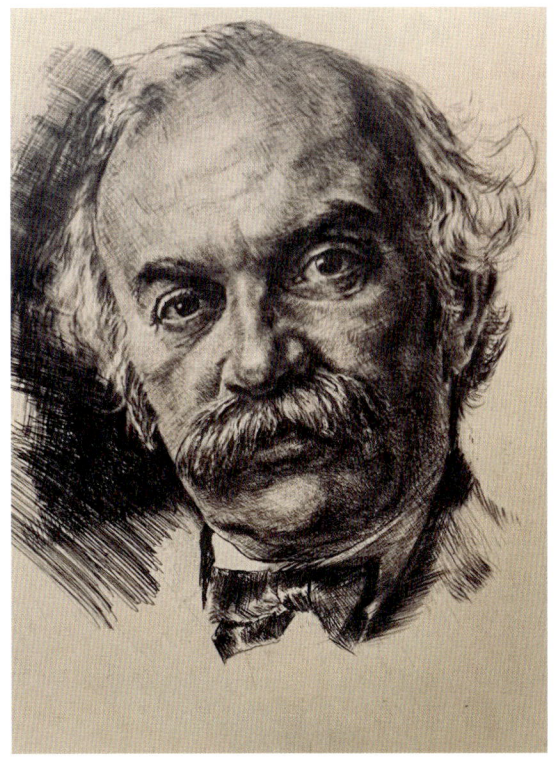

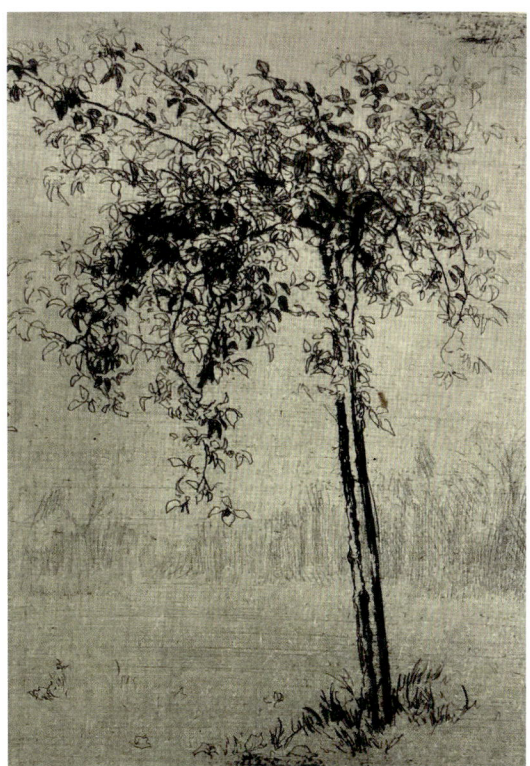

Professor Julius Tandler (1869–1936) was an Austrian physician and anatomist, as well as a Social Democratic politician. He was a major proponent of social services, family planning, and public health.

"Blooming Rosebush" (1913)

actually be represented somewhere in this book (pages 54 & 55?). The portrait of Lilian Koerner (no. 3) is unattested. The portraits of Professor Ehrmann and Mrs. Subotka have eluded exemplification. The others can be found here at the pages listed:

Archduke Eugen of Habsburg (page 151).
Wedding in Bretagne (page 57).
Portrait of the Artist's Mother (page 232).
Edmonde Guy, French Dancer (page 13).
Archduke Otto of Austria (page 149).
Chief Justice Hughes (page 171).

Justice Stone (page 135).

Justice Roberts (page 143).

Justice Reed (page 142).

Justice Douglas (page 124).

Justice Murphy (page 144).

Justice Frankfurter (page 139).

Justice Black (page 136).

Ambassador George S. Messersmith (page 72).

President Franklin Delano Roosevelt (pages 96 & 99).

Secretary of State Cordell Hull (page 108).

Assistant Secretary of State Breckinridge Long (page 111).

Prince Francis of Liechtenstein (page 151).

Sir Arthur Wauchope (page 39).

Study of a Tree (page 166).

Professor Tandler (page 159).

Maria Jeritza as Elisabeth, Tannhäuser (page 52).

Miss Lotte Brociner (page 40).

Queen Marie of Romania (page 151).

One only wishes that photographs of the exhibition could be found.

Oskar had a practical problem here that may not be immediately apparent. As Graeme noted in her review, he was staying in Washington in hopes of having more portraits commissioned. But once people have seen that an artist has portrayed dignitaries such as the president, all the justices, and European royalty, who would step forward to say, "I want one, too"? A mere congressional representative or senator probably wouldn't: it might be seen as presumptuous, especially in the days when personal modesty was a prized attribute. A lower-court judge wouldn't: it might suggest unseemly notions of grandeur. ("Are you putting yourself on the level of a Supreme Court justice?") Would a businessman or journalist or professor come forward? Probably not. Meanwhile, Oskar needed sitters whose portraits would sell—either to the subject personally (for distribution to friends and family) or to the public.

And that's another problem. Oskar was selling his portraits from the Corcoran Gallery, which generously agreed (as the brochure mentions) to take no commission on the sales. But who wants to frame and display any of the portraits listed above? Romanian royals? Austrian royals? A Liechtenstein royal? Americans didn't admire European royalty, especially not in the midst of World War II. Oskar's mother? George Messersmith? Breckinridge Long? Perhaps an ardent Democrat might want an FDR portrait, especially if the president would sign it. And perhaps a lawyer close to one of the justices might buy an etching to request an inscription from the subject—and then to hang in the law office. These would have been few. Oskar's sales as well as his further commissions were surely a disappointment.

Generally speaking, Americans buy art depicting things like seascapes, fields of flowers, children at play, boating parties, sumptuous interiors, street scenes, classical architecture, and so on. In short, Oskar might have done much better if he had stuck to his erstwhile passion for cityscapes and country landscapes. Even a well-wrought White House, Supreme Court building, or New York thoroughfare would have sold better than what he was offering.

As an artist, however skillful, Oskar was finding that his business plan was failing him.

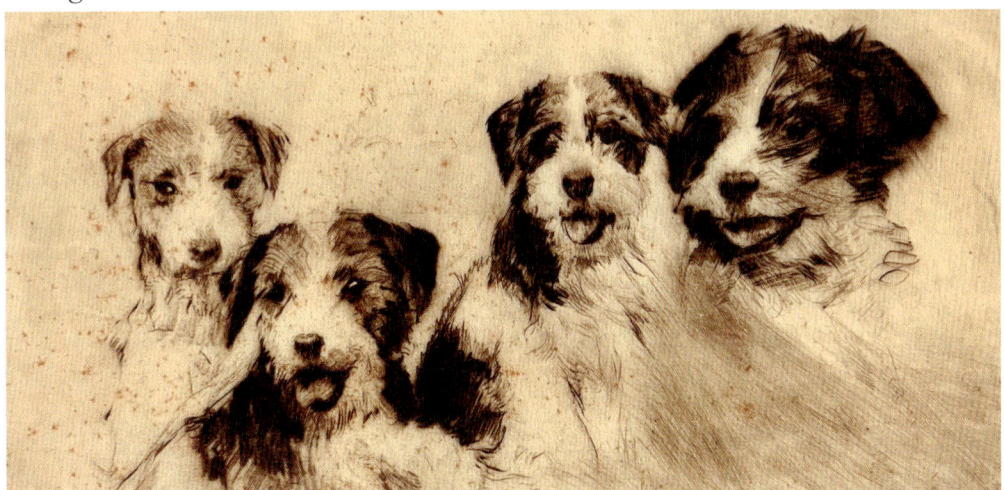

Four fox terriers (mid-1920s)

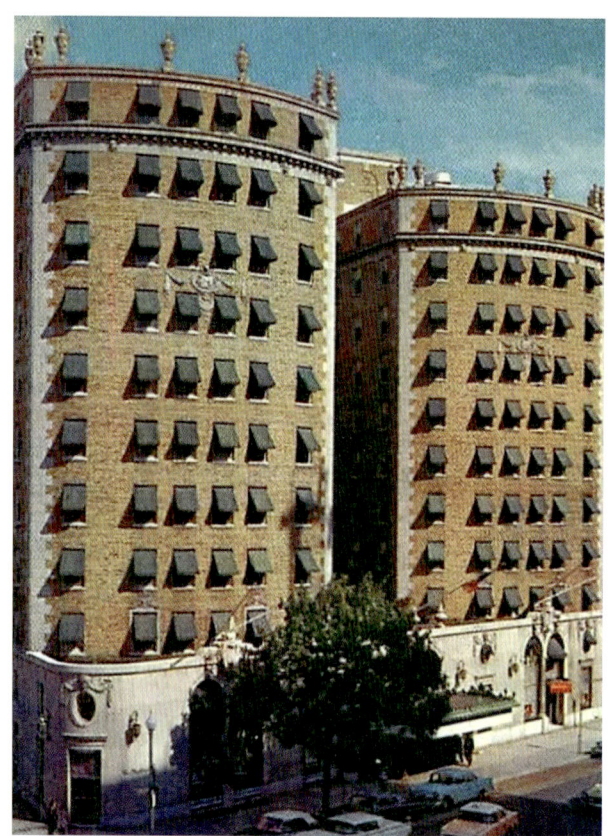

The front of the Mayflower Hotel as it looked in the 1940s

CHAPTER 21

Selling at the American Law Institute

J USTICE STONE had been working to help Oskar stage an exhibit of etchings at the prestigious American Law Institute, which at the time met at
the Mayflower Hotel in Washington. In 1941, the ALI comprised 787 of the
most accomplished judges, lawyers, and law professors in the nation. Like unof-
ficial legislators, they gathered for three days to a week each May—as they still
do—to compose and approve restatements of American law. Justice Stone had
obtained the ALI's approval for Oskar to set up his portraits near the registration
table May 5 through May 7.[1] Justice Stone and Oskar had surely discussed the
matter before Stone wrote this letter:

April 18, 1941.

Dear Mr. Stoessel:

I think I have arranged so that you can exhibit your etchings at the Mayflower Hotel in Washington at the meeting of the American Law Institute to
be held there on May 5, 6, and 7.

I enclose herewith a copy of a letter from Judge Goodrich,[2] who is connected
with the Law Institute, which will explain the situation to you.

I also enclose a note of introduction to Miss Paul.

When you come to Washington on the 5th if you will drop in to see me I will
make any suggestions that I can to be of assistance.

With kind regards, I am,

Yours sincerely,
Harlan F. Stone[3]

---

1. Judge Herbert F. Goodrich to Chief Justice Harlan Fiske Stone, typed letter, Apr. 15, 1941,
   Stone Papers, Library of Congress.
2. Judge Herbert Funk Goodrich of the U.S. Court of Appeals for the Third Circuit was influential in the ALI. He didn't become director until 1947, so his precise role in the arrangements isn't known.
3. Stone to Oskar Stoessel, typed letter, Apr. 18, 1941, Stone Papers, Library of Congress.

Unfortunately, the ALI archives contain no photographs of the 1941 annual meeting. But one can imagine Oskar seated in the long corridor of the Mayflower, surrounded by easels displaying his work and occasionally making a sale.

That same month, before the ALI meeting, Justice Stone was encouraging his wife to sit for a Stoessel portrait. Disappointingly, she would not consent. Stone wrote to Oskar at the Lee Hotel in D.C.:

April 30, 1941.

Dear Mr. Stoessel:

    I have had a talk with Mrs. Stone about sitting for you.

    She has not been very well this winter and is quite tired, and thinks for that reason that the picture would not be a success. She thinks it would be better to wait until after we have been away for the summer when perhaps she will feel and look more like it.

    At your convenience, will you print for me a half dozen of the portraits you have made of me? I should like to have you sign them, of course, if you feel like doing so.

    With kind regards, I am,

Yours sincerely,
Harlan F. Stone[4]

This suggests that Oskar stayed at a Washington hotel for most of a month—from early April through at least May 7. He does seem to have returned to Carnegie Hall for a few days. In any event, the additional portraits ordered by Chief Justice Stone netted Oskar an additional $120, and whatever judicial portraits he sold to the prominent lawyers of the ALI would more than defray his expenses. Stone doubtless attended parts of the meeting, given that he had long been a leading member, and his presence would have encouraged further sales. Other justices, too, might have made appearances and stopped by to greet Oskar. Having arranged sittings with all the justices, Stone seemed to feel as if he had a vested interest in Oskar's success. If sales were slow among the most prestigious lawyers in America, that would have embarrassed Stone. Within

---

4.   Stone to Stoessel, typed letter, Apr. 30, 1941, Stone Papers, Library of Congress.

the bounds of decorum and propriety, Stone was doing what he reasonably could to boost Oskar.

He certainly kept busy doing that in the copious correspondence he was sending from his chambers.

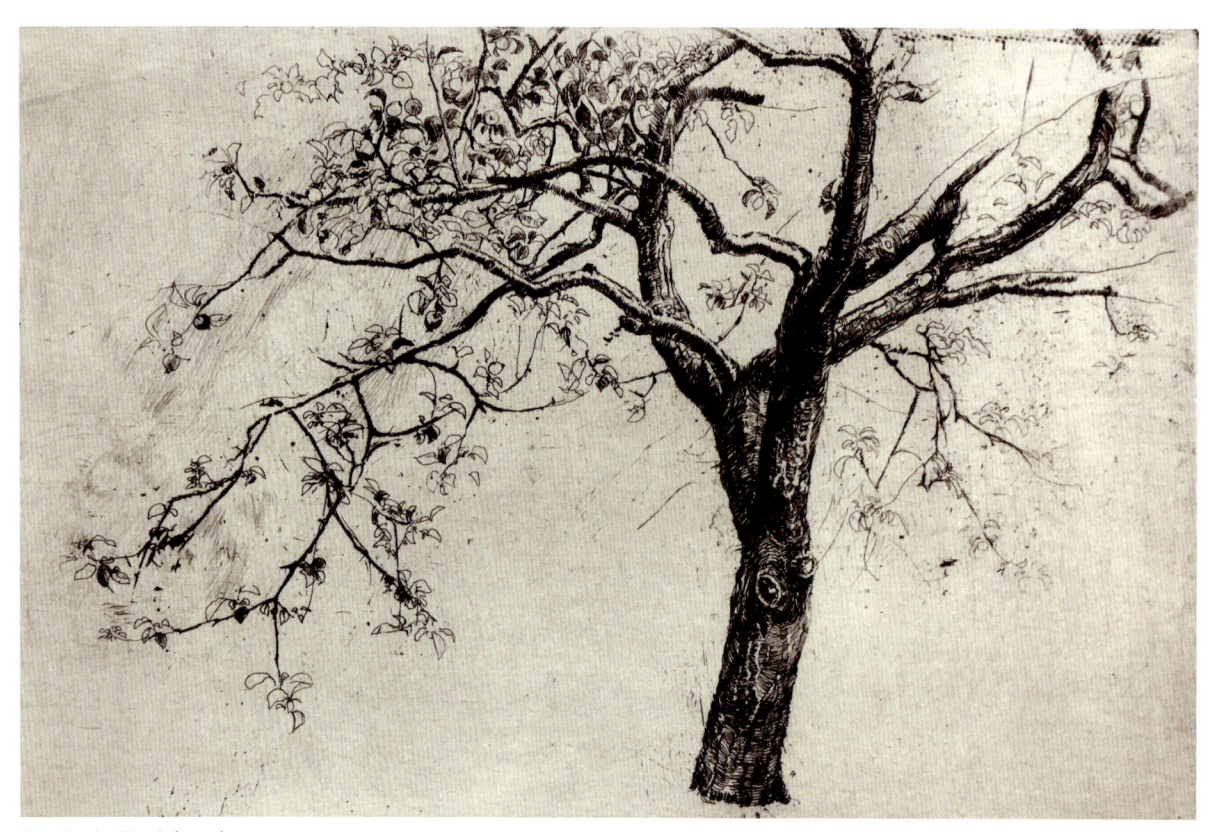

"Study of a Tree" (1920)

CHAPTER 22

Would Gladly Teach

Tᴏᴇ day after the ALI annual meeting concluded, Justice Stone wrote to Mrs. Charlotte Augusta Lea, a major benefactor to the Philadelphia Museum of Art. She had given more than 5,000 engravings to the museum.[1] Stone wrote that Oskar was "anxious to secure an opportunity to teach his art," adding: "I am wondering whether you think it likely that there would be any possibility of his getting such an opportunity in Philadelphia and, if so, if you would indicate to me how he should go about it."[2] Stone asked Lea not to trouble herself about the matter, but asked for any information she might readily give: "I feel confidence enough in his competence," he said, "both as an artist and a teacher, to write any necessary letter of recommendation."[3] The next day, Mrs. Lea responded warmly: "I am glad of any opportunity to help an artist."[4] She planned to meet the president and vice president of the Philadelphia Museum and also to propose an exhibition of Oskar's portraits at the Philadelphia Print Club.[5] Stone soon thanked her, saying that he would suggest to Oskar a trip to Philadelphia.[6] "But in any case," he urged Mrs. Lea, "do not let my interest in Mr. Stoessel become a burden to you."[7]

That same day, Justice Stone wrote to Oskar:

---

1. See *Fifty-Second Annual Report of the Philadelphia Museum and School of Industrial Art* (1928), 22.
2. Justice Harlan Fiske Stone to Mrs. Charles Lea, typed letter, May 8, 1941, Stone Papers, Library of Congress.
3. Stone to Lea, May 8, 1941.
4. Charlotte Augusta Lea to Stone, handwritten letter, May 9, 1941, Stone Papers, Library of Congress.
5. Lea to Stone, May 9, 1941.
6. Stone to Mrs. Lea, typed letter, May 12, 1941, Stone Papers, Library of Congress.
7. Stone to Lea, May 12, 1941.

May 12, 1941

Dear Mr. Stoessel:

I have had some correspondence with my friend Mrs. Charles Lea, an old resident of Philadelphia, who has many connections there and much interest in both the Art Museum and the Print Club, to which she and her husband have made many contributions.

I enclose herewith an excerpt from her letter, written to me yesterday, and also a note of introduction to Mrs. Andrew Wright Crawford, the Curator of the Print Club in Philadelphia.

Mrs. Lea is returning to her country home at Devon, Pennsylvania, near Philadelphia, this week, and I would suggest that you arrange to make a visit to Philadelphia sometime after her arrival there, with the purpose of calling on Mrs. Crawford and also on Mr. Jenks and Mr. Stokes, who are associated with the Museum, if in the meantime Mrs. Lea has had some opportunity to speak with them. Whenever I hear further from her on the subject I will drop you a line.

With kind regards, I am,

Yours sincerely,
Harlan F. Stone[8]

Oskar was soon making plans to visit Philadelphia. He wrote to Stone about the prospect:

May 25th, 1941

The Honorable Mr. Justice Harlan F. Stone.

Dear Mr. Justice:

I thank you very much indeed for your kind letter and for the great help you are giving me.

I intend going to Philadelphia sometime next week where I hope to be able to get in touch with Mrs. Andrew Wright Crawford, the Curator of the Print Club in Philadelphia. I shall take along with me some of my etchings and I do hope I shall succeed in taking some steps toward the arrangement of an exhibition there. From this exhibition some valuable connections that might lead to a teaching appointment may result and help me realize a favourite plan.

Yesterday I sent you 6 proofs of your portrait and I enclosed one for your secretary. She has been so nice to me and I should like to please her.

8.   Stone to Oskar Stoessel, typed letter, May 12, 1941, Stone Papers, Library of Congress.

I have started on the print of the set and I shall be very happy if you will very kindly accept one of these sets which I print for you hoping that you may enjoy this modest gift from an artist's workshop.

Thanking you again I am very respectfully

Yours

Oskar Stoessel.[9]

Stone's grateful reply came just two days later:

May 27, 1941.

Dear Mr. Stoessel:

Many thanks for the proofs, which have arrived, and which are excellent.

I have delivered Miss Jenkins's copy to her and she is delighted with it.

I shall indeed be glad to have a set of the portraits of my brethren whenever you can find it convenient to make them, and if I am not trespassing too much on your generosity.

You omitted to send me a bill for the six proofs. Please let me know how much I owe you.

Yours sincerely,

Harlan F. Stone.

P.S. I hope you have good success with your trip to Philadelphia.[10]

Perhaps Oskar phoned to say that the amount owed was $120, or perhaps he simply sent an invoice. Whatever the arrangements, his next letter acknowledged receipt of payment and further suggested his hope to put down permanent roots in America:

June 5th 1941.

The Honorable Mr. Justice Harlan F. Stone.
Washington, D.C.

Dear Mr. Justice,

Thank [sic] for your kind letter of June 2nd and for the check of $120. Thank you very much for the great help you are giving me. I am now printing the whole day, and when I have finished some sets, I will reserve the best proofs for you. I am so happy that I succeeded to get in touch with you, and I hope I can show

9.   Stoessel to Stone, handwritten letter, May 25, 1941, Stone Papers, Library of Congress.
10.   Stone to Stoessel, typed letter, May 27, 1941, Stone Papers, Library of Congress.

you in the future that I will do a usefull [sic] work in this country that I hope will be my new home. Thanking you again, and wishing you a good summer I am
 Very respectfully yours
  Oskar Stoessel.

P.S. I thank also Mrs. Jenkins for her kind letter.[11]

The correspondence never mentions whether he met Mrs. Andrew Wright Crawford at the Philadelphia Print Club. But the Club's archives have no copies of any correspondence from him and no exhibition was ever held, so it appears that nothing came of Oskar's trip to Philadelphia.

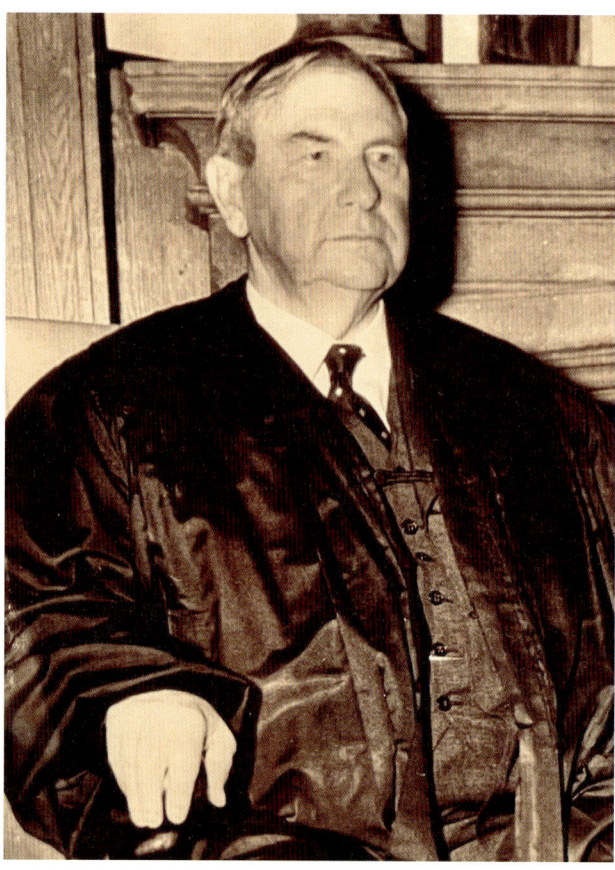

Stone donned his robe at home to celebrate his 69th birthday (Oct. 4, 1941).

11. Stoessel to Stone, handwritten letter, June 5, 1941, Stone Papers, Library of Congress.

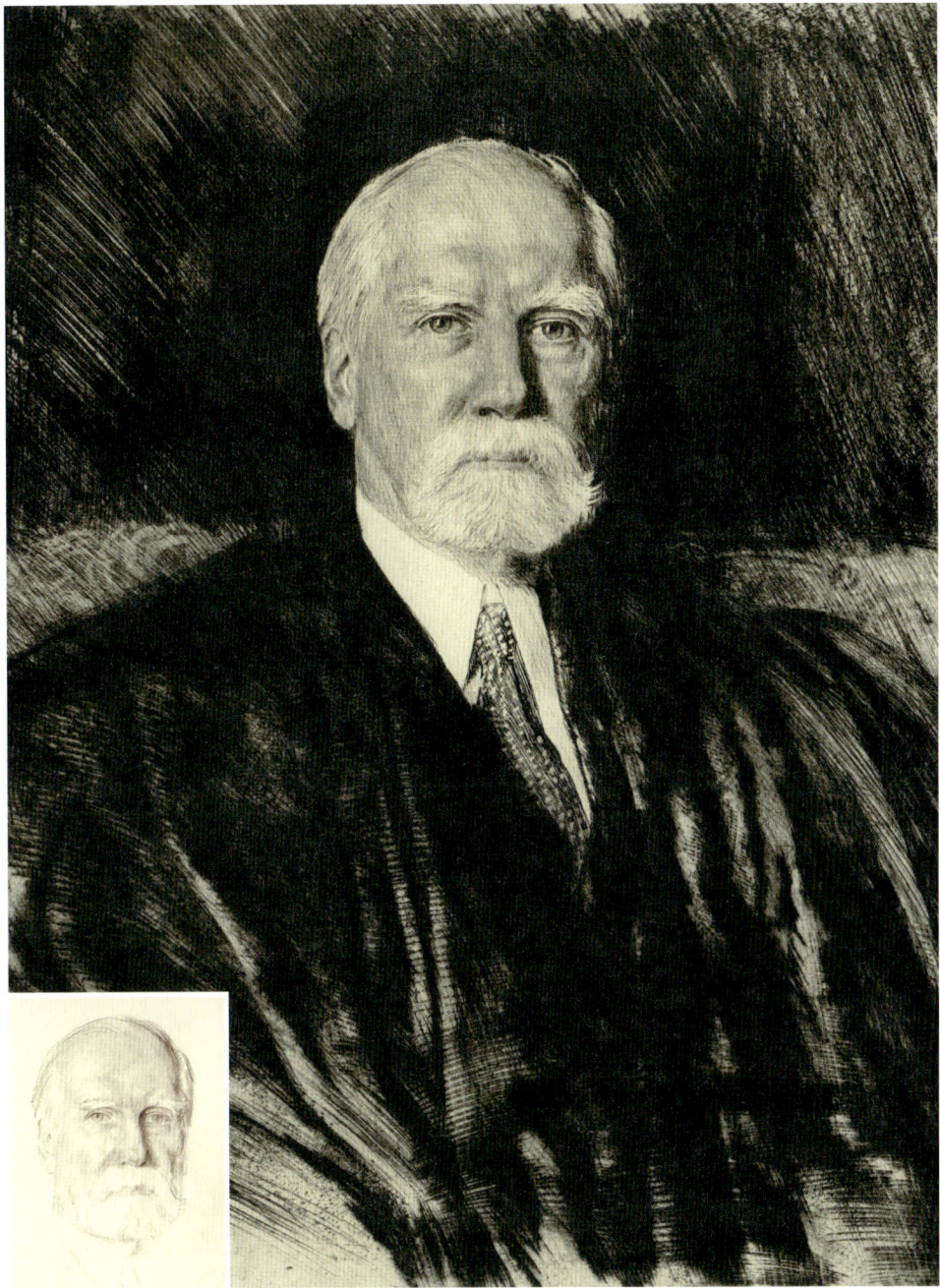

Oskar's etching of Chief Justice Charles Evans Hughes. He served not only as chief justice (1930–1941) but also as associate justice (1910–1916), as secretary of state (1921–1925), and as governor of New York (1907–1910). He was the Republican nominee in the 1916 presidential election, losing narrowly to Woodrow Wilson.
INSET: *Oskar's initial pencil drawing (courtesy of the Supreme Court of the United States)*

Supreme Court of the United States
Washington, D.C.

June 3, 1941.

My dear Brethren:

I shall always treasure the generous words of your letter. I keenly regret the necessity of giving up the privilege of our daily association and I shall carry into my retirement an abiding and precious memory of the good will and friendly consideration you have invariably shown me in the intimacy of our common endeavor. Despite my withdrawal from active service, I trust that our companionship may still continue and I extend to each of you the assurance of my high esteem and my earnest wish for your health and happiness.

Faithfully yours,

Charles E. Hughes

Mr. Justice Stone.
Mr. Justice Roberts.
Mr. Justice Black.
Mr. Justice Reed.
Mr. Justice Frankfurter.
Mr. Justice Douglas.
Mr. Justice Murphy.

Letter of Chief Justice Hughes announcing his retirement from the Court

CHAPTER 23

The Ascent of Stone

IN June 1941, Chief Justice Charles Evans Hughes announced his retirement (see opposite), and a month later Harlan Fiske Stone was confirmed as his successor.[1] Taking Stone's place as associate justice was Robert H. Jackson (confirmed July 11, 1941). At the same time, James F. Byrnes (confirmed June 25, 1941) was appointed to take the place of Justice James Clark McReynolds, who had retired in January. Meanwhile, Chief Justice Stone's new position made him chancellor of the Smithsonian Institution and chair of the board of trustees for the newly founded National Gallery of Art.[2]

Shortly after the beginning of the Court's new term, Chief Justice Stone wrote identical letters to Justices Byrnes and Jackson:

October 8, 1941.

Dear Justice Jackson:

During the last term of the Court, Mr. Oskar Stoessel, a distinguished artist, asked and received the privilege of etching each of the members of the Court. While there was some variation in his work I thought he did an extremely successful job, and some were superb.

He asks the privilege of etching you and Justice Byrnes. He takes very little time, two or three sittings at the most of about a half hour each time, and I very much hope that you will give him the desired sittings so that the set may be made complete.

His rather special terms, made to all the members of the Court, are: The sitter is under no obligation of any kind to take any of the etchings. He will present

---

1. *American National Biography* (1999), "Stone, Harlan Fiske [11 Oct. 1872–22 Apr. 1946]" ("On 2 June 1941 Chief Justice Charles E. Hughes retired, and President Roosevelt named Stone to succeed him. Some people thought the appointment a reward for his defense of New Deal measures, but as the justice himself noted, 'Washington is under no illusion that I am a New Dealer.'").

2. Alpheus Thomas Mason, *Harlan Fiske Stone: Pillar of the Law* (Viking, 1956), 758.

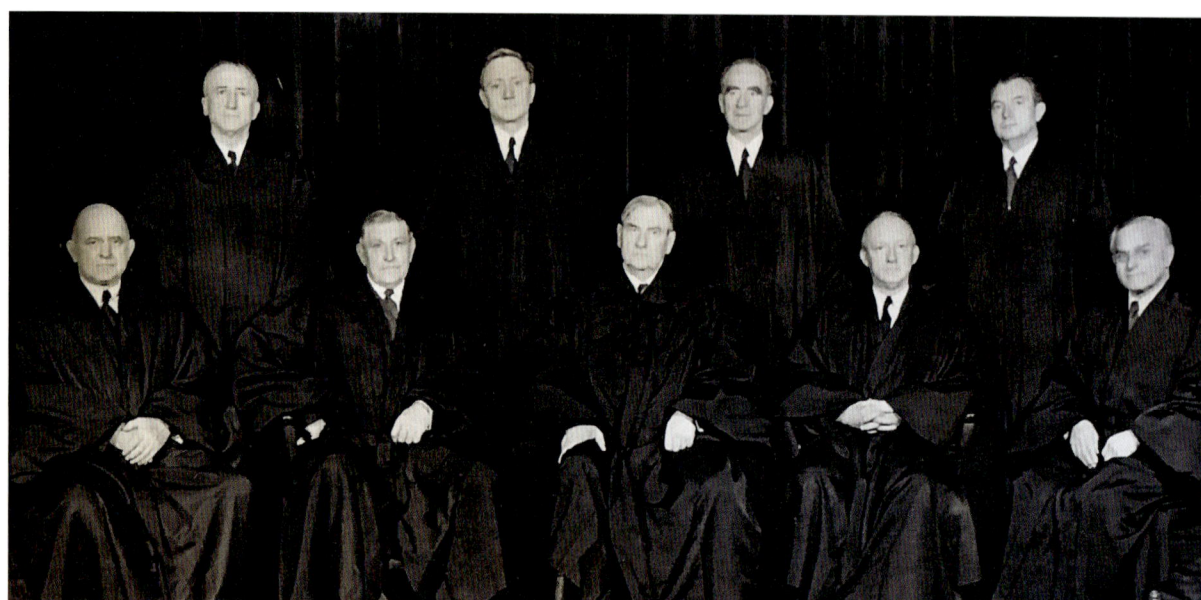

The Stone Court (seated left to right): Reed & Roberts JJ., Stone C.J., and Black & Frankfurter JJ.; (standing): Byrnes, Douglas, Murphy & Jackson JJ. Relationships among these justices were strained: Douglas and Frankfurter JJ. detested each other, and Black J. harbored enmity toward Roberts J. This roster on the Court has often been referred to as "scorpions."

one proof of the portrait to each sitter without charge, and then if they desire additional proofs he will supply them at $20 each.

If you are interested and will tell me so I will give him a card of introduction to you.

Yours faithfully,
Harlan F. Stone.[3]

Justice Byrnes answered the next day, with a letter equally formal. It was on Supreme Court letterhead, and the sender signed not "Jim" or "Jimmy" but "James F. Byrnes" above the typed name in all capitals.

No further letters exist from Justice Byrnes, but Justice Jackson maintained records of his correspondence with Oskar. Jackson's detailed in-chambers appointments calendar for October 27, 1941, contains two notations about Oskar's

---

3   Chief Justice Harlan Fiske Stone to Justice Robert H. Jackson, typed letter, Oct. 8, 1941, Stone Papers and Jackson Papers, Library of Congress.

meeting. They appear to be in the handwriting of Ruth Sternberg, Jackson's secretary. The first notation wasn't really in a time slot but seemed to mark the day for Oskar's visit. The second was probably added later, when the time was pinned down at 12:45 p.m. This may have been Jackson's only sitting with Oskar, no other having been recorded.

Oskar wrote to Justice Stone toward the end of the year, seemingly about two matters. The letter doesn't reside in the Stone Papers, but we do have two letters dated December 16 referring to Oskar's letter. The first is to Duncan Phillips, di-

Supreme Court of the United States
Washington, D.C.

October 9, 1941

Dear Mr. Chief Justice:

    I shall be glad to sit for Mr. Oskar Stoessel to make an etching and suggest that he come to my office some morning at 9:30.

Sincerely yours,

JAMES F. BYRNES.

The Chief Justice.

rector of the Phillips Memorial Gallery in Washington, stating: "A letter just received from Mr. Stoessel tells me that the Mendelsohn family, formerly of Vienna,[4] are now living in this country. They have a valuable collection of pictures which they are obliged to place on the market."[5] Among other items the Mendelsohns were selling were two Manets and a Van Gogh.[6] Whether or not Phillips

---

4. The reference seems to be to Erich Mendelsohn and his family. Mendelsohn was "arguably the most successful German architect until Hitler's takeover in 1933, when because of his Jewishness, he was forced to emigrate." *American National Biography* (1999), "Mendelsohn, Erich [1887–1953]." At the time of this letter, Mendelsohn was living and working in New York City.

5. Stone to Duncan Phillips, typed letter, Dec. 16, 1941, Stone Papers, Library of Congress.

6. Stone to Phillips, Dec. 16, 1941.

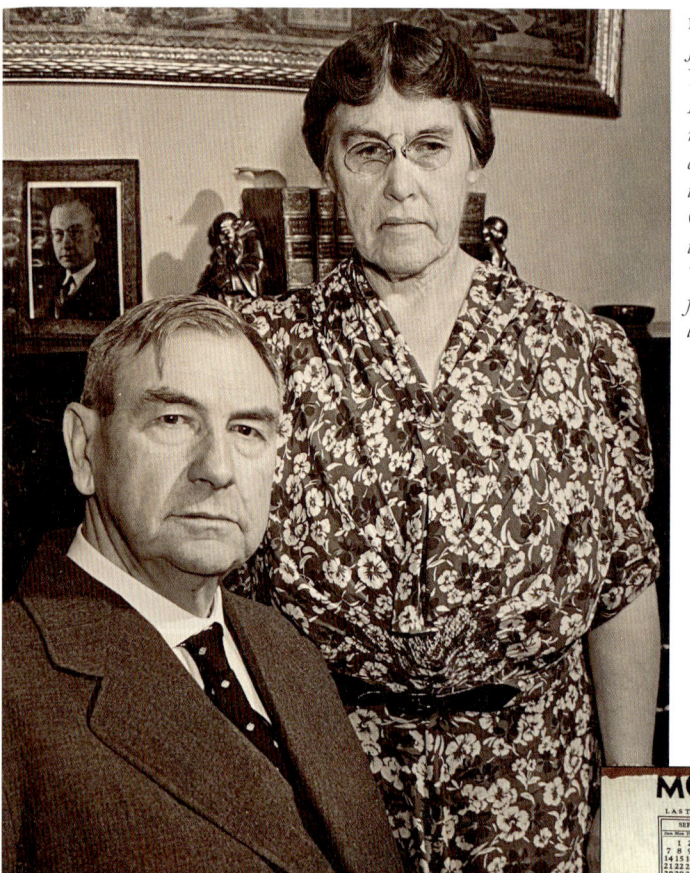

LEFT: *Justice and Mrs. Stone on June 13, 1941, in Brooklyn, New York, at the home of their son Lauson. Although he had just been nominated for the chief justiceship and was therefore busy with interviews, he may well have visited Oskar at Carnegie Hall on this trip. He commented to one reporter: "I don't know whether one should feel gratification at assuming such large responsibility."*

Justice Jackson's appointments calendar showing his only recorded meeting with Oskar——on October 27, 1941 (bottom line). The page has been ripped at the top.

was interested in buying, the chief justice recommended a meeting with Oskar: "He is a gentleman, something of a print collector himself, and a very agreeable person to know."[7] Phillips responded warmly, offering to see Oskar but saying: "We are not in the market for such valuable paintings as the Manets and the Van Gogh." Then he corrected something Oskar had said in his letter: "[Stoessel] is wrong in saying that we have no important Manet for there is no better example of the artist's first period than our 'Ballet Espagnol.' However 'Le Port de Bordeaux' is also a masterpiece which I know very well and I only wish we were in a position to acquire it. Your introduction of Mr. Stoessel will certainly make him a very welcome visitor."[8]

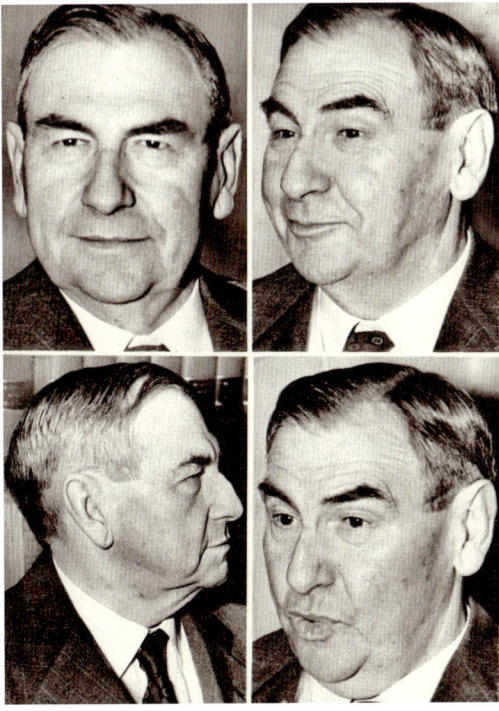

In June 1941, the Associated Press ran this series of photos of the nominee for chief justice, calling it a study in facial expressions.

7. Stone to Phillips, Dec. 16, 1941.
8. Phillips to Stone, typed letter (on Phillips Memorial Gallery letterhead), Dec. 20, 1941, Stone Papers, Library of Congress.

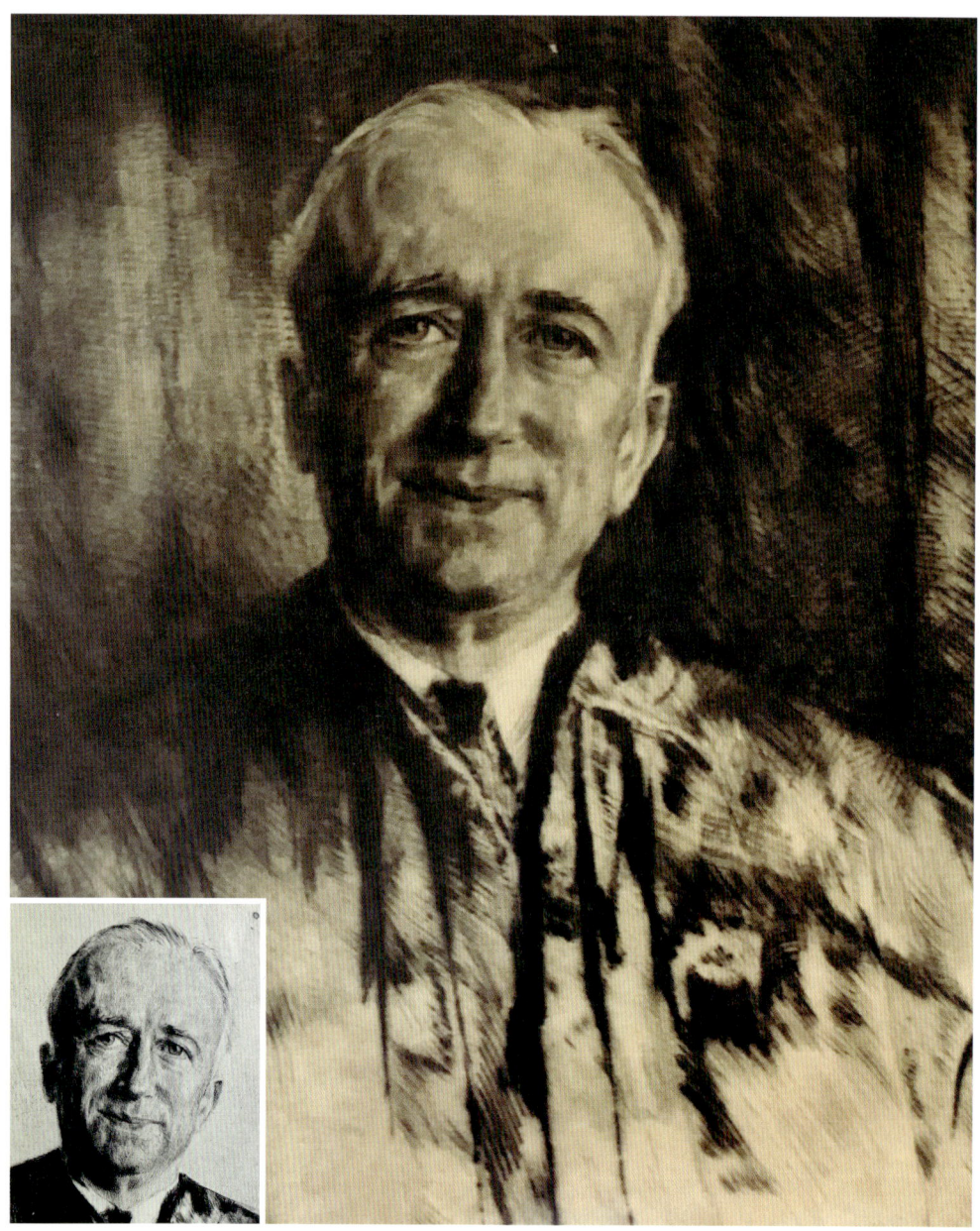

Oskar's 1942 etching of Justice James F. Byrnes. One or more sittings occurred probably in October–November 1941. See pages 174 & 181. (Inset: the trial proof.) Justice Byrnes sat on the Court for only one term——the second-shortest tenure in history. As a senator, Byrnes blocked antilynching legislation by arguing that lynching was a necessity "to hold in check the Negro in the South." Serving as governor of South Carolina from 1951 to 1955, Byrnes infamously opposed Brown v. Board of Education *and sought to defend "separate but equal" schooling for the races.*

CHAPTER 24

The Law Put in Focus

S UPREME COURT justices rarely give anyone private legal advice. Though they might informally make an exception for a close friend, it's hard to imagine one ghostwriting a request to the Justice Department. But it happened.

Apparently Oskar wrote to Chief Justice Stone, posing a legal question about the possession of a camera. Although we don't have Oskar's letter, we can assume that it was written sometime on or after December 7, 1941—the date of the Japanese air raid on Pearl Harbor. Late that day, after the bombing and in conjunction with the forthcoming declaration of war, President Roosevelt issued a proclamation ordering alien enemies to surrender their cameras, among other things. Oskar wanted to continue his practice of photographing his subjects. Surely there was talk about the war and this proclamation among the artists at Carnegie Hall, some of whom were photographers. In any event, Oskar either wrote to the chief justice or called his chambers about the issue. Chief Justice Stone's letter was written nine days after the Pearl Harbor bombing and eight days after the United States had officially entered World War II:

December 16, 1941.

Dear Mr. Stoessel:

Referring to your inquiry about the use of a camera, there is a statute of the United States forbidding the use of a camera for obtaining information respecting the National Defense, with quite heavy penalties.

The only other statute that I know of, which might apply to you, is the provision in the regulations promulgated by the President pursuant to statutes of the United States, in which it is provided that "No alien enemy shall have in his possession, custody or control at any time or place or use or operate any of the following enumerated articles . . . (j) cameras."

You were, as I understand it, a citizen of Austria, at least until the German occupation and have, I assume, never voluntarily assumed German citizenship and, as I understand it, this country has never recognized German sovereignty over Austrian territory.

In the peculiar circumstances of this case, I should think it would be well for you to address a letter to the Attorney General of the United States and to the State Department stating the following facts, if such are the facts:

That you were born in Austria, having lived there until the date you departed from it (giving the date);

That you are a citizen of Austria, not a citizen of Germany, and have never sought to become a citizen of Germany;

That you have resided in the United States ever since your arrival here, giving the date and place of entry;

That you are an artist and in connection with your work in the preparation of etchings, you have occasion to use a camera, and request a ruling whether you are an alien enemy within the meaning of the President's Proclamation of December 7, 1941, under 22, 23 and 24, of Title 50 of the United States Code.

Yours sincerely,
[no typed name][1]

Chief Justice Stone provided Oskar with a matter-of-fact wording that might elicit an opinion from the Department of Justice or from the State Department. Even if no opinion resulted, Oskar's letter would have created a protective paper trail that might insulate him from legal troubles.

It isn't known whether Oskar actually wrote to the Department of Justice, and if so whether a response was sent. Normally, the Department doesn't give legal advice other than to the Executive Branch, as it is required to do by law. Its mandate isn't to respond to third-party inquiries, so any reply might have been a routine acknowledgment of receipt. Then again, the heightened sensitivities in the wake of Pearl Harbor might have sparked further inquiry into Oskar's activities in the United States. But that doesn't seem to have happened.

----

1.   Chief Justice Harlan Fiske Stone to Oskar Stoessel, typed letter, Dec. 16, 1941, Stone Papers, Library of Congress.

On Christmas Day 1941, Chief Justice Stone went to the Court and wrote two letters relating to Oskar—one to him and one about him. The letter to Oskar expressed doubts about the Phillips Memorial Gallery's ability to purchase the Manets and the Van Gogh but encouraged Oskar to meet Duncan Phillips the next time he'd be in Washington. Stone signed off, "With kind regards, and with the hope that you can find some holiday cheer in this troubled world."[2] The other letter was to Duncan Phillips, serving as a formal introduction of Oskar, concluding: "My association with Mr. Stoessel has been most pleasant."[3]

Oskar's response, three days later, showed ebullient gratitude:

December 28th 1941.

The Honorable The Chief Justice
Mr. Harlan F. Stone.

Sir:

I have received your two kind letters giving me the liberty to give you as a reference and with the letter of introduction to Mr. Phillips, and I thank you for the great kindness. I will never forget what great moral help you are giving me in this hard times [sic], and I can only say, I am happy being in a country where the law and justice is in hands like yours. God bless you and your family for the kindness you are giving to others, and I wish you a very happy 1942.

I hope to come in the next two or three weeks for one or two days to Washington, and will bring with me the proofs of Mr. Justice Jackson and Mr. Justice Byrnes.

I have the honor to remain,

Yours respectfully,
Oskar Stoessel.[4]

2.   Stone to Stoessel, typed letter, Dec. 25, 1941, Stone Papers, Library of Congress.
3.   Stone to Duncan Phillips, typed letter, Dec. 25, 1941, Stone Papers, Library of Congress.
4.   Stoessel to Stone, handwritten letter, Dec. 28, 1941, Stone Papers, Library of Congress.

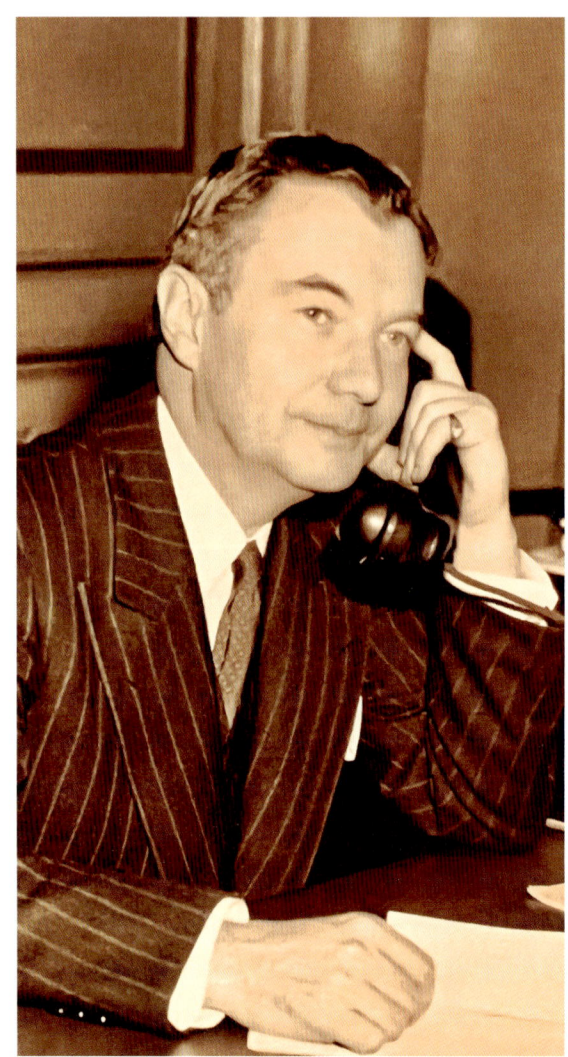

Justice Robert H. Jackson

CHAPTER 25

The Affable Justice Jackson

URING 1942, the Stoessel letters to and from the Court were primarily with Justice Jackson, who was waiting for Stoessel's trial proof from the sitting on October 27, 1941. By May 1942 the process was well along, as we can deduce from this letter:

May 20, 1942

Dear Mr. Stoessel:

I am wondering whether you have found time to complete the etching, and whether any proofs are available.

I suppose you have been pressed for time, but I would appreciate learning from you whether they will be available in the near future.

With regards and good wishes,

Sincerely yours,

Robert H. Jackson[1]

Handwritten as always, Oskar's response was sent six days later. A notation on the letter ("no ans." in the top right) shows that Justice Jackson didn't answer it directly. No longer working toward an exhibition of justices' portraits, Oskar had fallen behind in his work:

May 26th 1942.

The Honorable Mr. Robert H. Jackson
Justice of the Supreme Court
Washington, D.C.

Sir:

I have your kind letter of May 20th and it is true I have been pressed for time, so I am still working on the copperplate of your etching, but it is now ready for

---

1. Justice Robert H. Jackson to Oskar Stoessel, typed letter, May 20, 1942, Jackson Papers, Library of Congress.

printing and I make this week the first trial proofs and I will send you the first proof and I shall be glad to know how you like it, and I can make those corrections if necessary, but I think it will be complete as far as I can see on the plate.

I have the honor to remain,

Yours very truly,
Oskar Stoessel.[2]

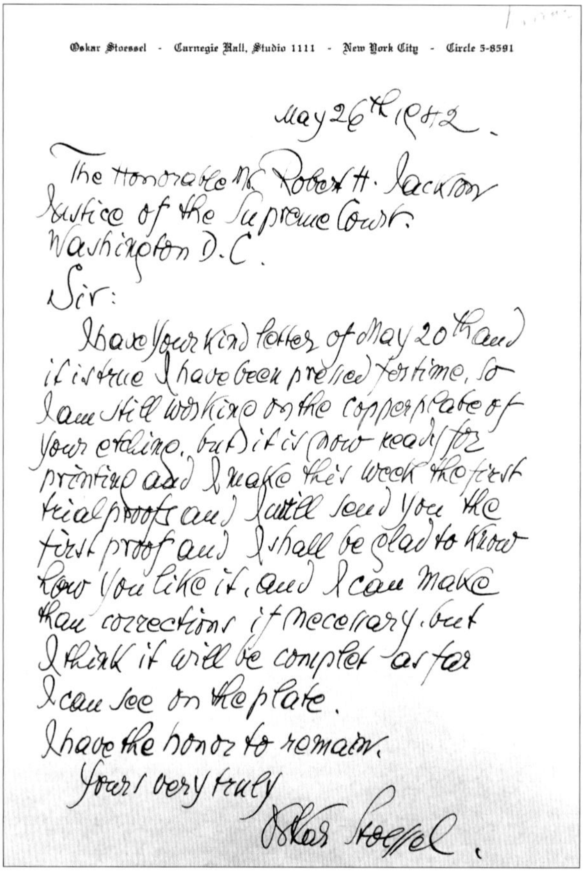

Within two weeks, Oskar followed up with another letter. He expressed gratitude for the opportunity to work with Justice Jackson. He had also apparently established a cordial relationship with Jackson's secretary.

---

2.   Stoessel to Jackson, handwritten letter, May 26, 1942, Jackson Papers, Library of Congress.

June 7th 1942

The Honorable Mr. Robert H. Jackson
Justice of the Supreme Court.

Sir:

I have your kind letter of May 20th and I have answered some days ago and now I send you the first print of your etching and I hope you may like it.

I should be glad if you take this print as a sign of my thankfulness, for your kindness you have given me your time, so that I could finish the whole set of the members of the Supreme High Court. And I have now also finished the etching of Mr. Justice Byrns [sic] and I shall be able to send the first print to Mr. Justice Byrns this week. I send a trial proof and I should be very glad if you would be kind enough to sign it for me. If you like the etching, and I hope you will do it, I send also one print to your secretary. The following proofs I charge $20 for each print, but there is no obligation for you to buy any proofs. The first proof is free of any charge and I am happy if you enjoy it.

I have the honor to remain,

Yours very truly
Oskar Stoessel.[3]

Justice Jackson asked for no alterations in the etching, which he found to be quite good:

June 10, 1942

My dear Mr. Stoessel:

I am grateful to you for the print. I like the etching very much and am glad to sign and return to you the trial proof.

I enclose a check for $20 for which please send me an additional proof.

Do you prefer to have the trial proof signed in ink or pencil?

With all good wishes,

Sincerely,
Robert H. Jackson[4]

Two weeks later, Oskar responded enthusiastically. Perhaps the warm salutation of Jackson's letter ("My dear Mr. Stoessel"), along with the unreserved praise

---

3. Stoessel to Jackson, handwritten letter, June 7, 1942, Jackson Papers, Library of Congress.
4. Jackson to Stoessel, typed letter, June 10, 1942, Jackson Papers, Library of Congress.

of the etching, encouraged Oskar for the first time to ignore formalities such as the "Honorable" front matter that characterized most of his letters. Indeed, his salutation was unabashedly exclamatory:

June 24th 1942.

Sir!

I thank you very much indeed for your kind letter and I am very happy you like the etching. I thank also for the check $20, and I make another print and I will send it to you. I got now the paper for printing. It is the good French paper. [Note that France was then Nazi-occupied.]

I thank also for signing the trial proof for me, and it is possible to sign on this paper in ink. I shall enclose another print for your secretary. I had promised her a proof when I had the opportunity to make the etching. Thanking very much for your kindness I have the honor to remain,

Yours very truly,
Oskar Stoessel[5]

Jackson didn't intend to answer: he wrote "No ans." (a typical note for his chambers). Perhaps Jackson was simply waiting for the additional etching. When he hadn't received it by early September, Jackson wrote with muted impatience:

September 10, 1942

Dear Mr. Stoessel:

Some time ago I ordered an additional etching. I had promised it to my friend Mr. Blair, who is a friend of Mitzi Steiner[6] and who was much interested in you and your work on account of it. The etching has not come, and I have wondered if it has miscarried through the mail.

Sincerely yours,
Robert H. Jackson[7]

---

5. Stoessel to Jackson, handwritten letter, June 24, 1942, Jackson Papers, Library of Congress.
6. Marie "Mitzi" Steiner, prominent in Viennese theater, was the mother of the noted film composer Max Steiner, who wrote the scores for *Casablanca*, *Gone with the Wind*, and many other movies.
7. Jackson to Stoessel, typed letter, Sept. 10, 1942, Jackson Papers, Library of Congress.

The response came in a letter from Los Angeles, California, where Oskar was visiting his younger brother Ludwig, the actor. Using Ludwig's personal stationery, Oskar replied:

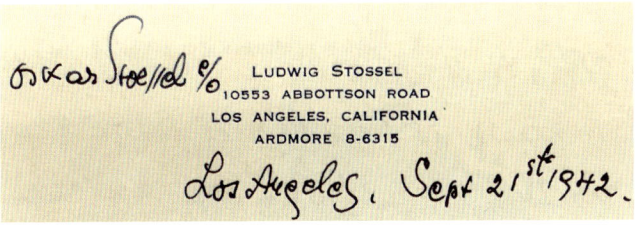

The Honorable Mr. Justice Robert H. Jackson.
Supreme Court of the United States, Washington, D.C.

Sir.

I am sorry. You have not yet received the ordered etching. Before I had left for California, where I am staying, I had prepared two of your etchings. One you have been so kind to order, and one I had promised to send for your secretary. The package containing the two proofs is prepared, and a friend of mine has promised me to take them from my studio and mail them. Will you kindly excuse the matter. I come back the first week of October and if the package is still there I will mail it instantly. If it has been miscarried through the mail, I send you two other proofs of the etching.

Please excuse this delay.

Very respectfully
Yours
Oskar Stoessel.[8]

Perhaps it was Austrian modesty that kept Oskar from saying more about his brother, other than using his stationery. Each had reason to be proud of the other, but neither ever boasted about their relationship.

---

8.   Stoessel to Jackson, handwritten letter, Sept. 21, 1942, Jackson Papers, Library of Congress.

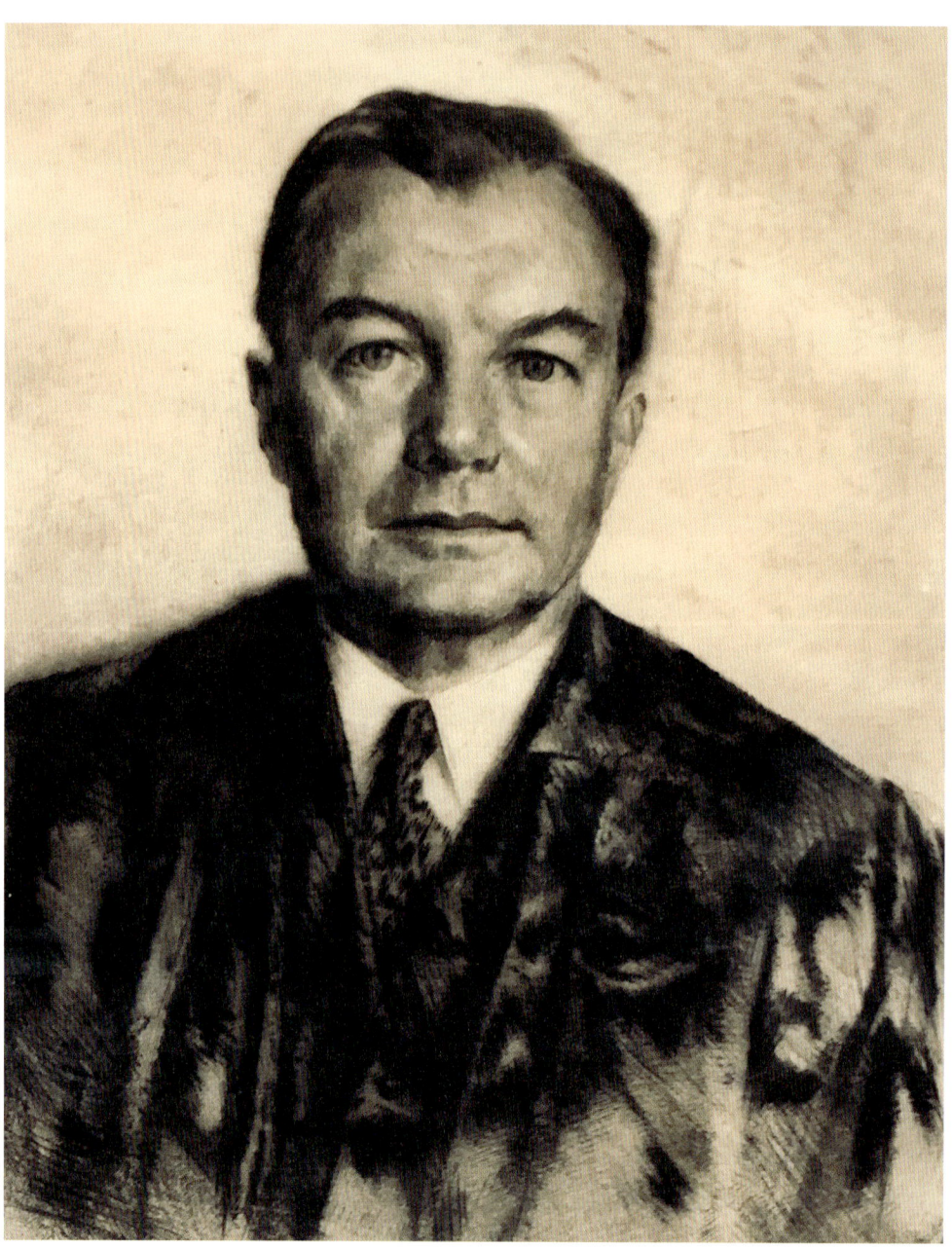

Oskar's 1942 etching of Justice Robert Jackson, the only person to have served as U.S. solicitor general, U.S. attorney general, and justice of the Supreme Court. Widely considered the most eloquent writer ever to have sat on the Court, Jackson took a break from his judicial work to serve as chief U.S. prosecutor at the Nuremberg Trials after World War II. Justice Jackson corresponded more extensively with Oskar than did any other member of the Court apart from Chief Justice Stone.

CHAPTER 26

Reunion in Hollywood

FROM the age of 17, in 1900, Ludwig Stössel started taking as many theater jobs as he could get in Austria and then in Germany. At first, he earned mere pennies for his work as a stagehand. Then he began acting in small parts in stage plays. Never formally trained as an actor, he once lost a job because he spoke in a guttural dialect.[1] He cured this problem by practicing in the manner of the ancient Greek orator Demosthenes, who famously spoke with pebbles in his mouth. Ludwig improved his speech by putting a cork in his mouth—a technique that seemed to help. His stage roles slowly improved over the years. In 1926, he broke into German silent movies. Then came sound movies. Like many other Jewish actors, he left Berlin in 1933, when the Nazis came into power.

During the Berlin years, he worked with many people who would become major figures in Hollywood, such as Otto Preminger, Peter Lorre, and Hedy Lamarr. After the rise of the Nazis, many people that Ludwig had been working with began emigrating—some going directly to the United States, if Hollywood studios made offers. Ludwig, though, returned to Vienna. As early as 1937, Ludwig was in touch with British film producers, presumably anticipating the need to leave. These contacts probably made it easier for him and his wife to get visas to enter Britain in 1938.[2]

Readily finding work in England, Ludwig made three films during 1939. Eager to journey to America, he arrived in Hollywood in 1940. Fortunately, his predecessors had established a colony for helping immigrant actors and providing financial support through the European Film Fund, to which they contributed 1% of their income. Those without employment could withdraw money from

1. Thomas Ziegler, "Der Filmschauspieler Ludwig Stössel—Von Burgenland nach Hollywood" (diploma thesis, Univ. of Vienna, 2015), 12–13, https://doi.org/10.25365/thesis.38111.
2. Ziegler, 83.

this fund.[3] Ludwig landed his first job just six months after arriving, but despite relatively steady work, his first few roles were minor and didn't pay very well. He sometimes had to rely on the fund to stay afloat.[4]

Ludwig was probably less affected than Oskar by antisemitism. Even so, Hollywood was acutely aware of its existence, particularly the notion that Jews controlled Hollywood.[5] Not surprisingly, many immigrant actors, as well as the studios, sought to downplay or conceal Jewish heritage.

In late 1942, while staying with Ludwig and his wife Eleonore for about a month, Oskar must have found the environment in Los Angeles—and Hollywood in particular—to be rather dreamlike. The flora there and the beaches would have been unlike anything he had ever seen.

If Ludwig took Oskar to any of the popular restaurants that actors frequented, they might have encountered stars who had acted with Ludwig. He had already appeared in films with these actors:

> Ingrid Bergman (*Casablanca*, 1942).
> Humphrey Bogart (*All Through the Night*, 1942; *Casablanca*, 1942).
> Gary Cooper (*Pride of the Yankees*, 1942).
> William Demarest (*All Through the Night*, 1942).
> Marlene Dietrich (*Nachtkabarett* [Berlin], 1928; *Pittsburgh*, 1942).
> Jackie Gleason (*All Through the Night*, 1942).
> Laurel & Hardy (*Great Guns*, 1941).
> Peter Lorre (*All Through the Night*, 1942; *Casablanca*, 1942).
> Claude Rains (*King's Row*, 1942; *Casablanca*, 1942).
> Ronald Reagan (*King's Row*, 1942).
> Randolph Scott (*Pittsburgh*, 1942).
> Phil Silvers (*All Through the Night*, 1942).
> John Wayne (*Pittsburgh*, 1942).
> Theresa Wright (*Pride of the Yankees*, 1942).

---

3. Aljean Harmetz, *The Making of* Casablanca*: Bogart, Bergman, and World War II* (Hyperion, 2002), 220.
4. Harmetz, 221.
5. Omer Bartov, *The "Jew" in Cinema: From* The Golem *to* Don't Touch My Holocaust (Ind. Univ. Press, 2005), 35.

If chance encounters with such film celebrities occurred, Oskar would doubtless have enjoyed them. Although he wasn't the type to be star-struck, Oskar must have been gratified to see the success that his younger brother was now enjoying.

So busy was Ludwig that he might have taken Oskar on set as a spectator. In late 1942, Ludwig was filming two movies that would be released the following year. In both, he played Nazis. One was *The Strange Death of Adolf Hitler*, in which he was cast as a lowly civil servant in Nazi-controlled Vienna—a character who follows instructions unquestioningly. The other was *Hitler's Madman*, starring John Carradine and Patricia Morison. In that film, Ludwig played the opportunistic mayor of a small town, a perpetrator of crimes who later becomes a victim.[6] Ludwig had personal experiences to draw on: in Vienna in 1938, he had been arrested and briefly jailed three times by the Nazis.[7]

---

6.   Ziegler, "Der Filmschauspieler," 91–101.
7.   See Don MacLean, "Meet Ludwig Stossel," *Fitchburg Sentinel* (Mass.), Sept. 27, 1971, 4.

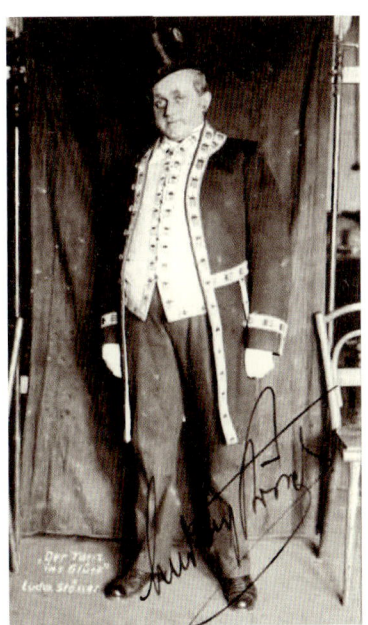

Ludwig in character in the German film Der Tanz Ins Glück *(1930). Note the autograph, which he supplied for his niece Elsa.*

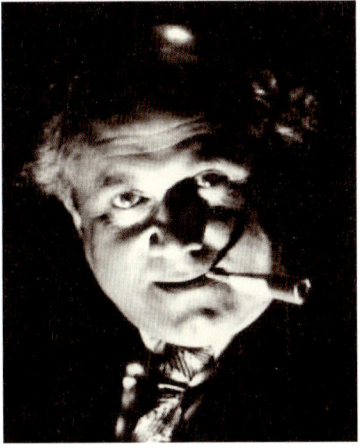

Ludwig in a 1930s German film

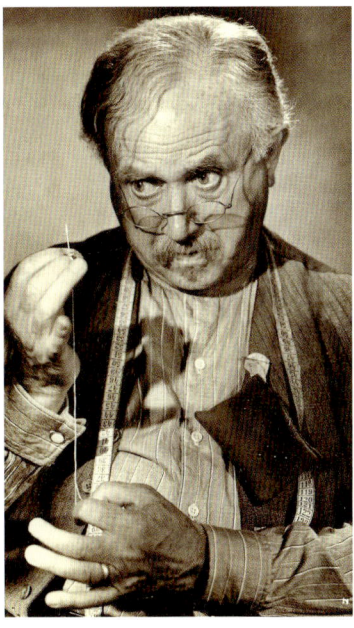

Ludwig in No Time for Flowers *(RKO, 1952)*

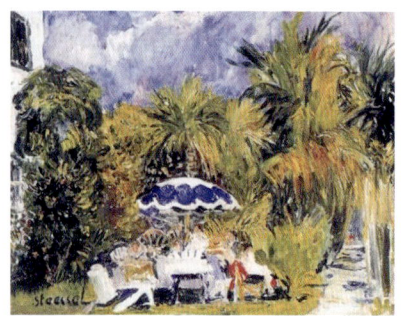

A garden scene that Oskar painted while visiting Ludwig (Glendale, Cal.)

Ludwig's thick accent and impressive range of facial expressions, from benevolent to sinister, brought him steady employment as a character actor in a variety of genres. Among film buffs, Ludwig will always be best remembered as Mr. Leuchtag, the husband of the German-speaking couple who are fleeing the Nazis in *Casablanca*. That film was shot between May and August of 1942—so it had finished just a few weeks before Oskar arrived in Los Angeles. The world premiere would occur in New York on November 26, 1942. One imagines that Oskar, back in Carnegie Hall by then, attended.

Ludwig acted opposite Ilka Grüning, another Austrian émigré who had found her way to Hollywood. Their dialogue in *Casablanca* provided comic relief, as they proclaim to Carl, the amiable waiter at Rick's Cafe, their proficiency in English. Carl brings the couple brandy. At first, they exchange words in German and then switch to English. As Carl pours brandy, this dialogue ensues:

Husband:	Come sit down. Have a brandy with us.
Wife:	To celebrate our leaving for America tomorrow.
Carl:	Oh, thank you very much. I thought you would ask me, so I brought the good brandy. And a third glass.
Wife:	At last, the day is came!
Husband:	Mareichtag and I are speaking nothing but English now.
Wife:	So we should feel at home when we get to America.
Carl:	A very nice idea. Mm-hmm.
Husband:	[Toasting.] To America!
Wife:	To America.
Carl:	To America.

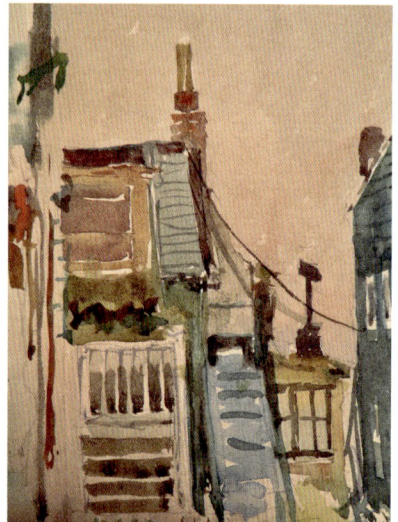

A California scene that Oskar painted in watercolor ca. 1942

Husband:	Liebchen . . . Sweetnessheart. What watch?
Wife:	[Looking at wristwatch.] Ten watch.
Husband:	Such much?
Carl:	You will get along beautifully in America. Mm-hmm.

In retrospect, the scene is all the more moving given its verisimilitude to Ludwig and Oskar's own lives.

During his European film career, Ludwig collected his reviews, carefully pasting them into 13 scrapbooks from 1926 to 1938. These were so precious to him that he carried them out of Austria and kept them for the rest of his life. Perhaps he would need proof of his acting prowess—something to show American producers and directors if they questioned his experience. Or perhaps he did it from sheer sentimentality, or for his mother.

Things would change. Apart from one 1950 clipping, Ludwig discontinued the habit after coming to America.[8]

---

8.   Ziegler, "Der Filmschauspieler," 11.

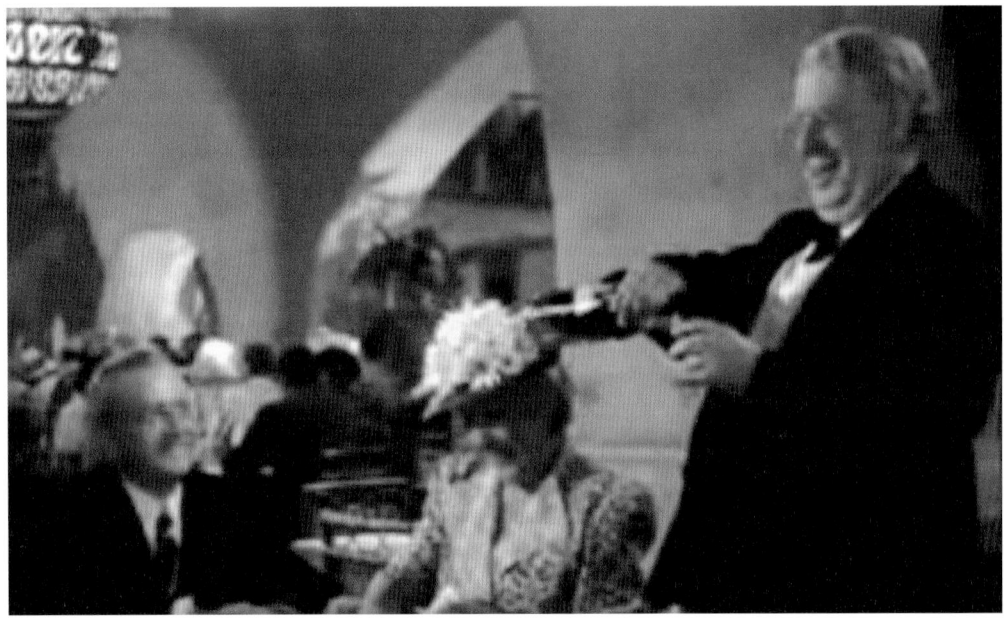

Ludwig (left) in Casablanca

October 17th 1942.

The Honorable Mr. Justice Robert H. Jackson.

Washington D.C.

Sir!

I am sorry that the two proofs I had ordered to send to your address. have not been sent. So will you please . excuse that I send them now. I am back from California, and I find that California is the most beautiful country I ever have seen . one of the two etchings is for your secretary. I thank for your Kindness and I am very   Respectfully

Yours

Oskar Stoessel.

CHAPTER 27

The Unsent Package at Carnegie Hall

WHEN Oskar returned to New York after his monthlong stay with
Ludwig, he discovered that his friend hadn't mailed the two etchings he had promised to send to Justice Jackson. So he hastened to
mail them:

October 17th 1942.

The Honorable Mr. Justice Robert H. Jackson.
Washington, D.C.

Sir!

I am sorry that the two proofs I had ordered to send to your address have
not been sent. So will you, please, excuse that I send them now. I am back from
California, and I find that California is the most beautiful country I ever have
seen. One of the two etchings is for your secretary. I thank for your kindness and
I am very

Respectfully
Yours
Oskar Stoessel.[1]

Twelve days later, Justice Jackson wrote to his friend John L. Blair[2] of Warren, Pennsylvania, informing Blair that he was sending an etching: "At last my

---

1. Oskar Stoessel to Justice Robert H. Jackson, handwritten letter, Oct. 17, 1942, Jackson Papers,
   Library of Congress. Just two weeks before, on October 3, Justice Byrnes had announced his
   retirement from the Court so that, at President Roosevelt's request, he could carry out new
   responsibilities as President Roosevelt's Director of the Office of Economic Stabilization.
2. A lifelong friend of Justice Jackson, John L. Blair (1888–1962) was a lawyer and successful
   businessman. He advised Roosevelt on strategies for his 1932 presidential campaign. Later he
   conferred with Treasury Secretary Henry Morgenthau Jr. about ways to help the economy
   recover from the Great Depression. Many of Blair's suggestions were adopted and proved
   effective.

old friend the Viennese artist Oskar Stoessel has come through with his etching. Opinions may differ about how good a likeness it is, but those who know how to value such things say it is a fine job from a technical point of view. Such as it is, it is on the way."[3] Jackson inscribed it and sent it, return receipt requested, as a gift to Blair and his wife, who answered by Western Union telegram: "Thanks for remarkably fine etching. Proud to frame for home. Maude [&] John Blair."[4] At some later point, probably after Justice Jackson's death, the Blairs gave the etching to Jackson's son Bill, who kept it for the rest of his life (d. 1999). Bill Jackson's family later donated it to the Jackson Center in Jamestown, New York, where it now hangs.

———
3. Jackson to John L. Blair, typed letter, Oct. 29, 1942, Jackson Papers, Library of Congress.
4. Blair to Jackson, Western Union telegram, Jackson Papers, Library of Congress.

CHAPTER 28

Would-Be Soldier

SOMETIME in 1942, Oskar did something that he didn't share with his various correspondents. At the age of 63, while a resident alien in the United States, he registered for the draft. He filled out the card by hand, noting that his occupation was "Painter—Portrait Etcher—Printer of Etchings."[1] Although nothing seems to have come of it, this five-foot-five-inch sexagenarian submitted himself to serve on behalf of the United States.[2]

Oskar may have thought that he was required to register even though he wasn't a U.S. citizen. After the attack on Pearl Harbor in December 1941 and the United States' entrance into the war, a new Selective Service Act—the "Fourth Registration" or "old man's draft"—required the registration of nonmilitary men who were born on or between April 28, 1877, and February 16, 1897 (men between 45 and 64). But these men wouldn't be drafted into military service; the goal of having them register was to provide a complete inventory of manpower resources and labor skills that could be used in the war effort. Between November 1940 and October 1946, more than 10 million American men registered under the statute. Given that Oskar wasn't a U.S. citizen, he wasn't required by law to register—but the fact that he did suggests that he felt a sense of loyalty and responsibility to the country that had taken him in.

On the registration card on page 198, you'll notice that Oskar spelled his name "Oscar" at the top but then reverted to the usual spelling in his signature

---

1. Draft registration serial number 3638, "Oscar [sic] Stoessel." In the box "Name and address of person who will always know your address," he named Hans Schutz of 40 West 89th Street, New York, New York. His signature showed his characteristic flourish.
2. We know his height from the ship's manifest by which he sailed to the United States in 1939. See note 18 on page 82.

at the bottom. This is the only known instance in which he used the -c- spelling. Perhaps, given that he was proposing to fight the Nazis, he wanted to present himself in a less "Germanic" way. But then he unselfconsciously signed in
his habitual manner.

*Oskar's registration card
for the "old man's draft"*

CHAPTER 29

Invisible Means of Support

D URING the 1940s and 1950s, Oskar supported himself primarily by sell-ing his own collection of rare prints by the European Old Masters—including the ones he somehow took or sent out of Vienna to evade Nazi confiscation and displayed at the Corcoran Gallery. He may well have been continuing a practice that he had engaged in before leaving Vienna. That is, one might deduce from the known record that his close ties to the Albertina Mu-seum involved his brokering purchases of art that he had identified as worthy of collecting. If this suggestion is correct, the Albertina came to rely on Oskar's considerable expertise when making acquisitions.

But like many other art scouts and brokers, Oskar had a significant collection of his own. He began trying to sell pieces as early as 1940. In late November or early December of that year, he called on Elizabeth Mongan, who was curator of the Alverthorpe Gallery in Jenkintown, Pennsylvania.[1] That private gallery held the notable collection assembled by Lessing J. Rosenwald, a business magnate who a year before had stepped down as chair of Sears, Roebuck & Co. to dedicate himself to full-time collecting of rare books and art, especially prints. In less than a year, he would be one of the founding donors of the National Gallery of Art. In the end, he would give nearly 25,000 pieces of art to the National Gallery.

Unsurprisingly, Oskar came to know about Rosenwald and paid his library a visit. He sought to sell several engravings, among which were *The Great Trium-phal Car* by Albrecht Dürer (1471–1528) (see page 200) and *Marie Antoinette* by Jean François Janinet (1752–1814) (see page 203). Oskar described the lat-ter as "the rarest print of the French eighteenth century in perfect state."[2] On

---

1. Oskar Stoessel to Elizabeth Mongan, handwritten letter, Dec. 20, 1940, box 28, Rosenwald Papers, National Gallery of Art.
2. Stoessel to Mongan, Dec. 20, 1940.

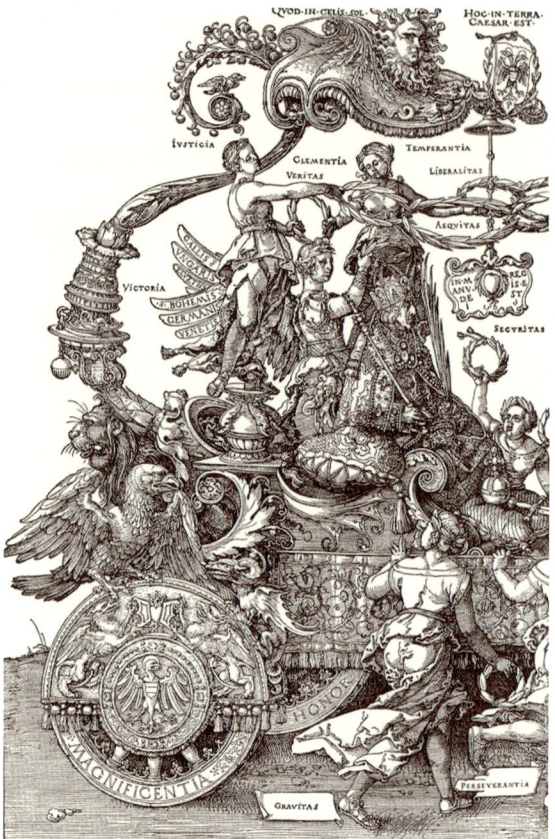

Dürer's "The Great Triumphal Car" (1522)——the left-most of eight prints making up the whole

that first visit to the Alverthorpe, Oskar left the Dürer on approval and showed a photograph of the Janinet.[3] Whether Oskar met with both Rosenwald and Mongan, or just Mongan alone, isn't clear.

On or just after that visit, Rosenwald did acquire one important work: *Christ Before Pilate* (ca. 1480), by Martin Schongauer (1450–1491). This piece became one of the highlights of the Rosenwald Collection, which already contained more than 80 Schongauer prints. The purchase price isn't known, but Rosenwald would later acknowledge that he had acquired the piece from Oskar.[4]

The other negotiations took a while. In early January 1941, Rosenwald's secretary wrote to Oskar, asking the price of the Dürer—requesting that he respond to Mongan.[5] Oskar responded, asking $3,000 for the Dürer ("I have paid a high price," he said) and $2,000 for the Janinet ("in this state and condition of utmost rarity, I do not know whether there is one exemplar in the U.S.").

3.   Mongan to Stoessel, typed letter, Dec. 23, 1940, box 28, Rosenwald Papers, National Gallery of Art.

4.   See Ruth E. Fine, *Lessing J. Rosenwald: Tribute to a Collector* (National Gallery of Art, 1982), 146 (noting that Rosenwald acquired the piece in 1940).

5.   E. Wellens to Stoessel, typed letter, Jan. 2, 1941, box 28, Rosenwald Papers, National Gallery of Art.

At the top of Oskar's letter, Rosenwald or Mongan wrote in pencil, "Send back Triumphal Car" (the Dürer). Mongan then wrote to Oskar: "The Dürer 'Triumphal Car' is an interesting print, but under present circumstances Mr. Rosenwald feels it is too expensive. I appreciate your having left it here for such a long time."[6]

Oskar reacted predictably as one might in a negotiation in which the seller really needed to sell: "As it is my intention to dispose of this print I shall be very grateful indeed if you would be kind enough to give me an idea as to what the amount would be Mr. Lessing Rosenwald might think interesting."[7] Mongan kindly replied that Rosenwald would be out for the next two weeks but would consider the question upon his return.[8]

This response prompted from Oskar a handwritten note that sounded almost desperate: "As I mentioned in my previous letter I am anxious to sell as the support of my family makes the sale of a part of my collection imperative. I hope you may understand my position and forgive me for being so frank."[9] Atop this letter, to note the decision, either Rosenwald or Mongan wrote, again in pencil, "Won't make offer."

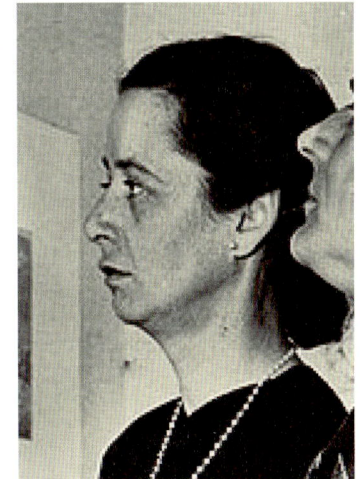

Elizabeth Mongan

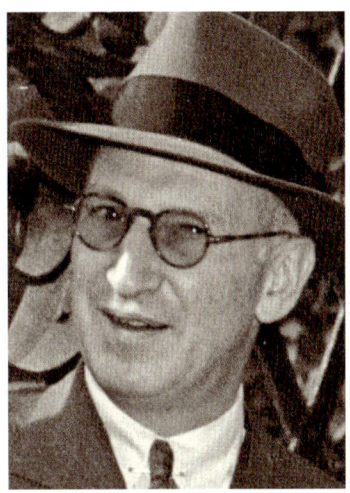

Lessing J. Rosenwald

6. Mongan to Stoessel, typed letter, Jan. 13, 1941, box 28, Rosenwald Papers, National Gallery of Art.

7. Stoessel to Mongan, handwritten letter, Jan. 23, 1941, box 28, Rosenwald Papers, National Gallery of Art.

8. Mongan to Stoessel, typed letter, Jan. 24, 1941, box 28, Rosenwald Papers, National Gallery of Art.

9. Stoessel to Mongan, handwritten letter, Feb. 4, 1941, box 28, Rosenwald Papers, National Gallery of Art.

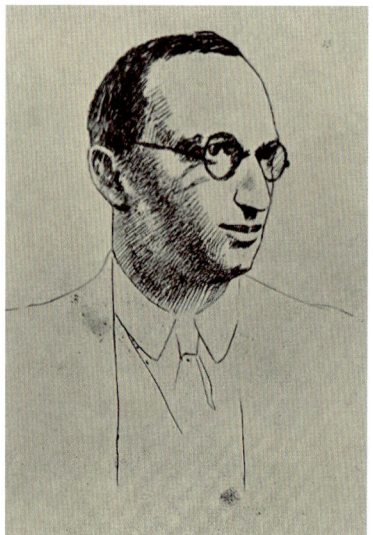

James McBey's 1930 portrait etching of Lessing J. Rosenwald. A largely self-taught Scottish artist, McBey had a style that was simpler and more rudimentary than Oskar's. Rosenwald never commissioned a portrait from Oskar.

Rosenwald was an accomplished negotiator. He refused to make an offer but instead wanted Oskar to bargain against himself. Now seven weeks into the negotiations, Mongan wrote to Oskar: "Mr. Rosenwald has a fixed policy of not making prices. He feels that you ought to set your own price on the print and then he will let you know if he is interested in it at your figure or not." She added: "I am sorry that it has to be this way, but it seems the only reasonable way for a private collector to proceed."[10]

By this point, it was mid-February 1941, a busy time for Oskar. All the justices of the Supreme Court had cemented their agreement to sit for him about this time. Oskar responded to Mongan with a price reduction of more than 25%: "As I am determined to liquidate I wish to ask you if an offer of $2,200 for the first German edition of the 'Triumph-Car' of Dürer would seem reasonable and what Mr. Lessing J. Rosenwald would think of it. I shall be glad to hear of you soon."[11] At the foot of this letter is a pencil notation: "Seems out [of] line still. Bargain price."

Mongan's response, arriving more than a week later, could not have been heartening for Oskar—whose financial obligations almost certainly weren't being met by his work on portraits: "Mr. Rosenwald . . . has asked me to tell you that he really would not be interested in buying it [the *Triumphal Car*] unless it were offered at a great bargain."[12] Rosenwald struck the shrewd negotiating pose of being

10. Mongan to Stoessel, typed letter, Feb. 8, 1941, box 28, Rosenwald Papers, National Gallery of Art.
11. Stoessel to Mongan, handwritten letter, Feb. 12, 1941, box 28, Rosenwald Papers, National Gallery of Art.
12. Mongan to Stoessel, typed letter, Feb. 21, 1941, box 28, Rosenwald Papers, National Gallery of Art.

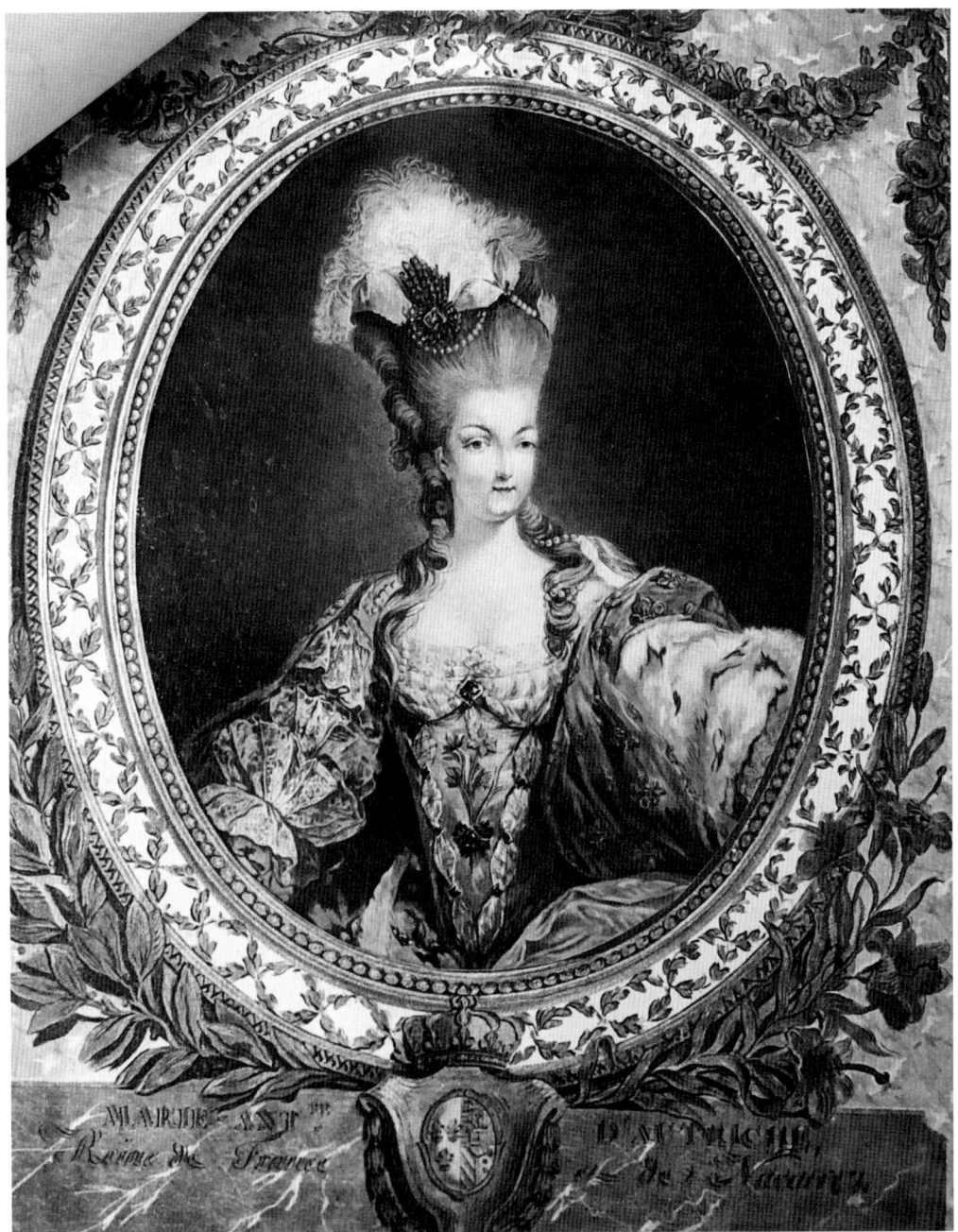

The photograph that Oskar gave to Elizabeth Mongan depicting Janinet's engraved portrait of Marie Antoinette

largely uninterested, and yet Oskar knew that he probably had a keener interest in prints than anyone else in the United States. Mongan added: "He [Rosenwald] does not feel necessarily you should offer it [at a great bargain], but he does not want that particular print enough to pay any great price for it."[13]

Oskar didn't immediately capitulate to a lower price, we know, because two years later he was still offering this item along with six others.[14] But he didn't act miffed in any way: his letters to Mongan and later to Rosenwald displayed great tact.

A few months later, Oskar offered to Rosenwald an even scarcer Dürer, a counterproof of *The Dream of the Doctor*. A counterproof is a print taken off an-

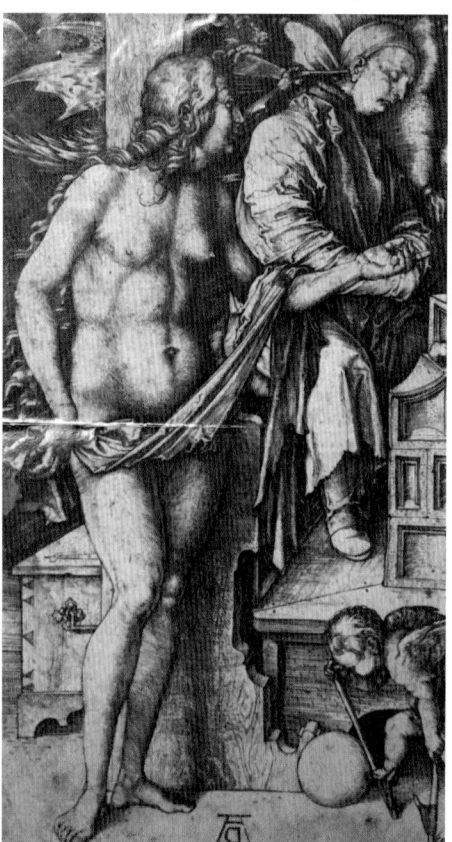

other print that is still wet, so that the copy on the second print is in reverse. Print-makers sometimes use counterproofs to inspect the quality of the original print.

As far as anyone knew, this Dürer counterproof was a one-of-a-kind item. In fact, it is the earliest known example of a counterproof from any artist[15]—and the artist happens to be Dürer! But the response from the Alverthorpe once again dashed Oskar's hopes: "Mr. Rosenwald feels that although this is a very interesting proof, he does not want to purchase the impression at the present time."[16]

Oskar's counterproof of Dürer's "The Dream of the Doctor"

13. Mongan to Stoessel, Feb. 21, 1941.
14. Stoessel to Lessing J. Rosenwald, handwritten letter, Jan. 26, 1943, box 28, Rosenwald Papers, National Gallery of Art.
15. See Fine, *Lessing J. Rosenwald*, 224.
16. Mongan to Stoessel, typed letter, June 19, 1941, box 28, Rosenwald Papers, National Gallery of Art.

Rosenwald's austere refusals to negotiate must have been seriously discouraging, since Oskar knew what dealers in New York City were obtaining for similar and lesser works. Two years later, in January 1943, Oskar wrote to Rosenwald directly instead of through Mongan, who had been acting as an intermediary. Once again he offered the Janinet, the two Dürers, and four other early engravings. He noted that he had finished his Supreme Court portraits, and he invited both Rosenwald and Mongan to his Harlow Gallery exhibition. Then he wrote, in tones suggesting personal anguish:

> It is now very difficult to work etchings because it is impossible to get any commissions, and I have invested all my money in my work. I have no connections to get a place as teacher, or to do any work for the government, so I must see to sell some of my old prints. I should be very happy if you would decide to buy something, and I write you a list of the prints that may interest you. I must sell something otherwise I must give up my studio, and then the work I did till now is lost. If I could get a place as teacher I should be very happy. I should be very happy if you could give me an advise in this matter.[17]

The penciled notation on this letter, in the same hand as all the other pencilings, says, "L.J.R. will go to exhibition." This suggests that all the earlier notes had been written by Mongan.

The known correspondence between Oskar and the Alverthorpe then comes to a halt. Oskar had no luck with selling the piece they'd been negotiating about for so long. And no teaching position ever materialized for Oskar.

But we do know that Rosenwald finally bought the Dürer counterproof of *The Dream of the Doctor*, undoubtedly at a greatly reduced price. That piece now resides at the National Gallery of Art in the Rosenwald Collection, with an accession date of 1947. But back in 1943, a bibliographer of Dürer's work called Oskar's piece "an undescribed counterproof" that was "all the more interesting as no other instance seems to be known at so early a date."[18] The counterproof also became

---

17. Stoessel to Rosenwald, handwritten letter, Jan. 26, 1943, box 28, Rosenwald Papers, National Gallery of Art.

18. Erwin Panofsky, *Albrecht Dürer: Handlist, Concordances, and Illustrations* (Princeton Univ. Press, 1943), 227 (information about Stoessel's ownership attributed by Panofsky to Rosenwald).

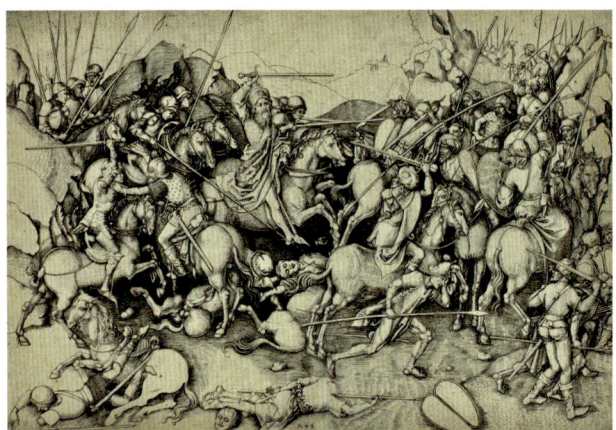

Schongauer's "The Battle of St. James the Greater at Clavijo"
(ca. 1470)

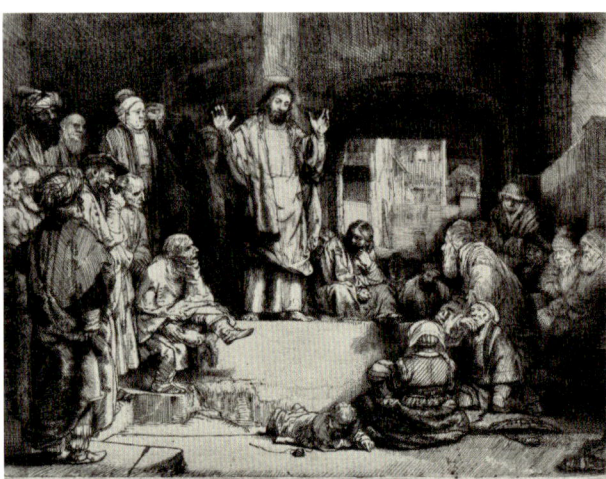

Rembrandt's "La Petite Tombe" (ca. 1652)

part of an unprecedented pairing, since Rosenwald already owned the engraving for which it was the mirror image.

In the end, Rosenwald's acquisition from Oskar was important enough to be listed among his 100 most significant prints. It is reproduced in the 1982 book *Lessing J. Rosenwald: Tribute to a Collector*, published by the National Gallery of Art.[19] Rosenwald's "perceptiveness and generosity" are notable, it is said, and his "discrimination as a collector is acknowledged throughout the world."[20]

At the same time as he acquired the counterproof of *The Dream of the Doctor*, Rosenwald purchased another important Schongauer engraving from Oskar: *The Battle of St. James the Greater at Clavijo* (ca. 1470).[21] At this point in negotiating with Rosenwald, Oskar probably approached the matter with an almost defeatist attitude. Any sale had to be an extreme bargain for the buyer. For Oskar, quite unlike Rosenwald, it was a matter of subsistence.

Oskar's attempts to sell his own precious collection must have been both time-consuming and dispiriting. Soon he decided to retain a New York City gallery to do this work for him: Schaeffer Galleries, owned by Hanns and Kate

---

19. Fine, *Lessing J. Rosenwald*, 226 (no. 81).
20. Fine, 7.
21. See Fine, 224 (noting that Rosenwald acquired the piece in 1940). This book, however, may be wrong: there is evidence that it wasn't acquired until after 1943.

Schaeffer.[22] Their gallery was located on East 58th Street, and by the mid-1940s the Schaeffers were friends of Oskar's. Through them he sold 15th-century engravings by Israhel van Meckenem (1445–1503) and 17th-century etchings by Rembrandt (1606–1669), among others. The Schaeffer Galleries' archives contain records of several transactions with Oskar, mostly in German.[23] Perhaps the most notable of these was the Rembrandt etching *La Petite Tombe*, depicting Jesus preaching—for which Oskar sought to net $4,000.[24] One doubts that he received that.

---

22. Hanns and Kate Schaeffer were native Germans who operated their first art gallery in Berlin beginning in 1921. (At that time, she was also an opera singer.) Later they had galleries in London and San Francisco before settling in New York City in 1936. He died in the early 1960s, she in 2001 (at the age of 102). In 1961, James J. Rorimer, the curator of the Metropolitan Museum of Art in New York, was quoted as saying: "The Schaeffers are among the most serious, knowledgeable and helpful art dealers who are enabling American museums to grow for the benefit of our public. They are friends who share unstintingly in helping curators, directors and trustees to choose with care the works of art which redound to the credit of their museums." Eric Pace, "Kate Born Schaeffer, 102, Owner of Art Gallery," *N.Y. Times*, 7 Jan. 2001.

23. The Schaeffer Galleries Records are held at the Getty Research Institute in Los Angeles. The Institute kindly provided me with copies of all the records relating to Stoessel.

24. Versions of this etching are now housed at several major museums around the world. In recent years, at auction, the etching has fetched $20,000–$25,000.

You are cordially invited to an

Exhibition of Portrait

Etchings and Drawings

by

OSKAR STOESSEL

Including present and ex-Justices of the
Supreme Court, the President and
Secretary of State, reproduced herein

During March

ARTHUR H. HARLOW & CO., Inc.
42 East 57th Street, New York
Tel. Eldorado 5-2882

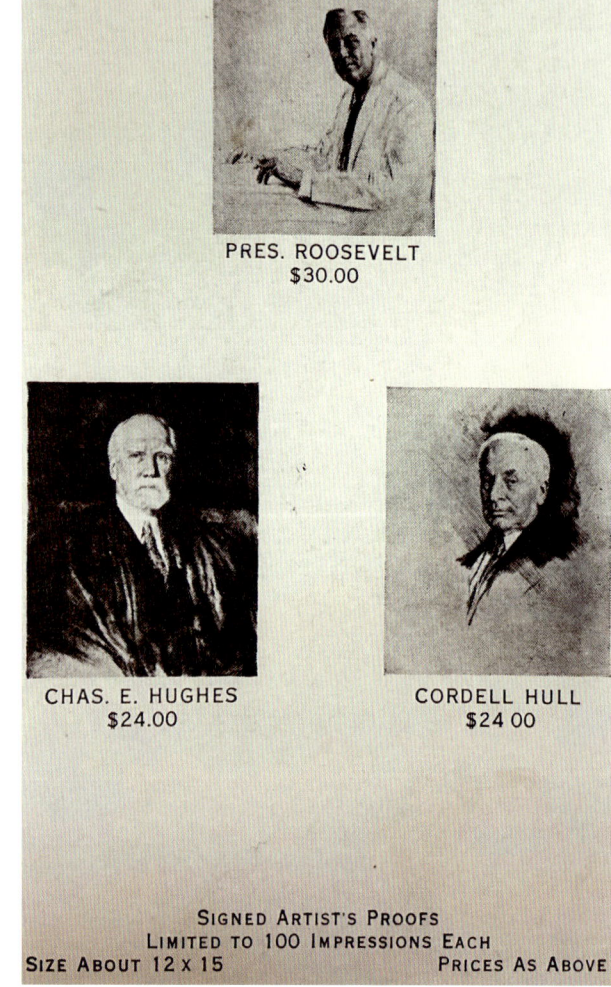

PRES. ROOSEVELT
$30.00

CHAS. E. HUGHES
$24.00

CORDELL HULL
$24 00

SIGNED ARTIST'S PROOFS
LIMITED TO 100 IMPRESSIONS EACH
SIZE ABOUT 12 x 15   PRICES AS ABOVE

The back of the brochure—invitation printed for the Harlow Gallery in New York for Oskar's one-man show in March 1943. Although in 1935 an article noted that Oskar generally made small editions of only 20 prints, here he advertises limited editions of 100. Unlike Oskar's D.C. exhibition two years earlier, this one——perhaps because it was more commercial——received comparatively little press coverage.

CHAPTER 30

Persistent Unemployment

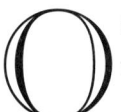N January 6, 1943, Oskar wrote to Chief Justice Stone to alert him to an upcoming exhibition of his work in New York:

January 6th 1943.

The Honorable Chief Justice
Mr. Harlan Fiske Stone.
Washington D.C.

Sir:

I thank very much [sic] for your kind letter[1] and I am pleased you enjoy the prints of Mr. Justice Jackson and Mr. Justice Byrnes. In February I have an exhibition of the Portraits of all the members of the Supreme-High-Court at Harlow, New York. It will be a one man show and I intend also to exhibit other portraits. It would be a great honor for me if Mr. Chief Justice would visit the exhibition when you are occasionally here in New York, and I could know if you are at any time in February in New York. I have the possibility to make the exhibition at this time.

I thank also for your kind wishes. In this times [sic] it is almost impossible to make my living with art work, and now having finished the set of the Honorable members of the Supreme-High-Court, I had the idea to work all the important personalities in this country in connection with the war. I should be very happy if I could make plates for the Government Printing Office. I think it could be a very interesting work for the future also, and I should be very happy to get such a job for the Government.

You have been allways [sic] so kind to me, so I dare to ask what steps I should make to reach this kind of job. I think I could do a usefull [sic] work and I should be happy just to make my living in doing this work.

---

1.   The letter referred to here cannot be located.

Thanking for your kindness I am with all good wishes for you and Mrs. Stone.
Yours respectfully
Oskar Stoessel.[2]

In retrospect, Oskar's suggestion seems entirely reasonable: if the government could supply him with copperplates, ink, and paper, he could make first-rate portraits of countless notable Americans. And he could do it for a modest salary. It would take imagination to create such a position—and ingenuity to fund it. Perhaps Congress would subsidize the portraits of all its members over a period of years. Perhaps a publisher would subsidize an undertaking for a reference book—just as Max and Albert Rosenthal had done in the 19th century, when they were commissioned by P.W. Ziegler & Co. to create portraits of all the justices who had ever served on the United States Supreme Court for *The History of the Supreme Court of the United States* (1902).

Chief Justice Stone was by now deeply involved in the formation of the newly founded Committee for the Protection and Conservation of Historical Monuments in Europe, established to save art that had been plundered by the Nazis.[3] He replied to Oskar's letter two weeks later, saying that he had delegated three avenues of inquiry to his secretary, Gertrude Jenkins, but that the responses were disappointing:

---

2.   Oskar Stoessel to Chief Justice Harlan Fiske Stone, handwritten letter, Jan. 6, 1943, Stone Papers, Library of Congress.

3.   David E. Finley to Stone, Nov. 30, 1942, Stone Papers, Library of Congress ("You will note that we have recommended the establishment of two committees; one, an official Committee, of which we hope you yourself will act as Chairman, with an executive secretary located preferably in Washington where the work could be done with the least amount of inconvenience to you; and second, a subcommittee of experts in the different fields of art and archeology."); Stone to President Franklin Delano Roosevelt, Dec. 8, 1942, Stone Papers, Library of Congress (beginning, "My dear Mr. President: I write as Chairman Ex-officio of the Board of Trustees of the National Gallery of Art, to ask your support of a plan for the creation of an organization functioning under the auspices of the Government, for the protection and conservation of works of art and of artistic or historic monuments and records in Europe."); FDR to Stone, Dec. 28, 1942, Stone Papers, Library of Congress (acknowledging receipt and thanking the chief justice).

January 20, 1943

Dear Mr. Stoessel:

I am so busy that I think there is very little prospect of my coming to New York between now and late in the spring, so I think you should set the date of your exhibition without reference to me. If I should come over while it is in progress I shall be very glad to come and see it.

Miss Jenkins has made inquiry at the Government Printing Office, the Bureau of Printing and Engraving, and the Treasury Department, and finds that there are no posts for one of your qualifications, and too all employees must be American citizens with a Civil Service status.

I understand that the American Bank Note Company are always in need of exceptionally fine steel plate engravers, and I wonder if you have skill in steel engraving and if you would be interested in this type of work. If so, let me know and I may be able to help you in obtaining employment there.

With kind regards and all good wishes, I am,

Yours sincerely,

Harlan F. Stone.[4]

The job opportunities were proving elusive, and as Oskar had already acknowledged, he was having a hard time making a living as an artist. But he didn't dwell on that point in his correspondence. To an artist of Oskar's caliber, the idea of helping engrave bank notes couldn't have been appealing. The chief justice was suggesting a different craft that involved more artisanship and less artistry:

January 25th 1943.

The Honorable Chief Justice
Mr. Harlan Fiske Stone.

Sir.

I thank you very much indeed for your kind letter, and I hesitated to answer because it is so difficult for me to decide what to do in this case. I am sure I could do this job after learning it, but I do not know if I can succeed because one must be young to begin with engraving. I have no experience in steel-engraving. Etching is a quite different technique. I use sometimes the [diamond] engraver, but only to strengthen some outlines.

---

4.   Stone to Stoessel, typed letter, Jan. 20, 1943, Stone Papers, Library of Congress.

Now I should disappoint you when I have not the ability to satisfy in this work. I hear that some artists are working for Mr. Elmer Davis[5] and I will ask him whether he is interested in my work. May I ask you to excuse I make you so much troubles, but you have been always so kind to me, and it is now quite impossible to get private commissions. I am so sorry that I cannot show you my exhibition. I intend to exhibit etchings, drawings, watercolors, and perhaps some oil paintings. May I tell my sincerest thank you for your kindness.

I am Respectfully

Yours

Oskar Stoessel.

P.S. I am member of the College-Art Association and I will try to get a place as teacher here in New-York.[6]

Resolute in wanting to help Oskar find a job, the tenacious if unimaginative chief justice answered two days later. An art connoisseur himself, Stone seemed defensively curt about making clear that he knew something about the etcher's and engraver's arts:

January 27, 1943.

Dear Mr. Stoessel:

Thank you for your letter of the 25th.

I, of course, know that etchers are not necessarily engravers. I will make further inquiries to see if there is any further possibility for your work here.

Yours sincerely,

Harlan F. Stone.[7]

Meanwhile, Arthur H. Harlow & Co., the New York art gallery, had begun representing Oskar. In March 1943—not February, as Oskar had originally suggested to Chief Justice Stone—Oskar mounted an exhibition there, at 42 East 57th Street. The brochure shows three samples of his signed artist's proofs: Presi-

---

5.   Davis was a successful author and radio commentator. In June 1942, President Roosevelt had appointed him director of the Office of War Information, with a budget of some $25 million and about 30,000 employees. *American National Biography* (1999), "Davis, Elmer [13 Jan. 1890–18 May 1958]."

6.   Stoessel to Stone, handwritten letter, Jan. 25, 1943, Stone Papers, Library of Congress.

7.   Stone to Stoessel, typed letter, Jan. 27, 1943, Stone Papers, Library of Congress.

dent Roosevelt (available at a cost of $30), Chief Justice Charles Evans Hughes ($24), and Secretary of State Cordell Hull ($24) (see page 208).

A notice of the exhibition caught the attention of Stone, who must have noticed that Chief Justice Hughes, his predecessor, was given top billing. Even so, Stone was characteristically generous in writing to Oskar:

March 23, 1943

Dear Mr. Stoessel:

I am happy to note in this week's issue of *The Art Digest* a very interesting write-up of your exhibition of etchings and water colors at the Harlow Galleries.[8] The article speaks highly of your work. I hope there will be many visitors and that it will bring you some purchasers.

With congratulations, and with kind regards, I am,

Yours sincerely,
Harlan F. Stone.[9]

Oskar's grateful reply followed five days later:

March 28th 1943.

The Honorable Chief Justice
Mr. Harlan Fiske Stone

Sir, I have your kind letter of March 23, and may I thank you very much for your kind interest. It encourages me very much to see you think still on my modest work. The exhibition was a good success more in a moral way and I had very good criticism in *New York Times*[10] and *Herald Tribune*. (Mr. Royal Cortissoz

---

8.   "Great Americans Etched by Noted European," *Art Digest*, Mar. 15, 1943, 20 ("The artist places extreme emphasis on the sitter's countenance to disclose the intrinsic character of his subject. . . . Stoessel has arrived at a mature expressiveness of the master artists; his work is convincing and his artistic message is sufficiently significant to deserve American acclaim."). See also *ArtNews* 42, Mar. 15, 1943, 23 ("His etchings and drawings include all the important figures in the Executive and Judiciary branches of our Government. His approach to art is as conservative as the opinions of Mr. Justice Roberts, whom he has so ably depicted. Realistic, pleasant, not without dignity, these portraits should appeal to a large public.").

9.   Stone to Stoessel, typed letter, Mar. 23, 1943, Stone Papers, Library of Congress.

10. Howard Devree, "From a Reviewer's Notebook," *N.Y. Times*, Mar. 14, 1943, X8 ("Oils, water-colors, and prints by Oskar Stoessel, late of Vienna, have been placed on view at the Harlow Gallery. Graphics are essentially his medium as the large drypoints of the individual members of the United States Supreme Court amply testify. One water-color—an interior—

wrote very nicely.)[11] In April I have to make a private portrait in Washington, D.C., and I hope I shall have opportunity to see you. I will try it. Thanking again for your kind letter I must say I am very proud of it.

Respectfully

Yours

Oskar Stoessel.

My respectful regards to Mrs. Stone and Miss Jenkins [Stone's secretary, Gertrude Jenkins].[12]

The two men would see each other three months later, in June 1943. Three years had now passed since Chief Justice Stone's first attempt to boost Oskar Stoessel's career with Frederick Paul Keppel in New York and C.P. Minnigerode in Washington, D.C. Although exhibitions had resulted at the Corcoran (D.C.) and at Harlow (N.Y.), Oskar still hadn't found full-time employment. At last, his prospects seemed to be improving:

June 24, 1943.

Dear Mr. Stoessel:

Confirming my telephone conversation with you, after I saw you this morning I called on Mr. David E. Finley of the National Gallery of Art (Mellon Gallery). I talked with him about you and your aspirations to be doing more work, and he said he would be very glad if you would call and see him. He would like to have an opportunity to talk with you.

Fortunately there happened to be present Colonel McBride, who is connected with the Gallery, and who had seen your exhibition in New York and spoke very favorably of it.

---

is fluent and bold. But it is to the graphic portraits that one returns with considerable admiration.").

11. Royal Cortissoz (1869–1948) was a New York art critic. See Royal Cortissoz, "American and Foreign Artists," *N.Y. Herald Trib.*, Mar. 14, 1943, VI5 ("I cannot too warmly commend these prints as characterizations and as examples of expert workmanship. Mr. Stoessel is a finished draughtsman, using his instrument with equal firmness and freedom. He studies his sitter in a natural pose and then etches him with fluent directness. He has no flourish of style, to be sure, but his simple and straightforward approach secures good results. . . . For his authentic quality as an artist he is cordially to be greeted.").

12. Stoessel to Stone, handwritten letter, Mar. 28, 1943, Stone Papers, Library of Congress.

I think if you tell Mr. Finley of your interest in etching, also in painting, and also in collecting, that he may find opportunities for you.

With kind regards, I am,

Yours sincerely,
Harlan F. Stone.[13]

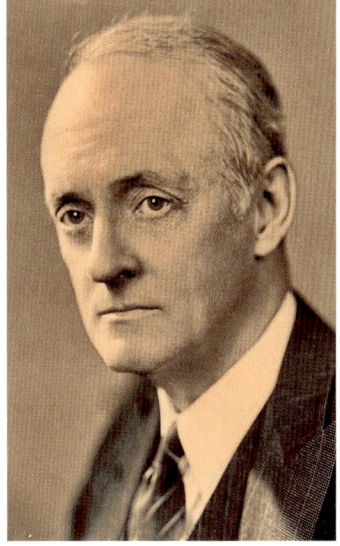

David E. Finley, first director of the National Gallery of Art

In the late summer of 1943, Oskar spent six weeks in California—perhaps most of that time with his brother Ludwig.[14]

The work of the Commission for the Protection and Salvage of Artistic and Historic Monuments in Europe was getting underway. When Chief Justice Stone declined to chair it, the task fell to Justice Owen Roberts,[15] hence its informal name the "Roberts Commission." Surprisingly—considering his expertise in the field and Justice Roberts's presumed knowledge of that expertise—Oskar seems not to have been asked to participate in any of the Commission's work, even though he applied for a position. Pulling the laboring oar for the Commission, Finley became engrossed in his work, and nothing of consequence materialized by way of work for Oskar. It might have been otherwise if Stone had chaired the Commission.

---

13. Stone to Stoessel, typed letter, June 24, 1943, Stone Papers, Library of Congress.

14. Stoessel to unknown art dealer, handwritten letter, July 29, 1943 (on file with author).

15. Finley to Stone, Western Union telegram, Aug. 24, 1943, Stone Papers, Library of Congress ("Organization meeting of Salvage Committee will be held with Justice Roberts as chairman at National Gallery Tomorrow Wednesday morning. We shall miss you but will send you report of proceedings.").

No. 5953502

Name .... STOESSEL, Oskar ....

residing at Carnegie Hall, New York, New York, NY

Age ... 65 ... years. Date of order of admission .. May 4, 1944

Date certificate issued .... May 4, 1944 .... by the

U. S. District .... Court at ... **New York City, New York**

Petition No. 483019 2150102

(Complete and true signature of holder)

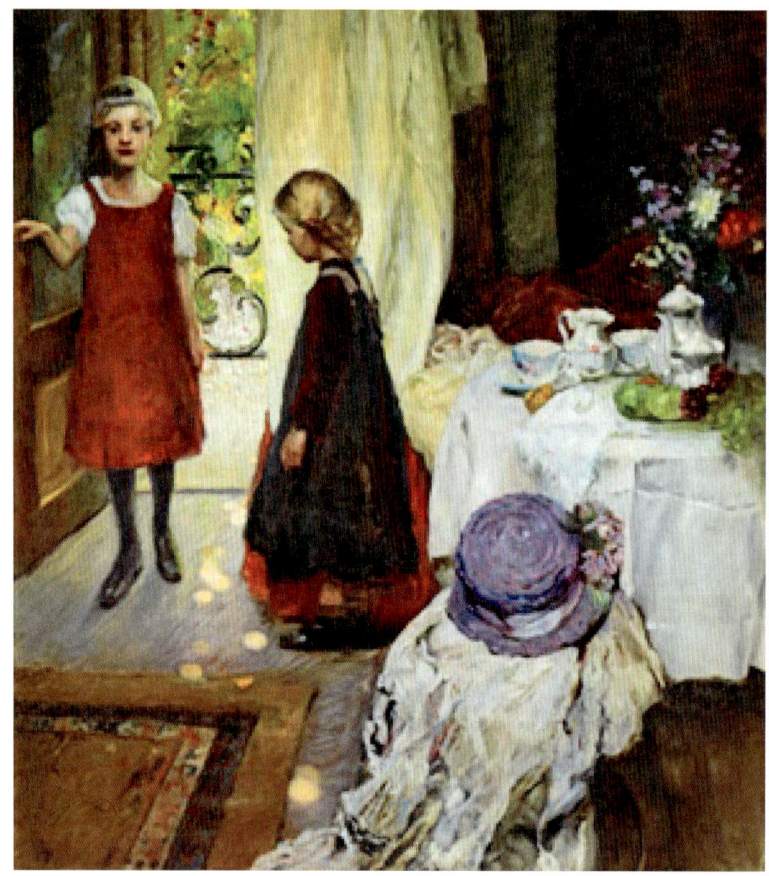

Oskar's "Sonnenkringeln" (1910), an early painting of children

CHAPTER 31

New American Citizen

Iɴ the new year, Chief Justice Stone acknowledged receipt of Oskar's artistic New Year's card (see page 219, bottom left)—a rather edgy rendering of the Madonna (with halo) and child in the foreground and the Star of Bethlehem in the background:

> January 6, 1944
>
> Dear Mr. Stoessel:
>
> Many thanks for your attractive New Year's card.
>
> I wish for you the best kind of a New Year.
>
> Last evening we saw Mr. and Mrs. Somary,[1] who told us that you were painting some very interesting children's pictures.
>
> With kind regards, I am,
>
> > Yours sincerely,
> >
> > Harlan F. Stone.[2]

Perhaps the Christian-themed New Year's cards were intended only for Oskar's Christian friends. They might seem strange for a Jewish artist who hadn't converted to Christianity, but these were exceedingly common in Roman Catholic Austria.

Oskar must have been quite busy with these paintings and other projects. Not until May 1944, it appears, did Oskar again write to the chief justice. He was exuberant about the news he could share:

---

1. Felix Somary (1881–1956), an Austrian-Swiss banker, moved to Washington, D.C., and advised the Defense Department from 1941 to 1943 on finance issues. His wife was an Austrian countess (née May Demblin).
2. Chief Justice Harlan Fiske Stone to Oskar Stoessel, typed letter, Jan. 6, 1944, Stone Papers, Library of Congress.

May 23rd 1944.

The Honorable Chief Justice Harlan Fiske Stone
    Washington, D.C.
Sir,

    This week I have got my second papers and I am now citizen of U.S.A. and I am very happy.[3] May I say my gratitude for the help you always have given me. Since the time I had the honour to know you I had the feeling that I belong to this country, and I thank you for having given me this feeling of security, and I can promise to do all I can, to be a useful and good citizen of this country. In June I hope to come for some days to Washington and I should be very glad to see you. I hope you are well and I am

                    Respectfully
            Yours
                    Oskar Stoessel.[4]

Ever gracious and generous as a correspondent, the chief justice hastened to send felicitations to the new American:

June 7, 1944

Dear Mr. Stoessel:

    Congratulations on your becoming an American citizen. I am convinced that you will find the United States will be a safer and a happier place in which to live than a great many others in the world—and I may add that we are glad to have you as citizen.

    I hope you will find plenty of interesting work here and if there is anything I can do to assist you know that I shall be glad to do it.

    Do you still have some copies of the etching which you made of me? It may be that some of my friends will wish to secure copies.

    With kind regards, I am,

                    Yours sincerely,
                    Harlan F. Stone.[5]

---

3.   Oskar's certificate of citizenship was issued May 4, 1944, by the federal court in the Southern District of New York. He was 65. Petition no. 483019.
4.   Stoessel to Stone, handwritten letter, May 23, 1944, Stone Papers, Library of Congress.
5.   Stone to Stoessel, typed letter, June 7, 1944, Stone Papers, Library of Congress.

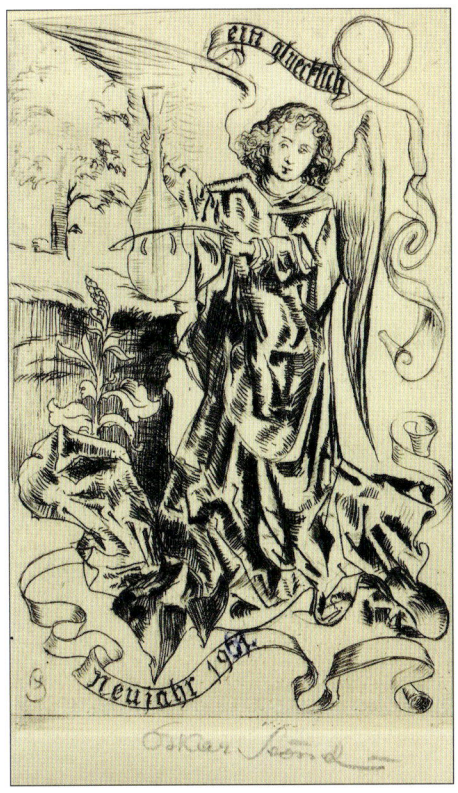

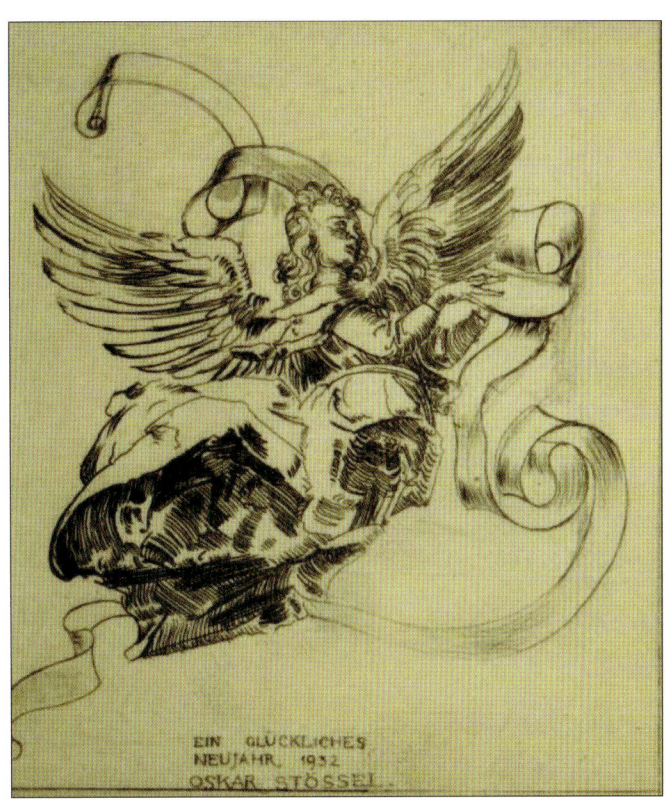

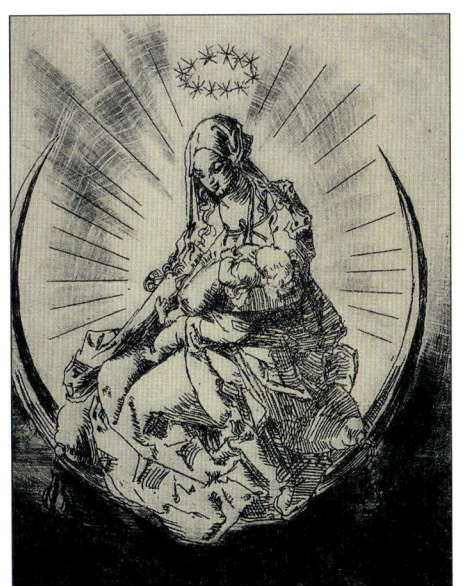

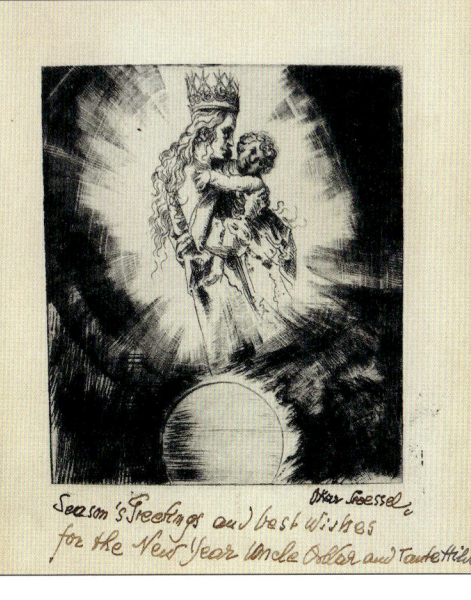

Oskar created his own New Year's greeting cards, here from 1931 (top left), 1932 (top right), 1944 (bottom left), and 1953 (bottom right). The bottom-right image, inscribed from "Uncle Oskar and Tante [Aunt] Hilde," was sent to Oskar's niece Elsa (courtesy of David & Jill Heichler).

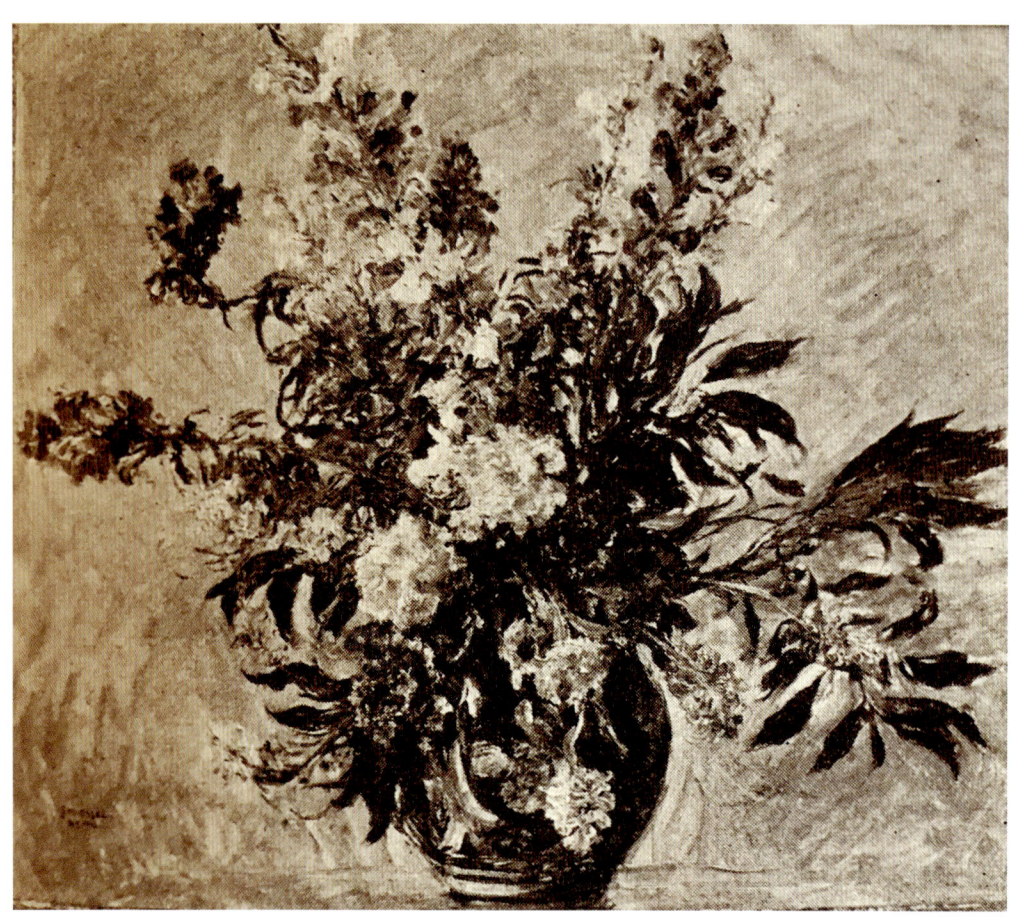

Oskar's "Large Floral Vase" (1945), as shown in the auction brochure for the Carnegie Hall Art Gallery

CHAPTER 32

Oskar's Bouquets

MORE than a year passed before the correspondence between the chief justice and Oskar resumed. Both Franklin Roosevelt and Adolf Hitler were dead, and the war in Europe had come to an end. Oskar was doubtless inspired by the Allied victory and wished to commemorate its American heroes:

June 14th 1945.

The Honorable Chief Justice Mr. Harlan Fiske Stone.
Washington, D.C.

Dear Sir,

I hoped all the time to come to Washington before vacation, but I do not know when I can. So I want to wish you a very good vacation. I am often thinking gratefully on you. You have done so much for me, so I have the feeling I succeeded to find a new home in this country. In fall I hope to come to Washington, and I shall try to make some etchings of the great commanders of the armies of U.S.A. I think it would be a great thing to have etchings of those famous men. I think eventually to make a group of the High-Command.

I have now finished an etching of Mr. Morgenthau,[1] the father of the Secretary of the Treasury.[2] He spoke very highly of you, and I have to give you his best regards.

---

1. See *American National Biography* (1999), "Morgenthau, Henry [26 Apr. 1856–25 Nov. 1946]" (born in Mannheim, Germany, he moved at age ten with his parents to the United States, where he would become a successful lawyer, developer, supporter of Jewish causes, and ultimately chair of the Democratic National Committee's finance committee in 1912; in old age, he was a strong supporter of the New Deal). No image of the Morgenthau etching has been located.

2. See *American National Biography* (1999), "Morgenthau, Henry Jr. [11 May 1891–6 Feb. 1967]" (born in NYC, he escaped his father's influence by becoming a farmer in Texas in 1911, but then in 1913 his father helped him purchase 1,700 acres in Dutchess County, NY, where he came to know Franklin Delano Roosevelt, whom he considered an "alternative father"; beginning in

I hope, Mr. Chief Justice, that you will stay in full health on the high place, and help the humanity for many years. Wishing you a very fine vacation, I should be happy to see you soon.

I am Respectfully

Yours
Oskar Stoessel

Please give my respectful regards to Mrs. Stone and Miss Jenkins.[3]

The Court's term would end on June 30, and Oskar had apparently become sufficiently acquainted with the Court's schedule to know this. Though busy, the chief justice made time to acknowledge his friend (though his salutations remained formal):

June 19, 1945

Dear Mr. Stoessel:

Many thanks for your letter of the 14th.

A short time ago I gave your name and address to Mr. Sam Lewisohn, the well known collector of modern art.[4] He recently saw a copy of the etching which you made of me, which he liked very much, and I have suggested to him that he ask you to do some work for him. I think he would like to have Mrs. Lewisohn's portrait etched.

Next fall or winter I should like to try again to persuade Mrs. Stone to have you etch her portrait if you are likely to be in Washington on any other errand. Write and let me know when you think of coming and then I can talk with her about it.

1928, he served as agricultural commissioner in Roosevelt's gubernatorial administration, as head of the Federal Farm Board in Roosevelt's first presidential administration, and beginning in 1934 as secretary of the treasury for 11 years; he was said to be "often inarticulate and awkward in press conferences and other public appearances, causing many to underrate his competence").

3. Oskar Stoessel to Chief Justice Harlan Fiske Stone, handwritten letter, June 14, 1945, Stone Papers, Library of Congress.

4. Sam A. Lewisohn (1884–1951) was an American lawyer, financier, philanthropist, and art collector in New York City.

Whenever you wish to make etchings of some of the military men I should be glad to do whatever I can to assist you. General Marshall,[5] who is one of the great military men of this time, I know quite well. Some of the others I know less well.

I am leaving town very soon now for the summer and will not be back until October.

With kind regards and all good wishes for a pleasant summer, I am,

Yours sincerely,

Harlan F. Stone.[6]

A month later, a public auction of paintings and bronzes was held at the Carnegie Hall Art Gallery. Sponsored by the Artists of Carnegie Hall Inc., the sale featured works not only by Oskar but also by such notable artists as Wilford Conrow (1880–1957), Ethel Myers (1881–1960),[7] and Walter Russell (1871–1963). The auction catalogue provides a glimpse of the life Oskar led at Carnegie Hall with the other artists. It was Oskar's first major sale as an American citizen. Four of his paintings were auctioned off: *Venice* (starting bid of $250), *Large Floral Vase* ($150), *Peonies* ($120), and *Carnations* ($120). The sale shows that Oskar had continued painting as well as etching. His minimum bids were comparable to those of the other Carnegie artists.

---

5.   General George Marshall (1880–1959), U.S. Army Chief of Staff during World War II.
6.   Stone to Stoessel, typed letter, June 19, 1945, Stone Papers, Library of Congress.
7.   See *American National Biography* (1999), "Myers, Ethel [23 Aug. 1881–24 May 1960]" (mentioning her ceramics studio at Carnegie Hall and her direction of the fine arts and ceramics department of Christodora House in New York in the 1930s and 1940s).

February 23rd 1946.

The Honorable Chief Justice Harlan Fiske Stone,

Dear Sir.

I have your kind letter and I am very glad to know you agree on the matter of purchasing drawings and engravings of the old masters. I thank for your kind words about the passing away of my dear mother. I wrote her often how kind you are allways to me.

End of next week or beginning March I hope to come to Washington D.C. and I shall be very happy to see you, and to have an opportunity to talk about the matter of the Museum.

Thanking again for your kindness I am with best wishes for you and Mrs. Stone   Yours Respectfully

Oskar Stoessel.

Oskar's last known letter to Chief Justice Stone

CHAPTER 33

Inextinguishable Memories

THE next letter from Oskar to Chief Justice Stone—over seven months later—was extraordinary, and Stone knew it. He had his secretary type a fair copy from Oskar's handwritten original, which isn't in the Library of Congress file. But we're fortunate to have the typed version, with one blank where Miss Jenkins couldn't make out a name. The letter begs to be read closely, for it's the most important of all:

January 30, 1946

The Honorable Chief Justice Harlan Fiske Stone

Sir:

I have tried to come to Washington several times but I could never get a room. I think it is better now and I hope to come in the near future.

News from my former home, Vienna, are bad, and I have the feeling most of the people did not learn from the experience they had. But there is some good people there, and I have a letter from my former pupil, and she is now so poor and I am trying to help her with food packages. She saved my plates in Vienna, although she had to suffer all the time. [This was Hildegarde Hofmann, Oskar's former student in Vienna (see pages 84–85).] She had to work in a factory welding iron. Now she hopes the work is over, and I will help her as far as I can. This people is starving and I think America could educated this people best by helping them, and I have an idea how they could help also the United States.

In Vienna is the most famous collection of old engravings, etchings, and drawings. The "Albertina." In U.S. is not one collection even to compare with it. In Vienna there are several dozens of Durer drawings.[1] America has only one important drawing in the Morgan collection. I do not want to rob Vienna of her great treasures, but they can give some of their duplicates and some of the

---

1. Albrecht Dürer (1471–1528) was the noted German artist of the Renaissance.

drawings without losing much of their importance. It is a very important matter that the young American artists have the opportunity to see some of these masterpieces here and it is more important that people is not starving there, and sooner or later they will sell those things to art collectors. It would be much better when it would be bought direct by the [National Gallery?—a blank is left here]. I hear Mr. Stix[2] is again on the Board of Directors of Albertina, and he is a very fine and honest man. If I could be of any help selecting officially a collection of drawings, very useful for America, I should be glad to give my service to my new home.

I have only my pupil there, a very fine lady.[3]

My relatives are no more in life. My dear mother died in Switzerland. My sister [Isabella], my brother in law, and a niece were murdered by the Nazis. So I try to extinguish all memories of Austria in my mind.

I think America could make a fair deal with Austria, and I think it is of great importance that America should have a collection of drawings of the old masters, and when Vienna gives only a small part of those away it would still have more than the British Museum.

May I ask your opinion on this matter and Austria would get enough help to build up a healthy and good-minded population.

I hope that you are in good health and when I come to Washington I should be very happy seeing you.

With my greetings to you and Mrs. Stone,
Respectfully Yours,
Oskar Stoessel.[4]

"I try," wrote Oskar, "to extinguish all memories of Austria in my mind." His erstwhile source of group identity—being an Austrian—had been shattered. That was a common feeling among Austrian Jews exiled after the Anschluss. The writer Jean Améry is the archetypal example. Having grown up in a Jewish family that, like many cultural elites, had only loose ties with Judaism and celebrated

---

2.   Alfred Stix (1882–1957) was an Austrian art historian and museum director.
3.   Again, Hildegarde Hofmann.
4.   Oskar Stoessel to Chief Justice Harlan Fiske Stone, typed letter (apparently transcribed in Stone's chambers from a handwritten letter), Jan. 30, 1946, Stone Papers, Library of Congress.

Christmas as a secular holiday, Améry "saw himself as part of Austria's cultural and historical landscape."[5] Because his sense of homeland was inseparable from his self-image, his exile entailed a diminished self: he "felt as if he had never been a part of the society with which he had so much identified and he could not fool himself into believing that he was still part of an Austrian community."[6] Améry "tried to forget his memories of Austria's history and its landscape" and therefore suffered "a diminished sense of self."[7] Not really self-pity, homesickness amounted to "self-destruction."[8] These feelings weren't unique to Améry; many others had them, and Oskar was surely among them.

Chief Justice Stone's reply arrived less than two weeks later. It was a severely underwhelming letter of condolence. It was also probably the last letter Oskar would receive from Stone. At this point, among members of the Court, only the chief justice appears to have maintained correspondence with the artist. Still living at Carnegie Hall, and having his studio there, Oskar might have been both heartened and disappointed by the letter (note the startlingly understated euphemism "unhappy experience"):

February 12, 1946

Dear Mr. Stoessel:

I was glad to hear from you, although sorry indeed to learn of the unhappy experience of your family, and especially the death of your mother. Please accept my sincere sympathy.

If the Collection of drawings of old masters, or a substantial part of it, is likely to be available for purchase, I agree with you that it would be very important that they should come to the United States. It is possible that we might find someone who would be willing to buy them to add to our collection of prints and drawings at the National Gallery. I will make inquiry to see what the possibilities are of raising money for that purpose, and you perhaps could tell me how best to proceed to make purchases there if such articles are likely to be available.

---

5.   Jacqueline Vansant, *Reclaiming* Heimat*: Trauma and Mourning in Memoirs by Jewish Austrian Reémigrés* (Wayne State Univ. Press, 2001), 35.
6.   Vansant, 37.
7.   Vansant, 39.
8.   Vansant, 39.

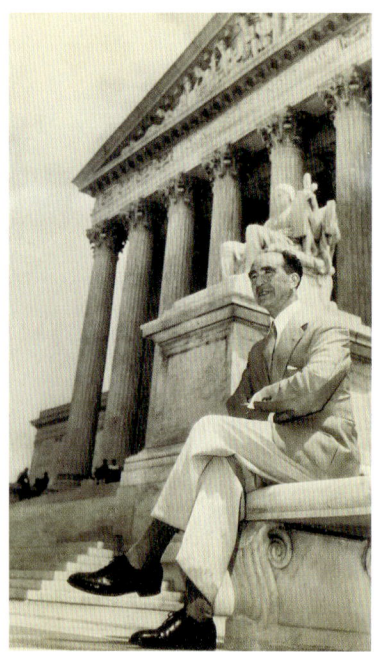

Justice Frank Murphy sits outside the Supreme Court as arguments are presented for and against seven Nazi saboteurs. As an active lieutenant colonel in the U.S. Army, he was disqualified from sitting on the case.

When you next come to Washington come in and see me and we will talk about it.

With kind regards, I am,

Yours sincerely
Harlan F. Stone.[9]

The chief justice's extreme reserve in expressing condolences about the Nazi atrocities may have stemmed from his judicial responsibilities. Some may find this explanation a craven rationalization, but in fairness it ought to be stated. A careful man, Stone studiously avoided saying things, especially in writing, that might damage the image of either himself or the Court as an impartial decision-maker. He had sat on Nazi-related cases before, and he knew that he might do so again. Just four years before, in 1942, Justice Frank Murphy had to recuse himself from a case, *Ex parte Quirin*.[10] In that case seven Nazi saboteurs, who had been tried by a military tribunal that Roosevelt created solely for them, appealed to the Supreme Court for writs of habeas corpus. Because Justice Murphy was on active duty in the U.S. Army as a lieutenant colonel, he was disqualified from hearing the case. While his colleagues heard oral arguments, Justice Murphy went to the front of the Supreme Court building and sat on a marble bench as press photographers snapped his photo. Although in the end the opinion was unanimous in denying the writs, the case provoked great strife on the Court. Justice Jackson wrote a long draft concurrence (ultimately withdrawn) in which he touted sweeping presidential power during wartime. Justice Felix Frankfurter wrote a "soliloquy" addressed to the Nazi petitioners, but circulated only within the Court, in which he entreated the members of the Court to be unanimous.

---

9.   Stone to Stoessel, typed letter, Feb. 12, 1946, Stone Papers, Library of Congress.
10.   317 U.S. 1 (1942).

To this day, *Ex parte Quirin* remains controversial on the constitutionality of a president's power to create a nonstatutory military tribunal.

Whatever one makes of the chief justice's letter, Oskar answered 11 days later, with words of hope about the reunion of the two men:

February 23rd 1946

The Honorable Chief Justice Harlan Fiske Stone.

Dear Sir,

I have your kind letter and I am very glad to know you agree on the matter of purchasing drawings and engravings of the old masters. I thank for your kind words about the passing away of my dear mother. I wrote her often how kind you are always to me.

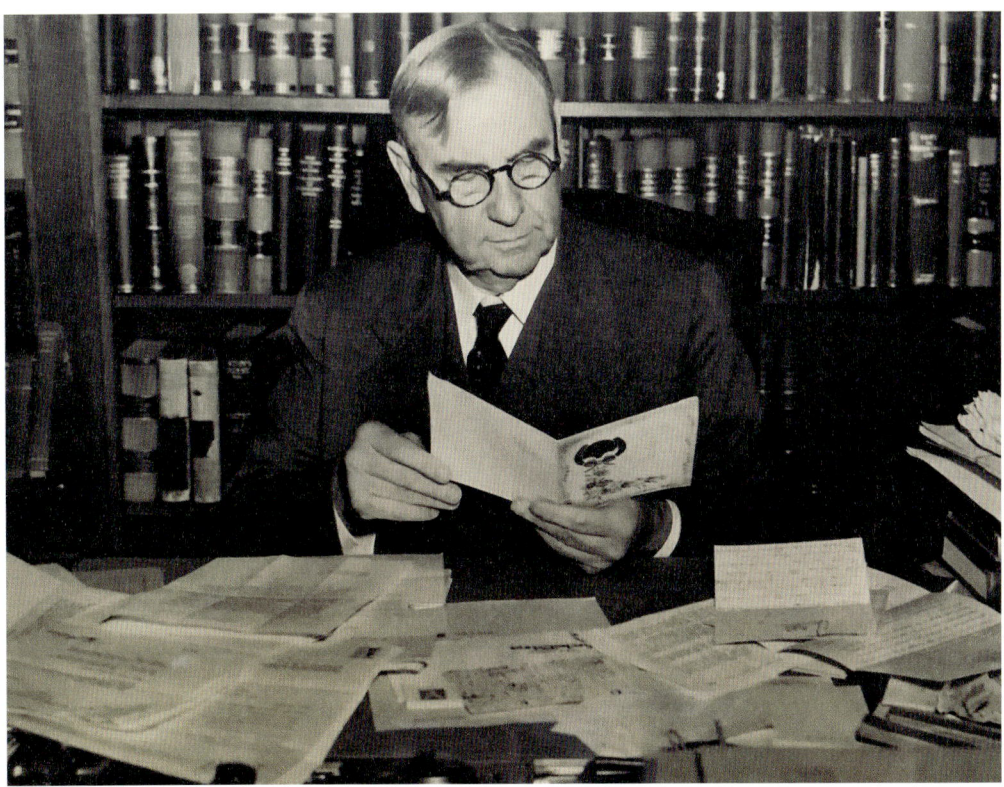

On October 11, 1944, Chief Justice Stone was photographed at his desk reading birthday greetings. He turned 72 that day.

End of next week or beginning March I hope to come to Washington, D.C., and I shall be very happy to see you, and to have an opportunity to talk about the matter of the purchase.

Thanking again for your kindness, I am with best wishes for you and Mrs. Stone.

Yours Respectfully,
Oskar Stoessel.[11]

Whether this reunion occurred is unknown.

What actually happened to Oskar's family in the Holocaust? Official records show that Oskar's sister Isabella was deported with her husband Max Stessel from Vienna to the Theresienstadt ghetto in Czechoslovakia. She was 62; he was 74. Then, on September 10, 1942, they were taken to the Treblinka extermination camp in Mazowiecke, Poland, where, shortly after arriving on September 29, 1942, they were murdered.

Their daughter Hilda, at the age of 30, was taken to the camp in Auschwitz, Poland, where on September 7, 1942, she was murdered.

Oskar also had two cousins who were killed in camps. They were the sons of his father's brother Farcas Stössel. Their names were Max Mordechai Zwi Stössel (1880–1944) and Emanuel Mayer Stoesel (1886–1941). Max was murdered at Auschwitz on October 9, 1944. Emanuel was taken to the gruesome ghetto at Litzmannstadt (or Lodz), Poland, where many Jews died of malnutrition. Many others were shot there. Emanuel died on September 19, 1941.

Similar fates befell the entire network of people whom Oskar knew as extended family members. They died excruciating deaths at the hands of the ruthlessly efficient Nazis.

---

11.   Stoessel to Stone, handwritten letter, Feb. 23, 1946, Stone Papers, Library of Congress.

CHAPTER 34

Stone's Judicial Finale

THE Supreme Court session on April 22, 1946, was a dramatic one. The Court had just announced the decision in *Girouard v. United States*, in which a Canadian had petitioned to become an American citizen. In an interview, he had said that, being a Seventh-Day Adventist, he would not fight to defend the United States but would willingly serve in a noncombatant position. The Supreme Court overturned an act of Congress, holding that denying him citizenship on this basis violated the First Amendment's guarantee of freedom of religion.

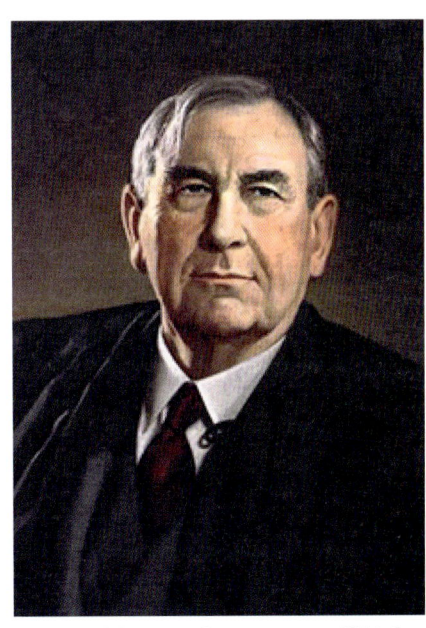

The official Supreme Court portrait of Chief Justice Harlan Fiske Stone (by C.J. Fox)

Chief Justice Stone dissented, declaring: "It is not the function of this Court to disregard the will of Congress in the exercise of its constitutional power."[1] It must have been a moment of frustration and stress.[2] The chief justice may well have known, through conversation, that his friend Oskar Stoessel had registered for the "old-man's draft" before petitioning to become an American citizen.

---

1. *Girouard v. United States*, 328 U.S. 61, 79 (1946) (Stone C.J. dissenting).
2. See *American National Biography* (1999), "Stone, Harlan Fiske" (stating, in reference to Stone's final years, "The demands of the job, as well as the constant refereeing among the justices, took their toll.").

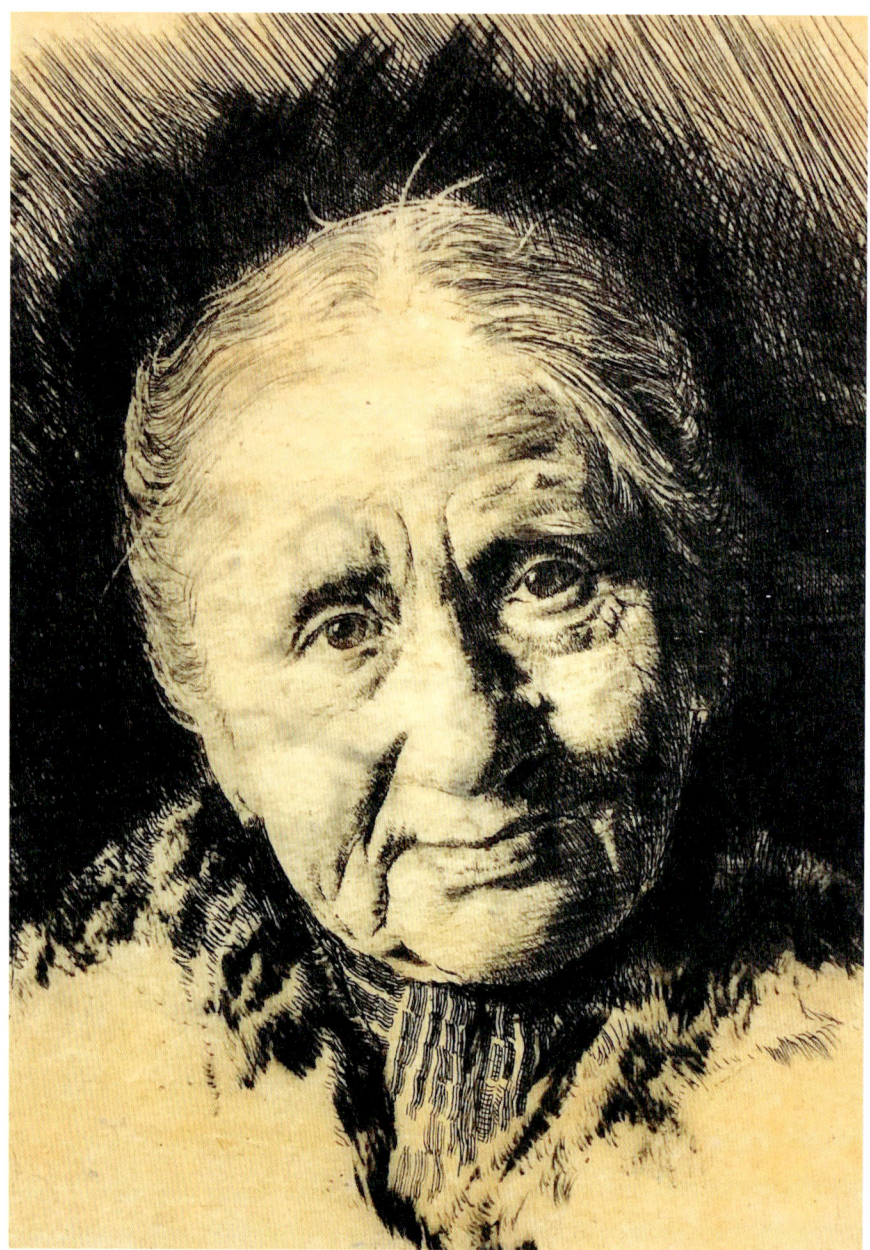

Oskar's mother, Berta, toward the end of her life. She died in Switzerland during the war.

Just after he had finished reading his dissent, it was Chief Justice Stone's turn to deliver three more decisions.[3] But several moments of awkward silence passed, and then Stone began mumbling. Perceiving that something was wrong, Justice Hugo Black called for a 45-minute recess, until 2:30 p.m., and physicians were summoned.

Justices Black and Reed helped Stone off the bench, and he lay unconscious on a couch in a washroom off the conference chamber. Soon there was reassuring news: a physician had diagnosed the illness as a "small case of indigestion." Stone's own personal physician took a more somber view but "held out hope for recovery."[4] In fact, he was having a severe cerebral hemorrhage. About 3:30 p.m., an ambulance took the stricken chief justice not to a hospital, but home—where he never regained consciousness. Shortly after, he died.

3.   Alpheus Thomas Mason, *Harlan Fiske Stone: Pillar of the Law* (Viking, 1956), 806.
4.   Mason, 806.

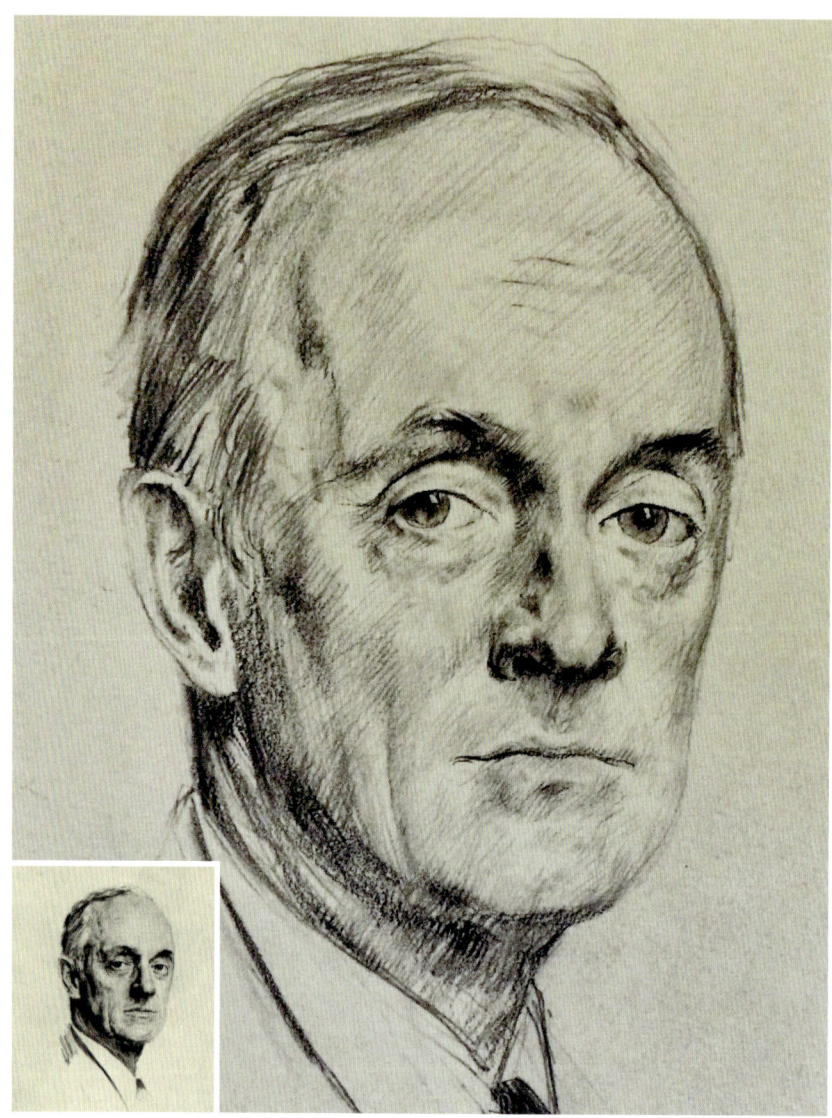

David E. Finley Jr. (1890—1977) was an American cultural standard-bearer in the mid-20th century. He was not only the first director of the National Gallery of Art but also the founding chair of the National Trust for Historic Preservation (1949), the founding chair of the White House Historical Association (1961), and the moving force behind the founding of the National Portrait Gallery (1962). He was also head of the Roberts Commission during and after World War II——meaning, in pop-culture terms, that he was directing the "Monuments Men" who saved Nazi-plundered art. Shown here is Oskar's pencil sketch of a thinner-faced Finley (1946), probably made after the first trial proof (inset), which in Finley's view made the subject too jowly and heavyset. The copperplate for the etching is shown on page 3.

CHAPTER 35

Hopes for the National Gallery

Now 67, Oskar seems not to have corresponded further with any of the justices. Although he had surely heard of Justice Robert H. Jackson's role as lead prosecutor in the Nuremberg Trials against Nazi war criminals, Oskar seems not to have written to him again despite their having corresponded so heavily and warmly in 1942. Nor is there any record of later correspondence with George Messersmith.

But about the time of Chief Justice Stone's death, Oskar's relationship with David E. Finley of the National Gallery of Art was warming. Finley had sat for a portrait (see page 234), and in July 1946 Oskar sent him two copies of the first version. Finley had negotiated to receive each state of the portrait,[1] as well as the copperplates.

As with many other Stoessel portraits, the background was blank in the floating-head technique—with only the barest hint of Finley's suit. Upon receiving the first trial proof, Finley wrote to Oskar to say he liked the uncompleted background, and so did his wife.[2] "I am very happy to have a portrait by such a distinguished artist," wrote Finley, "and I am most grateful for the trouble you have taken about it."[3] Finley enclosed what must have been a generous check to reimburse Oskar for his expenses.

Both Finley and his wife wanted some refinements: "As is usually the case with a family in the matter of portraits, she [Mrs. Finley] had some reservations about

1. Oskar Stoessel to David E. Finley, handwritten letter, July 10, 1946, Finley Papers, National Gallery of Art.
2. Finley to Stoessel, typed letter, July 10, 1946, Finley Papers, National Gallery of Art.
3. Finley to Stoessel, July 10, 1946.

the likeness in the lower part of the face."[4] He appeared to have jowls: "She thinks you have given me too heavy a jaw, particularly the muscles on the right side of the face—the left-hand side looking at the picture. I told her that the portrait was not quite finished, and that perhaps you expected to take off a few pounds from my face before it was completed!"[5]

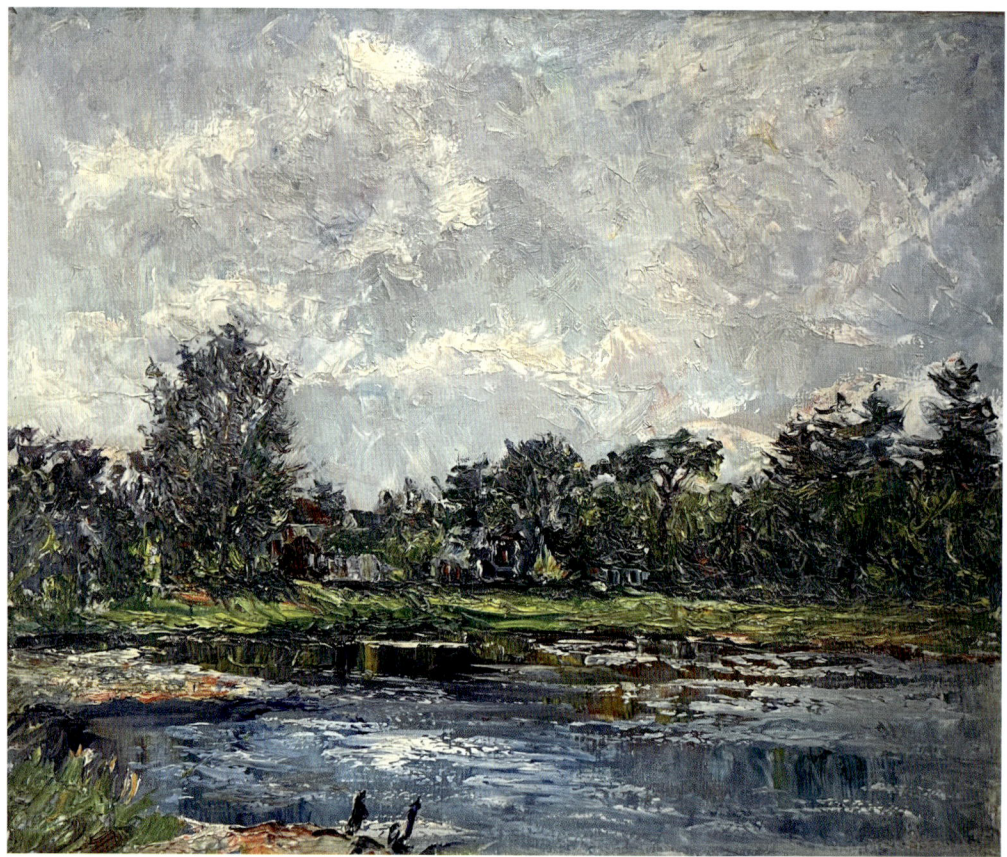

In November 1946, while staying in Lake Placid in upstate New York, Oskar painted this scene. It belonged to a family in Scarsdale, New York, until it came into the Garner Collection in 2023.

---

4.   Finley to Stoessel, July 10, 1946.
5.   Finley to Stoessel, July 10, 1946.

Oskar spent most of November 1946 in a hotel in Lake Placid, New York. Copies of his correspondence were being forwarded to him. Oskar tactfully assured Finley that the finished etching would be "a great improvement." And it must have been, since Finley would later write when it was complete: "I cannot tell you how grateful I am for the effort you have expended on my portrait, or how pleased I am with the result."[6] He asked for ten to twelve additional prints and wanted to know the cost.[7]

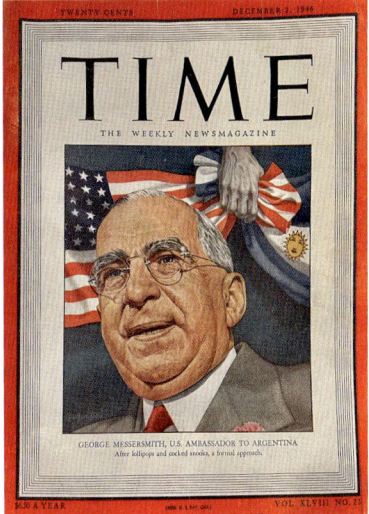

About the time of Oskar's stay in Lake Placid, his friend George Messersmith—whose portrait Oskar had completed a decade before (see page 72)—appeared on the cover of Time *as the new U.S. ambassador to Argentina. It is unknown whether the two men still remained in touch with each other.*

Perhaps still hoping for a job with the National Gallery, Oskar pledged to send Finley a dozen copies as a gift: "I am very pleased to make the prints for you, and there is nothing to pay. I shall be pleased to make this and offer it to you as a sign of the great esteem I have for you."[8] In the end, Oskar sent 13, asking Finley to sign one and return it to Oskar. He wrote: "It would remind me always on the pleasant sittings I had the honor of having with you."[9] Finley soon returned the signed etching, noting that he had given away several of the others to "persons who received them with great enthusiasm."[10]

In the new year, probably sometime in January 1947, Oskar had a health crisis that caused him "to stay for some time," as he told Finley, in the Roosevelt

6.   Finley to Stoessel, typed letter, Nov. 27, 1946, Finley Papers, National Gallery of Art.
7.   Finley to Stoessel, Nov. 27, 1946.
8.   Stoessel to Finley, handwritten letter, Dec. 5, 1946, Finley Papers, National Gallery of Art.
9.   Stoessel to Finley, handwritten letter, Dec. 23, 1946, Finley Papers, National Gallery of Art.
10. Finley to Stoessel, typed letter, Dec. 27, 1946, Finley Papers, National Gallery of Art.

Hospital[11]—now known as Mount Sinai West. He was discharged on February 13.[12] His doctor instructed him not to work at all for two weeks after going home.[13]

What was the problem? It might well have been a heart attack. In the 1940s, the usual treatment was essentially to do nothing apart from keeping the patient about a month in the hospital and then prescribing rest for two weeks. But there are countless possibilities: surgery, pneumonia, or some other condition. My own suspicion is that he had his first heart attack.

Oskar's correspondence was slowing down. In March, Finley expressed sympathy about Oskar's having "been ill." Four months later, Oskar asked to see Finley and offered to bring him the copperplate of his etching, together with additional prints. "I should also," wrote Oskar in one more plea for employment, "be very glad to learn if you have also interest for the making of other important personalities in Washington, D.C."[14]

Finley confirmed an appointment on July 17, saying he would be delighted to see Oskar.[15] The two men must have met on that date, and the gift of the copperplate doubtless occurred then. No further letters are known to have been exchanged between the men.

And no job prospects were forthcoming. In fact, Oskar seems never to have found the kind of full-time employment he so earnestly sought. As his hopes waned, his artwork slowed. At some point he made an etching of the view from the window of his studio at Carnegie Hall. It has been recorded as having been sold at auction, but no version of it has been located. Somehow the image brought forth in the mind is sobering: the lonely artist looking out his window at the bustling world of New York City.

---

11.   Stoessel to Finley, handwritten letter, Feb. 14, 1947, Finley Papers, National Gallery of Art.
12.   Stoessel to Finley, Feb. 14, 1947.
13.   Stoessel to Finley, Feb. 14, 1947.
14.   Stoessel to Finley, handwritten letter, July 10, 1947, Finley Papers, National Gallery of Art.
15.   Finley to Stoessel, typed letter, July 11, 1947, Finley Papers, National Gallery of Art.

CHAPTER 36

New Chief Justice

IN the late 1940s, Oskar resumed his activities at the Supreme Court by arranging to make a portrait for the new chief justice, Fred M. Vinson. Because of his health problems, Oskar had slowed down radically. Vinson sat for him on May 20, 1949, for 30 minutes and then again for nearly an hour two months later. But nothing materialized for another two years.

In March 1951, from the Hotel Statler in D.C., Oskar wrote to Chief Justice Vinson, saying that he had finally made a trial proof of his etching. He had been in Europe for a few months, and he had been ill for quite some time.[1] Oskar probably met with the chief justice during that D.C. visit, since a postscript to the letter noted that he would be reachable at the Hotel Statler for "the next few days."[2] Perhaps, following his normal practice, Oskar adjusted the portrait to make it more acceptable to the subject.

Nine weeks later, Oskar penned a solicitous letter to the chief justice:

May 22nd 1951.

The Honorable Chief Justice
Fred Vinson

Sir!

I have now finished the etching of you, and I hope you will like it, and should like to give you two of the first prints I have made, and to ask you to sign me a few proofs. I have made an etching for the Kress-Foundation, and Mr. Kress would be very gratefull [sic] to have a print signed by Your Honor. May I ask for

1. Oskar Stoessel to Chief Justice Fred Vinson, handwritten letter, Mar. 15, 1951, Vinson Papers, University of Kentucky.
2. Stoessel to Vinson, Mar. 15, 1951.

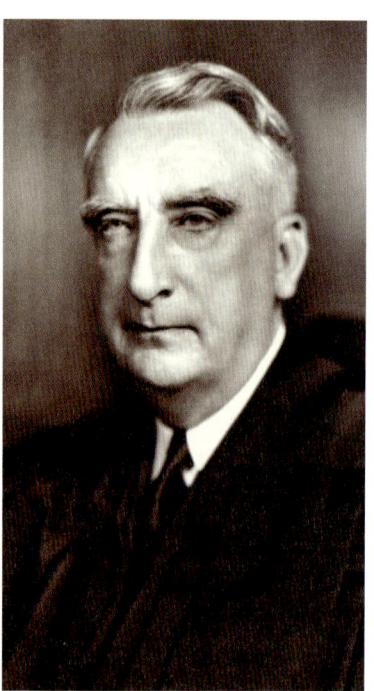

*Chief Justice
Fred M. Vinson
(in office 1946—1953)*

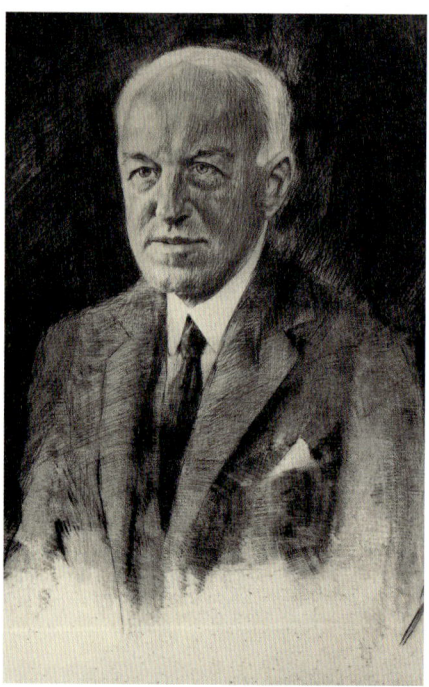

*Oskar's portrait
of Samuel Henry
Kress (ca. 1951).
A businessman
and philanthro-
pist, Kress made
his fortune from
S.H. Kress & Co.,
a national chain
of five-and-dime
stores. He was an
important collector
of European art,
particularly from
the Italian Renais-
sance. In 1941, he
joined Paul Mellon
to make a large gift
that established the
National Gallery of
Art in Washington,
D.C.*

the honor to come in your office to see you just for a few minutes, then I would
come for a day to Washington D.C.

My health is not so good and I should like to go for a short time for a recovery to Europe. Then I hope to come back to New-York in fall. I should be very
grateful to know a few days (2 or 3) in advance when I can come to Washington
D.C. Thanking you very much.

Respectfully Yours
Oskar Stoessel.[3]

If Chief Justice Stone had been formal in his correspondence with Oskar, his
successor was far more so. Even though his appointments calendar notes that
Oskar is an artist "and friend,"[4] the tone in reply was stiff—perhaps because it
was ghostwritten by a secretary:

---

3. Stoessel to Vinson, handwritten letter, May 22, 1951, Vinson Papers, University of Kentucky.
4. Chief Justice Vinson's appointments calendar for June 12, 1951, Vinson Papers, University of
    Kentucky.

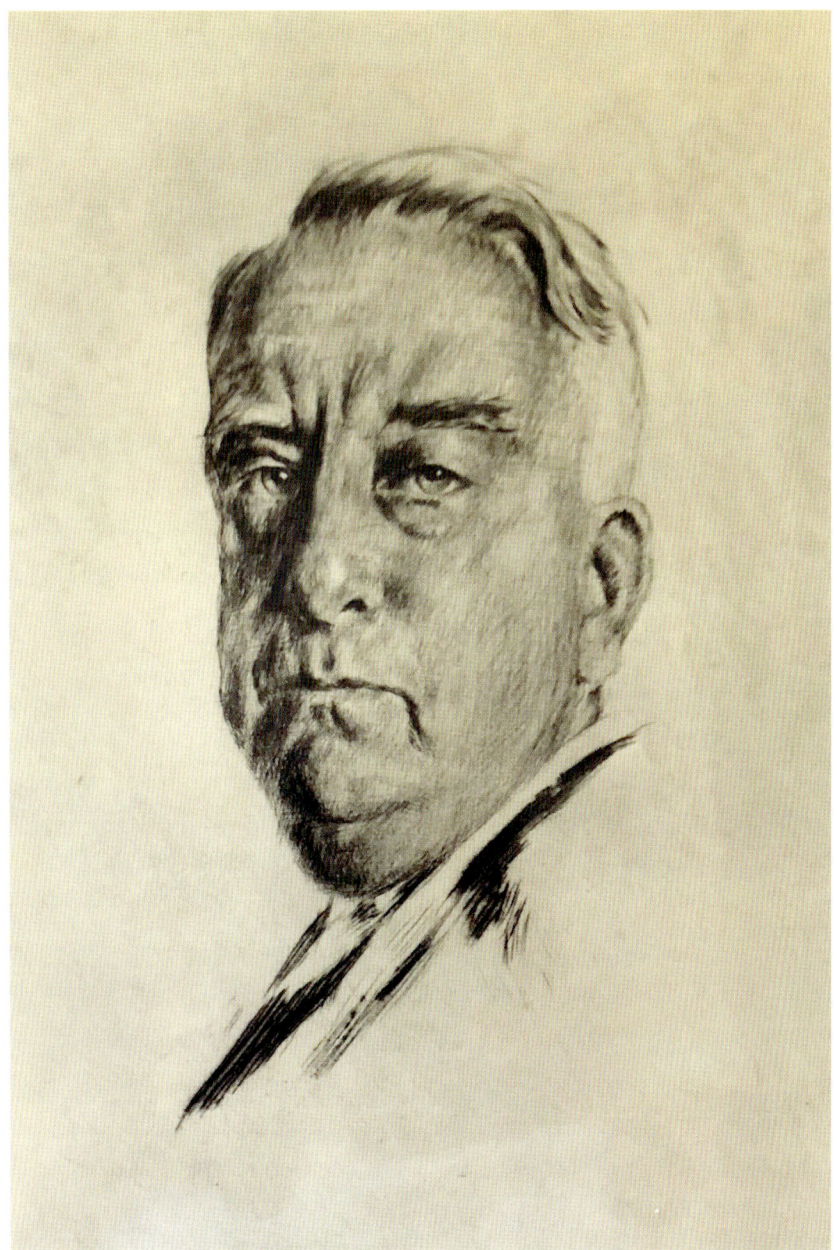

Oskar's etching of Chief Justice Fred Vinson (1951). Vinson held several key government positions before President Truman appointed him to the Supreme Court in 1946; he died unexpectedly of a heart attack in 1953.

8 June 1951

Dear Mr. Stoessel:

Thank you for your kind letter of May 22nd.

If you care to make a trip to Washington, I will be glad to see you on Tuesday, June 12th, at 3:00 p.m.

Would you please let me know whether or not this appointment is convenient for you.

With kind regards.

Sincerely,
Fred M. Vinson[5]

The chief justice's calendar shows that he reserved 15 minutes for Oskar, from 3:10 to 3:25 p.m.—with another appointment immediately following for a 26-year-old law student named E. Barrett Prettyman Jr. (after whose father the federal appellate courthouse in Washington, D.C., is named). It was a busy afternoon for the Chief, who was in the office from 11:15 to 5:35 and had six meetings during that time.

Not long after returning to New York, Oskar thanked Chief Justice Vinson for the opportunity to see him.[6] Apparently Vinson had signed two of the etchings, and Oskar gave one of those to Samuel Henry Kress, the arts benefactor whose portrait Oskar was doing at about the same time.[7] Oskar said he'd be sailing the next day (July 3, 1951) for Europe with the intention of spending some time in Bad Gastein, a health-resort town outside Salzburg.[8] "If you want to have some more prints," the etcher wrote, "please let me know it. Your kind words have encouraged me for future working. Thanks."[9]

---

5.   Vinson to Stoessel, typed letter, June 8, 1951, Vinson Papers, University of Kentucky.
6.   Stoessel to Vinson, handwritten letter, July 2, 1951, Vinson Papers, University of Kentucky.
7.   Stoessel to Vinson, July 2, 1951.
8.   Stoessel to Vinson, July 2, 1951.
9.   Stoessel to Vinson, July 2, 1951.

CHAPTER 37

Reuniting with Hilde

I N 1950, Hildegarde Hofmann, or "Hilde" as she was familiarly known, sailed to New York aboard the S.S. *America*, listing Oskar's apartment as her destination. By July 1951, Oskar and Hilde were considering marriage.

Just who was she? Was she the former student whose portrait Oskar had painted before he fled Austria? The brave woman who had protected Oskar's copperplates in Vienna and to whom he sent food packages after the war? The evidence strongly suggests so.

We know that in 1945, she was still in Vienna, now occupied by Soviet soldiers and soon to be partitioned by the Allies, and she had written to Oskar asking for help. During the war, Vienna had endured more than 50 Allied bombing raids, which destroyed 20% of the city's housing—about 37,000 houses and 80,000 apartments. Food was always scarce. Many people, Hilde included, had to work jobs to support the Nazi war efforts. The last days of the war saw street-to-street combat as the Soviets invaded. When the German troops abandoned Vienna, Soviet soldiers brutalized the civilians and looted the city. Lawlessness prevailed until other Allied troops arrived and began to impose order. We can only imagine Hilde's suffering during these years.

The Allies divided Vienna into six separate occupied zones, each with its own entry and exit points. The Soviets held the largest single zone and a second smaller zone. They also controlled the territory around Vienna, stretching all the way to Styria. Leaving Vienna required a special visa from the Soviets and much patience in waiting and hoping that it would issue.

Yet it's uncertain whether Hilde remained in Vienna. Some evidence indicates that she didn't. In 1947, she wrote to the Academy of Fine Arts to request a copy of her transcript. Maybe she was employed during the hours that the school's records office was open and unable to request her transcript in person. Or it might have been too difficult to reach the school because she'd have to travel through several occupied zones. She signed the request for her transcript "Hildegarde Winnar," a relatively uncommon surname.

The Graz directory for 1949 shows that a professional painter named Hildegarde Winnar resided there as an independent woman. If Hilde did indeed manage to leave Vienna, she was evidently widowed or divorced. In Graz, she could study art and be closer to her family in Tamsweg. And she might have had some support from her husband's family.

Hilde was probably widowed and continued using her married name in respectable widowhood. Many Austrian men of all ages were drafted into the German Army, so it's probable that Hilde's husband became a soldier. He may have been killed in action or died after the war, possibly of war-related injuries. The residential directory for Graz in 1949 includes several people named Winnar besides Hilde. They may have been related to her late husband. If she was a widow, the family might have provided her with emotional and practical support. They may also have disapproved of her growing relationship with a Jewish émigré. Such disapproval could motivate a woman to reclaim her maiden name and start her life over. Hilde's life decisions at this point cannot have been easy.

Oskar's behavior also suggests that it was his former student who would become his wife. Although Oskar had written to Chief Justice Stone that he wished to forget Austria, ships' passenger lists show that he sailed to Europe every year from 1948 to 1950. His family was gone, and he'd lost touch with everyone else during the war. As far as we know, only his former student contacted him after the war ended, and

FAMILY NAME—GIVEN NAME DESTINATION IN UNITED STATES	AGE (Years)	SEX (F–M)	MAR-RIED OR SINGLE	TRAVEL DOC. NO. NATIONALITY	NUMBER AND DESCRIPTION OF PIECES OF BAGGAGE	HEAD TAX COL-LECTED	THIS COLUMN FOR USE OF MASTER, SURGEON, AND U. S. OFFICERS
STOESSEL, Hildegarde Carnegie-Hall Studio 1111, New York City	56	F	M	I-1370991 AUSTRIA	3	Yes	
STOESSEL, Oskar, Prof. –do–	73 (USC)	M	M	USPP 630161 AUSTRIA	4	USC No	U. S. CIT.

The manifest for the S.S. United States, *which sailed to Le Havre just after Oskar and Hilde's 1952 marriage in New York City. They would return to New York in 1953 after a few months in Europe.*

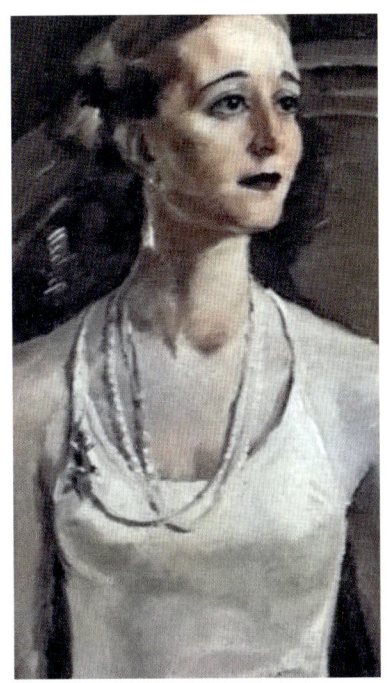

Hilde's portrait (cropped and colorized). For the full portrait, see page 84.

we know he cared about her. He stayed for months each time he visited. No records show where he went or what his purpose was, but seemingly having had a heart attack in 1947 and suffering a decline in his health, he made a visit to Bad Gastein the following year. Trains ran between there and Vienna (and Graz), so it would have been easy for him to visit Hilde and see how she was faring. In late 1950, Hildegarde Hofmann returned to the United States with him. They sailed to and from Europe again in 1951 to visit Bad Gastein once more. The next year, they married in New York.

The timeline for Hilde's journey to America fits with her beginning an application in 1947 or 1948 and finally being able to leave in 1950. Postwar life in Austria was hard. Food shortages were worsened by crop failures. The Soviet Union had won control of the newly created East Germany, including the divided city of Berlin. Fearful of Soviet annexation, a substantial percentage of Austria's population sought to leave the country. To prevent mass flight, the Soviets made sure that applications were expensive and slowly processed; any complaint would cause an application to be moved to the bottom of the pile. With expedited processing, it would take three years to obtain approval for an application for a passport and visa to leave Austria. The United States wasn't helpful; it was similarly slow to grant visas to Austrians seeking to immigrate.

Although we can imagine what Hilde's general experiences were like, not much is actually known about her except that she was much younger—less than half Oskar's age (36 to his 73). The alert reader will have noticed something curious about her. On page 85, she is said to have been born in 1915. College records show that she entered the Academy of Fine Arts in Vienna in 1937. In the caption accompanying her portrait on page 84, she is said to have been about 23, and the etching is said to be circa 1938. But as shown here, the ship's manifest from 1952 records her age as 56, meaning that she would have been born in 1895 or 1896.

Why the discrepancy in her age? Perhaps she wasn't the Viennese art student who had been born in 1915 in Styria, near Graz. Oskar could have met another Hilde Hofmann in Austria, perhaps in Bad Gastein. Or maybe the presumption that Hilde's portrait was painted in 1938 was wrong. The Peer catalogue raisonné records the painting on page 84 as having been done circa 1930. The future art student would have been a mere 15 years old then—and the portrait is certainly not of an adolescent. Could it be a 34-year-old woman? Perhaps, but most observers estimate the woman to be between 20 and 25. It's also possible that Oskar painted one Hilde Hofmann in the 1930s and married another one in the 1950s—one who had never been an art student but who also hailed from Vienna. Possible but highly implausible. Hilde Hofmann Winnar was Oskar's only real connection to Austria and the only person who could give him reason to return.

Might Hilde have lied about her age and added 20 years when obtaining a visa and passport to travel to America? Why would she do that? Women (and men) of a certain age don't normally pretend to be significantly older than they actually are. But perhaps it's explainable.

Prewar and postwar photographs of many Europeans show drastic changes in their visages. They were constantly in fear of bombings, under stress from chronic food and housing shortages, forced to toil for the Nazi machine or else unemployed, and in fear of neighbors who might report transgressions, real or imagined, to the Nazi authorities. It's conceivable that a young, beautiful woman like Hilde could have looked 10 or even 20 years older than she really was by 1950. It would have been painful for her to admit that she was only in her 30s when she looked more like a grandmother. It may not have been difficult to add years to her age after the war, given her aged appearance—and perhaps to subtly alter a handwritten "1915" to "1895" on a birth or baptismal certificate.

Hilde might have raised her age for another reason: to avoid scandal. Think of a ship as a microcosm of society at large. She was traveling with her 73-year-old fiancé, who was in poor health. He'd had a heart attack five years before. She was less than half his age: she was still 36 when they sailed in 1952. There would be talk. At the time, a strong social stigma attached to such an age difference between spouses. The ship's crew would come to know of the 36-year-old bride with her elderly husband, and so would other passengers. She might have claimed to be older to forestall gossip. Perhaps she even acted the part of a woman more advanced in years. And perhaps it didn't take so much acting for someone who had suffered the privations of war-torn Austria in the 1940s.

Finally, Oskar had a paternal instinct toward Hilde—understandable, perhaps, given their age difference. In a letter to his niece Elsa, in December 1956, he wrote: "I feel toward my beloved wife as though she were my own child."[1] That statement was in the context of Uncle Oskar's expressing how much pride he knew Elsa must take in her young son David. Oskar being childless, the comparison by simile was surely meant to express empathy.

Certainty in this matter remains elusive. But there's a touch of romance in the version here suggested: Hilde met Oskar when she was 22 and he was 58; the war intervened, and she was forced to become not an artist but a welder. While keeping Oskar's copperplates safe in Nazi-controlled Vienna, she married someone else and was probably widowed. After the war, she wrote to Oskar, who was sorrowing over the fate of his family and wanted to forget everything about his homeland, yet he was worried about his former student and sent her packages of food. He traveled back to Austria and saw her again, and the two fell in love. She reclaimed her maiden name, alienating her late husband's family. In 1950, with Oskar's financial support, the 34-year-old woman traveled to New York, her destination being his studio apartment. With their longtime affection and shared memories, they began a new life together.

Hilde was a loving, supportive wife. Beginning in 1952 she organized most of Oskar's dealings with Hanns and Kate Schaeffer, who were selling on consignment

---

1.   Oskar Stoessel to Elsa Heichler, handwritten letter, Dec. 16, 1956 (courtesy of David and Jill Heichler; on file with the author) ("Ich empfinde meine liebe Frau, Hilde, wie ein eigenes Kind.").

what remained of Oskar's personal collection of prints by Old Masters. In 1960, when Oskar had surely become almost entirely inactive as an etcher, she even helped him negotiate the sale of his etching press.[2] When his hand had become unsteady, she would write out his dictated letters in her own hand for his signature.[3]

Oskar had reached the age of 77 and had slowed significantly. Very little art was created after he was 68—perhaps only the etched portraits of David E. Finley, Samuel H. Kress, Rush H. Kress, and Chief Justice Vinson.

But even his earlier years in America produced nothing like his prodigious output of the prewar years. Of the 400 or so images shown in the Peer cata-

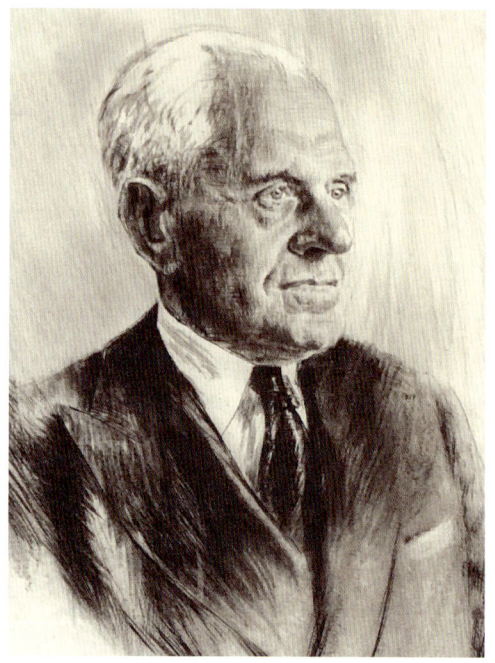

Oskar's portrait of Rush H. Kress (ca. 1951), who headed the Kress Foundation after his brother Samuel suffered an incapacitating stroke in 1945. Under Rush Kress's leadership, the Foundation gave away 31,000 pieces of art to American museums.

logue raisonné, only 20—some 5%—postdate his emigration from Austria in 1939, when he was 60. This text adds some 30 to that number, including the portraits of most of the justices. Hence of the known Stoessel artwork, about 12% was created after 1939. His floruit was 1911 to 1938. Gradually the work of etching, with its attendant handling of heavy copperplates, became unduly arduous for him.

---

2.   Five letters, Lotte Jacobi Papers, University of New Hampshire.
3.   Five letters.

CHAPTER 38

Returning to Austria

I**N 1959, for Oskar's 80th birthday, the Viennese Künstlerhaus, the most prestigious artists' society in Austria, tried to send a congratulatory message to
him in the United States. But he was reported to be living in "absolute pri-
vacy" and couldn't be reached. The next year, in 1960, he and Hilde returned per-
manently to Austria. Four years later, for his 85th birthday, the mayor of Vienna
honored Oskar in some way.[1]

The dysphoria that Oskar must have experienced upon returning to Austria
shouldn't be overlooked. Of the 130,000
Austrian Jews who were exiled (as opposed to killed) during the war, only 4%
to 10% returned afterward.[2] Their own experiences were "notably absent from the
collective memories of the general Austrian population."[3] The Austria to which
they returned was populated by gentiles
who opposed their return and "continued
to misrepresent the past and to deny responsibility for the injustices suffered by

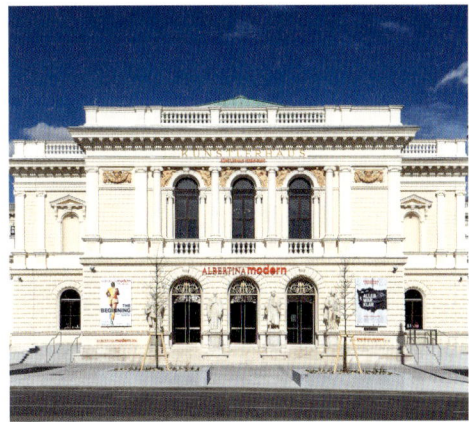

The Künstlerhaus, Vienna

1. Ludwig Stössel to Elsa Heichler, handwritten letter, Feb. 6, 1964 (courtesy of David and Jill
   Heichler; on file with the author ["I forgot to tell you that Oskar celebrated his 85th birthday
   on January 10th. He was very honored by the mayor of Vienna."]). Ludwig seems to have been
   mistaken about Oskar's birthdate. The official Report of the Death of an American Citizen
   shows January 11. Or perhaps the city's celebration took place the day before his birthday.
2. Jacqueline Vansant, *Reclaiming* Heimat: *Trauma and Mourning in Memoirs by Jewish Austrian
   Reémigrés* (Wayne State Univ. Press, 2001), 13.
3. Vansant, 14.

Jews."[4] Stories of exile were unwelcome because they threatened other Austrians' claims of victimhood. The gentiles who had lived in Austria through the war "assigned themselves the role of victims of Hitler's aggression and Allied bombings."[5]

Meanwhile, within exile communities, there was disagreement about whether a return was morally defensible. Oskar couldn't have escaped discussions about this point after the war. Some living in exile saw a return to the homeland as a moral failing: "How could people return to a country that had thrown them out and murdered their friends and relatives?"[6] Many exiled expatriates thought that the Austrian people themselves had shown complicity in failing to rise up against Hitler.

Seemingly like Oskar, most exiled Jews who returned to Austria were married to gentiles.[7] (We can deduce that Hilde was almost certainly not Jewish, given that she continued to live in Austria and worked during the war.) So the sense of alienation was very much individual, not communal. Oskar was returning to a place that had once been his home but had become a deathtrap for his family.

But Oskar's position was even more fraught with personal and emotional difficulties. He was an American—and he had famously done a portrait of Herr Rosenfeld, as Franklin Roosevelt was known in Austria.[8] In the average Austrian's view, Herr Rosenfeld had "caused the poverty and bombed-out cities."[9] That history is wildly inaccurate, of course, and the chronology reversed. But a reémigré in Oskar's position was viewed as "the cause of Austrian misery."[10] To the extent that Oskar's personal history with Roosevelt and other U.S. government officials became known to his acquaintances in Austria, he would have been considered socially unacceptable.

---

4.   Vansant, 29.
5.   Vansant, 29.
6.   Vansant, 41.
7.   Bruce F. Pauley, "Austria," in *The World Reacts to the Holocaust*, ed. David S. Wyman (Johns Hopkins Univ. Press, 1996), 493.
8.   Vansant, *Reclaiming* Heimat, 47.
9.   Vansant, 48.
10.   Vansant, 48.

It's understandable that reémigrés typically experienced not a recovery of their home-land, but a second loss of it. Although they "defined themselves as Austrians first and Jews second,"[11] they were "perceived first as Jews and . . . were often absurdly reproached for having left Austria even if staying would have meant certain death."[12] Their return caused them to feel brutally alienated from the homeland they had once loved and from their former selves. One reémigré wrote: "Here, where my roots reach so deep in the earth like no other place, I am a total stranger, so removed in time and space, like a ghostly revenant."[13]

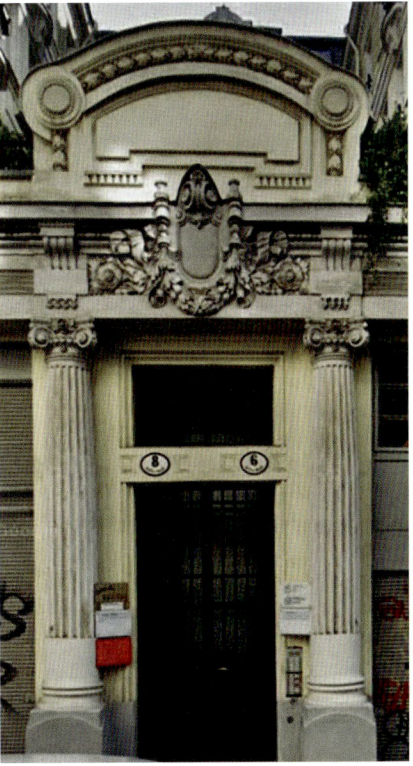

The facade of Oskar's last residence: Koestler-gasse 8, Vienna. It's a ten-minute walk from the Academy, where in 1908 Oskar began his studies with Ferdinand Schmutzer.

By the time Oskar and Hilde returned to Austria, he had already turned 81. She was in her mid-40s. They had lived as husband and wife in New York City for eight years, and undoubtedly they discussed her future, whether she could continue living in Carne-gie Hall, and whether she would be comfortable continuing to live in New York City without him. Together, they decided to return to Vienna. Oskar wanted a good future for his still-young wife, for whom he had a paternal instinct. He surely knew that after his death, she would thrive best in her native Austria.

Four years after his return to Vienna, Oskar Stoessel died of coronary sclero-sis.[14] The day was July 17, 1964. He was 85. Almost nothing is known about the last

---

11. Vansant, 153.
12. Vansant, 49.
13. Hilde Spiel, *Rückkehr nach Wien* (Nymphenburger Verlagshandlung, 1968), 54–55 (as trans-lated in Vansant, *Reclaiming* Heimat, 50).
14. Form FS-192 for Oskar Stoessel, "Report of the Death of an American Citizen," Office of

few years of his life. One imagines that Oskar, a man who seemed predisposed to gregarious cheer, had sadly fallen into the final category mentioned by the scholar who writes: "While a considerable number of Austrian emigrants quickly or not so quickly adapted to the new life in America, not even wanting to go back, others never found a firm footing in American society longing for their—real or imagined—Austrian homeland, and again others were either living in both worlds or unable to put down roots in either America or Austria."[15]

A letter that Oskar sent to New York less than a month before his death: "The etching of Pres. Roosevelt will be sent today, but it probably won't be delivered for about 14 days. I would be happy to hear from you again, and also whether the etching arrived without a problem."

Special Consular Services, dated Aug. 3, 1964, signed by Vice Consul Richard T. Conroy. According to the report, a death certificate (no. 859/64) was issued ten days after the death by the Standesamt Innere Stadt-Mariahilf in Vienna. He died at Koestlergasse 8/I. He was interred at Vienna Central Cemetery, group 5a, row 23, grave 13. His personal effects were declared to be "in custody of widow, Mrs. Hildegarde Stoessel." His social-security number was 088-20-3109. Copies of the report were sent to Hildegarde Stoessel in Vienna and to Ludwig Stössel in Los Angeles.

A week after the death, a Freemasons lodge to which Stoessel belonged in Manhattan ran a death notice in the *New York Times*: "STOESSEL, Oskar. Humanitas Lodge No. 1123, F. and A.M., mourns the loss of its esteemed member, age 85. Death and burial in Vienna, Austria." Otherwise, the death seems to have received little notice in the United States (but see page 255).

15. Volker Depkat, "The Challenges of Biography and Migration History," in *Quiet Invaders Revisited: Biographies of Twentieth Century Immigrants to the United States*, ed. Günter Bischof (StudienVerlag, 2017), 308.

CHAPTER 39

Two Brothers' Legacies

I
N 1962, two years after Oskar returned to Austria—the country he had unsuccessfully tried to obliterate from his mind—President John F. Kennedy signed
legislation creating a National Portrait Gallery as a bureau of the Smithsonian
Institution. David E. Finley, then retired as director of the National Gallery of Art,
contributed four portraits that constituted the first official accessions of the newly
created museum: "he donated a group of portrait etchings by Oskar Stoessel of
Franklin D. Roosevelt, Harlan F. Stone, James F. Byrnes, and William O. Douglas."[1] Whether Oskar ever knew about this great honor is unknown.

After Finley died in 1977, the National Portrait Gallery Commission adopted
a resolution in his memory "because it was recognized by everyone around the
table that without David Finley the National Portrait Gallery would simply not
exist."[2] Included in its holdings today is the etching of Finley done by Oskar
Stoessel, along with the copperplate (see pages 3 and 234).

There is also an etching in the Smithsonian's collection of Oskar's mother (see
page 232), one of the artist's favorite and most recurrent subjects. When her two
sons left her with friends in Switzerland, she must have been exceedingly worried
about them and their future. Both sons would make their mark in America.

* * *

AMONG Oskar's and Ludwig's nieces and nephews, Ludwig was known as the
famous one in the family. Although he was a prolific Hollywood character actor,
his most famous role turned out to be in television commercials—as the "Little

---

1. David A. Doheny, *David Finley: Quiet Force for America's Arts* (National Trust for Historic
Preservation, 2006), 331. Finley later gave a Stoessel portrait etching of himself to the National Portrait Gallery (Smithsonian object no. NPG.65.2).

2. Doheny, 336.

253

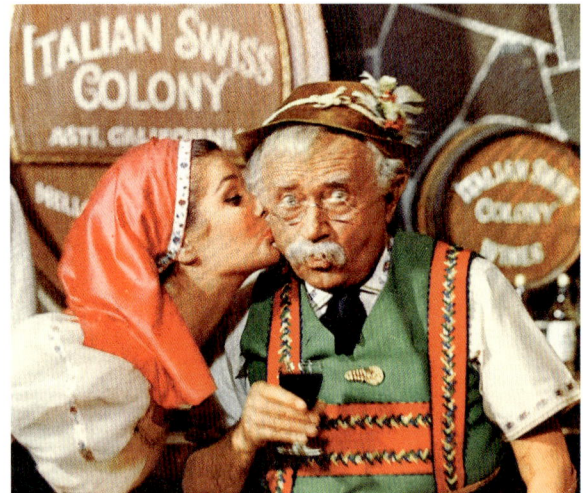

Ludwig Stössel as "That Little Old Winemaker, Me" in TV ads for Italian Swiss Colony wines

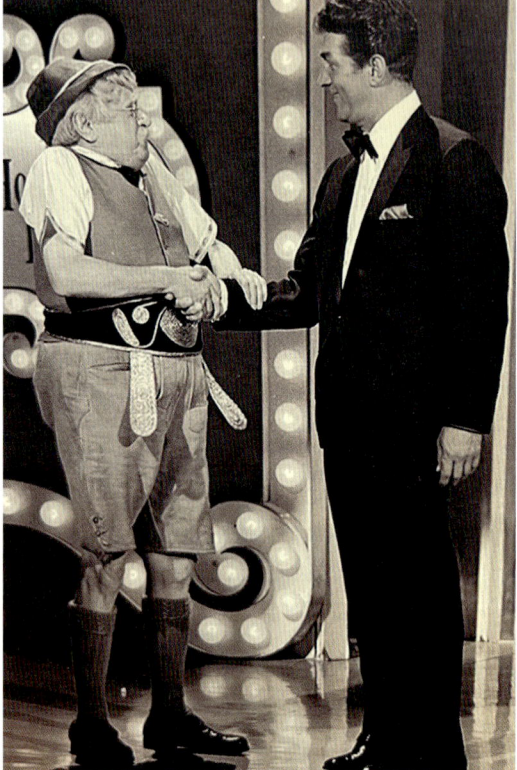

Old Winemaker" in Italian Swiss Colony wine commercials. David Heichler, niece Elsa's son, remembers much family talk about the renowned Ludwig, but little about Oskar.

Ludwig as "Little Old Winemaker" on Hollywood Palace, *with Dean Martin, March 7, 1964*

Born in 1883, Ludwig died in Hollywood in 1973—just short of his 90th birthday. He had been called "the dean of character actors in Hollywood, being the oldest working actor listed in the Academy Players Directory."[3] His obituary credited him with appearances in more than 200 European and American films.[4] He also made frequent appearances on television shows, such as *Perry Mason*, *Father Knows Best*, *The Phil Silvers Show*, *Man with a Camera*, *My Three Sons*, *Crusader*, and *Science Fiction*. His wife of 53 years, Eleonore Birn Stössel, survived him. They had met in 1920 in the Viennese theater, where Eleonore was an operetta star. They had no children but two nieces.[5]

3.   Don MacLean, "Meet Ludwig Stossel," *Fitchburg Sentinel* (Mass.), Sept. 27, 1971, 4.

4.   "Ludwig Stossel, 89, TV's 'Little Old Winemaker,' Dies," *L.A. Times*, Jan. 30, 1973, 3.

5.   "Ludwig Stossel, 89," 3. Presumably, these were Elsa and Grete (Margarethe), Isabella's two daughters, who emigrated before the Anschluss. Both married, Elsa Heichler immigrated to

Oskar Stoessel gestorben

In diesen Tagen ist der Maler und Radierer Professor Oskar Stoessel im 86. Lebensjahre in Wien gestorben. Der "Aufbau" hat anlässlich des 85. Geburtstages Stoessels am 10. April eine ausführliche Würdigung der lange Reihe von Kunstwerken gebracht, die Stoessel geschaffen hat. Sein berühmtestes Portrait, das er in der USA gemalt hatte, war das des Präsidenten Roosevelt, das Frau Eleanor Roosevelt als das beste Bild ihres Mannes bezeichnet und in ihrem letzten Willen ihrem Arzt, Dr. Gurevitsch, vermacht hat. Stoessel ist auch der erste und einzige gewesen, der Radierungen des gesamten Supreme Court unter seinen Werken buchen kann. Von seinen Arbeiten sind u.a. die Portraits des ehemaligen US-Secretary of State, Cordell Hull, des Chirurgen Dr. Davidoff, des Gründers der Kress-Foundation, Mr. Kress, besonders bekannt geworden.

Stoessel, der nach 20jährigem Schaffen in den USA vor 5 Jahren nach Wien zurückgekehrt war, hatte die Freude, viele seiner Bilder von berühmten Museen der Welt (u.a. vom Metropolitan Museum und British Museum) angekauft zu sehen.

Oskar Stoessel hinterlässt seine Gattin Hildegarde und seinen Bruder, den bekannten Schauspieler Ludwig Stoessel, der im Februar v. J. 80 Jahre alt wurde.

Obituary in Aufbau, *a New York City newspaper founded in 1934 for German-speaking Jews (July 31, 1964). The first paragraph, after announcing Oskar's death, reminds readers that* Aufbau *had marked Oskar's 85th birthday with a tribute to his longtime output. It goes on to describe his most famous American work, FDR's portrait, and his other etchings of famous or notable Americans. The second paragraph notes that Oskar had returned to Vienna 5 years earlier, after a 20-year stay in America. It states that Oskar had the pleasure of seeing his works purchased by famous museums such as New York's Metropolitan Museum and the British Museum. It ends by recognizing Hilde and Ludwig as his surviving family.*

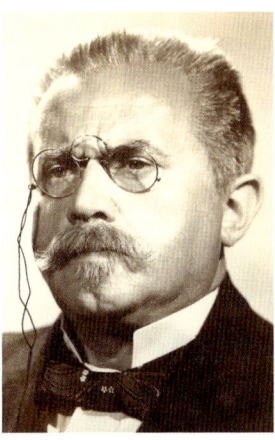

Ludwig in the 1940 film Jennie, *directed by David Burton. His character, Fritz Schermer, is the patriarch of a German American family in Ohio.*

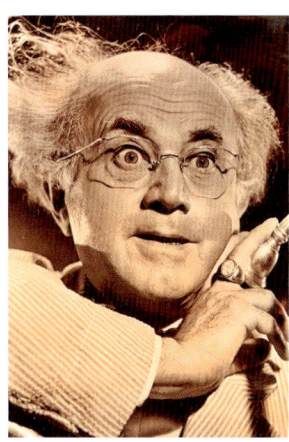

Ludwig in the 1948 American film A Song Is Born, *directed by Howard Hawks*

Interestingly, Ludwig's hobby was collecting rare prints.[6] We might deduce that there was a practical reason for print-collecting: Oskar and Ludwig may have known that acquiring rare prints in prewar Europe was the most feasible

---

the United States, and Grete Berger to Palestine.

6.   "Veteran Actor Plays Role of Anton Kovac," *Honolulu Star-Bulletin*, Feb. 28, 1959, 15.

way for Jewish refugees like them to leave Austria with valuable property. Oskar doubtless guided Ludwig in his early collecting.

Imbued with different talents in the fine arts, both Oskar Stoessel and Ludwig Stössel made their mark. It was Oskar, the elder son, who in 1939 first sailed to the United States—under conditions of fear and duress. Through his creative genius, he became a significant preserver of his new country's heritage.

CHAPTER 40

An Unsolved Mystery

T HERE remains another mystery in this story. The known Stoessel works include two enigmatic pencil drawings of women dating from the mid-1940s. These both derive from the same Vienna archive that contained the pencil drawings of Chief Justice Harlan Fiske Stone (1940) and David Finley (1946)—the only source I've found for Oskar's pencil drawings. We know that Oskar would make pencil sketches and then, from those, would create his copperplates for printing the etchings.

The pencils that Oskar used in the United States differed from those he'd used earlier in Europe: they were finer-tipped, almost like sharp no. 2 pencils. The ones he used in the earlier period were more like charcoal pencils, sometimes colored ones.

Only six of the American-style pencil drawings are known to exist: Stone, Finley, Chief Justice Charles Evans Hughes, Justice Stanley Reed, and the two mystery women. The Hughes and Reed drawings are now in the collection of the U.S. Supreme Court (see insets on pages 142 & 171); the other four are part of my own collection.

The mystery women may be identifiable. One appears to be a very preliminary idealization of Eleanor Roosevelt, for which Oskar might have used the First Lady's somewhat earlier hairstyle with a flatteringly younger face (see page 258). The other appears to be Lucy Mercer Rutherford (1891–1948), Eleanor's social secretary from 1914 to 1917—a woman with whom Roosevelt had two affairs (one from 1916 to 1917, and the other from 1941 to 1945, after she married Winthrop Rutherford).

In the drawing of Eleanor, she wears her hair as she often had for many years before—swept up. She had a characteristic turn of the head. The widow's peak is

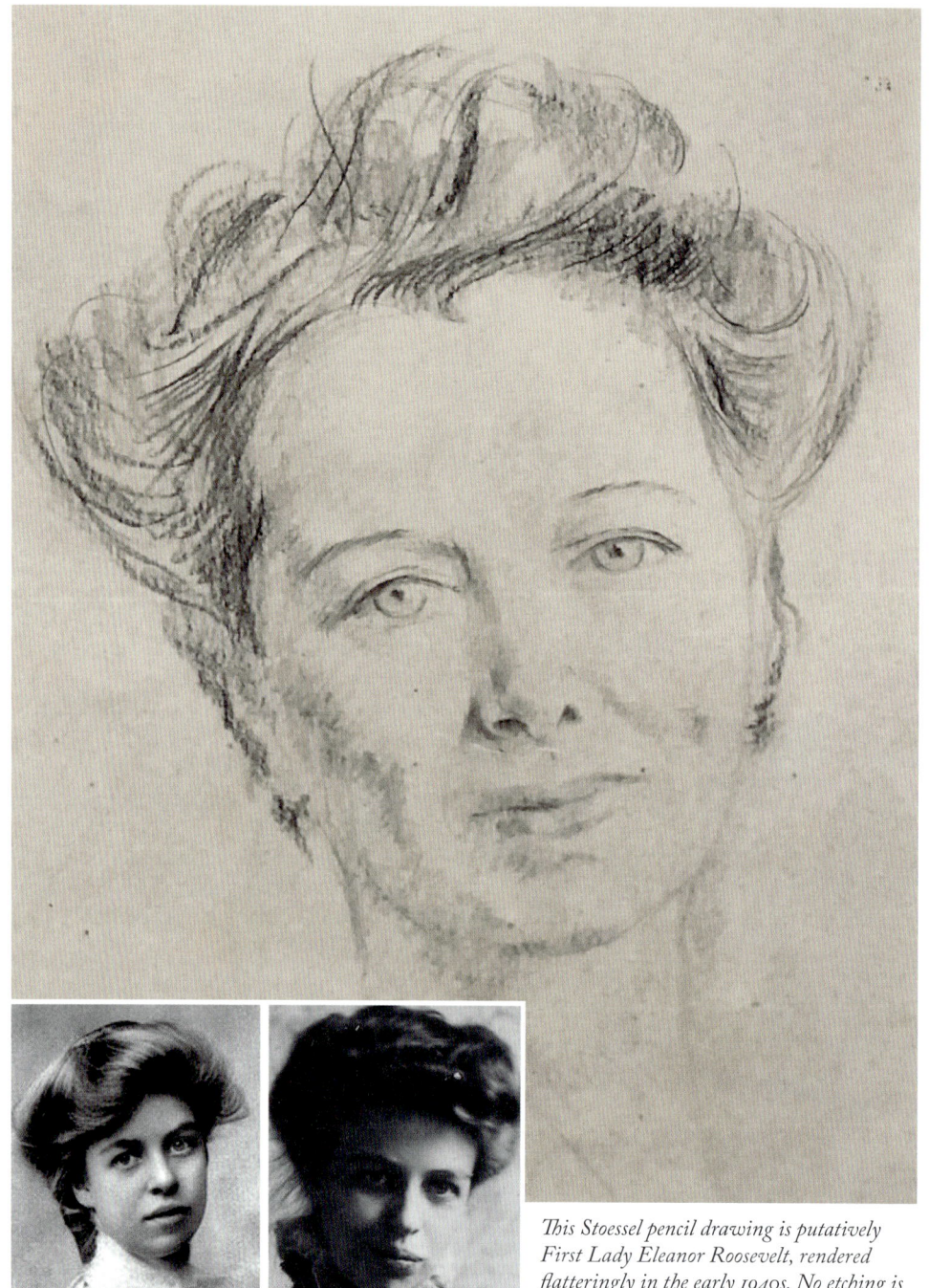

This Stoessel pencil drawing is putatively First Lady Eleanor Roosevelt, rendered flatteringly in the early 1940s. No etching is known to have resulted from this drawing.

just right (as confirmed by a comparison with other photos). The pursed lips seem to hide her orthodontic issues. A side-by-side comparison shows the similarity. But it must be emphasized that Oskar's pencil drawing appears to be idealized or even romanticized.

As for the putative Mercer drawing (see page 260), the likeness seems every bit as compelling. The part in her hair seems to be opposite to the part in the photo, but much else about the hairline looks similar. The nose seems the same, though the angle is different, and the discontinuity in the right eyebrow appears in both the photo and the drawing. We also know that Mercer had an interest in portraiture: on the day of Roosevelt's death, she and her friend Elizabeth Shoumatoff (1888–1980), the well-known artist, were visiting the president for the purpose of making his portrait. When Eleanor discovered Shoumatoff's unfinished watercolor portrait among Roosevelt's effects after his death, she mailed it to Lucy, who responded cordially with condolences.

It's not known whether etchings ever resulted from these drawings. None seems to have materialized. The reason is an interesting source of speculation. Did Roosevelt ask for them but then die before they could be completed? Roosevelt would have known how much Eleanor admired Oskar's portrait of him. He might well have wanted an etched portrait of Eleanor. We also know that during the last year of his life, Lucy met with Roosevelt many times at private dinners on the second floor of the White House—all without Eleanor's knowledge. If Oskar made the drawings during that year, perhaps Roosevelt's death intervened and caused Oskar to discontinue the project. That possibility seems plausible.

Yet the Roosevelt papers contain no evidence that Oskar visited the White House after 1940.

We know that Oskar's portraits were almost exclusively of notable people, so it seems hard to believe that Oskar made drawings of two women who were not prominent. Because of where they were found, it's reasonable to believe that the drawings are related to Oskar's visits to Washington, D.C. If they are preliminary portraits of the two women most important to Roosevelt, as they appear to be, the president might have asked for etchings and then died before they could be completed. It's also possible that Oskar undertook the portraits on his own. Either way, he almost certainly would have used photographs rather than having the subjects sit for him. Nothing indicates that Eleanor or Lucy ever knew about the sketches. The truth in this matter may well be irrecoverable.

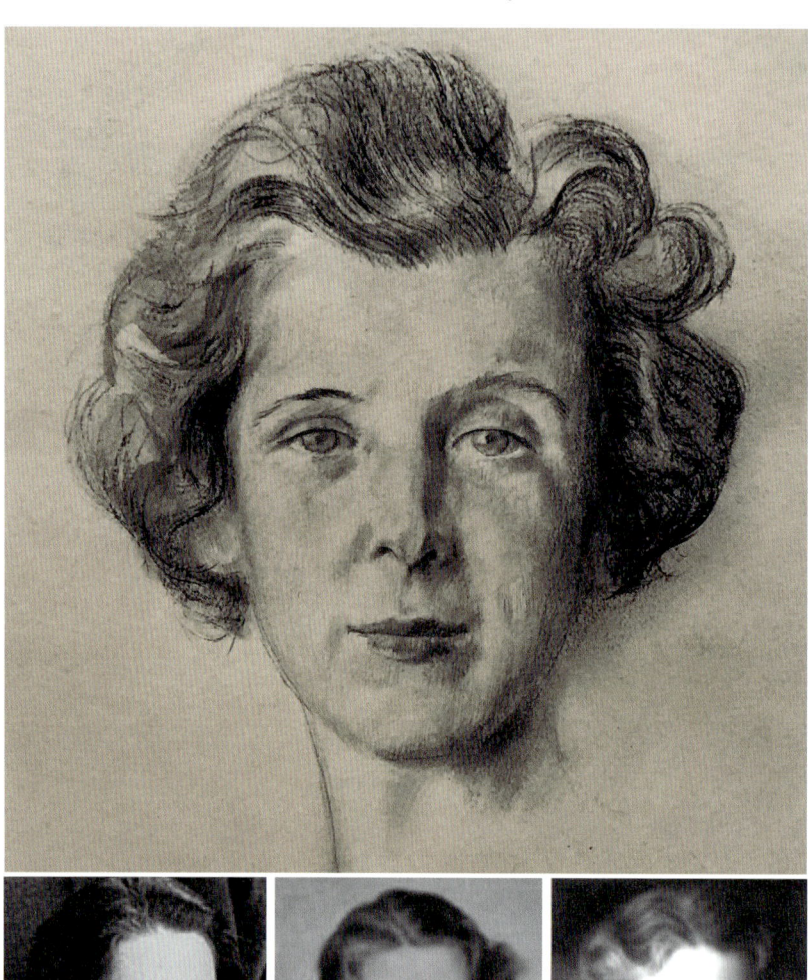

This Stoessel pencil drawing is putatively of Lucy Mercer Rutherford (1891—1948), with whom FDR had two affairs.

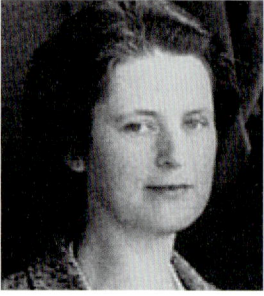
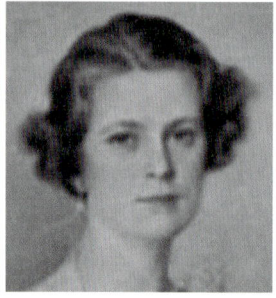
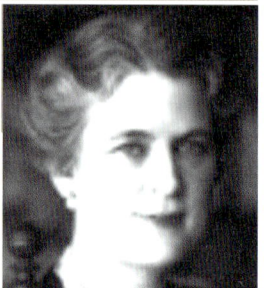

EPILOGUE

As with so many other things in life, the antecedents to this book were serendipitous matters of chance.

It all started in August 2014 with a visit to Meyer Boswell Books in San Francisco. The owner, Joe Luttrell, sold me two etched portraits that were inscribed by their subjects: Justice William O. Douglas and Justice Robert H. Jackson. The portraits had come from the estate of Judge Thomas F. McAllister of Grand Rapids, Michigan—a judge who sat on the Michigan Supreme Court (1938–1941) and was then appointed by President Franklin D. Roosevelt to the U.S. Court of Appeals for the Sixth Circuit (1941–1963).

I knew a bit about McAllister: on a memorable day in Lansing more than a decade before, an antiquarian bookseller had sold me 15 or so books that had come from McAllister's personal library. The most noteworthy of these was a five-volume set of Roscoe Pound's monumental work *Jurisprudence*, with McAllister's name embossed on the covers and Pound's shaky signature inside (see page 268). Given this jewel in my collection of autographed books, I was predisposed to like all things associated with McAllister.

Once Luttrell's shipment of the portraits arrived in Dallas, I had them professionally reframed with acid-free materials, carefully preserving the inscriptions. Soon they were hanging in my library, where I could admire them daily.

One day in November 2014, as Justice Antonin Scalia and I worked together in my library on one of our joint books, he caught sight of the Jackson portrait. When he asked who the artist was, I couldn't say offhand. We peered together at the lower right-hand corner to see whether we could make out the signature. It was plainly "Oskar Stoessel"—in tiny handwriting (uncharacteristically small for Oskar). "Who was Oskar Stoessel?" he asked. I had no idea.

After Justice Scalia returned to Washington, D.C., I searched the internet to find out more about Stoessel, including the remarkable fact that in the 1940s he had etched portraits for the entire U.S. Supreme Court. More searching revealed some of his works for sale online from a Viennese dealer, including an original pencil drawing of an "American gentleman" I recognized as Chief Justice Harlan Fiske Stone. I bought it at once, together with another pencil drawing of another "American gentleman," who turned out to be David E. Finley, the first director of the National Gallery of Art. I learned Finley's identity by crowdsourcing on Twitter: a definitive answer came quickly, together with an image of the final etching, which is held by the National Gallery of Art in Washington, D.C.

By mid-2015, I was hooked on Stoessel. I went back to the online art dealer in Vienna and learned that the 20 or so items he possessed had been part of Oskar's personal archive. Because Oskar died childless—or perhaps because his widow did—his archive was given to an artists' collective. After the collective became insolvent, its holdings were acquired by another Viennese art dealer. Toward the end of that dealer's life in the 1990s, he sold his holdings to my source. From him I bought the entire remaining archive in one fell swoop, increasing my Stoessel collection to 24 pieces.

Over the next couple of years, I acquired a few more Stoessels here and there. By June 2018, my collection had grown to 30 pieces. That month, I found 18 more post-1939 pieces in the files of a dealer in New York City, including most of the justices. The count was now 48.

In December 2018, my wife, Karolyne, and I traveled to Austria for three purposes: to meet Dr. Peter Peer, the Neue Galerie Graz/Universalmuseum Joanneum director who had compiled Stoessel's catalogue raisonné; to see the museum's collection of 150 Stoessels; and to acquire more pieces if they could be found. All three missions succeeded, and we found a cache of 16 Stoessels in the personal collection of an Austrian art dealer, who was delighted to see that they'd find a good home with me.

In November 2021, I located yet another archive in New York City, adding another 35 etchings to the assemblage.

Today, my collection stands at 136 Stoessels.

As I was accumulating all this artwork, my fascination grew more intense. Who was this man?

Dr. Peer put me in touch with a prodigious collector, Dr. Roman Carbon of Erlangen, Germany, who kindly helped me identify the subjects of some of the portraits and other Stoessel-related art. And Peer's catalogue raisonné proved extremely valuable. But like me, both Peer and Carbon knew only the bare-bones facts about Stoessel the man. We all wanted to know more.

It occurred to me that the justices must have corresponded with Oskar. So I went to the manuscripts division of the Library of Congress to see what I could find in the justices' archives. The first visit was in May 2018. The Library contains a trove of information: in eight visits over a one-year period, I assembled much of the original research reported here. On each visit, handling original letters to and from Oskar and about him, my enthusiasm for the artist and his work grew keener. I was working with the raw materials of history, and I'd found a story that had never been told.

This account has been gleaned from library archives of the eminent people whose portraits Oskar etched; from contemporaneous newspapers; from museum archives in Europe and America; from small stashes of Oskar's work in European and American art galleries; from official government documents; and from the files of Oskar's only known living relative, David Heichler of Indiana— Oskar's great-nephew.[1] Oskar's story, as it emerges from these disparate sources, is both edifying and enchanting.

*　*　*

IT's not unheard of for a figure such as Oskar Stoessel to fall into near-oblivion. But those who find his story compelling might rescue his reputation from that undeserved fate.

People come and go in this world. Stoessel came and went. Messersmith. FDR. Hull. Stone. Jackson. Finley. Eleanor Roosevelt. They strutted and fretted their hour on the stage, and then were heard no more. Those with a historical bent know the names to one degree or another. They were famous, but fame is fleeting. Oskar Stoessel's plunge into obscurity is particularly fascinating.

---

1.   Mr. Heichler's aunt, Grete Berger (1907–1991), resided in Israel with her three children. Oskar may have lost contact with the family before or during the war.

It may have something to do with his life's having had three discrete phases: European (1879–1938), American (1939–1960), and European again (1960–1964). In none of those phases, it seems, did he develop strong institutional ties: he had personal ties but not institutional ones. And his medium—etching—didn't and still doesn't have the cachet that painting and sculpture do. Also, portraiture is generally more gratifying to the subject than to anyone else; etched portraits, no matter how masterly, are unlikely to attract prestige to an artist. In December 2018, as we were inquiring of art dealers throughout Austria, I found that Stoessel's name isn't nearly as well known as that of his teacher Ferdinand Schmutzer. Most dealers in Graz and Vienna had no idea who Stoessel was.

In most of art history, etchers and engravers were seen as copyists. From the 17th century to the 19th, painters made portraits and then etchers copied them for mass consumption. That's certainly what happened with Joshua Reynolds's portraits in Great Britain. The etchers' or engravers' names are almost always obscure. Their craft generally comes "after" a painting by Reynolds or someone else. Yet Schmutzer, Stoessel, and Max Pollak (another Schmutzer student) perfected etching from their own initial drawings: they weren't copyists but instead viewed etchings as original works of art.

Schmutzer himself became somewhat more famous as an early master of photography. Just as Oskar was mastering etching, photography was displacing it as the more fashionable artistic medium. Before photographs, the primary way to know what some noteworthy person looked like was to have an etching. Up to about 1900, books were filled with etched portraits. After that, any contemporary likeness tended to be a photograph. Etchings were expensive, and they were seen as passé.

As an art form, etching has always experienced ebbs and flows in popularity. In the United States, it enjoyed great popularity in the 19th century, when American artists such as James Abbot McNeill Whistler produced his superlative prints. But by the end of the century, the art had fallen out of fashion again. After World War I, American interest revived as collectors began acquiring prints by Old Masters. During this resurgence, outstanding modern etchers such as John Sloane, Edward Hopper, and Reginald Marsh produced fine prints that were much sought after. Print clubs in major cities—such as the Print Society of Philadelphia and the Society of Etchers in Chicago—held competitions and awarded prizes. At least three major publications, *The Print Society Quarterly*, *Print Connoisseur*, and *Fine Prints of the Year*, reviewed and reproduced outstanding etchings.[2] But less-skilled artists, eager to meet the growing demand, came on the scene. As a result, "by the end of the 1930s, the market was glutted with the junk produced by hacks, and the public turned its interest to other things."[3]

Oskar's arrival in 1939 made the artistic timing unfortunate.

World War II created a shortage of teachers in America, including art teachers, and a shortage of students as well.[4] With low demand for etchings, few schools were interested in adding a master etcher to the faculty. Limiting himself geographically to New York and Washington, Oskar may have overlooked opportunities in California, perhaps near his brother's home in Hollywood. The noted American etcher Mildred Bryant Brooks lived and taught in California, eventually becoming a professor at the University of Southern California. From 1938 to 1941, she gave a series of lectures all over the state on "The Romance of Etching," together with demonstrations of the art.[5] But unlike Californians, most Americans had lost interest in etching.

Other factors militated against greater success for Oskar in America. It wasn't just that he was Jewish, that he was etching, and that he was doing portraiture. It was also that he had done portraiture for subjects like royal families, pet dogs and cats, industrialists, and the Supreme Court. In the art world, these would have

---

2. Elton W. Hall, "R. Swain Gifford and the New York Etching Club," in *Prints and Printmakers of New York State 1825–1940*, ed. David Tatham (Syracuse Univ. Press, 1986), 210.

3. Hall, 211.

4. William H. Young and Nancy K. Young, *World War II and the Postwar Years in America* (ABC-CLIO, 2010), 294.

5. See, e.g., "Romance of Etching to Be Subject at Club," *Whittier News* (Calif.), Mar. 9, 1939, 2; "Noted Etcher Talks, Gives Demonstration," *San Bernardino County Sun* (Calif.), Mar. 18, 1940, 7; "Children to See Etching Made," *Santa Barbara News-Press* (Calif.), Apr. 15, 1941, 8.

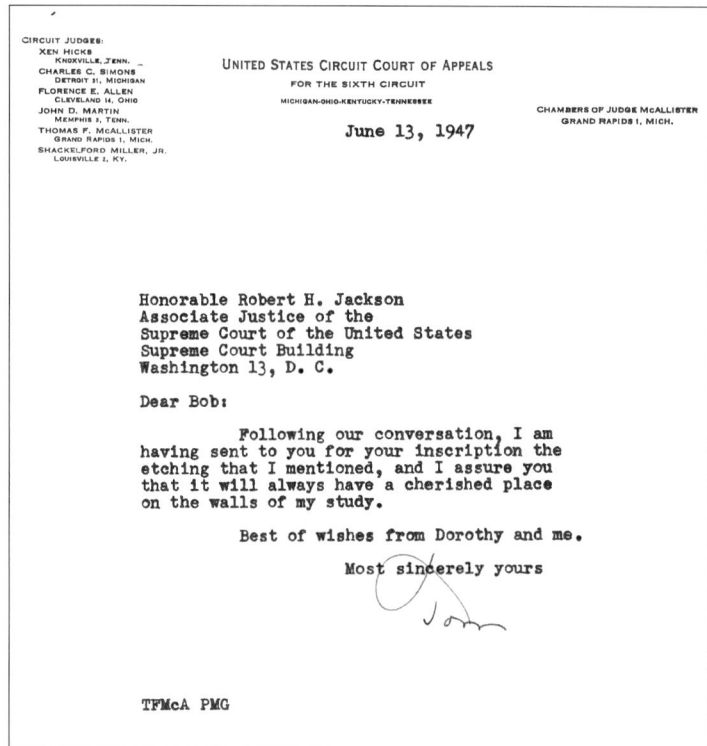

been marks against him, not in his favor. Perhaps he knew all this; perhaps he didn't.

Although we don't know Oskar's perspective on photography—apart from the query he put to Chief Justice Stone about the legality of his owning a camera— we do know that photographic images of him are exceedingly scarce. The only known photograph of the artist resides in the files of Oskar's great-nephew David H. Heichler, the only living relative I could locate. It's a good image of Oskar wearing a bow tie and a three-piece suit. It appears opposite the title page of this book.

Oskar Stoessel was an unassuming man. He would likely be surprised to learn that in the 21st century, people collect his art not because of the subjects but because of the artist. He was a modest man with little cause to be modest.

*   *   *

AMONG the Jackson Papers at the Library of Congress is a 1947 letter from Judge Thomas McAllister to Justice Jackson. It seems that McAllister had acquired Oskar's portrait of Jackson, perhaps from a New York gallery or perhaps from the artist himself.

On July 2, Justice Jackson wrote a brief note that began, "Dear Tom: I am returning the etching with pleasure." He had signed the portrait with this inscription: "For Thomas and Dorothy McAllister with friendship and esteem. Robert H. Jackson." This is the signed etching that hangs in my library—the one that Justice Scalia noticed in 2014 to prompt my research into Stoessel.

I keep a copy of all the Jackson–McAllister letters in a desk beneath the inscribed portrait. The first letter in the file is one that McAllister wrote to Jackson, acknowledging the latter's role in securing McAllister's federal judgeship:

April 25, 1942

Justice Robert H. Jackson
United States Supreme Court
Washington, D.C.

Dear Bob:

A year ago today, the President sent my name to the Senate for confirmation as Judge of the United States Circuit Court of Appeals; and as the day returns, I think of you with deep appreciation. Although, at the time, my work as a Justice of the Supreme Court of Michigan gave me pleasure and satisfaction, I realized that a judgeship on this Federal Court was an aspiration cherished, in the states of this circuit, by every lawyer and every judge devoted to the profession. But it was to you, that the fulfillment of this hope was due; and while I will always appreciate your decisive action on my behalf, more than that, I can dissociate myself from my good fortune and admire the generous spirit and thoughtfulness that, in the midst of arduous duties and political turmoil, made you remember the situation and act so promptly on my behalf. For this, rather than because of my having the judgeship, I take pride in having your name on my commission—and for this, I think of you from day to day. It is a satisfaction that life seldom offers.

Dorothy joins me in kindest remembrances; and I hope to have the pleasure of soon seeing you again.

Most sincerely yours,
Tom

Justice Robert H. Jackson's penciled inscription for the Stoessel portrait. Justice Jackson signed on the mat instead of on the portrait itself.

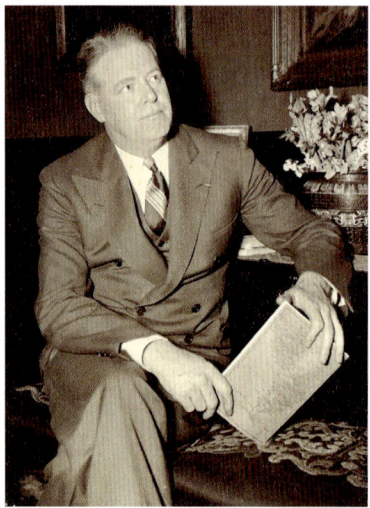

ABOVE: *Judge Thomas F. McAllister (1896–1976) of Grand Rapids served on the Supreme Court of Michigan from 1938 to 1941 and then on the U.S. Court of Appeals for the Sixth Circuit from 1941 until his death. As chief judge of the Sixth Circuit in 1959–1960, he served as a member of the U.S. Judicial Conference. In that capacity, he received an autographed copy of Roscoe Pound's magnum opus (see below).*

Perhaps we're getting far afield from Oskar. But perhaps not. McAllister's letter to Jackson is about friendship, personal indebtedness, and gratitude. That's mostly what this entire book is about. Oskar had a gift for friendship. People liked him and sought to help him. Oskar, in return, repaid his debts of gratitude both personally and in his enduring art.

For myself, I'm grateful to my late friend and coauthor Justice Scalia for asking, "Who was Oskar Stoessel?" This book has been my attempt to supply the answer.

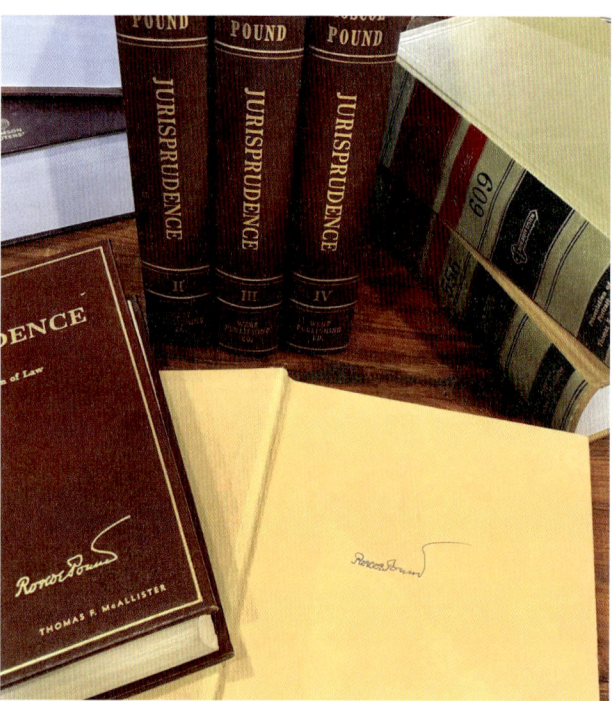

Judge Thomas F. McAllister's personalized copy of Roscoe Pound's five-volume masterwork Jurisprudence *(1959). Pound autographed it at the age of 89. This is the set I bought many years ago in Lansing (see page 261). To the right are two volumes of the* Federal Reporter *(second series) dedicated to McAllister.*

ACKNOWLEDGMENTS

I AM indebted to many friends and colleagues who read and commented on drafts of this piece and contributed in various ways. I would especially like to thank Dr. Roman Theo Carbon, the most prolific private collector of Oskar's work, for making his collection available and for lending his biographical and artistic insights. I'm also grateful to Dr. Peter Peer of Graz for his generosity in showing me the extensive holdings at the Neue Galerie Graz/Universalmuseum Joanneum. Among the others to whom I owe thanks are:

Dr. Amy Anderson
Mr. Ryden McComas Anderson
Professor John Q. Barrett
Professor Tim Bonyhady
Ms. Lindsey Bright
Dr. Eric Denker
Mr. Patrick Fahy
Dean Ward Farnsworth
Ms. Catherine Fitts
Mr. Gino Francesconi
Professor Gary T. Garner
Karolyne H.C. Garner, Esq.
Mr. Will Grogan
Herbert J. Hammond, Esq.
Mr. David H. Heichler
Ms. Jill Heichler
Ms. Lauren Hewes
Tiger Jackson, Esq.
Mr. Franz Jantzen
Mr. Anuradha Kasarabada
Ms. Jennifer King

Mr. Bernhard Kratzig
Hon. Harriet Lansing
Mr. Andreas Lendl
Dr. Steven Lomazow
Ms. Judith Martin
Ms. L. Rebecca Johnson Melvin
Becky R. Moler, Esq.
Mr. Eric Motley
Ms. Katharina Mraček-Gabalier
Dr. Paul Neubach
Jeff Newman, Esq.
Ms. Laura Pavona
The late John Simon
Mr. Curtis Small
Ms. Laura Ten Eyck
Randall M. Tietjen, Esq.
Professor John R. Trimble
Professor Ron Tyler
Professor Louise Weinberg
Ms. Michele Willens
Mr. Peter Znidaric

For reacting to Chief Justice Stone's letter to Oskar quoted in chapter 24, I am grateful to several legal scholars: John Q. Barrett, Noah Feldman, Charles Fried, Alberto R. Gonzalez, Neal Katyal, Sanford Levinson, Jeffrey P. Minear, Theodore B. Olson, Lucas A. Powe, and Elizabeth Shapiro. Was the chief justice giving legal advice? They were uniform in suggesting that today's judicial monasticism wasn't always the norm, and that the chief justice didn't overstep any boundaries. As Gonzalez explained, Oskar was probably "unaware of where to turn to get advice other than from his friend." Also, Stone's letter may not amount to legal advice at all because it says nothing about the application of the law to Oskar's particular situation.

Many institutions were helpful in my research. I am grateful for the cooperation received from the Library of Congress, the National Gallery of Art, the Franklin D. Roosevelt Presidential Library and Museum, the University of Kentucky, the Getty Research Institute, the University of Michigan, the University of New Hampshire, the Graz Museum, and the Neue Galerie Graz/Universalmuseum Joanneum in Graz.

My greatest debt is to my dear wife, Karolyne, who supports not just my research projects but my collecting as well. On legal matters, she is a fearless and incessant researcher, so she understands my drive to answer answerable questions. She's a treasure, and I'll always be grateful for her loving encouragement.

SELECT BIBLIOGRAPHY

Binder, Bruno. "Der Radierer Oskar Stössel." *Gesellschaft für vervielfältigende graphische Künste* 45 (1922): 99–105.

Binder, Bruno. "Der österreichische Maler und Radierer Oskar Stössel." *Westermann's Monatshefte* (Berlin), Apr. 1931, 105–12.

Binder, Bruno. "Oskar Stoessel and His Graphic Art." *Print Collector's Quarterly* 22 (July 1935): 245–64.

Birnbaum, Martin. *Catalogue of an Exhibition of Contemporary Graphic Art in Hungary, Bohemia, and Austria, Buffalo Fine Arts Academy, Jan. 4–Feb. 1st (1913–1914)*. De Vinne Press, 1913.

Connoisseur: An Illustrated Magazine for Collectors, The. 1915.

Martin, Christian Ludwig. *Ferdinand Schmutzer: Der Radierer und Maler*. Verlag Brüder Rosenbaum, 1958.

Peer, Peter. *Oskar Stössel (1879–1964): Portraitist der Gesellschaft*. Neue Galerie Graz am Landesmuseum Joanneum, 2008.

Stoessel, Oskar. "Special Exhibition: Etchings by Oskar Stoessel." Corcoran Gallery of Art, Washington, D.C., Apr. 5–27, 1941.

Weixlgärtner, Arpad. *Das radierte Werk von Ferdinand Schmutzer 1896–1921*. Fritz Mandel Kunstverlag, 1922.

ILLUSTRATION CREDITS

ii: Photo of Oskar Stoessel ca. 1942 courtesy of David & Jill Heichler. **viii:** Photo courtesy of Belvedere Museum in Vienna. **2:** Photos by author of Girardi (Peer plate 2), unknown subject 1920s (Peer plate 360), unknown subject 1923 (Peer plate 25), all held by Neue Galerie Graz/Universalmuseum Joanneum. **3:** Photo by author of copperplate held by National Gallery of Art, Washington, D.C. **4:** Photos by author of Wastian (Peer plate 24), unknown subject 1914 (Peer no. 45), Winterberg (Peer plate 37), and dachshund (Peer no. 150), all held by Neue Galerie Graz/Universalmuseum Joanneum. Spires (Peer plate 21) in Garner Collection. **5:** Photo by author of Ambrosi etching (Peer plate 43) held by Neue Galerie Graz/Universalmuseum Joanneum. **6:** Photo by author of village of Neunkirchen postcard in Garner Collection. Max Stössel photo courtesy of Dr. Roman Theo Carbon. **9:** Photo by author of Berta Stössel etching (Peer no. 24) held by Neue Galerie Graz/Universalmuseum Joanneum. Photo of press courtesy of Bernhard Kratzig. **10:** Photos by author of oil portraits of Robathin (not in Peer) and Janschitz (not in Peer), both in Garner Collection. **11:** Photos by author of rottweiler (Peer no. 148), Scottish terrier (not in Peer), fox terrier (Peer no. 144), German shepherd (not in Peer), cairn terriers (not in Peer), boxer (Peer no. 152), schnauzer (Peer no. 149), Doberman (Peer no. 145), Pekingese (not in Peer), all in Garner Collection. **12:** Photos by author of *Scene in Neumarkt, Steiermark* (Peer plate 4) held by Neue Galerie Graz/Universalmuseum Joanneum, and of *View of the Choir of the Parish Church* (Peer no. 105) in Garner Collection. **13:** Photo by author of Edmonde Guy (Peer no. 132) in Garner Collection. **14:** Photo by author of etching of Palazzo Contarini Fasan (Peer no. 23) in Garner Collection. **16:** Photo by author of *The Copyist at the Louvre* (Martin plate 22; Weixlgärtner plate 35) in Garner Collection. **17:** *Studio of the Sculptor Charles Korschann* (Weixlgärtner plate 30) in Garner Collection. **18:** Photo by author of Strauss portrait (cognate with Martin plate 29) in Garner Collection. **19:** Photos by author of Kainz etchings: head-on (Weixlgärtner plate 104) and looking over shoulder (Martin plate 27), both in Garner Collection. *Vienna Philharmonic* (Martin plate 34) in Garner Collection. **20:** Photo by Dr. Roman Theo Carbon of Freud etching (cognate with Martin plate 36) in Carbon Collection. Photo by author of Einstein etching (Weixlgärtner plate 232; Martin plate 35) in Garner Collection. **21:** Photo by author of Casals etching (Martin plate 33; Weixlgärtner plate 177) in Garner Collection. **22:** Photo by Dr. Roman Theo Carbon of *The Kiss* (Weixlgärtner plate 12) in Carbon Collection. **23:** Photos by author of Schmutzer's Hartmann (Weixlgärtner no. 185) and Stoessel's unknown subject (not in Peer), both in Garner Collection. **24:** Photo by author of Schmutzer WWI etching (not in Martin or Weixlgärtner) in Garner Collection. **26:** Photo by Dr. Roman Theo Carbon of Kaiser etching (Weixlgärtner plate 183) in Carbon Collection. Photo by author of 76ers (Peer no. 59) in Garner Collection. Photo by Dr. Roman Theo Carbon of Krasnik (Peer no. 63) in Carbon Collection. **28:** Photo by author of Mackensen (Peer plate 13) in Garner Collection. **29:** Photo by author of Austro-Hungarian Army (Peer plate 10) in Garner Collection. **30:** Photo by author of Silberbauer drawing (Peer p. ii) held by Neue Galerie Graz/Universalmuseum Joanneum. **32:** Photo by author of barracks etching (Peer plate 8) in Garner Collection. **33:** Photo by author of *Two Soldiers* (Peer no. 57) held by Neue Galerie Graz/Universalmuseum Joanneum. **34:** Photo by Dr. Roman Theo Carbon of aquatint street scene (not in Peer) in Carbon Collection. **36:** Photos by author of *View of Graz* (not in Peer) and *View of the City from the Schlossberg* (Peer plate 5), both in Garner Collection. **37:** Photo by author of unknown subject (not in Peer) in Garner Collection. **38:** Photos by author of Ertl etching (Peer plate 16) in Garner Collection. **39:** Photos by author of Wauchope etching (Peer plate 48) held by Neue Galerie Graz/Universalmuseum Joanneum; *Illustrated London News* in Garner Collection. **40:** Photos by author of Lotte Brociner (Peer plate 3) held by Neue Galerie Graz/Universalmuseum Joanneum; *The Ruins* (Peer plate 11) in Garner Collection; Radnay (Peer plate 18) in Garner Collection. **41:** Photo by Dr. Roman Theo Carbon of Princess Irene etching (Peer no. 292) in Carbon Collection. Photo by author of oil painting of Princess Irene (not in Peer) in Garner Collection. **42:** Photos by author of *Woman with a Lyre* (Peer no. 79) and Helen with King Michael (Peer plate 34), both held by Neue Galerie Graz/Universalmuseum Joanneum. Photo by author of *Sleeping Girl* (Peer no. 54) in Garner Collection. **43:** Photo by author of painting of Schielleiten Castle (Peer plate 70) in Garner Collection. **44:** Photo by author of *Two Kittens* (not in Peer) in Garner Collection. **45:** Photo by Dr. Roman Theo Carbon of *Betty Stein* (Peer no. 134) in Carbon Collection. **46:** Photo by author of Lake Wolfgang painting (not in Peer) in Garner Collection. **52:** Photos by Dr. Roman Theo Carbon of Jeritza etching (Peer no. 216) and *Female Nude* (Peer no. 135), both in Carbon Collection. **54:** Photo by author of Strasser etching (Peer no. 1) held by Neue Galerie Graz/Universalmuseum Joanneum. Photos by Dr. Roman Theo Carbon of *Pediatric Care* etching (not in Peer) and of calling card, both in Carbon Collection. **55:** Woman in green from unknown collection. Photos by author of *Portrait of a Woman* (Peer plate 38) and *Willow Shrub* (Peer no. 29), both in Garner Collection. Photo by author of unknown subject (Peer no. 241) held by Neue Galerie Graz/Universalmuseum Joanneum. **56:** Photo by author of *Unequal Pair* (Peer plate 19) held by Neue Galerie Graz/Universalmuseum Joanneum. **57:** Quartet etching from an unknown collection. Photos by author of *Print Collector's Quarterly* and *Farm Homestead* (Peer no. 213), both in Garner Collection. Photos by author of wedding etching (Peer plate 42) and *View of the Schlossberg and Clock Tower* (Peer no. 104), both held by Neue Galerie Graz/Universalmuseum Joanneum. **58:** Photo by author of dog-pair etching (not in Peer) in Garner Collection. **59:** Photo by author of *Sleeping Beauty* (Peer plate 1) held by Neue Galerie Graz/Universalmuseum Joanneum. **60:** Photo by author of Rupprecht etching (Peer no. 113) held by Neue Galerie Graz/Universalmuseum Joanneum. **61:** Photos by author of nine cynological etchings, all in Garner Collection. Only two are in Peer: the German shepherd (top right, Peer no. 151) and second-row left (Siegfried Jabornegg-Gamesenegg, Peer no. 125 [mislabeled Viktor]). **62:** Photo by author of Krauss etching (Peer plate 46) in Garner Collection. **63:** International News Photos (not under copyright). **64:** International News Photos (not under copyright). **65:** International News Photos (not under copyright). **66:** International News Photos (not under copyright). **67:** Acme Newspictures (not under copyright). **71:** International News Photos (not under copyright). **72:** Photo by author of Messersmith etching (not in Peer) held by Franklin D. Roosevelt Presidential Library and Museum. **80:** Photo by author of Paul Khuner etching (Peer no. 219) held by Neue Galerie Graz/Universalmuseum Joanneum. Photo by Dr. Roman Theo Carbon of first Georg Khuner etching (not in Peer) in Carbon Collection. Photo by author of second Georg Khuner etching (Peer no. 218) held by Neue Galerie Graz/Universalmuseum Joanneum. **83:** Photo by author of S.S. *Manhattan* postcard in Garner Collection. **84:** Photo by author of Hildegarde Hofmann portrait appearing as Peer plate 208 (location now unknown). **86:** Photo by author of Oskar's self-portrait in oil (not in Peer) held by Neue Galerie Graz/Universalmuseum Joanneum. **89:** Photos by author of Murray Hill Hotel postcard and Carnegie Hall brochure, both in Garner Collection. **91:** Photo by author of Callas portrait (not in Peer) held by Neue Galerie Graz/Universalmuseum Joanneum. **92:** Photo by author of oil portrait (Peer plate 75) in Garner Collection. **95:** Benisch etching (not in Peer) courtesy of Sydney Jewish Museum. **96:** Photo by author of FDR etching (Peer plate 52) in Garner Collection. **98:** Photo by author of

Messersmith letter held by Franklin D. Roosevelt Presidential Library and Museum. **99:** Photo by author of large FDR portrait (Peer plate 53) held by Neue Galerie Graz/Universalmuseum Joanneum. Photos by Dr. Roman Theo Carbon of the three variants (not in Peer) in Carbon Collection. **102:** Photo of Watson courtesy of Franklin D. Roosevelt Presidential Library and Museum. Photo by author of the White House memo held by Franklin D. Roosevelt Presidential Library and Museum. **104:** Photo by author of FDR's 1940 appointments calendar held by Franklin D. Roosevelt Presidential Library and Museum. **106:** Photo by author of remarque (from Peer plate 52) in Garner Collection. **107:** Photo by author of *New York Times* paragraph. Photo by Dr. Steven Lomazo of *The Nation* cover from his collection. **108:** Photo by author of Hull etching (Peer no. 253) in Garner Collection. **110:** International News Photos (not under copyright). **111:** Photo by author of Long etching (not in Peer, but cognate with Peer no. 316) in Garner Collection. 1933 photo: Harris-Ewing Photographic News Service. **112:** Photo of unknown origin; physical copy in Garner Collection. **118:** Photo of unknown origin. **124:** Photo by author of Douglas etching (not in Peer) in Garner Collection. Photo by author of inset held by National Portrait Gallery (not in Peer). **125:** Photo by author of tinted Douglas etching (not in Peer) in Garner Collection. **126:** Photo by author of Justice Stone's signature in Garner Collection. **128:** Photo by author of pencil sketch of Stone (not in Peer) in Garner Collection. **131:** Photo by author of initial Stone etching (not in Peer) in Garner Collection. **132:** Photo by author of another state of Stone etching (not in Peer) in Garner Collection. **133:** Photo by author of another state of Stone etching (not in Peer) in Garner Collection. **134:** Photo by author of another state of Stone etching (not in Peer) in Garner Collection. **135:** Photo by author of another state of Stone etching (not in Peer) held by United States Supreme Court Archives. **136:** Photo by author of Black etching (not in Peer) held by United States Supreme Court Archives. **138:** Photos by author of Lee Sheraton Hotel postcard in Garner Collection and of Justice Stone's calling card held by the Douglas Papers at the Library of Congress. **139:** Photos by author of various states of Frankfurter etching (not in Peer) in Garner Collection. **141:** Photo by author of letter held by the Stone Papers at the Library of Congress. **142:** Photo by author of Reed etching (not in Peer) in Garner Collection. Pencil sketch held by United States Supreme Court Archives. **143:** Photo by author of Roberts etching (not in Peer) held by United States Supreme Court Archives. **144:** Photos by author of two Murphy etchings (neither in Peer) in Garner Collection. **146:** Two AP Wirephotos (not under copyright). **148:** Photos by Dr. Roman Theo Carbon of sketch (Peer no. 290) and etching (not in Peer) of Helen of Greece and Denmark, both in Carbon Collection. **149:** Photo by author of Habsburg etching (Peer plate 50) held by Neue Galerie Graz/Universalmuseum Joanneum. **151:** Photos by author of Archduke Eugen etching (Peer plate 49) (upper left), Queen Marie etching (Peer no. 188), King Michael etching (Peer plate 35), and Prince Francis etching (Peer no. 127), all held by Neue Galerie Graz/Universalmuseum Joanneum. **154:** Photo by author of Corcoran Gallery postcard in Garner Collection. **155:** Photos by author of Corcoran Gallery brochure held by United States Supreme Court Archives. **159:** Photos by author of Tandler etching (Peer plate 44) and *Blooming Rosebush* (Peer no. 42), both held by Neue Galerie Graz/Universalmuseum Joanneum. **161:** Photo by author of fox-terrier etching (not in Peer) in Garner Collection. **162:** Photo by author of Mayflower Hotel postcard in Garner Collection. **166:** Photo by author of tree etching (Peer no. 85) held by Neue Galerie Graz/Universalmuseum Joanneum. **170:** AP Wire Photo (not under copyright). **171:** Photo by author of Hughes etching (not in Peer) and sketch (Peer no. 328), both held by United States Supreme Court Archives. **172:** Photo by author of Hughes letter held by the Stone Papers at the Library of Congress. **174:** Photo courtesy of United States Supreme Court Archives. **175:** Photo by author of Byrnes letter held by the Stone Papers at the Library of Congress. **176:** International News Photos (not under copyright). Photo by author of Jackson's appointments calendar held by the Jackson Papers at the Library of Congress. **177:** Associated Press photo sheet (not under copyright). **178:** Photo by author of Byrnes etching (not in Peer) in Garner Collection. **182:** Photo of unknown origin. Physical copy in Garner Collection. **184:** Photo by author of Stoessel letter to Jackson held by the Jackson Papers at the Library of Congress. **187:** Photo by author of Ludwig Stössel's letterhead held by the Jackson Papers at the Library of Congress. **188:** Photo by author of Jackson etching (not in Peer) in Garner Collection. **191:** Photo of Ludwig in 1930 film courtesy of David & Jill Heichler. Photos by author of two other photos, both in Garner Collection. **192:** Photos by Dr. Roman Theo Carbon of two California scenes (top, Peer plate 74; bottom, not in Peer), both in Carbon Collection. **194:** Photo by author of Jackson letter held by the Jackson Papers at the Library of Congress. **200:** Photo by author of Stoessel's photo of Dürer print—original held by National Gallery of Art. **201:** Photos of unknown origin. Physical copies in Garner Collection. **202:** Photo by author of 1930 McBey etching held by National Gallery of Art. **203:** Photo by author of Stoessel's photo of Janinet's portrait of

Marie Antoinette held by National Gallery of Art. **204:** Photo by author of Stoessel's counterproof held by Rosenwald Collection in National Gallery of Art. **208:** Photo by author of Harlow Gallery brochure held by the Stone Papers at the Library of Congress. **215:** Photo courtesy of National Gallery of Art. **216:** Painting (not in Peer) from an unknown collection. **219:** Photos by author of four New Year's greeting cards, upper left (Peer no. 212); three others not in Peer; bottom right courtesy of David & Jill Heichler. **220:** Photo by author of Carnegie Hall Art Gallery brochure (not in Peer) held by the Stone Papers at the Library of Congress. **224:** Photo by author of Stoessel letter held by the Stone Papers at the Library of Congress. **228:** AP Wirephoto (not under copyright). **229:** Acme Newspictures (not under copyright). **231:** Photo by author of Stone portrait by Fox held by Supreme Court Historical Society. **232:** Photo by author of Berta Stoessel etching (Peer no. 281) held by Neue Galerie Graz/Universalmuseum Joanneum. **234:** Photo by author of pencil sketch of Finley (Peer no. 313) in Garner Collection. Inset etching (Peer no. 256) held by National Portrait Gallery. **236:** Photo by author of Lake Placid painting (not in Peer) in Garner Collection. **240:** Photo by author of Samuel Kress etching (not in Peer) in Garner Collection. **241:** Photo by author of Vinson etching (not in Peer) in Garner Collection. **245:** Photo by author of cropped Hofmann portrait from Peer catalogue. **248:** Photo by author of Rush Kress etching (not in Peer) held by National Gallery of Art. **249:** Photo of unknown origin. **251:** Photo of unknown origin. **252:** Photo by author of Stoessel letter in Garner Collection. **254:** Photo by author of "Little Old Winemaker" postcard in Garner Collection. Dean Martin photo: Getty Images, ABC Photo Archives; physical copy in Garner Collection. **255:** Photo by author of *Aufbau* obituary in Garner Collection. *Jennie* photo: Twentieth Century Fox. *Song Is Born* photo: RKO Radio Pictures **258:** Photo by author of First Lady (putatively) sketch (Peer no. 325) in Garner Collection. **260:** Photo by author of Rutherford (putatively) sketch (Peer no. 305) in Garner Collection. **266:** Photo by author of McAllister letter held by the Jackson Papers at the Library of Congress. **267:** Photo by author of Jackson inscription in Garner Collection. **268:** Photo by author of signature alongside several books in Garner Collection.

INDEX